PALGRAVE *Studies in Oi*

Series Editors: Linda Shopes and Bruce M. Stave

Oral History Off the Record

Toward an Ethnography of Practice

Edited by
Anna Sheftel and Stacey Zembrzycki

Foreword by
Steven High

Afterword by
Alessandro Portelli

palgrave
macmillan

ORAL HISTORY OFF THE RECORD

Copyright © Anna Sheftel and Stacey Zembrzycki, 2013.

All rights reserved.

First published in 2013 by
PALGRAVE MACMILLAN®
in the United States—a division of St. Martin's Press LLC,
175 Fifth Avenue, New York, NY 10010.

Where this book is distributed in the UK, Europe and the rest of the world,
this is by Palgrave Macmillan, a division of Macmillan Publishers Limited,
registered in England, company number 785998, of Houndmills,
Basingstoke, Hampshire RG21 6XS.

Palgrave Macmillan is the global academic imprint of the above companies
and has companies and representatives throughout the world.

Palgrave® and Macmillan® are registered trademarks in the United States,
the United Kingdom, Europe and other countries.

ISBN: 978–1–137–33963–8 (hardcover)
ISBN: 978–1–137–33964–5 (paperback)

Library of Congress Cataloging-in-Publication Data

Oral history off the record: toward an ethnography of practice / edited by
Anna Sheftel and Stacey Zembrzycki; foreword by Steven High; afterword by
Alessandro Portelli.
    pages cm.—(Palgrave studies in oral history)
    ISBN 978–1–137–33963–8 (alk. paper)—
    ISBN 978–1–137–33964–5 (alk. paper)
    1. Oral history—Methodology. 2. Oral history—Moral and ethical aspects.
3. Oral history—Political aspects. I. Sheftel, Anna editor of compilation.
II. Zembrzycki, Stacey editor of compilation.

D16.14.O75 2013
907.2—dc23   2013011940

A catalogue record of the book is available from the British Library.

Design by Newgen Knowledge Works (P) Ltd., Chennai, India.

First edition: September 2013

10 9 8 7 6 5 4 3 2 1

For those who have shared their stories

Contents

CHAPTER 13

CHAPTER 14

Illustrations

Foreword

Steven High

Find voice, make sense. What else can we do?[1]

Off the record has its semantic origin in journalism. "Few terms are more widely used or abused than 'off the record,'" wrote *Time Magazine* in 1952.[2] "Even veteran Washington correspondents, who bump up against the term most often, have trouble agreeing on exactly what it means." Another early mention noted that off the record was useful as it allowed politicians to "let down their hair before the press without getting into trouble in the process."[3] When someone said that something was off the record, what they were really saying was "please don't quote me." It was also a way to arouse interest in what was about to be said, to connote a "hushed conversation."[4] Not much has changed in the intervening decades. A person's ability to determine what is off the record in a journalistic interview remains ambiguous.[5] New York University's current handbook on "good practice" for journalism students, for example, notes that in spite of its "murkiness" a source cannot say something and then claim it was off the record: "That's too late."[6]

Oral history is not journalism. Our codes of ethical conduct often emphasize informed consent, the mitigation of harm, and the right of withdrawal. In Canada, interviewees sign consent forms that indicate their willingness to be interviewed, to be named in publications, and, increasingly, the nature of subsequent diffusion. Is the interviewee agreeing to the use of the audio-video recording itself or just the transcribed words? Can the recording be posted online? Can it be integrated into an art installation or a live performance? To varying degrees, oral historians also practice something we call "sharing authority," where the collaborative relationship of the interview is extended outward to subsequent stages in the research process. In our work at the Centre for Oral History and Digital Storytelling, here in Montreal, this has meant the codirection of research projects as well as the coauthorship of online digital stories, radio programming, audio walks, and other public outcomes. The traditional line between the researcher and the researched has been blurred as community members become partners in research and not simply objects of study.

Oral History Off the Record originates in the work of the *Montreal Life Stories* project, a major collaborative research initiative that recorded the life stories of Montrealers displaced by war, genocide, and other human rights violations. As a "Community-University Research Alliance" (CURA), the project team included a broad range of university and community-based researchers, artists, activists, educators, and community partners, including a number of the contributors to this volume. Multisession interviews were conducted with almost five hundred people and their stories were integrated into live performances, radio programming, online digital stories, audio walks, museum exhibitions, art installations, and other media. A great deal of methodological and artistic experimentation occurred, raising questions about how things are usually done in university-based research.[7]

It was within this context that Stacey Zembrzycki and Anna Sheftel, the two editors of this collection, began to collaborate. They joined the project as staff members, coordinating interviews and training, before being awarded postdoctoral fellowships to work on intersecting projects. Their work together, however, led them to develop a new joint research project on Holocaust survivors who give public testimony. Given the informal talk in the *Montreal Life Stories* project, I was not surprised when Stacey and Anna told me that they were organizing an international workshop on the ethical, political, and personal struggles and negotiations between interviewer and interviewee outside the formal interview relationship. Oral history is messy business and we can learn much from people's candid interview stories. I was surprised, though, when Stacey and Anna told me that they had invited a who's who of global oral history. Was it too ambitious, I wondered? Would they come? Thanks to the organizational skills and vision of Stacey and Anna, and the generosity of participants, the workshop was a great success. The practice-based conversation that resulted is well represented here in the 14 chapters that follow as well as in the introductory essays. Figuratively at least, this collection is the result of our letting down our hair: speaking frankly about issues that matter to all of us.

Nobody has thought longer or harder about the interviewer-interviewee relationship than Valerie Yow. Her articles on interview ethics are foundational.[8] "We ask people to be honest," writes Yow, but "how do we handle this trust?"[9] In reflecting on her own practice, Yow notes that she has found herself "hesitating to ask some things of narrators for whom [she] felt affection lest [her] questions cause them discomfort."[10] Indeed, "[as] we pry into our narrator's private lives or the secrets of their public or professional lives, we often have to consider the effects of making public the whole story."[11] Yow now asks herself some hard questions: What was she feeling about this narrator? How did her views affect this process? Why was she doing the project in the first place? Being reflexive about our practice helps identify the wider logics in what we do and why we do it.[12]

Writing in the first person makes reflexive writing possible, yet there remains considerable resistance to personalizing our voice, at least within disciplines such as history. I have encountered this in the peer review process, as an editor and author. Personal scholarship is sometimes viewed as not scholarly enough. What does this mean precisely? Mary Patrice Erdmans, in her introductory essay to a special issue of the *Journal of American Ethnic History*, entitled "The Personal Is Political, but Is it Academic?" voices some of this uncertainty. She concedes that oral history is "a legitimate method today," at least when the authorial voice is scholarly, but not "personal narratives."[13] On this basis, two of the contributions to that special issue were presented as unconventional because they "did not resemble academic articles." To this end, she mused, they may be more "suitable" for a literary journal than a scholarly one. As it happens, one of these unconventional pieces was written by Pamela Sugiman, a contributor to this volume.[14] In it, Sugiman explored the deep personal significance of her research with Japanese Canadians who were interned in World War II. This was her family's story. She then spoke of how this research project entered her daughter's life too. Many of us take on research projects that are close to our hearts. The work we do is often intensely personal, as is made abundantly clear in the pages that follow.

In collaborative environments, however, self-reflexivity quickly becomes ethnographic as we reflect on our work together, raising ethical questions about what can and cannot be said. Scholars have been speaking of oral history as an "ethnographic encounter" since the 1980s.[15] Both fields were "founded upon a progressive impulse to give voice to the voiceless."[16] For Henry Glassie, "ethnography is interaction, collaboration."[17] So, too, is oral history. Where Glassie's work in Northern Ireland focused on the "daily round," how people "form their own lives" in everyday interactions, oral historians have traditionally sought meaning in the narrative accounts recorded during the interview and in the context of the interview itself.[18] In both instances, the *experience* of fieldwork—being in a study area or in the interview space with someone—is at the core.[19]

There are key differences of course, as the fields have developed independently. Whereas ethnography is at the disciplinary core of anthropology, oral history is still at the margins of the history discipline. Oral historians therefore come from a range of disciplines and, importantly, from outside the university academy altogether. There are other notable differences. Ethnographic informants go largely nameless in the published work of anthropologists, not so in the writings of oral historians. Oral historians also seem more interested in individual subjectivities than ethnographers. Ethnographers are more interested in observed behavior.[20] Participant observation, as historian Jean Barman writes, is "by its very nature concerned with what is."[21] Oral history, by contrast, is interested in the relationship between what was and what is: placing change over time and memory at its interpretative center.

If the subject of inquiry differs, my sense is that these methodological or disciplinary differences are not what they used to be. The mythic status of ethnographic fieldwork and the oral history interview have come under intense scrutiny in the past two decades and the subjectivity of our research practices is now widely acknowledged. As oral historians reflect more on what happens before, after, and within the interview, we have come into contact with ethnography like never before. Whole new scholarships have opened up for us. The rich exchange between anthropology and oral history is evident in the diverse disciplinary backgrounds of the contributors and in the essays themselves. What we see here is an autoethnography of oral history practice, as contributors step back and reflect on their collaborative work.

In reading the contributions to this remarkable collection, I asked myself the question: What more is being revealed here and why? Generally, contributors reflect on what appears on or remains off the record. My sense is that we sometimes use the phrase in much the same way as journalists do: to denote when the interviewee says something off-camera or when the researcher grapples with whether or not to disclose something noticed or heard. To do so might result in hurt feelings or even put an interviewee into danger. What is the "right" thing to do? In other instances, it is the oral historian's own practice that is the object of attention. How far should they go? Some time ago Henry Glassie conceded that his "problem" was to "be scientific, compassionate, respectful: it was to create an ethnography strong enough to cause disquiet in [his] world, but gentle enough to cause no discomfort among the people [he] wrote about."[22] The contributors to this volume struggle with the same dilemma.

When someone says something is "off the record," almost always she or he goes on to tell you what that something is. What is off the record is therefore not off-limits. As a result, we are not so much dealing with silences as we are going public with the kinds of issues that are often worked through in informal conversations with friends and colleagues. "Corridor talk,"[23] as Anna and Stacey say in their introduction, provides us with a relatively safe space to speak candidly about our interview experiences (and our interviewees themselves) and to grapple with the obstacles we face, the mistakes we make, and the embarrassing moments, failures, or ethical lapses we experience. These are not things we usually speak candidly about in our published work, perhaps not even in university corridors. It is always risky business when we reveal our personal vulnerability or professional fallibility. Some stories remain off-limits. To do otherwise is to risk hard-earned reputations. Younger scholars also face an unforgiving job market. It is therefore a great deal safer to direct our critical gaze at others, revealing only our "public faces." This is why this edited collection is so refreshing.

The 14 chapters that follow allow us to listen-in as the contributors chew on and work through some of the messiness of oral history. After all, we, too, are only human. A few years ago Michael Riordan approached a number of oral historians working with some of the most silenced communities about their practice. He asked them: "Who are you, why do you do this work, what drives you, what do you hope to accomplish?" His conclusion: "Find voice, make sense. What else can we do?"[24] What else, indeed.

Notes

1. Michael Riordon, *An Unauthorized Biography of the World: Oral History on the Front Lines* (Toronto: Between the Lines Press, 2004), 5, 7–8.
2. "A Semantic Jungle," *Time* 60, 10 (September 8, 1952).
3. "On the Record," *Time* 53, 3 (January 17, 1949).
4. Alleen Pace Nilsen, "How to Read between the Lines," *Change* 22, 3 (May/June 1990), 46.
5. From time to time, a public figure has gotten into trouble for something they said that may or may not have been on the record. US president Barack Obama's initial foreign affairs advisor, Samantha Power, was forced to resign in 2008 after making some disparaging remarks about Hilary Clinton during the Democratic nomination. She was quoted as saying, "She is a monster, too—that is off the record—she is stooping to everything." Howard Kurtz, "Obama Adviser Quits Over 'Off the Record' Crack at Clinton," *The Washington Post* (March 8, 2008).
6. Adam L. Penenberg, *New York University Journalism Handbook for Students: Ethics, Law and Good Practice* (New York University: Department of Journalism, no date). Available at: http://journalism.nyu.edu.
7. The *Montreal Life Stories* project (www.lifestoriesmontreal.ca) produced a wide range of scholarly publications. At present, three books have been published or are forthcoming: Michele Luchs and Elizabeth Miller, eds., *Mapping Memories: Participatory Media, Place-Based Stories & Refugee Youth* (Montreal: Self Published, 2011), freely available online at http://storytelling.concordia.ca/refugeeyouth; Steven High, Edward Little, and Thi Ry Duong, eds., *Remembering Mass Violence: Oral History, Digital Media and Performance* (Toronto: University of Toronto Press, forthcoming); Steven High, *Oral History at the Crossroads: Life Stories of Montrealers Displaced by War and Genocide* (Vancouver: University of British Columbia Press, forthcoming). On collaborative practice, see: Steven High, Lisa Ndejuru, and Kristen O'Hare, eds., Special Issue on "Sharing Authority: Building Community-University Research Alliances through Oral History, Digital Storytelling and Collaboration," *Journal of Canadian Studies* 43, 1 (2010). On interviewing, see: Anna Sheftel and Stacey Zembrzycki, "Only Human: A Reflection on the Ethical and Methodological Challenges of Working with 'Difficult' Stories," *Oral History Review* 37, 2 (2010): 191–214. On oral history performance, see the twin special issues of *alt.theatre*, especially: Hourig Attarian and Rachael Van Fossen, "*Stories Scorched from the Desert Sun*: Testimony as Process," *alt.theatre: cultural diversity and the stage* 9, 2 (2011): 30–39; Sandeep Bhagwati, "*Lamentations*: A Gestural

Repertoire in the Realm of Shadows," *alt.theatre: cultural diversity and the stage* 9, 1 (2011): 50–55; Nisha Sajnani, "Coming into Presence: Discovering the Ethics and Aesthetics of Performing Oral Histories within the Montreal Life Stories Project," *alt.theatre: cultural diversity and the stage* 9, 1 (2011): 40–49; as well as Nisha Sajnani, Warren Linds, Lisa Ndejuru, Alan Wong, and Members of the Living Histories Ensemble, "The Bridge: Toward Relational Aesthetic Inquiry in the Montreal Life Stories Project," *Canadian Theatre Review* 148 (Fall 2011): 19–24.

8. Valerie Yow, "Ethics and Interpersonal Relationships in Oral History Research," *Oral History Review* 22, 1 (Summer 1995): 51–66.

9. Ibid., 51–52.

10. Valerie Yow, "'Do I Like Them Too Much?': Effects of the Oral History Interview on the Interviewer and Vice-Versa," *Oral History Review* 24, 1 (1997): 76.

11. Ibid., 52.

12. For more on reflexivity, see: Natasha S. Mauthner and Andrea Doucet, "Reflexive Accounts and Accounts of Reflexivity in Qualitative Data Analysis," *Sociology* 37, 3 (2003): 413–31.

13. Mary Patrice Erdmans, "The Personal Is Political, but Is it Academic?" *Journal of American Ethnic History* 26, 4 (2007): 7–8.

14. Pamela Sugiman, "'A Million Hearts from Here': Japanese Canadian Mothers and Daughters and the Lessons of War," *Journal of American Ethnic History* 26, 4 (2007): 50–68.

15. Micaela di Leonardo, "Oral History as Ethnographic Encounter," *Oral History Review* 15 (Spring 1987): 2.

16. Ibid., 3.

17. Henry Glassie, *Passing the Time in Ballymenone: Culture and History of an Ulster Community* (Bloomington: Indiana University Press, 1995), 14.

18. Julie Cruikshank, *The Social Life of Stories: Narrative and Knowledge in the Yukon Territory* (Vancouver: University of British Columbia Press, 1998), xii–xiii.

19. Fern Ingersoll and Jasper Ingersoll, "Both a Borrower and a Lender Be: Ethnography, Oral History and Grounded Theory," *Oral History Review* 15 (Spring 1987): 81–102.

20. Di Leonardo, "Oral History as Ethnographic Encounter," 3–7.

21. Jean Barman, "'Oh, No! It Would Not Be Proper to Discuss That With You': Reflections on Gender and the Experience of Childhood," *Curriculum Inquiry* 24, 1 (Spring 1994), 55.

22. Glassie, *Passing the Time*, 13.

23. Yow, "'Do I Like Them Too Much?'" 55.

24. Riordon, *An Unauthorized Biography*, 5, 7–8.

Series Editors' Foreword

Oral history is grounded in the relationship between interviewee and interviewer—without both, there is no oral history. Furthermore, the quality of this relationship, the nature of the interviewee/interviewer interaction, has a determinative effect on the interview itself. Early practitioners recognized this as they spoke about the cultivation of rapport with narrators. More recently, we have spoken of intersubjectivity in oral history—that meaning is cocreated through dialogue. The 14 essayists included in *Oral History Off the Record: Toward an Ethnography of Practice*, masterfully edited by Anna Sheftel and Stacey Zembrzycki, address the implications of the oral history relationship in detail and in depth, based on their own work in oral history. They consider the intangibles surrounding the "talk" of an interview—the emotional demands, the cognitive dissonance that sometimes occurs, the role of intermediaries, the way relationships outside of the interview affect the interview, and the way relationships established through interviewing sometimes take on a life outside of the interview. The essays also reflect on ethical complexities of the interview relationship, particularly when the intended subject is politically charged. Cumulatively, they establish forcefully that the practice of oral history extends far beyond the actual interview, encompassing a range of relationships and charging us all with a range of obligations.

The essays in *Oral History Off the Record* are the product of an international workshop Sheftel and Zembrzycki organized in April 2011 at Concordia University in Montreal entitled "Off the Record: Unspoken Negotiations in Oral History." That conference in turn built on the work of Concordia's Centre for Oral History and Digital Storytelling, which has done much to revivify oral history in Canada; and especially the Centre's *Life Stories of Montrealers Displaced by War, Genocide, and other Human Rights Violations* project, which pressed to the fore some of the questions addressed in this volume. We are especially pleased that the volume brings together the considered reflections of longtime practitioners of oral history with newer voices, the latest generation of oral historians, who build upon, deepen, and sometimes challenge the work of their intellectual forebears. It makes for a particularly rich mix. While many of the essays focus on oral history done in Canada, many of the Canadian subjects have transnational dimensions, and one-third of the essays address interviewing conducted outside of North America, further expanding the international reach of Palgrave's *Studies in Oral History* series. While most books in the series continue to present the content of oral history interviews, *Oral History Off the Record*, the thirty-third volume in the series, joins several recent publications that offer more theoretical and methodological reflections, including Alexander Freund's and Alistair Thomson's *Oral History and Photography* (2011), Shelley Trower's *Place, Writing, and Voice in Oral History* (2011), and Sean Field's *Oral History, Community, and Displacement: Imagining Memories in Post-Apartheid South Africa* (2012).

LINDA SHOPES
Carlisle, Pennsylvania
BRUCE M. STAVE
University of Connecticut

Acknowledgments

Since this book addresses the "off the record" experiences we have had while doing oral history, it seems only fitting that we begin with an "off the record" story. In our "Introduction," we describe how the idea for this project originated in the collaborative partnership between its editors, Anna Sheftel and Stacey Zembrzycki. This is the more diplomatic way of telling you that it is really a tale about mutual harassment. We met at Concordia University five years ago—Anna was the associate director for the Centre for Oral History and Digital Storytelling (COHDS) at Concordia University and Stacey held a limited term appointment as an assistant professor in the Department of History there. Although we passed each other in the hallways, we did not get to know each other until we began to conduct interviews with Holocaust survivors for the *Montreal Life Stories* project. We had great chemistry during our interviews, but we truly became friends and collaborators, or as we usually put it—work wives—in the car rides after our interviews and in the long telephone conversations that always followed. During these informal debriefings, we pondered nearly every aspect of each interaction we had with our interviewees in excruciating detail.

The harassment began when Stacey proposed that we write a paper about those car rides and telephone calls, focusing on some of the ethical and political challenges that we experienced in our interviews. Anna's reaction was blunt: "That would make a brilliant paper, but we're not going to write it!" It felt too scary to raise some of the issues we faced in print. Stacey was, however, quite persistent and in October 2010, our article "Only Human: A Reflection on the Ethical and Methodological Challenges of Working with 'Difficult' Stories" was published in the *Oral History Review*. This piece not only formalized many of our thoughts on how collaborative interviewing works in practice, but also allowed us to articulate what our challenges taught us about ourselves, our interviewees, and oral history as a methodology.

In January 2010, we, both fairly nervous flyers, found ourselves teetering precariously in Israeli airspace on our way to a conference to present a draft of that very paper. This was some of the worst and most erratic turbulence that either of us had ever experienced. Just as we dipped down for the umpteenth time, and several people screamed while the man seated beside us nervously clutched an air sickness bag with white knuckles, Anna turned to Stacey and proposed that we organize a workshop to build on the discussion we started in "Only Human." Stacey looked at her with wide, and slightly queasy, eyes and blurted: "Are you nuts?" Anna continued to harass her throughout their two weeks in Israel, between mouthfuls of hummus, and later, during their daily telephone calls in Montreal. Stacey's, "Are you nuts?" slowly evolved into "Do you know how much work this sort of thing is?" and then to "So does the Social Sciences and Humanities Research Council of Canada (SSHRC) give workshop funding to postdoctoral fellows?"

Eventually Stacey gave in and in April 2011 a workshop, entitled "Off the Record: Unspoken Negotiations in Oral History," took place. We wanted it to be an intimate, interdisciplinary, intergenerational, and international space for reflecting on oral history practice. We imagined scholars who study genocide exchanging stories with scholars who study social movements. We imagined PhD students working on their first projects discussing their work with some of the most recognized names in the field. To this end, we set to work devising a "dream team" of oral historians. We challenged ourselves to look through the books on our shelves and come up with a list of people who inspired us. Once we had our list, we drafted invitations, closed our eyes, and pressed the send button on our emails. We were shocked that almost every person we invited accepted our offer. These amazing, generous, thoughtful people made *Oral History Off the Record* possible. We thank each and every one of our contributors for traveling to Montreal, participating in the workshop, and inspiring our thinking about oral history. We also thank them for submitting intelligent and nuanced pieces to this collection, and for being so willing to edit them many times. They are all strong and thoughtful writers, and although their chapters here may seem effortless, there are no words to describe their willingness to spend countless hours working with us to bring this book to fruition.

We were both postdoctoral fellows when the April 2011 workshop took place, under the encouraging supervision of Steven High. While it is unusual for junior scholars to take on this sort of endeavor and then go on to edit a collection, we were fortunate to benefit from an incredible amount of support throughout this process. Steven High has always pushed us to dream big, and he created the ideal environment in which we could do that. We must also acknowledge the funding agencies that awarded us our postdoctoral fellowships: SSHRC funded Stacey and the *Fonds québécois de recherche sur la société et la culture* (FQRSC) provided support for Anna. We are also grateful for the generous funding we received from three Canada Research Chairs—Steven High, Erica Lehrer, and Joy Parr—who believed in us from the beginning of this project and continued to encourage us throughout it. Concordia University's Department of History, its office of the Vice President for Research and Graduate Studies, and SSHRC, in the form of an Aid to Research Workshops and Conferences in Canada, also provided the funds necessary to make our workshop and this collection possible.

Financial support was not all that we benefitted from, however; the success of this project is also a testament to the vibrant community we found at COHDS and within the *Montreal Life Stories* project. In particular, we wish to thank Eve-Lyne Cayouette Ashby, Neal Santamaria, Gracia Dyer Jalea, and Audrey Mallet, our workshop assistant, for all of their help with the workshop and its aftermath. We were warmly received at both the Canadian Historical Association Annual Meeting in 2011 and at the Oral History Association Annual Meeting in 2012 when we put together panels highlighting some of the work coming out of this book. Thank you to all of those who attended the sessions and made comments that helped us contextualize our work within the wider field. We are also indebted to Linda Shopes, Chris Chappell, Bruce M. Stave, and Sarah Whalen at Palgrave Macmillan Press, as well as our two anonymous peer reviewers, for all of their enthusiastic support for this volume. Linda Shopes, in particular, flew to Montreal to participate in our workshop, answered every panicked email we sent her throughout the editorial process, and provided invaluable feedback on the manuscript that pushed us to make it stronger. We cannot thank her enough for her kind mentorship.

This collection is about reflecting on our interviews and research relationships, as well as on the stories that come out of both of them. And so we would be remiss if we did not acknowledge how grateful we are to all of the people who have let us into their lives by participating in oral history interviews. They are the inspiration for this collection. We know what it means to open up and share the most intimate, and sometimes difficult, moments of one's life with researchers, and so we are forever indebted to those who do.

Last, but not least, we thank our husbands for their love, support, and patience. It is not easy putting up with the demands that a third person—a work wife—places on a marriage. Robert Douglas and Graeme Williams constantly dealt with us ignoring them through a million telephone calls, meetings, and emails to discuss the workshop, the book, and anything else that happened to be on our minds. While they sometimes could not see why we needed to talk *so much*, they were unwavering in their encouragement. We only hope they realize that this project's conclusion does not mean an end to all of the talking!

Introduction

Anna Sheftel and Stacey Zembrzycki

I had never met anyone who was 104, except perhaps in movies, so I was a bit shocked—and worried—when Sylvie Thygeson's daughter led her out from her room in the convalescent hospital to the couch where I was waiting. Stylish, with her grey hair pulled back in a bun and adorned with a beautiful head band, she was frail and almost skeletal looking, her eyes appearing as black pools in an unbelievable sea of wrinkles. What had I gotten myself into, I wondered; what can this woman possibly remember? As someone called out bingo numbers in the background, Sylvie Thygeson remembered a lot. For the next hour, until she became tired, Thygeson eloquently recounted what she did to push along "the great evolutionary process." Thirty years later, I realized that I had interviewed Imogen Cunningham the previous day. Yet, that interview with Thygeson was such a profound experience that it remains ingrained in my memory, as the first one I did.

—Sherna Berger Gluck[1]

I came to my first interview with some experience in journalism but no oral history training whatsoever. Remembering the interview still makes me cringe because it is full of classical mistakes: no introduction, a television blaring in the background, family members walking through the room, and me not knowing my questions by heart and being continually distracted by unfamiliar recording equipment. There were mistakes specific to my project on German immigrant women in Vancouver, British Columbia, too. I accidentally conducted the interview in German rather than in English—even though my narrator felt more comfortable in English—and then I could not find a way to switch languages. This awful interview is the only one that I conducted but never transcribed.

Despite much of it going wrong, my interviewee drew me in with stories that I did not anticipate but which, nevertheless, raised important questions and stimulated research topics that occupied me for the following decade. Two stories stand out, continuing to be unique among the many that German post-war immigrants in North America have told me: first, the narrator's experiences as a single mother migrating and successfully establishing herself, against all obstacles, in postwar Canada; and second, her date with another European immigrant, which, under the shadow of the recent Nazi past, turned into a violent and public humiliation of her. I don't remember my narrator well, but I remember her son, who was a friend of mine from school. Thinking about the interview always makes me look at a painting in my apartment as well; the narrator's first husband, a famous German artist, drew it. Although the interview still makes me shudder, it also reminds me of the importance of training and experience, two things I now try to provide to community researchers and my students.

—Alexander Freund[2]

Do You Remember Your First Time?

When we asked our contributors to recall their initial forays into oral history, Sherna Berger Gluck and Alexander Freund were among the first to respond. Although much time has elapsed since these interviews, their memories of them are vivid, evoking anxiety, awe, and confusion. Do you remember your first oral history interview? What comes to mind? Were you nervous as you knocked on the door? What were your first impressions? Were you excited? Scared? How did the interview go? Did you talk too much or not enough? Were there deafening silences or awkward laughter? Did you hit it off or were you glad to leave? Did you ask yourself, as Gluck did, "what [have] I gotten myself into?" Does it still evoke particular memories for you, as it does for Freund?

What has changed since your initial experience? Does your heart no longer skip a beat when you ring the doorbell? Are you more comfortable with the pauses that occur in the middle of recorded conversations? Or, does every interview still feel like your first? Each interview, regardless of how many we conduct, can be daunting. Every one requires a tremendous amount of time, patience, energy, work, and thoughtfulness. Our interviewees, and the relationships we form with them—whether they are deep and long-lasting or short and sweet—mean that no two exchanges are ever the same. Nevertheless, we gain new insights the more we hone our skills as listeners. When we sit down and ask people to tell us about their lives, we try to understand the meanings behind their words, stories, and treasured secrets. This is a challenging task that has a formative impact on us—it shapes us into the oral historians we become. Our interview stories are important because they have the potential to improve our practice and strengthen the field of oral history.

Oral History Off the Record: Toward an Ethnography of Practice approaches interviewing as the precarious, fallible, and exciting human process that it is, exploring what we can learn about oral history, as both a methodology and a craft, when we honestly reflect on our experiences in the field. This collection argues for a shift away from hypothetical methodological and theoretical approaches to interviewing. We can learn more about how to do oral history by sharing our experiences, especially when discussing long-term and in-depth projects such as those that involve humanistic and engaged practices.[3] The authors in this collection, who are in different stages of their careers and employ various disciplinary approaches, share their interviewees' stories alongside their own. By examining the intersection between research processes and outcomes, and drawing attention to their fumbles, missed opportunities, and magical encounters, the authors have created an *ethnography of oral history practice*.[4] This holistic approach not only allows them to discover new layers of meaning in their own projects, but also deepens our understandings of oral history's potential.

Taking Our "Corridor Talk" Public

My earliest real "interview" was with Angela Sidney, a senior Tagish woman from the Canadian Subarctic, then in her seventies. It was 1973. I was beginning an oral history project in collaboration with several Indigenous women who suggested that I interview knowledgeable grandmothers, mothers, and aunts about their life histories. This, they proposed, might make a substantive contribution to the work that was engaging younger activists during the early stages of land claims research. One of Mrs. Sidney's granddaughters introduced me, and I remember feeling quite shy when we met. A quietly composed woman, Angela Sidney expected me that day and she asked me to tell her what I wanted to learn. I began with some careful questions, keeping her daughter's and granddaughters' concerns about land claims in mind.

As we sat in her small living room, I remember how she studied me intently, listening closely as I explained my interest in learning about the changes that engulfed Tagish women's lives during the twentieth century. She considered this thoughtfully. Then, completely ignoring my questions (or so it seemed to me), she suggested that I take down some stories that she thought I needed to know—"traditional" stories that others had told her as a young woman. In so doing, she took control of the interview, and drew on her own narrative conventions for describing complex life circumstances framed in terms unfamiliar to me. Our subsequent discussions, over almost two decades, provided my real education about how interviews are often co-created and how they develop as part of a relationship that may change the way researchers think about their questions. Her narrative arc led us to answers I never anticipated.

—Julie Cruikshank[5]

My "first interview" was with a Holocaust survivor I was interviewing for a psychological study on the ways that people construe moral dilemmas. "So you want to hear some 'real' moral dilemmas?" he asked. "Sure," I said. And from there [we went] to Auschwitz, Buchenwald, and other places of hell. Besides the content, I think part of the hook for me was having no idea what was coming next, but feeling—in a nice way—partly responsible for whatever did. It was that "in the zone" kind of relaxed focus, being trusted by someone older and obviously more experienced than I was, and the self-importance of feeling like a "confidant" [that drew me in].

—Henry Greenspan [6]

No matter how careful we are, interviews rarely go as planned. There are always surprises, as Cruikshank and Greenspan demonstrate. Interviewees often take us to places we did not know we needed to go. While the aforementioned surprises were formative moments in Cruikshank's and Greenspan's careers, shaping their work that was to come, this is not always the case. Sometimes we leave interviews contemplating what went wrong and how we could have done things differently. Much like first interviews, what we perceive as our best and worst ones leave lasting impressions on us. These experiences are what we tend to talk about when our colleagues ask about our projects. "Corridor talk," according to Valerie Yow, is the informal way that oral historians tend to debrief.[7] We speak candidly about our interview stories in person, and yet few of us are willing to put them into print.[8] Ann Oakley recognized this inherent contradiction more than 30 years ago, stating: "Interviewing is rather like marriage: everybody knows what it is, an awful lot of people do it, and yet behind each closed front door there is a world of secrets."[9] When they do make it into print, our experiences are usually relegated to introductions or epilogues—safe spaces for these sorts of personal remarks—as a way of adding texture to the interview *content* contained within the body of our work. This distinction, between process and content, is a construct that obfuscates how we listen to stories and shape them into narratives. Ethnographers have long examined how the two intersect, writing vulnerably so that they may understand and learn from the meanings therein.[10] Everything that happens within and outside of the conversations they have with their informants is important. Process and outcome are interconnected because they are shaped by the relationships that ethnographers build and nurture throughout their research projects. This collection asks how we might benefit from integrating some of these practices into our own work. What we learn from our interviewees is a direct result of the relationships we forge with them—our chemistry and sense of purpose; the moments we share before and after the recorder is turned on and off; the power differential between us and how it evolves; and everything that is relayed or goes unsaid.

Although there is a growing body of literature that treats interview experiences as a starting point for discussing oral history practice, it has largely been scattered in various journals and isolated in different edited collections.[11] It is time to bring these reflections together to create a sustained conversation that will help us learn from our rich and varied experiences. As the chapters in this collection make clear, our interview stories matter for many reasons. They tell us about our interviewees and they teach us about our strengths and weaknesses as interviewers and human beings. Studying the mistakes made by one oral historian might work to another's advantage. We cannot know this, however, unless we begin to discuss our experiences more openly. Conversations in corridors feel safer, but they do little to push oral history forward as a field. *Oral History Off the Record* enables us to begin to debrief as a community of practitioners.

When Theory and Practice Collide

Although it wasn't my first, one of my most formative interview experiences took place in rural Zimbabwe, where I spent my junior year of undergrad on a study abroad program. Along with eight women of various ages, I folded my legs beneath me as I sat down on the mat-covered floor. The circular, thatched *kitchini* (cooking hut) was soon filled with the sounds and smells of rural Zimbabwean cooking, but I was in the smoky, dim room to conduct interviews about motherhood. My original plan for the afternoon was to interview three women individually with the help of my host sister's translation. My sister was delayed, however, so my host mother, whose goal was to make me "the smartest student in the class," undertook the role. Amai rounded up all the women she could find and ordered them to be seated. She then quickly explained my project, ignoring my attempts to speak for myself. My intention was to follow the precedent established in previous interviews: introduce myself and the project and follow my meticulous interview guide to elicit a detailed life story of my interviewees' experiences of and thoughts about motherhood. Noticing this Shona-translated guide, my mother took it from me and proceeded to read each of the questions to the group. Losing control made me feel defeated.

Upon finishing the last question, the women began to speak at once. Wondering how I would be able to transcribe the cacophony of recorded voices, I internally railed against the waste of corrupted data and resented my sister for not arriving on time. It was then that my mother regained control, ordering everyone to be quiet and sending the youngest girl to find paper and pencils. Straining to maintain my composure, I told my mother that the women should talk about their answers, not write them. "This is not what the interview process is about!" I silently screamed in my head. In calm, deliberate English, my mother patiently explained to me that the women would discuss the questions among themselves to determine the truth and the youngest would write their answers down for me. It was then that I realized I was in the midst of an important anthropological moment. These women gave me more to think about than I ever could have gathered from dozens of "properly conducted" interviews. Being effectively occluded from my own interview was a fascinating, disorienting, humbling, and provocative experience.

—Monica Eileen Patterson[12]

Our methodological training is rooted in "best practices," which rarely, as Patterson demonstrates, hold up in the field. Why do we have problems discussing about this reality? Perhaps, as a progressive methodology that has struggled to prove its "legitimacy" vis-à-vis more traditional historical methods, we have been afraid to admit our weaknesses.[13] History can be a conservative discipline that has resisted the subjective turn,[14] and so there is no doubt that acknowledging the messiness of humanistic research complicates matters.[15] All of this volume's contributors—be they historians, sociologists, anthropologists, psychologists, or artists—worked hard to provide balanced narratives that honestly convey their experiences without sacrificing scholarly rigor. For many, this has meant reliving embarrassing moments; grappling with their own boundaries as well as those of their interviewees'; and pushing themselves to explore uncomfortable questions. Writing about their interview experiences clearly required courage, but it also raised many concerns. Chief among them was this question: If we position our interviewees' stories as products of a specific circumstance, influenced by who we are as interviewers and how we conduct ourselves in subsequent exchanges, do we undermine the integrity of their narratives? For many of us, analyzing and interpreting the stories that we hear and the lives of the people who tell them has become second nature. However, the reflection demanded in *Oral History Off the Record* necessitated turning the lens in the other direction, a prospect that made many of our authors uneasy. If we turn the spotlight onto ourselves, are we taking something away from those with whom we work?

The practice of self-reflexivity has been mired with such questions since it emerged, as researchers struggle to find the line between honesty and narcissism, and between what advances or undermines their work.[16] Most of us are drawn to interviewing because we believe that there is an inherent value in the stories we hear. Shifting attention to our own stories is, therefore, a fraught process. Our interest here is not to propose a particular approach to self-reflexivity that ought to be adopted by oral historians, but rather to ask how such tools might help us learn about our interviewees, ourselves, and oral history. Rather than engaging in these classic and rather dichotomous debates, we hope that these diverse reflections on practice—some more self-reflexive than others—will enable us to explore the potentials and pitfalls of doing this kind of work with more nuance. Our question is not whether or not we should be reflecting on our own roles in the research process; it is about how we should do so, in what contexts, and to what ends. What can we learn and what are our limits?

Oral History Off the Record ambitiously asks whether we can find a balance between feigning objectivity and becoming paralyzed by our always less-than-perfect methodologies. Our contributors demonstrate that it is possible to thoughtfully and critically reflect on interviewing experiences while still honoring the lives and stories of their interviewees. Our goal is to explore how a more holistic approach to the interview might help us better understand the work we do and the people with whom we engage. This is the purpose of building an *ethnography of oral history practice.*

Of course, ideas differ about what exactly oral history interviewing entails. Since contributors come from different methodological backgrounds, they offer a glimpse into a range of projects with various approaches. That said, all are rooted in a humanistic research ethos that values the lives of ordinary people and gives them space within research and writing. Most of our authors conducted life history interviews, listening for how stories and memories fit within the complicated and layered context of the life in question. Many of the interview stories they tell here are about silenced, marginalized, or disenfranchised people and communities, thus adding an additional ethical obligation not only to do justice to these experiences, but also to frame them carefully. To this end, contributors often expand on the ethic of "sharing authority" as a way of redressing power imbalances and fostering a collaborative and non-hierarchical interview environment.[17] And, it should come as no surprise that many identify specifically with the subfield of feminist oral history, as it was one of the first movements within the field to take on questions about power, subjectivity, marginalization, and the interviewer's often conflicted position as an academic, advocate, community member, and friend.[18] In many ways, *Oral History Off the Record* is a response to *Women's Words: The Feminist Practice of Oral History*, a seminal text that paved the way for generations of feminist oral historians because it encouraged us to have honest, critical, and self-reflective conversations about our interviews.[19]

As such, this collection aims to deepen our understanding of humanistic oral history practice. By this we are referring to interviews that acknowledge the humanity of the interviewer and interviewee, aim to create a collaborative and just interview space, and valorize the relationships that grow out of these encounters.[20] Humanistic interviews embrace the messiness of human experience and interaction, and treat speaking and listening as profound and imperfect processes that require time and commitment. Many of the contributors to this volume have spent years building relationships with their interviewees; their involvement with them and their communities goes far beyond recording stories for use in their monographs.

Starting the Conversation

> I guess [I felt] a mix of being bewildered and overwhelmed while I was also grateful that a total stranger took me into his intimacy. And guilty, very guilty for having opened up his wounds. I felt very, very responsible for that.
>
> —Hourig Attarian[21]

> My first interviews were done with my two closest Bosnian friends; I met them when I lived there. I remember feeling very nervous about interviewing them because we had an easy, fun, and carefree friendship, and it felt a bit like a violation to then ask them to tell me about their horrific wartime experiences. I knew they agreed to participate because I was their friend and they were generous people who wanted to help me. They came over to my apartment and I interviewed one of them and then the other. I made sure to have coffee and cookies, but I was nervous because hosting is a precise art in Bosnia and I knew that I would not be up to par with their ideals; for example, I was still terrible at preparing Turkish coffee and cringed at the idea of serving it to anyone but myself. The walls of my apartment were very thin, and my young neighbors'—several university students—laughter and music punctuated the interviews. I still hear this noise when I re-listen to those recordings.
>
> Despite my anxiety, the interviews went well. Even though I knew my friends would not have chosen to discuss their painful memories were they not helping a friend, they were thoughtful and considered all of my questions very carefully. At the end they even told me that it had been a valuable experience for them. The interviews were much shorter than I expected, and I wondered if I should have pushed us deeper, so as to sustain more of a conversation. I am pretty sure that I still worry about this sort of thing every time I do a new interview.
>
> —Anna Sheftel[22]

Since interview stories are at the heart of *Oral History Off the Record*, we have scattered our contributors' memories of their early interview experiences throughout this introduction. Taken together, they illustrate the plethora of anxieties and insights we have all had while learning to listen. As Sheftel makes clear, our insecurities are usually a normal part of the process. Listening, as Attarian tells us, can take a toll on both the interviewee and interviewer.

The idea for this collection also began in a story, and we would be remiss if we did not share it here. Its origins are rooted in the serendipitous research partnership that developed between the editors, Anna Sheftel and Stacey Zembrzycki. Although we met as colleagues at the Centre for Oral History and Digital Storytelling (COHDS) at Concordia University, we did not become close friends until we began to cointerview Montreal Holocaust survivors as part of the *Life Stories of Montrealers Displaced by War, Genocide and Other Human Rights Violations* project, also at Concordia University. This project, which aimed to collect 500 stories of people who came to Montreal from situations of mass violence, was rooted in a collaborative community-university research partnership. It was the project's policy to interview in pairs, a prospect that we both approached with trepidation as neither of us had done this before.[23] But we discovered that we had immediate chemistry as cointerviewers, and so our "corridor talk" quickly mushroomed into car talk, telephone talk, email talk, and coffee talk. COHDS is a hub for a diverse group of researchers who are all engaged in various kinds of oral history projects, and so our personal conversations easily melded with those that always seemed to be taking place there. We talked a lot. And as we talked among ourselves and with others, we began to realize that these conversations could be helpful for other oral historians. We were constantly debating how best to apply many of the principles that we had read about in the literature on humanistic oral history interviewing to our practice: for example, how *do* you share authority, exactly? We went on to formalize our "corridor talk" in an article in the *Oral History Review*: "Only Human: A Reflection on the Ethical and Methodological Challenges of Working with 'Difficult' Stories."[24]

Our hope in publishing this piece was to start a larger conversation about what often goes unsaid in oral history interviewing and what could be learned from it. The response was, and continues to be, significant. Researchers who are either close colleagues or strangers seem to identify with the particular challenges we faced, and our article also prompts them to share their own experiences. The proverbial Pandora's box has been opened. Buoyed by the response, we decided to organize a small workshop, inviting a diverse group of oral historians to Montreal to share their interview stories. We purposefully invited practitioners who were in different stages of their careers—scholars with decades of experience as well as those working on their very first graduate projects. Participants also came from different disciplinary circles and work on a range of regions and themes, such as Holocaust memory, collaborative work with Indigenous communities, Middle Eastern studies, refugee studies, immigration and ethnic history, postcolonial history, postconflict memory, and histories of marginalized peoples such as people of color, lesbian, gay, bisexual, transgender, and queer (LGBTQ) communities, working-class women, and others. These people often have little reason to speak to each other, and so we tried to find ways to discuss shared research experiences across these themes. After all, everyone, in the end, had one thing in common: our interviewing experiences.

On the opening night of the workshop, we asked a series of ambitious questions to set the tone for our exchanges, generated out of early drafts of the papers our participants had already submitted:

- What are our boundaries in the interview space and how do they translate into our research and writing?
- What are the burdens that we take on when we listen?
- What are the limits of sharing authority? Is it possible, or even desirable, in all circumstances?
- Can we envision other ways of characterizing our collaborative approaches?
- What is the boundary between deep and difficult listening? How far is too far, especially when we are listening in distressing situations?
- How do our identities shape the stories we hear and the ways that we interpret them?
- Can we like our interviewees too much? Do we have to like them at all?
- How do we select whom we write about and those we choose to never write about? How does this process of selection influence our scholarship?

We never arrived at any easy or definitive answers to these questions. The more time we spent debating and discussing them, the more questions we raised. This book is therefore a way for us to continue the important conversations we began in April 2011 and to broaden them. We are just as keen to initiate a wider conversation in the field now as we were when we published "Only Human." All 14 chapters in this collection may have originated at this workshop but they have continued to evolve since. The authors live, eat, and breathe their projects—as most of us do—illustrating the multiple ways in which we are implicated in our scholarship.

Oral History Off the Record is divided into four sections that, like the questions given earlier, speak to their own issues but are also interrelated. Part I, "Reflections on a Lifetime of Listening," invites four distinguished career oral historians, Sherna Berger Gluck, Julie Cruikshank and Tatiana Argounova-Low, and Joan Sangster, to take a long view of their past projects and revisit their understandings of them now. Gluck grapples with publishing unflattering details of progressive women she admires, making connections and building trust when interviewing in circumstances of severe political tension in Palestine, and adapting to the digital turn. In reflecting on their long-haul work with Indigenous peoples in two different projects, Cruikshank and Argounova-Low consider their struggles to collaborate with their interviewees and define their projects' purposes, rhythms, directions, and goals. The "record," as they illustrate, always holds different meanings for those involved. Sangster, for her part, recalls the first interviews she conducted with progressive Canadian women and uses her memories of these experiences to probe the limits of inviting discussions of subjectivity and self into work that aims to investigate the plight of disenfranchised peoples. Together, these chapters highlight the ways in which oral historians have always struggled with the specificities of working with marginalized people and how they have managed to do justice to their narrators' stories while also being rigorous, honest, and true to themselves and their craft.

The next section, "Encounters in Vulnerability, Familiarity, and Friendship," builds on the issues raised in part I and narrows the focus to research relationships. If an interview is a document that is cocreated by interviewer(s) and interviewee(s), then examining the dynamics of the relationships that evolve in the interview space are crucial to understanding how oral history works. In this vein, Martha Norkunas writes about being a "vulnerable listener," by which she means finding herself in emotionally and psychologically taxing interview contexts that forced her to navigate fragile moments, family secrets, and contentious emotions. How do we listen in these spaces? In an equally self-reflective piece, Alan Wong asks how familiarity, shared experience, and the telling of painful and divisive memories can complicate the interview space in the context of his work with gender-diverse people of color. Wong places his boundaries and those of his interviewees at the center of his analysis, examining how we speak and listen when these boundaries intersect or contradict. Elizabeth Miller, describing a group project with Montreal youth with refugee experiences, elaborates on the careful process that she and her collaborators nurtured to build mutually beneficial research spaces for their participants. Relationships were at the heart of her work, defining how she facilitated a healthy group dynamic that enabled the young Montrealers to navigate the dynamics of going public with their difficult pasts. And finally, Stacey Zembrzycki reflects on the long journey of building a relationship with one Holocaust survivor, Rena Schondorf, from their initial meeting, which was filled with suspicion, to their time spent together strolling arm in arm through the death camps of Poland. She ponders how their deep bond affected their interviews as well as her conception of what oral history relationships can be, should be, and are. These four chapters outline the tensions and possibilities that emerge from our interview relationships, highlighting the many forms they can take. This is not a controversial or new point in oral history methodology, but here it is elaborated in vivid detail.

Part III, "The Intersection of Ethics and Politics," uses our research relationships as a starting point to explore the ethical quandaries that arise when interviewing in contentious political situations. It not only asks how we can build trust during these tense and capricious moments, but also outlines how experiences that take place both in and outside of the interview space impact the stories told and the ways we listen to them. Pamela Sugiman begins by examining her relationship with a Japanese Canadian woman, Lois Hashimoto, and their exchanges about Hashimoto's wartime internment. Sugiman, herself an advocate for the rights and redress of interned Japanese Canadians, reflects on how they managed to speak across their conflicting politics, and on the ways in which these discussions forced each of them to humanize and reexamine their opposing views. Nadia Jones-Gailani then delves into the dynamics that structured her interviews with Iraqi women, exploring how those in the room—her interviewees, herself (an insider-outsider in the Iraqi community), and her stepmother (an insider translator)—shaped the often painful, and, in many cases, unresolved, memories that she heard. In a community where one's lived experience of violence is intimately related to one's social position and affiliation as an Iraqi, the intersection of these identities proved to be especially sensitive and significant for Jones-Gailani to navigate. Nancy Janovicek's chapter about the back-to-the-land movement in British Columbia asks how oral historians can build trust as well as research relationships in places where people are very conscious of the legacies they want to leave, the political battles that have marked them, and the tensions that remain. Finally, Monica Eileen Patterson turns to her work in South Africa, and specifically its Truth and Reconciliation Commission (TRC). Viewing the TRC as a form of oral history, she is critical of its mediated nature and how it placed particular value on stories that supported the state's political project. She questions the possibility of truly recounting one's Apartheid experiences in this context, where stories were and continue to be politically instrumentalized. If part II focuses on the relationships that we create while doing oral history, part III goes further to consider the multiple ways that troubling political contexts can impact these relationships, as well as the narratives we hear and the ethical commitments we make.

The final section, "Considering Silence," builds on this discussion by exploring how we may negotiate the potential meanings inherent in the various silences we encounter in our projects. Although silence is broadly addressed in the literature,[25] this section seeks to move us toward what Alexander Freund dubs an "ethics of silence." In his piece, Freund revisits two difficult interview experiences from early in his career, wherein "off the record" pronouncements on taboo topics strongly influenced how he came to understand his interviewees' lives and also prevented him from exploring those subjects further. He pushes us to consider how we can appreciate these sorts of difficult moments while still respecting the privacy of our interviewees. Considering another type of silence, Luis van Isschot draws on his academic work and activism in the politically tense Colombian community of Barrancabermeja, to reflect on the challenges of interviewing activists—many of whom were his contemporaries—who were used to carefully guarding their views and experiences out of fear for their lives.

As interviewees recounted Barrancabermeja's violent past, van Isschot negotiated how he could tell their stories without putting them at risk or undermining their struggle. Finally, Anna Sheftel uses her research on wartime memory in Bosnia-Herzegovina to delve into a previously ignored form of silence—that of refusing to be interviewed. She explores the meanings inherent in refusals, arguing that these experiences need to be treated as research findings and not just problems. When people declined her requests to be interviewed they were telling a story about their lives and their country's difficult past. Together these chapters ask oral historians to embrace silence as an important site of struggle and interpretation. For Freund, van Isschot, and Sheftel, silences emerged from the tenuous political contexts that they were trying so hard to understand.

All of these chapters ask us to travel to different parts of the world and grapple with many complex political contexts. By reflecting on sensitive, uncomfortable, and sometimes even dangerous moments in their research, contributors add texture to discussions of how oral history can and should be done. Rather than being a prescriptive methodological volume, *Oral History Off the Record* explores the potential of learning from the descriptive.

Toward an Ethnography of Oral History Practice

Her name was Mary Brydges and she was ninety years old. She had one week left to live in the home where she had spent much of her life; she was moving to a nursing home because she was losing her sight and hearing and found it hard to manage. She had a warm and friendly face—I felt welcome in her house—but she seemed just as shy and nervous as I felt. I largely failed to diffuse the situation. She was relatively quiet throughout our exchange and really downplayed the importance of her life: she was "just" a miner's wife, "just" a mother, "just" a woman. The dynamics, however, changed as soon as I turned off my recorder. The stories began to flow.

—Stacey Zembrzycki[26]

As best I can recall, my first bone fide interview was done in 1974, as an assignment in Martha Ross's oral history course at the University of Maryland. We were to interview someone who had been involved in the university's anti-war movement some years earlier...It turns out I knew someone who had been politically active at Maryland at that time. I too had been active in the antiwar movement, not at Maryland, but in Baltimore where I was living, and the person I wanted to interview also lived in Baltimore, and our paths had crossed socially. Significantly, he was a historian who studied history at Maryland [and]...taught at a local community college.

All of this is pertinent to the interview itself: I contacted him, he readily agreed to be interviewed, we set a date, I prepared thoroughly, and at the appointed time we did the interview. I believe it went well: partly because I was prepared, partly because we shared a certain political point of view that enhanced trust and rapport, partly because he was a historian who understood the historical significance and context of the interview topic, and partly because we already knew each other.

BUT THEN, disaster! When I went to listen to the interview, NOTHING HAD BEEN RECORDED. I have no idea how that happened: I don't recall being nervous, I had practiced with the recorder in advance, and I thought I had pressed the right buttons. What I didn't do was "stop" and check to make sure the recorder was, in fact, recording. Of course I panicked, but then I decided the only thing to do was re-contact the narrator and ask if we could do it again. Of course he agreed: he was a good guy, and he didn't want me to get a bad grade in the course—never mind the intrinsic value of the interview.

So, we redid it. And I'm afraid it was a bit flat. I already knew the story and I was not so engaged in it; he'd already told it and likely felt the same way. I've never been one to tout the value of "spontaneity" in an interview—often one's "spontaneous" response to a question is not very considered or thoughtful. Interviews deepen as time goes on. But this "repeat" interview wasn't a deepening of the story; it was a reiteration of it. I didn't have the original interview to go back to and see what else I could ask; and I didn't recall parts of it so as to give a new dimension to the second interview. Overall, it just wasn't any fun. No juice.

—Linda Shopes[27]

The title of this book, *Oral History Off the Record*, is a playful nod to the journalistic practice of differentiating between people's public and private pronouncements, and the difficulty of navigating the delineations between these two spheres; Zembrzycki learned about this in her first oral history interview. When a person discusses something "off the record" with a journalist, they often relay taboo information that they would rather not see in print; disclosing these sorts of details provides context and texture that is meant to inform the larger conversation. Similarly, this volume asks how our "off the record" experiences inform the stories we hear and the narratives we write. However, it goes further too, pondering the boundaries between remarks made "on" and "off the record." For example, what about unflattering memories that we record but our consciences compel us to censor? What is the line between being honest about what we hear and airing dirty laundry? Most oral historians implicitly protect their interviewees; even if interviewees agree to disclose unfavorable details, we often informally deliberate on the ramifications and decide whether they are worth making public. Our personal ethical commitments are far more nuanced and contextual than the terms set out in our consent forms.

Our intention in proposing an *ethnography of oral history practice* is to push past tired debates about whether self-reflexivity is crucial or self-indulgent and whether our job is to document facts or interpret meanings. Many scholars have already fought it out from both sides of these divides and we hope that our approach can be more conciliatory.[28] Rather, this collection demonstrates that studying process can be done in various ways. Just like the interview, no two approaches are the same and each makes for a different set of reflections. Some contributors' chapters are far more personal than others. Some put weight on relationships while others focus on emotion, ethics, or the mechanics of interviewing. Everyone is, however, trying to figure out what we can learn from closely studying our experiences and how the lessons that result may be useful to others. We hope that the range of insights presented in this volume will encourage readers to reflect on their own experiences. Examining practice need not subscribe to a particular academic ideology; it takes all kinds in this field.

Oral History Off the Record aims to narrow the divide between content and process, showing that our scholarship is made more rigorous by examining the intersection of the two. It also tries to demystify oral history. Even veteran oral historians, as Linda Shopes's recollection shows, did not always get it right. Novice interviewers must therefore be forewarned: you too will have your own imperfect, cringe-worthy "first" interview story. This is completely normal! We have all been nervous. We have all felt the burden of these stories on our shoulders. We have all fretted over our mistakes. These worries, negotiations, and vivid memories are all an integral part of what it means to do oral history. They never go away—you just learn to adjust and accept them for what they are. One of the things we love about oral history is its potential for lifelong learning.

Humanistic research in general and oral history interviewing in particular are complex engagements. There is no book, including this one, that can adequately convey the many kinds of experiences you will have in the field. However, the more interview stories we share, the more we will learn. *Oral History Off the Record* also shows how our work quickly, and often unconsciously, becomes intensely personal and transformative. When listening to stories it is easy to forget that we are researchers—we react in ways that are, simply put, human. Those of us who work with marginalized communities often feel that we have no choice but to practice an engaged scholarship that holds us responsible for our interviewees. Most of the authors in this book function within academic settings, where long-term engagement is not always valued, and the personal connections we form and the human ways we react to them can be difficult, if not taboo, to articulate. Our grant applications and job requirements reward research output rather than the relationships that are central to the long-haul work we do as oral historians. No wonder our reflections have been confined to the corridors. It is time to change that.

Oral history is not just about studying people; it is also about valuing them. This approach makes our work difficult and emotionally demanding, but it is the only way that we can try to truly understand people's lives. We must learn to acknowledge what happens "off the record" in our projects, because these encounters help us understand the humanity of interviewers, interviewees, and the process itself. As Alessandro Portelli beautifully conveys in his afterword to this collection, interviews can be transformative for both speaker and listener. We know that oral historians have been having these conversations for years. This collection brings them in from the fringes.

Notes

1. Sherna Berger Gluck, email message to authors, July 16, 2012.
2. Alexander Freund, email message to authors, July 19, 2012.
3. "Humanistic" refers to practices that acknowledge the humanity of interviewer and interviewee and foster collaborative and mutually respectful research environments as well as significant, long-term research relationships. Our use of the word "engaged" expands on how scholars have conceived of their political commitments to marginalized communities, highlighting the ways that oral history connects researchers to the people with whom they work in meaningful, committed, and often political ways. Practices based in social justice, solidarity, and care are central to all of our authors' work. For related discussions, see Nancy Scheper-Hughes, "The Primacy of the Ethical: Propositions for a Militant Anthropology," *Current Anthropology* 36, 3 (June 1995): 409–40; Paul Farmer, *Infections and Inequalities: The Modern Plagues* (Berkeley: University of California Press, 2001); Daniel Kerr, "'We Know What the Problem Is': Using Oral History to Develop a Collaborative Analysis of Homelessness From the Bottom Up," *Oral History Review* 30, 1 (2003): 27–45; Elizabeth Miller, "Building Participation in the Outreach for the Documentary *The Water Front*," *Journal of Canadian Studies* 43, 1 (Winter 2009): 59–86.
4. Although our use of the term "ethnography of practice" is somewhat more broad, we are indebted to Paula Hamilton and Linda Shopes for its creation. See Hamilton and Shopes, eds., *Oral History and Public Memories* (Philadelphia: Temple University Press, 2008), xiii.
5. Julie Cruikshank, email message to authors, July 16, 2012.
6. Henry Greenspan, email message to authors, July 15, 2012.
7. Valerie Yow, "'Do I Like Them Too Much?': Effects of the Oral History Interview on the Interviewer and Vice-Versa," *Oral History Review* 24, 1 (1997): 55.
8. Lynn Abrams, *Oral History Theory* (London: Routledge, 2010), 9.
9. Ann Oakley, quoted in ibid., 9.
10. We have been inspired by Ruth Behar, *The Vulnerable Observer: Anthropology That Breaks Your Heart* (Boston: Beacon Press, 1996); *Translated Woman: Crossing the*

Border with Esperanza's Story (Boston: Beacon Press, 1993); Barbara Myerhoff, *Number Our Days* (New York: Simon and Schuster, 1978); Caroline B. Brettell, *When They Read What We Write: The Politics of Ethnography* (Westport, CT: Bergin and Garvey, 1993).

11. See, for instance, Valerie Yow, "Ethics and Interpersonal Relationships in Oral History Research," *Oral History Review* 22, 1 (Summer 1995): 51–66; Lenore Layman, "Reticence in Oral History Interviews," *Oral History Review* 36, 2 (Summer/Fall 2009): 207–30; Pamela Sugiman, "'Life is Sweet': Vulnerability and Composure in the Wartime Narratives of Japanese Canadians," *Journal of Canadian Studies* 43, 1 (Winter 2009): 186–218; Katherine Borland, "'That's not what I said': Interpretive Conflict in Oral Narrative Research," in *Women's Words: The Feminist Practice of Oral History*, eds. Sherna Berger Gluck and Daphne Patai (New York: Routledge, 1991), 63–75; Stacey Zembrzycki, "Sharing Authority with Baba," *The Journal of Canadian Studies* 43, 1 (Winter 2009): 219–38; Alan Wong, "Conversations for the Real World: Shared Authority, Self-Reflexivity, and Process in the Oral History Interview," *Journal of Canadian Studies*, 43, 1 (2009): 239–258; Anna Sheftel and Stacey Zembrzycki, "Only Human: A Reflection on the Ethical and Methodological Challenges of Working with 'Difficult' Stories," *Oral History Review* 37, 2 (Summer–Fall 2010): 191–241. The following references also give attention to process and content: Abrams, *Oral History Theory*; Michael Riordan, *An Unauthorized Biography of the World* (Toronto: Between the Lines, 2004); Daniel James, *Doña María's Story: Life, History, Memory, and Political Identity* (Durham: Duke University Press, 2000).

12. Monica Eileen Patterson, email message to authors, September 12, 2012.

13. For a similar argument, see Sheftel and Zembrzycki, "Only Human," 195.

14. See Peter Novick, *That Noble Dream: The "Objectivity Question" and the American Historical Profession* (Cambridge: Cambridge University Press, 1988); Keith Jenkins, *Re-Thinking History* (London: Routledge, 1991).

15. Alessandro Portelli addressed this concern in his classic "The Peculiarities of Oral History," *History Workshop* 12 (Autumn 1981): 96–107.

16. On self-reflexivity, see Wanda S. Pillow, "Confession, Catharsis, or Cure? Rethinking the Uses of Reflexivity as Methodological Power in Qualitative Research," *Qualitative Studies in Education* 16, 2 (2003): 175–96. For more on the careful balancing act that is required when we turn to the subjective, see Franca Iacovetta, "Post-Modern Ethnography, Historical Materialism, and Decentring the (Male) Authorial Voice: A Feminist Conversation," *Histoire sociale/Social History* 32, 64 (November 1999): 275–93; Eric Mykhalovskiy, "Reconsidering Table Talk: Critical Thoughts on the Relationship between Sociology, Autobiography, and Self-indulgence," *Qualitative Sociology* 19, 1 (March 1996): 131–51.

17. Although they did not refer to it as "sharing authority" per se, feminist oral historians have always devoted themselves to this concern: Gluck and Patai, *Women's Words*. Michael Frisch's use of "shared authority" speaks to the inherent balancing of academic and experiential authority that typifies an interview: *A Shared Authority: Essays on the Craft and Meaning of Oral and Public History* (Albany: State University of New York Press, 1990). Frisch's notion has since been expanded to frame collaborative interview processes in general: "Shared Authority," Special Feature in *Oral History Review* 30, 1 (2003); Katharine C. Corbett and Howard

S. Miller, "A Shared Inquiry into Shared Inquiry," *Public Historian* 28 (2006): 15–38; Steven High, Lisa Ndejuru, and Kristen O'Hare, eds., "Special Issue of Sharing Authority: Community-University Collaboration in Oral History, Digital Storytelling, and Engaged Scholarship," *Journal of Canadian Studies* 43, 1 (Winter 2009).

18. See, for instance, Lisa M. Tillmann-Healy, "Friendship as Method," *Qualitative Inquiry* 9, 5 (2003): 729–49.

19. *Women's Words* was one of many texts to signal the beginning of this discussion; the last two decades of the twentieth century were a dynamic and exciting time for feminist oral historians. See, for instance, Meg Luxton, *More Than a Labour of Love: Three Generations of Women's Work in the Home* (Toronto: Women's Press, 1980); Elizabeth Roberts, *A Woman's Place: An Oral History of Working-Class Women* (Oxford: Basil Blackwell Publisher, 1984); Luisa Passerini, *Fascism in Popular Memory: The Cultural Experiences of the Turin Working-Class*, trans. Robert Lumley and Jude Bloomfield (Cambridge: Cambridge University Press, 1987); Julie Cruikshank, *Life Lived Like a Story: Life Stories of Three Yukon Native Elders* (Vancouver: University of British Columbia Press, 1990); Joy Parr, *The Gender of Breadwinners: Women, Men and Change in Two Industrial Towns, 1880–1950* (Toronto: University of Toronto Press, 1990); Franca Iacovetta, *Such Hardworking People: Italian Immigrants in Postwar Toronto* (Montreal and Kingston: McGill-Queen's University Press, 1992); Joan Sangster, *Earning Respect: The Lives of Working Women in Small-Town Ontario, 1920–1960* (Toronto: University of Toronto Press, 1995); Denyse Baillargeon, *Making Do: Women, Family and Home in Montreal During the Great Depression*, trans. Yvonne Klein (Waterloo, Ontario: Wilfred Laurier University Press, 1999).

20. Attaining these goals can be complicated, especially when interviewing those with whom our own values conflict. That said, Kathleen Blee's work with Ku Klux Klan members demonstrates the need, however trying and difficult, to build relationships so that we may understand the other: *Inside Organized Racism: Women in the Hate Movement* (Berkeley: University of California Press, 2003).

21. Hourig Attarian, email message to authors, July 16, 2012.

22. Anna Sheftel, first interview memories.

23. Undertaken with Montreal's Rwandan, Cambodian, Haitian, Jewish, and other Diaspora communities, *Montreal Life Stories* (http://www.lifestoriesmontreal.ca/) was a five-year project funded by a Social Sciences and Humanities Research Council of Canada (SSHRC) Community-University Research Alliance (CURA) grant that came to an end in July 2012.

24. Sheftel and Zembrzycki, "Only Human."

25. Luisa Passerini's work is a case in point: *Fascism in Popular Memory*.

26. Stacey Zembrzycki, first interview memories.

27. Linda Shopes, email message to authors, July 19, 2012.

28. For the great twentieth-century debates on the future of historical practice as it relates to objectivity, postmodernism, and engaged scholarship, see Novick, *That Noble Dream*; Jenkins, *Re-Thinking History*; Margaret MacMillan, *The Uses and Abuses of History* (Toronto: Viking Canada, 2009); W. J. Van Der Dussen and Lionel Rubinoff, eds., *Objectivity, Method, and Point of View: Essays in the*

Philosophy of History (Leiden: E. J. Brill, 1991); Thomas L. Haskell, *Objectivity Is Not Neutrality: Explanatory Schemes in History* (Baltimore: John Hopkins University Press, 1998); Joan Wallach Scott, *Gender and the Politics of History* (New York: Columbia University Press, 1988); Keith Jenkins and Alan Munslow, eds., *The Nature of History Reader* (London: Routledge, 2004); David Harlan, *The Degradation of American History* (Chicago: University of Chicago Press, 1997); Richard J. Evans, *In Defense of History* (New York: Norton, 1999).

PART I

Reflections on a Lifetime of Listening

Henry Greenspan

The four authors of the three opening chapters—Sherna Berger Gluck, coauthors Julie Cruikshank and Tatiana Argounova-Low, and Joan Sangster—have been our teachers for many years. And what they most centrally have taught us about, in these chapters as elsewhere, is power: especially, the power (and suppression) of women; the complexity of power in researcher-narrator relationships; the power of different approaches in oral history itself (including ones that they developed) both to inspire and constrain oral history practice; and the "powers-that-be," far beyond oral history practice, that may do their own inspiring or constraining. For all of the authors, as they reflect on lifetimes of practice, these threads are interwoven.

Philip Gourevitch notes that "power largely consists in the ability to make others inhabit your story of their reality."[1] The chapters in this section are founded in the authors' commitments to people narrating their own realities: feminists (especially Gluck), activists (all of the authors), Aboriginal peoples (Cruikshank and Argounova-Low), and working-class women both inside and outside of the Canadian labor movement (Sangster). Many (but not all) of those interviewed have themselves been involved in political struggles. That is, they have also been concerned with power. It is, therefore, not surprising that all of the authors recall initially approaching their narrators as allies, if not full partners, in struggle. And thus they imagined that they could overcome the distance that conventionally separated scholars from those whom they interviewed and publicized while creating new forms of collaboration.

As is now well-known, actualizing such aspirations became complicated. While collaborative ideals were realized, or at least approximated, in some instances, they were sorely challenged in others. Genuinely sharing power—or "sharing authority" as it came to be called—raised its own ethical and political questions. Explication of such dilemmas is especially detailed in Gluck's chapter. Beyond questions about who controls publication, or the often-gray line between honest scholarship and potentially hurtful revelation, Gluck focuses on the political consequences of making known what she has learned "off the record." To what extent could others use revelations opportunistically—to discredit political goals shared by researcher and interviewee? To what extent might publication put people in real danger? As these questions suggest, Gluck is keenly aware of the power of the researcher and its accompanying dilemmas. At the same time, as she emphasizes, narrators are anything but helpless. Indeed, she describes a range of ways in which it is usually "the narrator's terms and conditions that will govern the process." The more one enters into the social and cultural worlds of narrators—rather than simply trying to extract an interview *from* them—the more likely it becomes that *narrators'* terms begin to matter. Of course, there are no guarantees. But when one allows oneself to see things through the eyes, and within the lives, of one's participants, oral history practice becomes increasingly embedded in ethnography.

In a fascinating juxtaposition, Cruikshank and Argounova-Low also describe how much "speakers' insistence on speaking on their own terms" can challenge researchers' initial expectations. Reflecting on her 40 years of work with Aboriginal peoples in the Yukon, and Aboriginal women in particular, Cruikshank recalls having anticipated particular stories about the experience of colonialism and struggles against it. Instead, her narrators framed their individual life stories within traditional "folk" sagas of coherence and change, involving both the human and transhuman worlds, and it was these narratives that they wanted to transmit. Perhaps most essentially, both Cruikshank and Argonouva-Low learned how traditional stories served both to *frame* memories of resistance to colonialism even while their recreation—and especially their intergenerational retelling—were themselves *part* of resistance.

Questions about the place of "life story" interviewing run through all of the chapters in this section. The issue becomes particularly relevant in work with those who do not "naturally" think about their experiences in individual life-story terms: for example, the Palestinian activists with whom Gluck has worked or the Arctic peoples whom Cruikshank and Argounova-Low have engaged. Joan Sangster raises complementary questions, recalling that for many years she "avoided writing about a single life history." She was concerned that focusing on individual biography would distract from a history that was structured collectively, especially by class and gender. At the same time, stories retold by individuals could reveal dimensions lost in collective analyses, particularly about the development of agency and counternarratives. As for the other authors in this section, finding the right balance between individual and collective experience, analysis of subjectivity and societal structure, becomes a continuously evolving process. Indeed, contending with difficult balances, and the different contributions of different approaches, is the theme of Sangster's chapter more generally. She suggests, for example, that practitioners discussed critical questions about the ethical and methodological limits of "sharing authority" from the beginning. The vagaries of memory, the ethics and politics of public revelation, and the complexity of power balances and imbalances with interviewees were all part of these conversations. It was only that they became more "on the record," and popular, later. Sangster suggests a pattern with which, I think, all of the authors in this section would concur. Retelling one's professional "life story" (which is, after all, what reflecting on "a lifetime of listening" entails) rarely follows a linear, "onward and upward" pattern. There are, rather, spirals, revisions, and returns, as theory and practice not only inform each other (so we like to imagine!) but are themselves vehicles of memory—personal and guild. Immersed in new projects, and contending with new questions, one returns to old projects and old questions. Just as for our "interviewees," recounting a career facilitates hearing one's own story in a range of new, often unexpected, ways.

Such nonlinear, multileveled stories are not easy to tell, at least not with candor, complexity, and clarity. What is perhaps most impressive about the authors in this section is that they have managed to do precisely that, reconstructing careers and commitments while keeping ongoing questions "on the record." The result is both "thick description" of professional lives, or "ethnographies of practice" as this volume is subtitled, and confirmation that the adventures and ideals, which called many of us to oral history, do not fade with time. Amid changing historical and political circumstances, and all of the other contingencies in which oral history takes form, one "goes with the flow," as Gluck writes, while "making judgment calls continuously." In such nuanced telling of their own stories about power, activism, and scholarship, Gluck, Cruikshank and Argounova-Low, and Sangster empower us. They remind us that these are struggles that we are in together. In challenging times, we can be especially grateful for these teachers who led the way.

Note

1. Philip Gourevitch, *We Wish to Inform You That Tomorrow We Will Be Killed With Our Families: Stories from Rwanda* (New York: Picador, 1998), 181.

CHAPTER I

From California to Kufr Nameh and Back: Reflections on 40 Years of Feminist Oral History

Sherna Berger Gluck

Forty years ago, in 1972, I set off to the San Francisco Bay area in search of an apocryphal 104-year-old suffragist. In those early days of the US feminist oral history movement, one of my goals was to collect the stories of women. Like others whose work was inextricably linked to the women's liberation movement, I was determined to uncover our hidden history and, in the process, empower women and energize our movement.

My first interviews with Sylvie Thygeson and the renowned photographer Imogen Cunningham were evocative, moving, and thrilling experiences. Nestled between Thygeson and her 70-something-year-old daughter on a couch at the Convalescent Home where she was then residing, I listened to Thygeson's eloquently and elegantly performed narrative. Her belief in the "great evolutionary process" evoked a very different time. Despite her skeletal and fragile appearance, she was of more than sound mind, was quite proud of her accomplishments, very capable of making decisions, and even of controlling the interview. Her demeanor was in such contrast to the other residents who were sitting passively as they listened to the bingo numbers being called.

Equally in command of her narrative, but unlike Thygeson, the pixie-ish 89-year-old Imogen Cunningham was still spry and independent. Walking through her wonderfully untamed, fragrant garden to a little cottage in the back,

I was reminded of her famous self-portrait in which she is peeking from behind a tree, wearing the same kind of bandana on her head that she was wearing that day.

From these first remarkable interviews, where I was trying to capture the creativity and activism of women like Thygeson and Cunningham, to more recent years conducting interviews with women in Palestine, my thinking about the oral history process has gone through different stages. I went from being concerned about getting the names of Thygeson's coworkers in their 1910s illegal birth control clinic, to figuring out how to get "everywoman" to understand why her story was important, to wondering if I dare reveal unpleasant information that might undermine the credibility of my narrators. The growing willingness to be more critical of our work has made me uneasy, even embarrassed, by some of the early advice I proffered.[1] In fact, what I have learned from trying to be a feminist oral historian in a conflict zone, coupled with the implications of the digital revolution, leads me to dispute some of that early advice.

From Celebration to Critical Reconsideration

Before email and social media networking, feminist activists and academics in communities and classrooms across the continent were beginning to learn about each other's oral history projects. Just as the "new social historians" of the late 1960s had spawned a second generation of oral historians who were seeking to document the lives of diverse and ordinary Americans, feminist historians were seeking to add women's voices. More than an extension of the new social history movement, we were inextricably linked to the women's liberation movement and brought sensibilities from it to our work.

From the start, in the 1970s, we rejected the prescriptions for "neutrality" and "objectivity." Our roles as advocates and participants in the women's liberation movement were captured in our characterization of feminist research as being "by, for, and about" women. Only later would we problematize those "three little words."[2]

Our initial emphasis was on developing an interpersonal relationship and a collaborative process that was more consistent with nonhierarchical feminist principles. Shulamit Reinharz, for instance, posited an ideal process under the rubric of "collaborative experiential research."[3] Despite its perfect fit with feminist principles, few of us came even close to this "new ethic of participation." Joint construction of the interview was rare and usually succeeded only when the narrators were peers of the interviewers[4]; and collaboration in creating scholarly products derived from interviews was even more unusual.[5]

Moving beyond concern with the *ideal* of a nonhierarchical, collaborative relationship, many feminist oral historians began to more honestly examine the implications of the power differential between the interviewer and narrator—especially in the context of class privilege. Judith Stacey even argued that the delusion of an alliance places the "research subject at grave risk of manipulation and betrayal," concluding that the positivist, "masculinist" research methods might pose less of a risk.[6] Without necessarily embracing the positivist model, nevertheless, many of us began to ask if we were engaged in appropriation rather than empowerment.[7] Who, after all, shaped the transcript and/or any other products of the interview?

Whether or not we actually managed to implement the feminist ideal of collaboration and advocacy or its later iteration as shared authority, these remained guiding principles of our work. Yet, serious implications flow from this commitment, not only for the interview itself and its resulting products, but for what we do or do not disclose about our narrators, and even their narratives—implications for the scholarly integrity of our work.

Constraints of the Collaborative Process/Shared Authority

The context in which the 1970s US feminist oral history movement blossomed, with our celebration of women's agency and commitment to empowering women, complicated how we talked about our narrators and their narratives. Now, almost four decades later, we are more prepared to face contradictions head on and ask if our ideal of collaboration, including interpretive authority, might actually constrain us.

I cannot say if my very first oral history interviews in 1972 with 104-year-old suffragist and birth control advocate Sylvie Thygeson and renowned photographer Imogen Cunningham empowered them, but they certainly empowered me. The accounts by these foremothers of how they confronted traditional patriarchal values filled in those missing pages of women's history. They made us proud of our past and provided role models for my generation of activists. Both of these women were the kind of pathbreakers who contributed to the celebratory women's history of the time. Both were open and warm and applauded what I was doing. In fact, there was a mutual recognition and validation of each other, the kind of "feminist encounter" that I initially described as defining feminist oral history.[8] It was not too long, however, before my interviews with Grace Burnham McDonald challenged that assumption of mutuality.

McDonald was one of the founders, in the early 1920s, of the Workers Health Bureau, a research organization funded largely by the labor movement to expose serious health hazards for workers.[9] Despite its short-lived existence (1921–1929), it paved the way for labor-management negotiations on health and safety issues. A highly educated and privileged woman, McDonald maintained her lifelong advocacy of occupational health and safety and farm labor issues, using the considerable fortune that she inherited from her husband. In the 1970s, at the time of the interview, she was still publishing her widely respected *Newsletter*. In other words, she was another role model for feminists.

What, then, was I to do about her abusive treatment of the handful of young people working on the *Newsletter* in the small building on the premises? Would this information undermine her legitimacy as a workers' advocate? In describing the interview and my relationship with McDonald, I never mentioned it, instead alluding to problems establishing rapport. And although I referred to her determination to sanitize the history of the Workers Health Bureau, I did not mention how I had sanitized my description of the interview process in order to avoid exposing her elitism and exercise of class privilege. That was certainly an unfortunate historical erasure. In other words, both my concern about undermining her contribution and respecting my status as a guest in her home clashed with my obligations as a scholar. While I would be more open today, at the time, I did not even consider it.

When it comes to Mary Inman, I am still uncomfortable revealing some of my observations. She was a committed communist who challenged the conventional Marxist analysis of the "woman question" and she remains an extremely controversial figure in the history of the Communist Party. My dilemma in this case grows out of my concern about how her detractors might use my unflattering comments. Additionally, it feels like a betrayal of her trust since I was the only person to whom she ever granted an "interview" and welcomed into her little bungalow.[10]

While I usually managed to follow my own advice and achieve some semblance of balance between my agenda and the narrator's, Mary Inman completely controlled the agenda. Ultimately, what she revealed in fits and starts enabled me to piece together her development as a radical thinker and the trials and tribulations she faced in challenging the hegemonic discourse on the "woman question" in the Communist Party USA (CPUSA) during the 1930s and 1940s. Inman promoted her argument on the equal value of the production of life and of life's material requirements largely through her self-published second book and her four-page newsletter, *Facts for Women* (1941–1943).[11]

Although she retained her class analysis, Inman's ideas ran counter to the traditional Leninist position that women's advancement would be achieved through participation in the labor force. The ideas for which Inman was roundly castigated in the late 1930s to early 1940s were given new life by 1960s socialist feminists in the United States and England. In fact, "wages for housework" campaigns could have taken a page directly from Inman's 1943 "Program for Women."[12] Even though Inman was not particularly interested in being embraced by leftists in the women's liberation movement, their interest seems to have reignited the ideological battle in the CPUSA, with a renewed attack on Inman's theories in 1972.[13]

Despite her prescient contribution to feminist theory, Inman was all but erased from the histories of women and/or communism in the United States.[14] More recently, with rare exceptions, she has been totally discredited, even by feminist historians.[15] In fact, in what seems to have become a mantra promoted largely by CP advocates, Inman's persistent campaign to promote her ideas is portrayed as the ranting of an unstable woman who could not accept that her ideas were actually adopted without crediting her.[16] Part of the problem is that this argument is based largely on sources written by the very CP leaders with whom Inman clashed, especially Elizabeth Gurley Flynn.[17]

So what do my personal sessions with Inman reveal? Was she a woman whose obsessiveness and obstinacy verged on lunacy? Or was she, rather, a "premature feminist," as a former CP leader would tell me, but only in private?[18] There is no question that Inman was obsessive and obstinate; and there is also no question that her almost four decade battle to have her ideas legitimized embittered her. These are the kind of comments I normally would put on the record. But should I also add that she was a "cranky old woman," and even somewhat paranoid; that she was rigid, on the one hand, and quirky on the other; and that although she was ahead of her time in focusing on women's cultural oppression, she maintained classical 1950s Stalinist views. Her comment that "Marx was a family man, but that Engels was nothing but a damn hippie" might have given some clues of her views if they had been recorded.

Even if some insights might have been captured in a recorded interview, how do I handle some of my other observations? Because I remain concerned about how Inman's detractors might use my revelations, I am still hesitant to talk about her almost apoplectic reaction to a bumper sticker on my car opposing an antigay initiative. And what about the "Marxism-Leninism-Inmanism" label that she seemed to be trying out on me? As bizarre as that might seem, it was clear to me that this rather exaggerated sense of her own importance is what sustained her for more than four decades.

Ultimately, Mary Inman is just too important a figure in women's history and feminist thought for me to remain silent. As damning as they might be, these observations provide a fuller and more complex picture of her. Hopefully it might also help others to understand that what they took as signs of questionable mental stability are, instead, clues to the price paid by a woman who dared to challenge the hegemonic discourse of the CPUSA.

The dilemmas I have been discussing reflect some of the critical reconsiderations of feminist oral history practice. Other lessons were driven home for me by experiences interviewing Palestinian women during the first *intifada*. Those interviews were different from my earlier work that had focused on the past. This work, instead, was intended to document an historical uprising as it was happening; and it involved repeated interviews over a five-year period during very different sociopolitical-historical moments. Furthermore, they were done in what evolved into something akin to an ethnographic project.

Neither Spy Nor Merchant: Lessons from Kufr Nameh

I first went to Palestine in December 1988 with four other Jewish Americans in what was essentially a political tour. We traveled openly as Jews throughout the West Bank and Gaza and met with a range of political leaders and grassroots activists. Although these meetings included women activists, it was only afterward that I had the opportunity to interview urban leaders of the four women's groups.[19]

By and large, the initial interviews with these women were a lot like my experiences interviewing American radical and revolutionary women. Most of them had been in contact with Arab, if not Western, feminists and all spoke fluent English. I conducted these interviews in private spaces, and, with one exception, they were with a single narrator. My focus was on the evolution of their political activism and their gender consciousness. How much each of these narrators was willing to disclose about herself varied—not unusual for activists who have concerns about security, and in some cases, whose political ideology eschewed individual biography.[20]

Although I learned a lot about women's roles in the *intifada* from these women leaders, I wanted to learn more. After all, one of the most important features of the first *intifada* was the way in which the entire population of the 1967 occupied territories participated in the nonviolent uprising: those from urban centers as well as villages and refugee camps, and men and women of all ages. I wanted to capture this movement and historical moment and bring this story to an American audience.[21] So, I returned five months later to interview grassroots activists.

The interviews with these activists contrasted with the interviews I did with the urban leaders. Few of them spoke English, so I was accompanied by an English-speaking member of their respective committees. This provided both an invaluable opening, but also worked as an impediment at times when the translator seemed to impose her or her committee's views on the narrator. Furthermore, these interviews were rarely conducted in a private space or with a single narrator, and most of the time people came in and out of the room. In other words, these conditions were hardly compatible with the kind of good oral history practice I had earlier prescribed.

During my second or perhaps third visit to Kufr Nameh, one of my village hosts told me: "Three kinds of people come here to Kufr Nameh: spies, merchants, and friends," hastening to assure me that I was the latter. However, interviewing people during times of conflict is more complex than simply establishing that you are a "friend," an ally. For one thing, even a society united in struggle is not necessarily monolithic. In Palestine, during the first *intifada* and beyond this meant different class/family/clan loyalties, differing levels of religiosity and, above all, different political affiliations.

This complicated sociopolitical context, coupled with what clearly was an advocacy agenda on my part and a desperate call to be heard on their part, together with my growing sensitivity to cultural practices, governed my oral history work. It also taught me lessons that I took back to California; lessons that made me revise my thinking about the oral history process and, especially, the critical value of ethnography. I learned these lessons organically not only in Kufr Nameh but also in Issawiyeh and Jabalya Refugee Camp, outside Gaza City.

Political Tourism: Orchestrating Information

I was especially interested in Kufr Nameh because of its reputation as a "liberated village." Located high up in the hills 12 kilometers from Ramallah, this village embodied the spirit of the first *intifada*. It was not just because Palestinian flags usually waved freely throughout the village and nationalist graffiti covered the walls; or because forty of the two thousand villagers were in prison, two others had been martyred, and another four had been deported (including three women); or because eight houses had been demolished. Rather, this village, where all the Palestine Liberation Organization (PLO) factions as well as Islamic Jihad and Hamas had a presence, symbolized the way a new social order was being created: a community medical clinic was beginning to service the area; an agricultural cooperative was producing at least some of the products that could replace the boycotted Israeli goods; and the four women's committees, numbering one hundred members, were each running their own cooperative projects and kindergartens.

My initial visit to Kufr Nameh in June 1989 was quite unexpected. A local Union of Palestinian Women's Committees (UPWC) activist from Qadura Refugee Camp in the heart of Ramallah met me at the kindergarten where I had spent the morning. She took me to her home in the camp where she lived with her 90-year-old father and 60-some-year old mother. Like my interviewing experiences with the urban activists earlier that year, we spoke one-on-one and in English. However, unlike the more equivocating feminism of the leader of her own group, this Iraqi-educated science teacher was explicit about her feminism.

After noisy confrontations outside the iron gates of the camp subsided and we could hear no more gunshots, we headed to the edge of Ramallah and boarded the one lone bus parked there. Only then did Ghada tell me that we were going to Kufr Nameh. After a bumpy 30-minute ride, the bus cleared the rise to the village and stopped. We disembarked and followed a young fellow passenger across the road to a small building in what appeared to be a compound of several homes. Seeing the relatively bare room with a circle of chairs set up, I realized that this was going to be another political tourism visit. I joined the several local men who were already seated, and for the next hour I listened to the translated account of one of the villagers, Salim, who had just been released after serving a three-year prison sentence.

Following that, after a quick tour of the newly built chicken hatchery, we entered another compound off the highway, where three sisters-in-law and their multiple children were waiting for us in a small, detached sitting room—another example of how carefully orchestrated this visit was. The women, in their late twenties and early thirties, were all dressed in what I came to call "transitional dress," long, red velour robes that were so common among the married village women. The women's recitation of their committee's projects and activities initially was fairly routine: visiting homes of the wounded and imprisoned; joining the 1,000-women march on International Women's Day; running a kindergarten and a literacy class. Their tone changed dramatically, however, when they started talking about their *zaatar* cooperative. They explained how they gathered the wild thyme—an activity they laughingly said had become all the more popular since the Israelis had declared it illegal—and prepared it with sesame seeds and salt. All during this group interview, the young children played on the floor in front of us and the men either peered in or came in and sat respectfully silent.

Although this initial visit to Kufr Nameh seemed like an extension of my 1988 political tour, it was an important beginning of what was to become an evolving relationship as a "friend," at least to this political grouping. I returned to Kufr Nameh a week later with a university student from another committee and interviewed a group of young women who were involved in a sewing cooperative. However, it was not until the following winter that the nature of my relationship to the village and to individual women began to deepen.

From Political Tourist to Participant-Observer-Ethnographer

That 1990 winter visit started when I joined a group of American students who, like me, had come to Palestine to participate in the New Year's Day "Hands across Jerusalem" international solidarity event. Accompanying them on *their* political tour gave me an opportunity to reintroduce myself to the villagers and make arrangements for a stay. As we dismounted the bus, I immediately recognized the open expanse of the compound and building where I had first met Salim, the recently released political prisoner.

Several days later I returned to the village with Helena, a committee activist from Ramallah. We headed straight for the compound where I had first met with the three sisters-in-law and where Amal and her aunt seemed to be waiting for us. This was my first interview with Amal, who was cradling her infant. Much like "ordinary" women in the United States responded when I approached them for an interview, she asked, "Who me?" As before, Amal's husband Mahmoud kept peeking in. His presence outside the room might have contributed to Amal's shyness and reticence, and so too might his teasing remark: "You aren't telling her all our secrets, are you?" Indeed, Amal's off-handed joking response to what would be different in a future Palestinian state probably revealed a lot more than I initially understood. No sooner had she responded laughingly that "men will take two wives," then she immediately asked Helena not to translate.

Only years later, after Amal personalized her comment a bit more, and especially after I stayed in her household many times, did I come to understand what she might have been signaling. Watching her clean up the scattered sunflower seed shells on the floor following the nightly stream of male visitors, or spending hours stooped inside the *taboun* (the outdoor clay oven) baking bread, or the countless other chores that consumed her days and sapped her energy, I could understand how cowives might very well provide some welcome relief.

My second interview that evening was with Zahra, an older committee activist. When I arrived at her house with Mahmoud, who was going to serve as my translator, half a dozen men were already seated in the room. As we sat down, the ubiquitous small electric heater was pulled toward us and Farhid, Zahra's husband, served us coffee and tea. Despite Mahmoud's efforts to impose what he thought was my agenda, Zahra formulated her own. Of all the activities of her women's committee, it was the literacy class that she emphasized. Clearly, learning to read and write in just six months empowered her. This was another one of those nuggets that I was learning to appreciate from these *intifada*-focused interviews with married village women.

These interviews were becoming just one element in what was evolving organically into more of an ethnographic project. I was becoming a participant in the life of the community, joining in the nightly visiting pattern; and at times my guest status was almost forgotten as people went about the business of their own lives. All the time, of course, I was also an observer, and was seeking to understand the complicated dynamics of the relationships among the people in the village.

Communalism and Individualism

During my several visits and stays in Kufr Nameh that winter, meeting with and interviewing members of all four women's committees, including some of the more confident younger women, I managed to conduct only one conventional life history interview in private. Maryam ordered her entire extended family outside the house for two hours and told me her story through my German Palestinian translator as the three of us huddled over a little electric heater.[22] I am still not sure why she was so willing to do this highly personal interview, standing out more as an individual than an integral part of the collective/communal experience. Perhaps her organizing trips to other villages made her more like the urban activists; or perhaps she was simply relieved to find sympathetic listeners to hear her very sad story. Only later, remembering the level of disclosure of Issawiyeh committee members, did I wonder if it was perhaps a reflection of the more explicit feminism of her particular committee. In any event, the sleepover at Maryam's house and breakfasting and visiting with the extended family in the compound the next morning helped me to appreciate more deeply the complex relationships among and between the villagers: couples in their thirties with young children, older women, young single women, and the men connected to these women.

When I first visited Kufr Nameh in the summer of 1989 and heard Salim's prison story, I was in awe of this man who had just finished serving his second term as a political prisoner. Six months later, after staying in his household and observing his interactions with his wife, Rawwa, his children, and his brothers—and especially after basking in the warmth of the sun together on a cold winter morning—I was able to relate to him and the others in the village as ordinary mortals, even as I continued to admire their courage. One of my most enduring images of Kufr Nameh is of Salim coming out of the kitchen to say goodbye as I was about to board the last bus to Ramallah. Without embarrassment, he came out of the kitchen and extended his elbow to bid me farewell. In the midst of making bread dough, his hands were completely covered with flour.[23]

Despite my admiration and appreciation for the way that the villagers were simultaneously struggling against Israeli oppression and forging a democratic future, my deepening understanding also exposed the warts—especially during my next two trips in 1991 and 1994.[24]

Changing Historical Moments, Changing Relationships

By 1991, my interactions with the villagers with whom I had developed warm relationships became more relaxed. The men talked openly with me about difficult subjects, such as the cheering from the rooftops as Iraqi scuds hit Israel; and they were as eager to hear my views as I was to hear theirs. The women recognized me immediately and greeted me with warm embraces. Amal and the younger ones had grown more self-confident and did not hang back during the men's political discussions. They were also more open in *our* discussions during which we often challenged each other's assumptions. As Mahmoud, my usual host and guide in the village, explained: "I was not traveling with a group or just passing through, but spent time with them—and returned." Perhaps it was also because I was more at ease and not as intent on recording their stories.

I had also gained a deeper appreciation of the complexity of interviewing in changing political contexts, particularly of conducting interviews *during* a historical uprising rather than in retrospect.[25] Not only had the participants themselves changed, especially the women, but the "narrative moment" in 1991 was far different than 1989 or even 1990, at the height of the *intifada*. Then, many of the village projects were thriving and the women's committee, to which Amal and Zahra belonged, had not only expanded their kindergarten, but were still running their literacy project, had started an English class, and were engaged in tutoring some of the "slow people" in the village. There was more open discussion about women's roles, and the women were discussing Arab feminist writers.[26] The *intifada* had taken a different turn by 1991 and there was more self-reflection and evaluation, even as people were settling in for the long haul. Certainly, they were no longer breathing politics all the time.

By the time I returned in 1994, the mood had changed dramatically throughout Palestine, except perhaps among Fateh activists who were welcoming Yasser Arafat's recent return. Not only had the *intifada* gone through its last dying gasps by then, but there were few signs of the grassroots activism that had sparked the hope of building a democratic civil society. In Kufr Nameh, half of the village activists were involved in Hamas, with declining numbers in the left committees. Except for the medical clinic and one cooperative, most of the *intifada* projects had closed down, including the centers of the various women's committee and their child care programs. The only two that remained were run by Fateh and the mosque.

The Kufr Nameh women who I had come to know best over the years were generally discouraged and pessimistic. Although Muna was pleased with her expanded role at the medical clinic after receiving specialized training in women's health, she was despondent over her unsuccessful efforts to reenergize the members of her committee. Most of the other young activists had married and were constrained in their outside activities. Zahra, noting that she was the only older woman still involved in the committee, felt that things had gone back to the way they were before; that she was once again trapped in her home. The *taboun* bread collective that she had started when Farhid was in prison did not survive as a collective enterprise. Farhid himself noted that the women did not have anything to do outside the home anymore. The pessimism of those who I had befriended over the years in Kufr Nameh, those in whose houses I had slept and eaten, was best summed up by Muna at the end of her interview: "Before we had one occupation, now we have two."[27]

Historicizing the Narrative Moment

The changing political context in Palestine between 1989 and 1994, and the accompanying changing moods of villagers of Kufr Nameh along with my own changing role, raises a host of questions about oral history work. While acknowledging that it is a method used by people in a range of disciplines, the emphasis is usually on the past. But when does the past begin; and what are the differences between interviewing participants during the course of a social movement and retrospectively?

If I were to try to conduct interviews today as a newcomer, when the first *intifada* is no longer a living moment, how would I conduct them, and what would the women even tell me? Would their memories be of their 1994 gloomy assessment, or of the empowerment they felt from the projects in which they had earlier participated? Perhaps if I were able to conduct more biographical interviews, if not full life histories, the changing nature of their *intifada* activities and its effects might be evident. However, the political context today would probably produce a narrative moment that is more akin to 1994. Even more to the point, in today's context, with greater distrust and fewer international visitors to the village, it is doubtful if I could even establish the kind of relationships that had enabled me to become a participant-observer-interviewer.

The importance of the narrative moment in my interviews in Palestine was brought home rather forcefully in analyzing the interviews that I conducted with the urban women leaders over the years. At different political moments in the nationalist struggle they characterized their gender consciousness quite differently. While they downplayed their feminism at the height of nationalist unity during the early days of the *intifada*, when that unity was torn asunder, they were more forthcoming about their feminist beliefs.[28]

Regardless of the historical moment in which interviews are conducted, questions about the appropriateness of doing individual life histories remain. At the time, it was primarily the real life cultural context in which I was working, where the constant presence of extended family members and neighbors made individual interviews, let alone life histories, impossible. More than that, however, it quickly became apparent how inappropriate the life history interview was in this context. My Palestinian narrators and I shared an advocacy agenda, a belief that their stories could help educate Americans about Palestine; and this framed what they thought was relevant. For instance, why would I want to know about their childhoods? Usually, the only memory they related was of playing Israeli soldiers and Palestinian fighters—the equivalent of our cops and robbers. Ironically, the Israelis were actually both cops and robbers!

Beyond this, there is the ethical issue that Margaretta Jolly has raised about her interviews with former British women's liberation movement activists. Namely, is it really appropriate to do individual life histories with members of a movement that eschewed individualism in favor of collectivism?[29] Although that rejection of individualism might not have been as clearly enunciated in the Palestinian women's movement, it was certainly a guiding principle of the grassroots village activists in the early days of the *intifada*. Zahra's 1994 lament about the privatization of the bakery that the women had earlier established, certainly points to an earlier commitment to collectivism.

From Kufr Nameh to Watts

By the time I started my life history interview of Johnnie Tillmon in the spring of 1991, I had already come away with some lessons from Kufr Nameh. I was no stranger to Tillmon, a founder of the first grassroots welfare rights group in the early 1960s who went on to become a leader in the national movement. I had conducted a topical interview with her in 1984 focused on the "ANC Mothers of Watts Anonymous" and had maintained contact with her over the years.[30]

Tillmon was pleased when I approached her in 1991 about being interviewed as part of a project I was doing with my students on re-envisioning the history of "the" women's movement.[31] She thought that perhaps she could use the interviews to write her autobiography. Retired and in poor health, she was largely confined to her small bungalow in Watts, not far from the housing project where she resided at the time she started ANC Mothers of Watts Anonymous with Ardelphia Hickey. We quickly established a warm relationship, fostered no doubt by our political discussions before and after the interviews. These ranged from Palestine to the impact of the recession. Although President Bill Clinton had not yet made his 1992 campaign promise to "end welfare as we know it," it was already clear that the kinds of programs for which Tillmon had fought would not survive. This climate undoubtedly played a role in the construction of her narrative.

I had earlier advised that, if at all possible, life history interviews should be conducted in a quiet space where the narrator felt comfortable, with as few distractions as possible. When I arrived at Tillmon's house for our first session, it was pretty clear that this interview would be more akin to my experiences with grassroots activists in Palestine. Tillmon's husband, blues musician Harmonica Fats, was on the telephone in the back room arranging gigs and periodically shouted out to her for a phone number. Various adult children came in and out of the front door, heading to the kitchen just behind where we were sitting. At one point, her son came in with a load of laundry and started the washing machine. So not only were people coming and going, but there were repeated interruptions.

Nevertheless, I did not stop the tape recorder and we did not stop the interview—except for quick introductions as various family members came and went. Rather, as I learned from my experiences in Kufr Nameh, I went with the flow. This did not produce the best audio quality, but I did a series of interviews with Johnnie Tillmon that accommodated her lifestyle and her cultural context—a bit like the extended family context in Kufr Nameh. Accustomed to these interruptions, this key leader of the poor women's movement in the United States spoke openly and freely and on her terms.

That, I think, is one of the most important lessons that I learned in Kufr Nameh. Yes, I still believed in trying to develop a shared agenda, or at least to balance the narrator's and interviewer's agendas. But like it or not, ultimately, it is the narrator's terms and conditions that govern the process. That might mean conducting an interview in a somewhat chaotic setting and ending up with less-than-desirable audio quality. In other words, an authentic interview experience might well mean that we cannot follow "best practices." Even as I write this and wholly subscribe to it, I am troubled. Although it might be necessary "to go with the flow," it might run counter to our obligations as scholars to create the best possible historical record. This becomes particularly troublesome when we want to take advantage of digital technology and put that document on the web.

I Won't Ask, and Don't You Tell: Oral History on the Web

In Kufr Nameh and throughout Palestine, I would not have dreamed of asking questions that might possibly jeopardize those I was interviewing; and trying to be culturally sensitive, I was cautious about asking highly personal questions. Although we were not this cautious in our early interviews in the United States, today, with our interest in posting oral histories on the web, I believe that we have to think differently.[32]

While a narrator might not hesitate to discuss very personal matters in an oral history destined for an archive, the potential of wider and relatively unrestricted public access is a different matter. For instance, when I spoke with the women whose transcribed oral histories I edited for my *Rosie the Riveter Revisited* book, I was surprised when one of them commented that she was upset about the passage where she mentioned using a diaphragm.[33] "But, Marie, I said, you approved that in your transcript." "Yes, but a book is different!" she replied. Indeed. And placing an oral history on the web is a quantum leap in distribution that has implications for our work.

Furthermore, the current proliferation of legislation to monitor and even prosecute American citizens for political activism should make us think more carefully about how our interviews might be used. This concern is heightened by the realization that there is little we can do to protect our interviews from government snooping. [34] For me, being attentive to what we record and deposit, let alone what we place on the web, means following what I call the golden rule of interviewing: never ask a question that you would not want to answer; or today, which you would not want posted on the web. In other words, today I might monitor both myself and my narrators more than I did in the past. The danger, of course, is that this cautionary approach can stifle the spontaneity of the interview. Unfortunately, that might be one of the tradeoffs that we have to live with, especially if we want to make oral histories available on the web. For while the new technological advances have enabled us to implement the democratic promise of widely sharing our materials, it has brought with it perils, as well.

Rather than a new conundrum, perhaps this harks back to the contradictions inherent in our earlier ideal of a collaborative feminist process. After all, my own reluctance to expose damaging observations about Mary Inman was based on the potential use of those observations to undermine a significant precursor of later feminist theorizing.

Conclusion

In the early days of the US feminist oral history movement, most of us believed that we were engaged in a process that empowered—or at least validated—both us and our narrators. I went so far as to suggest that it was a "feminist encounter, even if the narrator is not herself a feminist."[35] Today, after 40 years of interviewing women in both the United States and Palestine, I wonder what both the narrator and interviewer really gain from the experience.

It was a sense of mutuality in Kufr Nameh that made me reflect on my past encounters. Amal, a woman I interviewed repeatedly and in whose household I stayed, commented during my second visit: "Your questions are good; they make us think. We discussed them at our meeting." In turn, the interviews with her and the other women challenged me and turned my Western feminist ideas on their head. So, while these interviews might have been a "feminist encounter" of sorts, I cannot vouch for other interviews I have conducted over the years. I suspect that the greater mutuality I experienced in Kufr Nameh was a result of my repeated visits and the relationships that evolved over time.

The cultural context and the collective nature of the interviews in Kufr Nameh also made me doubt our glorification of individual life history interviews. Perhaps because oral history in England has been so enmeshed in community history, practitioners there seem more attuned to the contradictions inherent in the practice. While Margaretta Jolly raised a question about doing individual life histories, Graham Smith was more direct, noting how oral historians had contributed to "gross individualism."[36]

So, instead of doing a life history with Johnnie Tillmon, should I have conducted a joint interview with her and ANC Mothers of Watts cofounder Ardelphia Hickey? Or, as I have advised in the past, should I have done individual interviews first, to be followed by a collective interview? Might this be a way to honor the work/life of an individual without promoting "gross individualism?" In any event, perhaps it is time to reconsider the practice of life history interviewing, particularly for social movement activists or people who were part of a collective experience.[37]

Twenty years ago, in an earlier reflection on my experiences in Palestine, I was struggling with the contradictory demands of advocacy oral history and scholarly integrity.[38] Today, with more reflection—and technological advances— I am convinced that it is not advocacy oral history that presents us with these challenges, but rather the general commitment to collaboration. For instance, from a scholarly standpoint, including best practices for documenting our interviews, how should we handle observations about our narrators that might reflect poorly on them; observations that we might feel too uncomfortable to share with them? And, given the potential risks posed by wide distribution of their interviews, with few effective controls over use, how can we safeguard their narratives? Should we be less ready to try to get the "whole story," perhaps even avoiding certain questions or even dissuading our narrators from revealing certain information? What kind of historical document would we be creating or, rather, not creating?

I suppose that the response to all of these questions—some of which might be viewed as heretical—is that we have to maintain complete flexibility and act according to the dictates of each situation. In other words, we have to do our best to balance the competing demands of scholarly integrity with collaboration and respect for the narrator and the cultural context. Ultimately, we have to make judgment calls continually. We can best do that if we continue to reflect not only on our own experiences, but also on those of practitioners from a variety of disciplines and backgrounds, taking lessons from them to better contextualize and make sense of our interviews. Certainly from history, we should pay more attention to the sociopolitical context of the narrative moment; and from anthropology, perhaps we should incorporate more ethnographic fieldwork practices in order to deepen our understanding of cultural meanings.

While we thought we were forging new ground 40 years ago, the practice of oral history has changed a great deal since then, becoming more complex. Yet, it still remains a remarkable way to capture the human spirit. I have learned so much from all of the women that I have interviewed over the years, be they more illustrious and "accomplished" or unrecognized ordinary women. I will never know how or even if my interviews impacted them; I know that they certainly had a tremendous influence on me and for that—as well as their stories—I am profoundly grateful.[39]

Notes

1. Sherna Berger Gluck, "What's So Special About Women? Women's Oral History," *Frontiers* 2, 2 (1977): 3–13. Reprinted in Susan H. Armitage, Patricia Hart, and Karen Weathermon, eds., *Women's Oral History: The Frontiers Reader* (Lincoln: University of Nebraska Press, 2002), 3–20.
2. Sherna Berger Gluck and Daphne Patai, eds., *Women's Words: The Feminist Practice of Oral History* (New York: Routledge, 1991), 1–5.
3. Shulamit Reinharz, "Experiential Analysis," in *Theories of Women's Studies*, eds. Gloria Bowles and Renati Duelli Klein (London: Routledge & Kegan Paul, 1983), 182.

4. For example, see Maria Mies, "Towards a Methodology of Feminist Research," in Bowles and Klein, *Theories of Women's Studies*, 117–39.

5. See Lorraine Sitzia, "Shared Authority: An Impossible Goal," *Oral History Review* 30, 1 (2003): 87–101, for a rare example of this kind of collaboration.

6. Judith Stacey, "Can There Be A Feminist Ethnography?" in Gluck and Patai, *Women's Words*, 113–14.

7. This was the focus of a roundtable at the 1988 US Oral History Association conference.

8. Gluck, "What's So Special About Women?"

9. The 1973 interview with McDonald and my interviewer comments can be found at www.csulb.edu/voaha. Charlotte (Todes) Stern's discussion of the WHB can also be accessed there.

10. Inman never permitted me to record a formal interview. Following our dialogic conversations that lasted as long as three hours, I immediately summarized our conversation. As a result, I can vouch only for the accuracy of a few short memorable quotes or phrases from the two unrecorded sessions (March 17, and July 14, 1978).

11. *Woman Power* (Los Angeles: Committee to Organize the Advancement of Women, 1942).

12. See the final edition of *Facts for Women*, nos. 39–40 (April–May 1943).

13. Margaret Cowl, "Inman's 'Maternity as a Social Function,'" *Public Affairs* (January 1973): 56.

14. The first serious acknowledgment of Inman in any history of the left was Dan Georgakakas's solicitation of an entry for the *Encyclopedia of the American Left* (New York/Oxford: Oxford University Press, 1998), 363–64.

15. Kate Wiegand, *Red Feminism: American Communism and the Making of Women's Liberation* (Baltimore: John Hopkins University Press, 2001). Rosalyn Fraad Baxandall has been the rare exception: "Precursors and Bridges: Was the CPUSA Unique?" *Science and Society* 66, 4 (2002–2003): 500–505.

16. With the exception of Baxandall, the contributors to the special issue of *Science and Society* basically followed Wiegand's line.

17. In a private communication, biographer Rosalyn Fraad Baxandall noted that Flynn ultimately toed the party line.

18. Personal conversation with Dorothy Healey. The term "premature" feminist alludes to the House Un-American Activities Committee (HUAC) designation of CP members as "premature anti-fascists." In a communication to the author, Baxandall noted that in her own private conversation with Healey she was "almost sympathetic to Inman." Nevertheless, Healey echoed the personal disparagement of Inman in the special issue of *Science and Society.*

19. The four groups, each of which was aligned with a faction of the Palestine Liberation Organization, were: Union of Palestinian Women's Committees (UPWC), Women's Action Committee (WAC), Women's Social Work Committee (WSWC), and Women's Work Committee (WWC).

20. For similar observations, see the chapters by Nadia Jones-Gailani and Luis van Isschot in this collection.

21. See Sherna Berger Gluck, *An American Feminist in Palestine: The Intifada Years* (Philadelphia: Temple University Press, 1994).

22. Her story is partially recounted in ibid., 135–40.

23. Ibid., 135.

24. My book was already in publication at the time of my 1994 trip.

25. Gluck, "Advocacy Oral History: Palestinian Women in Resistance," in Gluck and Patai, *Women's Words*, 205–19.

26. Because many of them could not read, these works were read aloud and then discussed.

27. She was referring to the return of Arafat and the entourage of Fateh leaders who supplanted the more democratic civil society organizations with the older, patriarchal clan structure.

28. Sherna Berger Gluck, "The Representation of Politics and the Politics of Representation: Historicizing Palestinian Women's Narratives," in *Living with Stories: Telling, Re-Telling and Remembering*, ed. William Schneider (Logan: Utah State University Press, 2008), 120–33.

29. Margaretta Jolly, Polly Russell, and Rachel Cohen, "Sisterhood and After: Individualism, Ethics and an Oral History of the Women's Liberation Movement," *Social Movement Studies* 11, 2 (2012): 1–16.

30. Their name was taken from the Aid to Needy Children Program extant at that time.

31. See Sherna Berger Gluck with Maylei Blackwell, Sharon Cotrell, and Karen Harper, "Whose History, Whose Feminism: Reflections on Excavating the History of (the) US Women's Movement(s)," in *Community Activism and Feminism Politics: Organizing Across Race, Class and Gender*, ed. Nancy Naples (New York, London: Routledge, 1998), 31–56.

32. The following reflections are based on a presentation at the 2006 International Oral History Association conference, Sydney, Australia, and published in Spanish in *Historia Antropologia y Fuentes Orales* 36 (2006): 5–16.

33. Sherna Berger Gluck, *Rosie the Riveter Revisited: Women, the War, and Social Change* (Boston: G.K. Hall, 1987).

34. Besides an earlier incident of the Federal Bureau of Investigation (FBI) subpoenaing Karl Braden's interviews deposited at Wisconsin Historical in 2011–2012, the British government fought to gain access to closed Boston College interviews with Irish Republican Army (IRA) activists.

35. Gluck, "What's So Special About Women?" 5.

36. Sherna Berger Gluck, "Has Feminist Oral History Lost its Radical/Subversive Edge?" *Oral History* 39, 2 (2011), 67.

37. In fact, at a 2011 US Oral History Association roundtable, one participant suggested that perhaps it was time to ask "When, not if, should we abandon the life history interview?"

38. Gluck, "Advocacy Oral History," 205–19.

39. This echoes the remarks made by Alessandro Portelli in the afterword.

CHAPTER 2

"On" and "Off" the Record in Shifting Times and Circumstances

Julie Cruikshank and Tatiana Argounova-Low

The title of this collection, *Oral History Off the Record: Toward an Ethnography of Practice*, points to questions about "the record" as a concept that may have divergent meanings for oral historians and our interlocutors. Might unspoken negotiations alert us to tensions, especially in collaborative projects where we researchers cannot necessarily control outcomes? Should we be surprised that discrepancies about what should constitute the record arise, especially when our questions and expectations may clash with other narrative practices? Rather than posing a methodological problem, we argue here, questions about what appears on or remains off the record may provide opportunities, even further insights into what oral histories can contribute to understanding past and present.

Our chapter examines what initially appeared on, and what seemingly remained off, the record in two different oral history projects. One draws on Cruikshank's long-term research in northwestern Canada, the Yukon Territory, since the 1970s. The second discusses a more circumscribed oral history project where Argounova and Cruikshank collaborated in the mid-1990s as part of Argounova's ongoing research in the Russian Far East. While different in scope, each project began with the explicit goal of documenting difficult imperial histories from perspectives of Indigenous peoples who had firsthand experience of the process. In both cases, accounts offered "on the record" initially diverged from our expectations, in surprisingly similar ways. Specifically, our interlocutors downplayed personal, autobiographical themes even when documenting life stories was the shared objective. We have come to appreciate speakers' insistence on speaking on their own terms when they choose to participate with us in these endeavors and this has taken us down avenues that might have otherwise remained unexplored.

We begin by outlining circumstances of the research, initial expectations, and then some surprises in each case. We go on to discuss concepts that became explicit in each location: narrative practices, notions of personhood, and the significance of connecting story to place. We conclude by identifying insights that may follow from locating "the record" as part of—even an active agent in shaping—oral history projects.

Despite dramatically contrasting regional political histories, there were compelling similarities in processes occurring in northwestern Canada and in northeastern Siberia in the late twentieth century. Both populations are located in the circumpolar north where they are positioned far from centers of economic power, yet enmeshed in global economies through states that now govern them. Both were experiencing a moment of rare opportunity in the late twentieth century. In northern Canada, from the 1970s onward, Yukon First Nations were negotiating claims to land and self-governance with the government of Canada. In the Republic of Sakha (Yakutiia) during the 1990s, following the dissolution of Soviet power, Sakha (formerly called Yakut) were directing energies to constitutional and economic changes. These were exciting times, but also times of considerable risk. In each location we were working with senior, rural individuals, locally identified as experts, who wanted to record impressions of their changing times. Questions about what should be on or off the record were very much on the agenda of our collaborators. Our intention here is to document concepts they brought to this experience of recording oral history, specifically their agency in defining that record.

Yukon Territory, 1970s

Circumstances of my (Cruikshank's) Yukon research date back some decades. During the 1970s and early 1980s, I spent more than ten years living in the Yukon Territory and worked with several senior women who were eager to document life stories for younger generations. The context at the time was the energy and activism surrounding Indigenous claims to land and aspirations to self-governance. Young Aboriginal women my own age were absorbed in devising research strategies and procedures for negotiations with federal and territorial governments. They were aware that ethnographies included detailed accounts of men's hunting practices but less about women's lives and they were interested in what senior women could contribute. In the 1970s, recording life stories was deemed to be a project suitable for an outsider, like myself, willing to work with families while younger activists got on with the important job of building the case that would finally lead to a land claims settlement in the 1990s. They introduced me to mothers, aunts, and grandmothers who agreed that recording life histories in booklets for families was a project they wanted to pursue, work that continued for more than two decades and through many stages. This was all prior to formal training on my part—I returned to graduate studies in anthropology only in the mid-1980s.

Initially, I viewed my role as documenting the modernizing lives of women whose experiences spanned the end of the nineteenth century and most of the twentieth. The women with whom I worked had almost all been born just prior to or just following 1900, and my expectation was that I would hear stories associated with impacts of the Klondike gold rush in the late 1890s, Alaska Highway construction in the early 1940s, ongoing missionary activity, and the increasing intrusion of the state into regulation of family lives as Canada proceeded to "develop the North." I anticipated recording stories of struggle and survival, documenting the experience of colonialism in the words of women who had lived through extraordinary times. So I was initially taken aback when they responded to my careful and cautious questions about their life experiences with instructions that I take down stories I recognized as classical or "traditional." Those narratives entangled categories we now call nature and culture: they dramatized relationships between humans and animals who embodied more-than-human qualities. My attempts to redirect our conversations to themes that I took to be related to life stories were politely but firmly rebuffed. They were having none of this, and they deflected my shallow questions. They clearly had their own purposes—and I unexpectedly found myself preparing lengthy booklets of narratives under their direction, taking us far from what I took to be our original purpose. Significantly, they insisted on recording these stories in English, by then the first language for most young people following decades of residential schooling and later public day schools. In the process, we also documented long lists of place names and names of ancestors in local languages.

They rapidly made me aware that they were evaluating our relationship by my readiness—my slowly emerging capacity—to "think with" the stories they told me. Without this, they implied, they would be wasting their time, and mine. This was the key to our relationship: a coconstruction where they initially set the terms and I did my best to keep up. When they did later speak about their own experiences, they referred me back to those stories we had already recorded, citing them as reference points to explain choices they had made in their lifetime, from childhood to adulthood to middle and old age. "Remember that story I told you about?" they might ask, reminding me of a story we had already recorded. "That's the one I thought about then." When you know enough to ask the right questions, they seemed to be saying, then we can talk about these things. Rather than narratives of struggle, they told stories of coherence enabled by this narrative scaffolding, "as though life were inherently transformational and intrinsically subject to change."[1] When they talked about darker times or difficulties, this was usually in private conversations that were "off the record." In some cases, at their request, we even erased parts of recorded tapes if they felt they had spoken too freely. They had a clear vision of their audience: younger people whom they felt needed their fund of stories to guide them. The initial record we made was being directed to them.[2] Years later, when Angela Sidney, Annie Ned, Kitty Smith, and I coauthored a collaborative account of our work, *Life Lived Like a Story*,[3] they were intentionally expanding their audience to include readers beyond the Yukon. Following their lead, and themes in those stories, led me to archival documents that further illuminated how tellers (and now their descendants) continue to navigate historical memories of the twentieth century.[4]

Sakha Republic, 1990s

The Siberian project came later, in the mid-1990s. I (Argounova) was then investigating the consequences of Soviet rule for indigenous Sakha populations in one region of what is now the Republic of Sakha (Yakutiia), as part of my doctoral research at the University of Cambridge. Intrigued by how oral history might broaden my archival research, I invited Cruikshank to participate. Located in northeastern Siberia, this was the first region in the new Russian Federation to enthusiastically declare itself a sovereign republic with its own constitution in April 1992.[5] Ambivalent relations between Sakha and Russians date back to the seventeenth century and had become particularly fraught by the mid-twentieth century, the era at the center of my research.

One of our questions when we embarked on this project was comparative. In North America, there has been a growing awareness that oral traditions can contribute to varieties of historical understanding, especially where written documents are relatively recent or largely absent. But what does oral history—telling one's story—mean in a political context like the Russian Far East where memory was dangerous—even punishable by death—since the 1920s and then sought out as a virtue after 1990?[6] How do local representations of the past in states shedding totalitarian legacies differ from those in what we call liberal democracies? Can perspectives from one region contribute to our understanding of practices in another? We return to these questions in our conclusion.

Our oral history research centered on one rural administrative district or *ulus*—called Taatta ulus—across the Lena River and some 270 kilometers east of the capital, Yakutsk. We were invited there because of my ongoing research as well as my family's historical roots in the region. We initially spent three weeks in Yakutsk at the Sakha Institute of Humanistic Sciences (Institut Gumanitarnykh Issledovanii) then traveled by ferry across the Lena River and hitchhiked on to the village of Ytyk-Kuol', the main settlement in Taatta. Our hosts were expecting us and had carefully planned our days. Our guides included a long-standing resident who organized our expedition and drove us; his nephew, a young man 20 years of age who came with a video recorder to document our progress; two elder historians from two different communities; and an artist, Ernest Alekseev, who, in the early post-Soviet moment had begun building memorials—sculptures in wood—to commemorate resistance and survival during the darkest times of the twentieth century. A thoughtful man, Ernest inquired about our interests and when we raised the subject of oral tradition, he immediately connected this with his own work: "You have come to the right place," he told us. "Our folklore is in our material tradition. Certainly they go together. The epic *olonkho* is told in a beautiful place, so the material tradition is also important."[7]

Our days had a distinctly expeditionary flavor. Initially they were explicitly framed as an education for us, the researchers, in what we needed to know before we could ask appropriate questions and we spent long hours at local museums immersed in the history of Taatta *ulus*. We made no tape recordings ourselves: this was the prerogative of our hosts, largely because of uncertainties about confidentiality and concerns about risk, and our collaborators directed the young videographer about when and what to record. Argounova, a linguist and professional translator before studying anthropology, conducted interviews in Russian and Sakha; Cruikshank made detailed notes that we later expanded and reviewed together. Our exchanges allowed Cruikshank to pose frank questions that might have been more difficult for Argounova to ask, given her "insider" status and expectations about what she should already know.

Again, there were surprises. Learning about the ancient Sakha epic *olonkho* was deemed to be a crucial first step in our education. Sakha have Turkic linguistic and cultural roots. According to some theories they reached the Lena River several centuries ago as horse and cattle breeders, permitting their confident claims to status as the dominant Indigenous population.[8] Among forces crystallizing Sakha national identity throughout the republic in 1996 were *olonkho* performances. This epic begins in the Asian steppes and dramatizes ancestors' travels to the Far North. It depicts a cosmology in which upper, middle, and lower worlds must be negotiated and traces the Sakha struggle to stabilize human life in the middle world. As the only historical account prior to Russian documents, *olonkho* provides a rich narrative of competing and contrasting relationships—first, among these pastoralists and the hunters they encountered already living in the region, and later with advancing Russians.[9] Sung and spoken in archaic language, it remains central to any Sakha autohistory. *Olonkho* performances were eventually deemed to be evidence of "bourgeois nationalism" and were suppressed during the long Soviet era.

This region, Taatta, was targeted by Soviet authorities following accusations of *natsionalizm* directed at several Sakha poets, playwrights, and activists who drew inspiration from *olonkho* performers. By the 1930s, officials asserted that their writings directly challenged state power and arrests were made. During our visit, oral accounts of these events were part of lively conversation in Taatta among those trying to rebuild a sense of shared memory. A rich archival record became available as Soviet-era documents were slowly declassified in the 1990s. Elsewhere, Argounova has traced the sequence of events that followed when these writers were identified by scholars as "founders of Yakut literature" at a time when speaking their names was prohibited.[10] Charges against these writers were subsequently directed at the entire *ulus*. Students from Taatta district were not accepted to institutions of higher education during the 1950s. Economic investment in the region ceased. Retrospectively, these incidents are recalled as attempts to detach people from their past: storytellers were prosecuted; local place names were changed to Russian names; educational opportunities were denied to a generation. "They wanted to remove the roots from the ground so that no new cultural writers would emerge from this place," we were told.

Rather than speaking directly about their own personal experiences of these difficult times, our hosts recounted the lives of named nineteenth-century *olonkho* performers and the struggles of early-twentieth-century writers whose names could now again be spoken.[11] They expected us to document a process of commemoration, showing how contemporary artists and activists were drawing on this epic tradition to tell stories about the suppression of cultural practices during the Soviet era, especially in Taatta *ulus*. We were concerned about issues of confidentiality in a potentially unstable political situation, but also aware that in 1996 speakers insisted on the importance of telling their stories more broadly. Relying on social networks in Yakutiia, Argounova was able to ensure that elders and the artist accompanying us were satisfied with our overview before we published our article. The oral history record, then, centered on documentation of post-1989 commemorative practices.[12]

Shared Concepts: Narrative, Personhood, Place

Despite marked differences between these subarctic contexts, our collaborators in each region seemed to share certain concepts about goals and outcomes for these projects. Three themes, elaborated here, stand out in their accounts: first, respect for long-standing narrative strategies; second, culturally specific ideas about personhood; and third, attachment to specific places. Our intention here is not to generalize, but to identify various understandings of oral "history" that emerge and comingle in these two settings.

Anthropologist Carole McGranahan argues that "thinking of one's life as a story, as something that can be narrated, involves social processes and conventions operative well beyond individual processes of reflection or experience. Narrating one's life, then, is to situate oneself and to be situated in dialogue with society."[13] In each project, the agreed-upon objective was documentation of alternative histories recounted by individuals who had actually experienced unprecedented political changes first hand. What is striking in retrospect is how none of our collaborators took this as an opportunity to recount a personal narrative in any straightforward way—a genre often central to oral histories. Instead, narrators responded with what might be called classical stories, starting with ancient narratives and eventually linking them with events from recent history. Implicitly, foundational narratives provided reference points for talking about thoroughly modern issues or dilemmas they had confronted, scaffolding for framing life experiences. One senior Yukon woman, Angela Sidney, reinforced this by saying that this was how she advised anyone from her community who came to her with a problem—by thinking of an appropriate story that would give the visitor guidance, rather than definite answers. As she concluded one winter afternoon, "Well, I've tried to live my life right, just like a story." Similarly, Sakha participants emphasized material representations of narrative in sculptured wooden carvings.

Second, in each setting narratives addressed concepts of personhood that expanded the category of what it means to be fully human. Senior women in the Yukon stretched the boundaries of "personal narrative" to include ancestors, but also other sentient beings. In Sakha Republic, stories of oral storytellers (*olonkhosuts*) and the writers who listened, took inspiration from them, and later were punished for their convictions were also deemed personal. Genealogical connections and a sense of profound mutuality pervaded these accounts: "What happened to my kin happened to me." In both locations, ancestors were orally footnoted, making genealogical connections explicit: Annie Ned, for instance, would begin her Yukon narrative by orally footnoting: "This is my two grandpas' story, Big Jim's and Hutshi Chief's. Lots of people in those days, they told their story all the time. I'm telling this story not from myself, but because everybody knows this story. This is not just my story—lots of people tell it . . . That's why we put this on paper."[14]

Third, physical place was central in each location, and recording oral history was a mobile process. Stories were embedded in particular named places on the land, places of significance in the tellers' own lives or in the lives of ancestors. Senior Yukon women often stated the impossibility of talking about places where they had spent early years—or even recalling the names of these places—without physically visiting them. Being there, they insisted, brought back memories, names, and events. Traveling through landscape authenticates stories and is proof of belonging to land. So we began regular outings, in my

(Cruikshank's) vehicle, sometimes traveling for some distance. "I'm born here. I branch here…My roots grow in jackpine roots," Kitty Smith noted expansively, as she documented her connections to places we visited.

During the summer of 1979, Angela Sidney recorded 130 place names in Tagish, Tlingit, and English (languages coincidentally from three distinct language families). Traveling by car, boat, and on White Pass and Yukon Railway, we visited each location, making a record of names and stories:

> You go to that *K'aa' Detl'óoní*—that means "where arrows are tied up in a bundle." That's Tagish language: Tlingit (language) is *Chooneit Wusi.axu Yé*. Now they call it "Frying Pan Island," because it sometimes joins to the shore. It's across from Ten Mile, *Tsuxx'aaí*. They call that mountain behind that place *K'aa Deitl'óoní Dzéle'*. He's the one, Fox, gave Indian names to all those points on Tagish Lake.[15]

Hoisting herself into the front seat of my vehicle with her cane, one day, Annie Ned, by then in her eighties, announced cheerfully, "Chicago, here we come!" We launched our way that day into a crater-like zone of Alaska Highway (re)construction. Flanked by huge trucks, diggers, and dumpers, we passed the hill *Sánkäla* where she once lived with her second husband. She explained that it was once "owned" by his paternal grandfather, *Ajängakh*, a member of the Wolf moiety, though this was not ownership in the sense of private property, but more like a location from which to invite others to visit, hunt, and fish. "You don't know this place, so I am going to sing it for you," Annie Ned told me more than once, alerting me to stop at a location she was clearly seeing through eyes different from mine. After naming the composer and the circumstances under which that song was "made," she would begin to sing. In this way, we documented numerous place names she remembered from childhood, mapping genealogy and song onto place. She then pointed out Nichäla where she and her husband used to hunt on horseback and another hill where she went as a child with her aunties to hunt "gophers" (arctic ground squirrels). In this sense, oral traditions explore connections between land and Aboriginal title, and land becomes part of social relations rather than a thing in itself. Dodging construction equipment, some of it piloted by her grandsons who waved cheerfully to us as we passed, lent a particular irony to our conversation. She was "seeing" the same hills that were simultaneously being leveled to straighten the Alaska Highway in 1985.

In Siberia, in order to reach sites where Ernest Alekseev's memorials stand, our group of six—elder, artist, driver, videographer, and two researchers—squeezed into a jeep on a journey that provided vivid sensory experience of an "off road vehicle." Merely locating destinations provided the first challenge and constituted a significant part of the story we were learning: the forced relocation of residents from homesteads and concentration in larger settlements following collectivization in the 1920s and 1930s. We headed across taiga, sometimes with no regard for track or trail and other times on overgrown paths, our driver and elder trading navigational tips. This phase of our journey involved visiting several homesteads, then following seasonal movements from summer to winter sites, all long abandoned after collectivization was enforced.

The mysteries of piloting our vehicle in 1996 left an indelible impression that the landscape was being resocialized with human stories inscribed through memorials. Most startling were dramatic carvings of images from *olonkho*, including those representing an underworld that Ernest entitled "World of Evils" (see figures 2.1 and 2.2). He described them as depicting the "dark times" following the 1920s, and as "a mystic picture of terror engendering feelings of terror in the landscape." This is manifestly a memorial on many levels—commemorating the *olonkho* performer, of course, but also the difficult years when Sakha traditions were officially prohibited.

Materiality: What Is the Record?

What role does the record play here? What do our research partners identify as the record in each case? What is their objective in participating with us in these projects, and how does this shape what gets on or remains off the record? What might this reveal about collaborative oral histories? The oral historian's role in this process is clearly more than that of exotic secretary; but in addition to creating a record, we arguably need to attend to unfamiliar narrative strategies to see what they reveal and what new forces they bring into being.

In both 1970s Yukon Territory and 1990s Sakha Republic, speakers viewed their work with us as part of an ongoing dialogue with their own society. In addition, they wanted their accounts to reach a more distant "outside" world. What oral history reveals about the past is important, they would agree, but it also demonstrates the practical work that foundational stories can do in the modern world. Our interlocutors used ancient narratives (poetry, song, visual imagery) as reference points to reflect on twentieth-century experiences; as models for explaining choices made during difficult times; and as one way to reinstate forgotten ancestors to their rightful position in history. Their expectation was that we were there as intermediaries and mediators—perhaps even as proxies for that outside world—who could help them extend their work and stories to broader audiences. They expected us to comment on how "traditional" stories can be used in decidedly modern ways.

What remained "off the record"? In each setting, participants downplayed personal, autobiographical themes at the same time as they expanded the

Figure 2.1   This tree, carved by artist Ernest Alekseev, represents the upper and middle worlds from the *olonkho* epic, inhabited by humans, animals, and birds. Photograph by Julie Cruikshank.

Figure 2.2 Here, Ernest Alekseev's sculpture depicts the lower world, again from *olonkho*, the World of Evils, symbolized by these figures. Part of his extensive memorial, it stands near the birthplace of the Sakha literary figure Oyunskii (1893–1939) who died in a Russian prison. Photograph by Julie Cruikshank.

concept of personhood to include other dimensions: long-standing connections among humans past and future, with other sentient beings and with land. One of the things we learned from this comparison is that senior individuals in both 1970s Yukon and 1990s Siberia were equally circumspect—careful with words. What they left off (or erased from) the record was anything that they thought might harm or "make trouble" for living people. Inevitably, there were stories that could be told openly, and those that could not, all governed by normative understandings of history and knowledge. In both locations, Yukon Territory and Sakha Republic, our interlocutors chose to put recognizably classic narratives on the record in an attempt to ground and legitimize a public story, especially during difficult times.

In each case, expectations about the material record were made very clear. In the 1970s Yukon, for instance, the observation that researchers frequently left no record of local value—or worse, sent back only a jargon-filled thesis—was repeatedly raised. Our agreement from the outset was that individual booklets documenting each narrator's account in her own words, under her authorship, would provide the record of local interest. One afternoon, as I (Cruikshank) was recording a story, Kitty Smith pointed to her young grandchild sitting nearby. "See that Tina?" she asked, "She's six years old now. Pretty soon she's going to start school. Pretty soon paper is going to talk to her." Mrs. Smith's goal of having her work included in schools was straightforward.[16] She had seen the conventional record—the school books—and wanted to appropriate this medium and add her own voice. And so she did. When discussions arose about whether these narratives should be formatted in more standard English in published accounts, it was universally agreed at the time that it was more important that their words "sound like Grandma." Those early printed stories are still used as resources in variety of contexts: in classrooms, at storytelling festivals, and, more recently, in film and theater productions by Yukon Aboriginal artists and writers.[17]

Over time, in the Yukon, voices on tape have gained importance as another kind of record. Narrators retained copies of audio tapes, and in one instance, Annie Ned's grandchildren gave her what was known in the 1980s as a "boom box," a portable radio complete with flashing red lights synchronized with sound level. Sitting in front of her cabin, she would cheerfully listen and play the tapes for friends. Tape recordings, though, degrade. More recently, Cruikshank arranged for copies to be made on archival discs, now in the Yukon Archives. We negotiated an agreement with the Yukon Archives that stewardship of those tapes remains with a named family representative as the source of permissions for anyone who wants access. Like Alekseev's wooden sculptures in Sakha Republic, the lives of this record will be limited by the durability of the medium. Paper may outlast the recordings.

In Sakha Republic, Ernest's memorials placed in locations where individual *olonkhosuts* and writers once lived provide a record of ancestry for local people, their primary audience. Tolia Barbassytov, a young videographer acting on behalf of the community, provided an essential part of that record. The local television station loaned him the camera, possibly the only one in Taatta district at the time. There was never any question that he would accompany us, making his record of what was significant and topical at the moment for Taatta residents. He was documenting what people with legitimacy in the community—elders and artists—had to say, carefully streamlined for a local audience, material to which they (not the researchers) comfortably asserted rights. This video recording remains in Taatta as a record of this project. More recently, in Sakha communities where Argounova continues to conduct research, a young person is frequently assigned to record what is said, not for her records but for their museum or school. Our carefully vetted written account, in turn, provided a traveling "record-of-the-record" for a more limited audience, readers of an academic journal.[18] The sculptured material record does its real work "at home" while our account simply documents that work for a distant audience. Carved from wood, it will have a limited life history before it disappears. It provides a story of endurance through difficult times, safely lodged in a past where it can do no harm to living individuals but may build spaces for speaking more directly about difficult times. Public commemoration through monuments has a long history in Russia; Ernest is appropriating a well-known Russian medium.

Each of these projects, briefly described, demonstrates some of the tensions associated with collaborative projects, including divergence and convergence of participants' views. As Sophie McCall argues in her book *First Person Plural*, collaboration is not a solution to the problems of representation, but can nevertheless take us in productive directions.[19] Globalizing depictions of the "Indigenous," for instance, are not without problems, given the range of groups who now claim (and those who reject) this affiliation.[20] In mid-1990s Siberia, claims by Sakha to indigeneity were being questioned by numerically smaller populations—Eveny, Evenk, and Yukaghir—displaced when Sakha arrived some centuries ago.

To conclude, we suggest that collaborations of this kind make a contribution to both local participants and scholarly objectives. Globally, studies of oral tradition and oral narrative increasingly emphasize the human agency of narrators and the diverse strategies they employ in specific times and locations. Such projects have shifted from viewing oral history primarily as documenting the past, and toward investigating narrative forms for speaking about past and present. As historian Luise White argues in her compelling book *Speaking with Vampires*, it is precisely the unfamiliarity of some stories that makes them good historical sources. They provide a way of seeing the world as the narrators do, depicting states of vulnerability and the often unreasonable relationships that accompanied colonial visions.[21] Accounts passed on orally are more than just "data"; they are themselves products of historical composition. They document a particular kind of history-making; in other words, they are histories but they also *have* histories. Narratives that are "good to think with" (to cite Levi-Strauss's well-turned phrase) can provide serious commentary on changing circumstances, tacking among past, present, and future as well as between facts and the imaginary, and between memory and history.[22]

Returning to a question raised at this chapter's outset about whether perspectives from one region might contribute to our understanding of practices in another, we conclude with a general observation. In our experience, insights from one region did contribute to our appreciation of what we were hearing in the other along two registers: first, through *concepts* and second, through *intentions* that our interlocutors brought to each project. Questions about what should be on or off the record were very much on the agenda of our collaborators in each region. They persisted in framing their responses using local concepts: meaningful stories, culturally specific notions of personhood, and personal attachments to place. How those concepts were deployed differed in the two locations, subarctic Canada and the Russian Far East, but in each case they became the project's foundation. Our interlocutors' intentions and goals became clear in their close attention to the materiality of the record. They viewed the record as having an impact and wanted a clear role in defining its outcomes.

In both the Yukon Territory and in Sakha Republic, much has changed since the work described here began. By 1994, Yukon First Nations had successfully negotiated land claims and self-governance agreements; consequently, the state is required to relinquish some powers and to give more autonomy and control to local governance. In Sakha Republic, during the same period, there has been a massive withdrawal of the state from social services at the same time as the state reasserts itself with fresh vigor, under the auspices of privatization. Historical accounts, both written and oral, continue to be vigorously debated and discussed in each location. Narrators at the center of these oral history projects become authorities whose interpretations, in turn, may subsequently be contested. Far from presenting a unified historical narrative, oral accounts frequently acknowledge how conflict, consensus, and hierarchy enter into historical representation. The collaborations described here document moments in the creation of an enlarging record that will undoubtedly be reexamined critically as subsequent generations reevaluate their own histories. Walter Benjamin once described the obligation of historians as "to brush history against the grain."[23] Our hope would be that the ongoing lives of oral histories attune us to such brushing, and especially to the contributions that local social theories may contribute to scholarly narratives.

Notes

1. Peter Gow, *An Amazonian Myth and its History* (Oxford: Oxford University Press, 2001), 22, makes this very point.
2. Booklets were compiled between 1974 and 1976 with eight women: Rachel Dawson (Whitehorse); Mary McLeod (Dawson City); Kitty Smith (Whitehorse); Kitty Grant (Carcross); Bessie Johns (White River); Victoria Lord (Carcross); Pat Lindgren (Dawson City); and Louise Paul (Eagle, Alaska).
3. Julie Cruikshank, in collaboration with Angela Sidney, Kitty Smith, and Annie Ned, *Life Lived Like a Story* (Lincoln: University of Nebraska Press, 1990).
4. Cruikshank, *The Social Life of Stories: Narrative and Knowledge in the Yukon Territory* (Lincoln: University of Nebraska Press, 1990); *Do Glaciers Listen? Local Knowledge, Colonial Encounters and Social Imagination* (Vancouver: University of British Columbia Press, 2005).
5. Marjorie Mandelstam Balzer and Uliana Alekseevna Vinokurova, "Nationalism, Interethnic Relations, and Federalism: The Case Study of Sakha Republic (Yakutia)," *Europe-Asia Studies* 48, 1 (1996): 101–20.
6. See Daria Khubova, Andrei Ivankiev, and Tonia Sharova, "After Glasnost: Oral History in the Soviet Union," in *Memory and Totalitarianism*, ed. Luisa Passerini (Oxford: Oxford University Press, 1992), 89–101; Irina Sherbakova, "The Gulag in Memory," in Passerini, *Memory and Totalitarianism,* 103–15.
7. A detailed account of this project, including an extended discussion of this artist's work appears in Julie Cruikshank and Tatiana Argounova, "Reinscribing Meaning: Memory and Indigenous Identity in Sakha Republic (Yakutia)," *Arctic Anthropology* 37, 1 (2000): 96–119. Ernest Alelseev's comments appear on page 106.
8. A. I. Gogolev, "Cultural History of the Yakut (Sakha) People: The Work of A.I. Gogolev," *Anthropology and Archaeology of Eurasia* 31, 2 (1992): 1–84.
9. A. P. Okladnikov, *Yakutia: Before Its Incorporation Into the Russian State*, trans. Henry N. Michael, Arctic Institute of North America (Montreal: McGill-Queen's University Press, 1970), 263–76.
10. Tatiana Argounova, "Scapegoats of Natsionalizm: Ethnic Tensions in Sakha (Yakutia) Northeastern Russia" (PhD diss., University of Cambridge, 2001); Tatiana Argounova-Low, *Politics of Nationalism in the Republic of Sakha (Northeastern Siberia) 1900–2000* (Lewiston: Edwin Mellen Press, 2011).
11. We heard accounts of the lives of two *olonkhosuts* from this region, Teehan Petrov (1863–1919) remembered by the nickname "Teehan the Song" and Ivan Nikolaev (1860–1940) better remembered as "Tabakharov." Local writers they inspired included Aleksei Kulakovskii (1877–1926), Anempodist Sofronov (1886–1935), Nikolai Neustroev (1895–1935), Platon Sleptsov-Oyunskii (1893–1939), and others. All were from Taatta and are now widely remembered as key Sakha literary figures.
12. Cruikshank and Argounova, "Reinscribing Meaning."
13. Carole McGranahan, "Narrative Dispossession: Tibet and the Gendered Logics of Historical Possibility," *Comparative Studies in Society and History* 52, 4 (2010): 768.

14. Annie Ned, *Old People in Those Days, They Told Their Story all the Time* (Whitehorse: Yukon Native Languages Project, 1984), 44.

15. Cruikshank et al., *Life Lived Like a Story*, 87; see also Angela Sidney, *Place Names of the Tagish Region, Southern Yukon* (Whitehorse: Yukon Native Languages Project, 1980).

16. Kitty Smith, *Nindal Kwädindür: I'm Going to Tell You a Story* (Whitehorse: Council for Yukon Indians and Government of Yukon, 1982).

17. Angela Sidney, Kitty Smith, and Rachel Dawson, *My Stories Are My Wealth* (Whitehorse: Council for Yukon Indians, 1977); Angela Sidney, *Tagish Tlaagú: Tagish Stories* (Whitehorse: Council for Yukon Indians and Government of Yukon, 1982); *Haa Shagoon/Our Family History* (Whitehorse: Yukon Native Languages Project, 1983); Ned, *Old People in those Days*. See also note 2, earlier. More recently, Northern Native Broadcasting Yukon produced a film for television, *The Storyteller* (2008), celebrating the life and work of Angela Sidney. In 2012, Leonard Linklater published his play entitled *Justice* (directed by Floyd Favel and produced by the Gwaandak Theatre) based partly on oral histories recorded years earlier by elders Angela Sidney, Kitty Smith, and Annie Ned.

18. Cruikshank and Argounova, "Reinscribing Meaning."

19. Sophie McCall, *First Person Plural: Aboriginal Storytelling and the Ethics of Collaborative Authorship* (Vancouver: University of British Columbia Press, 2011).

20. Marisol De la Cadena and Orin Starn, eds., *Indigenous Experience Today* (Oxford: Berg, 2007).

21. Luise White, *Speaking with Vampires: Rumour and History in Colonial Africa* (Berkley: University of California Press, 2000), 10.

22. Alessandro Portelli, *The Death of Luigi Trastuli and Other Stories: Form and Meaning in Oral History.* (New York: State University of New York Press, 1991); Luise White, Stephan F. Miescher, and David William Cohen, *African Words, African Voices: Critical Practices in Oral History* (Bloomington: Indiana University Press, 2001).

23. Walter Benjamin, "Theses on the Philosophy of History," in *Illuminations*, ed. Hannah Arendt (New York: Schocken, 1968), 257.

CHAPTER 3

Politics and Praxis in Canadian Working-Class Oral History

Joan Sangster

Oral history theory and practice are inescapably intertwined, and both are molded by international currents of thought as well as more specific national, regional, intellectual, and social influences. Our theoretical discussions are also implicitly political: the assumptions we make about how to frame our studies, which questions to ask, what issues are important, and indeed, why we even *do* history, are all shaped by inherently political perspectives on our world. While this may be more explicitly stated in some oral history projects that announce their sympathies for the marginalized groups they are collaborating with, it is also true of oral histories of prominent individuals, or those studies that claim a more distanced empiricism.

This chapter explores two moments of oral history politics and practice over the past 30 years, illustrated by examples from my research on Canadian working-class history. During the first moment of recuperation, circa the 1970s, our oral history praxis was often linked to new currents in social history and to the energy and goals of social movements for justice and equality. The second moment, 20 years later, was associated with more attention to memory, subjectivity, and identity, and to the influence of poststructuralist theory, with its skepticism about grand narratives, the unified self, and a knowable experience. While recognizing a general movement in oral history writing from social science to cultural approaches,[1] from an emphasis on experience to one on subjectivity, my reflections suggest that these moments did not simply evolve as a linear trajectory: ideas from each period overlapped and informed each other, and there were some continuities as well as discontinuities in oral history research. Our current moment offers us an opportunity to develop a critical praxis that incorporates both the insights and oversights of past work: this is preferable to a Whig historiography that suggests an onward and upward story in which each new academic orientation theoretically surpasses the one before. Not only does such a perspective diminish the importance of locating our oral history praxis within the changing academic, political, and social context that shaped our research, but it also discourages us from identifying the acuity of previous work or the limitations of current writing, both of which may be useful in our future practice of oral history.

Interviewing Old Left Women

My own interest in oral history, like that of many other working-class historians, grew out of the intellectual zeitgeist of the new social history and 1970s movements for social transformation. We were interested in challenging the prevailing "history from above," reviving a class analysis that took into account experience and human agency, and recovering the lives of historical actors—both women and the working class—who had left fewer written records for posterity. Early working-class oral history projects were often examples of "movement history,"[2] linked to grassroots political initiatives, alternative presses, nascent labor studies programs, and by the 1980s, in Canada at least, to a new labor history journal (*Labour/Le Travail*) and its popular book series.[3] Certainly, previous labor historians had employed oral history,[4] however this moment was characterized by more emphasis on working-class, rather than institutional labor history, and on challenging the prevailing hierarchy of importance in historical studies by focusing on the everyday: domestic labor, family, community, leisure, resistance, waged work, unions, and so on. While a few traditional political historians dismissed the reliability of oral history, we should not exaggerate their influence; within social history, there was a keen openness to this method, especially in the overlapping circles of immigration, labor, and women's history.[5]

Emerging from this political moment, I was caught up in debates that crossed the activist/academic spectrum concerning the creation of hybrid Marxist-feminism and in a concurrent political praxis of socialist-feminist organizing. Our political interests and activities raised questions about the history of women on the Left, underlining the importance of linking the past and present in a critical dialogue: what theoretical positions had fostered women's equality; how was the sexual division of labor reproduced in political parties; how did one ensure that gender, sexual, and reproductive freedom remain integral to socialism? By focusing on both women in the Communist Party of Canada (CPC) and the social democratic Cooperative Commonwealth Federation (CCF) from 1920 to 1960, I could compare these two traditions, considering contemporary feminist questions about the efficacy of vanguard parties and the value of separate feminist organizing within socialist parties. Focusing on CPC and CCF women also implicitly challenged the prevailing two wave categorization of feminism, which had obscured socialist and communist women's activities, relegating them to a 40-year trough of supposed political somnolence. Both archival and oral sources suggested an alternative story, one that some of the women I interviewed very much wanted recuperated. Why, they asked me for instance, do contemporary feminists not realize that communist women had celebrated International Women's Day since the 1920s?

My questions for social democratic and communist women were not only prompted by the politics of the time; the interviews were likely also shaped by my age, ethnicity, class background, and the ideological similarity/distance that women felt in relation to me. The prevailing Thompsonian emphasis on experience, agency, and the active making of class also influenced my research; these themes seemed especially resonant for oral history research, with its potential for interviewees to recast their own history by recovering and revaluing aspects of working-class life. Although more critical pieces were emerging, warning us against a facile equation of oral history with "democratization,"[6] retrieving women's recollections and contextualizing them was still a key priority. Was this because I/we were focused on an uncritical project of recovery and celebration? I think our approach was more complicated. Most historians of the working class did not see interviews as a simple panacea for the paucity of sources, nor did they believe that eyewitness accounts were the be-and-end-all for research: interviews were understood to be fallible, variable sources, not simply truth, writ large. Information on the who, what, and how of organizing was sought out, to be sure, but unpacking the meaning events had for workers was also on our agenda. Women's posture, silences, language, and justifications were sometimes noted, but I did not feel I had academic permission to muse over these in print—even if I discussed them over the kitchen table with other researchers like Georgina Taylor, who was also interviewing CCF women.[7] To concentrate on these issues might seem to undermine the voices of women who had already been historically silenced; to focus on the fluidity or distortions of memory might reinforce a privileging of written sources. Moreover, reflecting inordinately on my role in the interview seemed too self-preoccupied. After all, I was not that interesting; these women were.

In retrospect, many of the methodological issues increasingly explicated by oral historians were ones I had encountered in a less choate, untheorized way: ethical issues (which I might have characterized as political concerns); the insider/outsider dilemma; the creation of a past to fit the present; the influence of the dominant ideology on interviewees; and the interview as interactive process.

Certainly, I was cognizant of the structural limitations on my interviewing; I was a graduate student doing a cross-country research tour, couch surfing, and not tarrying too long in one city, so I did almost no repeat interviews, which might have allowed me to develop more detailed, collective biographies. There was at least one exception to this pattern. One woman I visited a number of times in Brandon, Manitoba (where I was marooned and unemployed for a lonely year in 1983), provided welcome conversation amid my prairie isolation, but I only interviewed her once, as to do more interviews might have altered (I thought negatively) the nature of the friendship. Smart, reflective, and compassionate, her insights became part of a relationship, not a transcript. Despite the fact that I felt a sympathetic connection to some of these women, there remained boundaries between us. After all, I was assuming a role as an academic investigator, they were acting as informants; as social scientists argued, to deny the fact that we are implicitly "trading on" our professional identities in this process simply denies or masks our authorial power.[8]

I knew that these women's perceptions of my politics also affected the interview. There were anxieties from both groups. Some of the social democrats were party loyalists who would not have liked my (critical) views on the CCF (later the New Democratic Party or NDP), and they were also concerned that I might unfairly assess their past politics through the lens of a modern, judgmental feminism. In one instance, this came through in the language of approbation an interviewee used. Some women in the CCF never supported separate women's groups within the party, feeling this ghettoized women who should take on the challenge of equal activism with men. Sensing correctly I had some sympathies for feminism and autonomous women's organizing, one female trade unionist became quite emphatic about her opposition to such views: "*I* am no women's libber. I have *no* use for those who run around with signs screaming and yelling [ironic for someone who had been on many picket lines]. Also, no patience with mollycoddling women who can't do this or that till they talk to their husband."[9] There is also no doubt that I appreciated listening to dissidents who had left one or the other party because they seemed to offer more critical, "outsider" perspectives. The narrative of the "rise and decline" of the CCF as a socialist party offered by Eve Grey Smith, a smart, politically engaged, passionate woman who was an (expelled) refugee from David Lewis's Cold War CCF, was interesting to me precisely for this reason.[10]

For many communist women, the Cold War was still prescient in their memories, and unless you were from a known Party family (a dwindling number), they feared what you would publish from your research. Even some ex-Party members did not want to speak too critically of their past, jeopardizing relationships with friends still in the Party—not to mention the difficult personal dilemma of denigrating their own lifelong dedication to the movement. I did not press women for interviews, and listened to their instructions about what personal information I could not use; this was a political as much as an ethical issue as they had the right to be shielded from lingering anticommunism and ongoing state surveillance. At times, personal connections assuaged some fears. The mother of a university acquaintance, a longtime communist activist who was respected for her political work, offered me some names and addresses across the country; since I was able to write ahead, I could give these women time to contemplate my request and check me out. When I interviewed a group of communists involved in the On To Ottawa Trek,[11] the presence of my cointerviewer, Karen Teeple, the daughter of another deceased but well-liked Party member, likely helped to put the room at ease.

My questions and language also had to accommodate changing historical contexts. I was wary of imposing post-1960s feminist ideas on their lives; if my politics assumed reproductive and sexual choices were important priorities, I knew this was not necessarily true for them. One needed a two-sided approach that contextualized their political choices, but did not avoid all retrospective judgments since the latter are inherent to historical writing. Moreover, I had to listen, not just to *what* women said, but also the feeling they conveyed. Their *belief* that motherhood inevitably defined women's lives more than men's, their *investment* in an ideology of familial care came through as so genuine that I could hardly characterize both parties' relegation of women to home-centered issues as mere manipulation, as it might appear from written sources, and indeed, as other historians had argued.[12] The dominant cultural scripts of the time were internalized by left-wing women, though I could also see some subversion and rewriting of those scripts, with communist women's promotion of a more public, political, "militant" version of mothering.[13]

A few CCF women leaders, with a sense of their place in history, were used to being interviewed, and spoke with caution and reserve; I doubt, for instance, that Grace MacInnis, a well-known former member of parliament, told me anything that was not in another interview. Still, less prominent women might also scaffold their stories around conventional narrative forms: some communist women, for instance, framed their story of youthful political awakening as a difficult road to the discovery of an alternative political truth, an understandable narrative given that their truth was so diametrically different from the hegemonic values of society. Women's failure to remember key events, I also realized at the time, was not necessarily accidental: after all, "memory is what we forget with."[14] It was obvious that women interpreted their political past in light of their subsequent political lives and loyalties. Why were some communist women so unresponsive to discussion of how they understood the Hitler-Stalin Pact? In their stories, this period was downplayed, compared to some of the more successful, earlier Popular Front campaigns, or a later period that denoted a "high point" of political engagement for them. Internment of male communists in 1939 was discussed, but less so the Hitler-Stalin Pact. This was not so much "an organized structure of forgetting,"[15] as individuals coping with a subsequent history that was painful or discomforting. In my handwritten notes, I jotted an observation that suggests an explanation: "too embarrassing" to recall, especially for some Jewish activists who accepted the party line at the time, but subsequently felt differently about this pact with Nazi Germany. Forgetting the Pact also expunged negative aspects of Party history, namely, its loyalty to the Comintern and the bureaucratic control of the Canadian party by its Central Committee. Was there a way I could have engaged with them on this and other uncomfortable topics? I am not so sure, but it meant that I did not have material that might indicate *if* and *how* women did wrestle with problems of Stalinism. Never questioning women when they misremembered, altered, or romanticized (in my view) closed down an opportunity to understand how they came to justify—in some cases—the unjustifiable, such as the show trials in the late 1930s, or Stalinism more generally. My age and perhaps a certain youthful political naiveté did not help. I was deferential to my elders who I thought had seen a lot more of life and struggle than me. Still, we can censor others by censoring ourselves. In retrospect, I think the notion that oral historians should avoid challenging and contradicting our interviewees—a shared problem across the field of oral history—can be condescending, especially if, like these women, they lived lives of engaged, political, public activism and debate.

Some of women's hesitations and silences on particular issues such as sexuality had already been raised in public conversations between New Left and Old Left women.[16] Communist women often relayed a conception of politics that centered on the public, the Party, and the programmatic; their impression of the 1960s women's movement was that it focused *too much* on the private, the personal, and sexual liberation. My list of questions was thus designed to speak more to forms of public organizing (even though many involved family and domestic issues). Those few women who were in touch with current politics, deeply aware of feminism, or who had rebelled specifically against a male-dominated party, offered more comments on familial relations, the sexual double standard, and women's lack of reproductive freedom.

While some of their priorities were different from those of my generation, women in the Old Left believed in the *collective* project of working-class mobilization, a commitment that resonated politically with me. Did we take our interviewees' words as simple truths, our project being one of recovery and "uncritical celebration?"[17] I am not so sure that we can press oral history into a Whig narrative in which an initial emphasis on celebratory recovery is followed by more complex, cultural interrogation. The project of recovery did not disappear after the 1980s, and an interest in cultural analysis was already apparent in the 1970s. Canadian working-class history, for example, was deeply concerned with the contours of working-class culture, and working-class oral history was discussed with reference to the cultural Marxism associated with Raymond Williams.[18] Nonetheless, in the next moment, the way in which culture and society were perceived was to shift. My analysis of these early recuperative efforts has emphasized the imperative working-class historians saw in situating texts in their historical context, in analyzing oral history as historical evidence and practice, rather than concentrating primarily on the interview as text. An emphasis on deconstructing the text, and on self-reflection as an end in itself, became more visible in the next moment of oral history.

Working Women's Identities in Context

By the 1990s, debates and priorities in oral history had altered course, a direction described by two scholars—rather too dichotomously—as a move from "realism to narrativity."[19] This shift, evident in historical writing more generally, was characterized by more emphasis on subjectivity, identity, narrativity, performance, and memory. Oral historians reflected more openly on the provenance, meaning, and textuality of the interview, along with nontextual forms of communication such as silences, hesitations, and evasion. There was a discernable shift in oral history writing from the third- to the first-person voice, from the erasure of the historian's presence in the interview to a discussion of it, and from an emphasis on "events" to understanding the "meaning" those events held for interviewees.[20] Notions of "shared authority"[21] between interviewer and interviewee and the relationship between oral historians and the communities they collaborated with were explored in more depth, and attention to "Memory" replaced "individual memories" as memory and oral history, for some distinct, but for many others intimately interlaced, was explored.[22] In feminist scholarship, the cultural shift was perhaps especially noticeable, as interest shifted from "consciousness to language, from the denotive to the performative,"[23] though in working-class history, there may have been a residual resistance to the demolition of materialist ways of seeing. The continuing influence of feminism did encourage attention to the operation of multiple forms of power, both within our research processes, and as a discernable theme in the interviewee's life; this augmented attention to identity formation reinforced the project of integrating ethnicity, race, gender, and sexuality into working-class history.

Although reflection on the collaborative construction of the interview intensified under the influence of poststructuralist appraisals of knowledge production, critiques of objectivity and metanarratives already had a place within the discipline, particularly for radical movement history practitioners. Moreover, scholarship using oral history penned well into this second moment revealed strong continuities with earlier aims of recuperation: women's words were generally assumed to have a measure of authenticity, there was minimal reflection on the constructed, indeterminate nature of the interview process, and interviewers did not dwell in their monographs on the dialogic nature of their oral sources.[24] Perhaps most important, oral history was still seen as a source marked by its unique connection to living individuals who were revisioning their own histories. Oral history remained appealing to many labor historians precisely because it offered a window into experiences obscured in written sources, and suggested a story of working-class agency distinct from historical narratives of high politics and nation building.

Increased attention to the interview as process did give us the permission to reflect in print on why and how working-class women remembered the way they did, as well as the power dynamics shaping interviews. When I undertook research on the lives of wage-earning women in a small manufacturing city, international interdisciplinary debates in oral history stimulated my exploration of the interplay between women's narratives and the dominant ideological norms of the time, highlighting how both accommodation and resistance operated in the workplace.[25] As a means of exploring this second moment in oral history, I reexamined these interviews, asking if and how a new emphasis on identity and memory enriched my analysis. As an illustration, I want to reflect on the life of one woman I interviewed, in part because I always avoided writing about a singular life history; I was concerned that a biography might create the picture of a heroic individual rather than an understanding of working-class women. Yet, as Pamela Sugiman has argued, there is value in exploring personal memory in relation to collective history, in order to understand how and why women create the life stories they do.[26] Concentrating on one interview allows us to engage more fully with the personality, emotion, detail, and dialogue that can get lost in a group biography. The life of one woman may show that memory is not simply determined by "cultural scripts" for we can see the "role of the consciously reflective individual, or the role of experience in changing the ways in which individuals view the world."[27] Moreover, recounting one life story can also be an effective means of peeling back the many layers of memory that characterize women's multiple lives as workers, mothers, daughters, wives, providing us with insight into how class memory is bifurcated with experiences of gender, culture, and ethnicity.

I originally interviewed Corinne because she had worked at one of the city's largest factories, General Electric.[28] Her interview included a great deal of material on her teen years that I did not integrate into my chapter on youth, largely because she was an English war bride, and had not worked locally until after World War II. During the war, she joined the British women's land army as an underage teenager, by doctoring her birth certificate (although with her father's knowledge). Her teenage years were very vivid in her memory, more so than her factory experience, presumably because they represented a more carefree youth and a home she lost when she emigrated; the narrative style she used conveyed this well, as she spoke with humor, laughed, and offered great detail in describing her youth. Given that she had a number of children soon after arriving in Canada, and then had to support them with blue collar and service labor when she became a young widow, the association of fun with her youth, even during wartime bombing, was understandable. As an example of her rather cavalier teenage attitude toward life, Corinne told me that she chose the armed service according to pants: "I wasn't really patriotic but I loved the uniform [of the land corps]—jodhpurs, bright green jumpers, but I didn't like the hat so I went to the Timber Corps as I liked the hat...then [later] I joined the Army. [In that case] I wanted to wear slacks." Posted in northern England to read radar, she became a part-time physical education instructor, which had always been her career dream. She also became embroiled in a series of escapades and misdemeanors with a close friend who was "a bit of a devil." "But I was a devil too," she added with a laugh. When they were required to clean an officer's office as punishment for disobeying curfew, she and her "devil" friend found the "leave and rail pass book" on his desk. "So we wrote ourselves a few. And rail passes. We had a ball for awhile."

Her leave-taking from England was also described in some detail, and with reference to clothes. At a mere 19, she understandably had cold feet about going to Canada. She and her mother hatched a plan for a staged accident that would prevent her from leaving, but being already accident prone, she worried that she might actually be injured. In the end—unlike some other war brides she knew—she did not run away but caught "that retched boat." What she remembered especially was her mother admonishing her choice of goodbye outfit: it was a "red suit and she would not forgive me. She was heartbroken. She was so angry I was going to leave in a red suit that I had bought with all my army coupons...So I took the red suit off to please her." Clothes carry many meanings, and for her, they came to symbolize her life transitions, both those embraced and those dreaded.

In the book, however, I primarily drew on her descriptions of her wage work, working conditions, the family economy, coping with an ill husband, and how she integrated child care and wage work. Her identity was definitely shaped by paid work, particularly because she did not have the luxury of being a full-time homemaker, but also because, once she began to work as a cook, she felt considerable pride in the product and meaning of her labor. However, her identity was also shaped by her sense of being a British immigrant, and the alienation she felt in a city that seemed to her more like a "small village...a funny little place where buses just went round and round." When she first arrived, her alienation was augmented by the discomfort of living in the close quarters of a small house with a mother-in law she barely knew: "[She] was old. I did not know what to say to old people, and you know, when you are a young bride, you are embarrassed."

Perhaps some of her negative impressions of her new home were accentuated by her pride in her English background, and the hostility with which some people still greeted an English accent; however Anglo-centric small-town Ontario was, British accents were sometimes associated with a sense of superiority. Her English identity was juxtaposed in her mind to more unappealing aspects of her new Canadian home; indeed, her rendition of postwar Peterborough was rather uncomplimentary. People were just "rude," she said when describing her 50-cent-an-hour job serving in an ice cream parlor: "[There] were so many people and they were so rude. English people were so polite and here they weren't. [Here] they would say, gimme this, and never said thank you." She also associated her English and familial upbringing with a level of tolerance that she believed was missing in her new country, and indeed, she was initially puzzled by their definition of difference. People kept asking

> what you *are*, and they don't mean are you English or Scottish, but are you Protestant or Catholic…[My husband] and his friend Joe lived on the same street but because one was Anglican and one Catholic they did not know each other before the army…Jewish and Catholic people could not get into the golf club. It was disgusting. It was ignorant, the prejudice.

Her recollections were not those of other interviewees, who more often ignored, downplayed, or denied religious and ethnic divisions.

Her comments about religious prejudice are likely historically accurate, but were all cities in Britain tolerant and only Canadian ones small-minded? Even granting that the dichotomy she set up reflects the construction of memory—shaped by her ethnic identity and her homesickness—I would now put more emphasis on a discussion of cultural identity, using interviews that were anomalies, like hers, to raise the topic. It is also possible that my prior association with her through my children's lives elicited more open, forthcoming comments from her. For interviewees who I did not previously know, raising the issue of religious prejudice, by the 1980s recognized as unacceptable, perhaps seemed presumptuous, and thus elicited defensive or evasive responses. To them, I was an outsider who was making unwarranted assumptions about small-town intolerance.

While recognizing the benefits of exploring the distinct and unusual aspects of her story, Corinne's discussion of workplace conditions, accidents, child care, and so on were of critical importance in connecting the individual and the collective since the everyday aspects of her life often correlated to other women's lives. Her explanation of why she worked is a good example. Twice, when discussing her early life, she characterized her decision to work outside the home when she had young children as "selfish" because she was determined to take her children home to England to visit, not just occasionally, "but every year." Her self-designation as selfish was not only related to her identity as a British immigrant, it was also a response to the dominant ideology in much of the mainstream press that still associated good mothering with those who stayed at home, and selfish mothering with those who went out to work for so-called extras. Other women similarly felt they needed to explain or excuse their wage work, since it was viewed critically by society. If we presume that "subjectivity is not a romantic fiction of the self prior to socialization, but rather bears marks of the person's interaction with the world,"[29] then the powerful influence of social context can never be ignored. While academic discussions concerning narrativity and identity in oral history may have encouraged me to add interpretive threads to my analysis, the importance of placing texts in context, and of assessing the commonalities in interviewees' recollections as a form of historical evidence remained just as important as in the initial moment of oral history recuperation.

Conclusion: Reconciling Recovery and Memory?

Individual stories like Corinne's can tell us much about how and why women remember, however some atypical aspects of women's lives may inevitably be suppressed in our writing if we are analyzing the common, shared experience of class relations. An emphasis on individual stories, subjectivity, and the interview as text should not obscure our analysis of the various structures and ideologies shaping women's lives. Moreover, to what degree must we explore our own role, the process of interviewing, and memory construction in our writing? A singular focus on how the interview unfolds may well put the researcher in the limelight rather than the voices of the interviewees. At what point does self-reflection become autobiography? During the first moment of recovery, our sense that other women's stories, not ours, should be showcased had some merit: it was a valuable element of movement history. The theoretical insights of Raymond Williams, who was concerned with "the relationship between inherited culture and the individual," offered us a way of seeing oral histories as dynamic "works in progress" as individuals "grappled with the contradictions and complexities of their lives."[30]

Elements of this earlier project, I have argued, have had some staying power in historians' actual practice of working-class oral history. While acknowledging these continuities, there are some disjunctures between the dominant scholarly paradigms framing these two moments. There *are* divergences between a post-structuralist informed, discursively constituted subject on the one hand, and a reflective subject who is an agent of history on the other hand, between an emphasis on the determining power of language and on the importance of social determination, the latter a characteristic of the earlier moment of social history. A distinction can be made between the poststructuralist emphasis on the constitutive influence of cultural scripts on individual memory and an earlier understanding of the individual as a social being, shaped, but not determined by cultural and ideological forces. For scholars with poststructuralist inclinations, recovering the experience of women or the working class through oral histories may now seem a "seductive," but ultimately impossible, perhaps hazardous goal, opening the door to "nostalgia" and "essentialism,"[31] while to others, myself included, still grounded in more materialist analyses, it remains a valid analytic project, particularly in the historian's quest for subaltern voices. Is there a way forward in the current moment that integrates the insights and oversights of these two moments in oral history? Divergent theoretical assumptions, with different epistemological starting points, cannot be simply collapsed, integrated, or absorbed into each other. However, we might attend to some of the *issues* raised by poststructuralist theories as a means of fine-tuning an approach in which "the social" still figures most prominently. Paying attention to subjectivity, narrativity, and memory does not necessarily obscure the critical importance of historical context *if* we see subjectivity as rooted in social life.

Feminist discussions of standpoint, historical materialism, and the relations of ruling may be useful in this regard. Connecting feminism and oral history practice has often involved discussions of ethics, collaboration, and "who can speak for whom," however feminist theory can provide other critical insights into the social landscape in which our interviews unfold, keeping us focused on two sides of the same coin: the perspective of the interviewee *and* her social context. Dorothy Smith's suggestion that the standpoint of the interviewee should be the starting point for feminist inquiry is a case in point. This admonition does not assume that the interviewee offers an essentialized, superior, unmediated point of view, but rather that we need to think about the actualities of her relations with others: her working, her thinking, feeling, everyday life experiences. Both the interviewer and the interviewee's "location in the social order" matter, for the historical accumulation of our experiences shape our understandings of the world, a knowable world always "brought into being by human activity."[32]

Taking this maxim to heart may help us understand the "social relations pervading [our interviewee's] world, but perhaps invisible to it," and explore the way in which their experiences are bound up with prevailing ideologies and the relations of ruling.[33] Thinking about the standpoint of the interviewee does not assume that those on the margins—like the working class—always speak from an oppositional standpoint for the views of those "from below" are multiple and contradictory, sometimes critical of, but also "vulnerable to the dominant culture."[34] Indeed, as feminist theorists refined standpoint theory, they insisted that alternative, radical perspectives are not predetermined by experience, but are also "achieved" through human consciousness and reflection. The latter might be facilitated by the telling of one's life history, as an interviewee comes to articulate "counter memories"[35] that challenge, or are an uncomfortable fit with ruling ideas of the social order.

Second, we can pay close attention to subjectivity and narrativity by reading working-class interviews through theories of language that are historical, social, and materialist—but not determinist. As V. N. Volosinov argues, language is always "reciprocal, the product of the relationship between speaker and listener, addressee and addressor."[36] Meaning does not reside in "words" but rather words take on meaning through social interaction and human relations.[37] Similarly, drawing on Bakhtin, Dorothy Smith stresses the social and interactive nature of communication: "Active, relational, dialogic" language involves social communication, not merely "texts, statements, categories."[38] The way we tell our life history may embody certain themes, accents, meanings, and these will shift according to who is speaking, why, and the context, but the "life of language" resides in the "nexus of social relations, and in human relations of social conflict."[39] Not only does this approach avoid our captivity in the circuit of discourse, but the emphasis on interaction and conflict may help us understand the nature of working-class consciousness without making it unitary, homogenous, and unchanging. A worker's recollections, for example, may reveal both oppositional discourses and a language of accommodation to the social order. As she makes sense of her life, she may help us understand under what conditions, in what moments, in what ideological spaces alternative views come to the fore, how they are developed, or perhaps silenced, pushed to the back recesses of memory.

Finally, our attempts to theorize oral history might benefit from engagement with broader debates about historical interpretation, particularly concerning the reclamation of the subject and human agency. Writing on oral history often stresses how fundamentally different it is from other forms of evidence, yet written sources are not simply "mute and frozen"[40] as some might suggest. Some of the challenges assumed to be particular to oral history have resonances across historical methodologies: asking "hard critical questions" of one's sources or connecting the "the horizontal linkages" in workers' experiences are issues many working-class historians wrestle with. [41] Written records are not static, and they too may convey affect, or elicit emotional responses, depending on the reader, and the context of the reading. The case files I read of criminalized women were similarly interpreted in a subjective, interactive manner, colored by my own politics, emotions, and assumptions. Women's words in these files might be collected—in contrast to oral sources—*against the will* of the informant, with transcriptions of their conversations then becoming public documents, raising ethical issues (as in oral history) ranging from the protection of one's sources to how we use them and convey them to others. They also elicit questions about how memory is shaped by the context in which the subject is speaking. An incarcerated woman, whose words may appear to be recorded verbatim, may change her story, according to who she is speaking to, and yet each utterance may incorporate certain truths. While we should not discount the methodological differences between our use of oral and written sources, a theoretical dialogue that crosses these boundaries may still enrich our understanding of both oral and written histories.

The risk of collapsing voice into discourse, memory into contingency, is not just a theoretical but a political question, relating to our views concerning the agency of the working class and the possibility of change. While the enriching impact of increased attention to cultural scripts, memory, and subjectivity on oral history writing is evident in much current scholarship, the recuperation of working-class experience has proven a resilient theme for some labor historians. Political questions still animate our scholarship: how do social being and social consciousness interact; what stimulates changes in collective consciousness; what makes systems of inequality, oppression, and exploitation tick, and what renders them untenable? Those questions, I believe, cannot be satisfactorily explained by focusing only on the discursive and subjective, at the expense of also recognizing the difficult experiences of disparity and struggle that permeated many workers' lives, and continue to shape how they interpret their past and the present.

Notes

1. Lynn Abrams, *Oral History Theory* (London: Routledge, 2010), 7.
2. Jim Green, *Taking History to Heart: The Power of the Past in Building Social Movements* (Amherst: University of Massachusetts Press, 2000), 2.
3. Bryan Palmer, ed., *Jack Scott: A Communist Life* (St. John's: Canadian Committee on Labour History [CCLH], 1988); Gil Levine, ed., *Patrick Lenihan: From Irish Rebel to Founder of Canadian Public Sector Unionism* (St. John's: CCLH, 1998). Two other examples are Sara Diamond, *Chambermaids and Whistlepunks: An Oral History of Women in B.C. Labour, 1930–55* (Vancouver: Press Gang, 1983); Wayne Roberts: *Where Angels Fear to Tread: Eileen Tallman and the Labour Movement* (Hamilton: McMaster Labour Studies, 1979).
4. Irving Abella, *Nationalism, Communism and Canadian Labour: The CIO, the Communist Party, and the CCL, 1935–56* (Toronto: University of Toronto Press, 1973).
5. The tendency to exaggerate the "anger and sarcasm" that greeted oral history is found in Steven High, "Sharing Authority in the Writing of Canadian History: The Case of Oral History," in *Contesting Clio's Craft: New Directions and Debates in Canadian History*, eds. Christopher Dummitt and Michael Dawson (London: Institute for the Study of the Americas, 2009), 23. The evidence High cites from popular reviews in the *Globe* and *Mail* suggests a less categorical rejection.

6. Luisa Passerini, "Work, Ideology and Consensus under Italian Fascism," *History Workshop Journal*, 8 (1979): 82–108.

7. Joan Sangster, "Women of the New Era: Women in the Early CCF" and Georgina Taylor, "The Women...Shall Help to Lead the Way: Saskatchewan CCF-NDP Women Candidates in Provincial and Federal Elections, 1934–65," in *Building the Cooperative Commonwealth: Essays on the Democratic Socialist Tradition in Canada*, ed. W. Brennan (Regina: University of Regina, 1985), 69–97, 141–60.

8. Janet Finch, "It's great to have someone to talk to: The Ethics and Politics of Interviewing Women," in *Social Researching: Politics, Problems, Practice*, eds. C. Bell and H. Roberts (London: Routledge, Kegan and Paul, 1984), 78.

9. Margot Thompson, interview by author, October 6, 1981.

10. Valerie Yow, "'Do I Like Them Too Much?' Effects of the Oral History Interview on the Interviewer and Vice-Versa," *Oral History Review* 42, 1 (Summer 1997): 55–79.

11. The On to Ottawa Trek involved unemployed men from western Canada who were riding the rails to Ottawa to confront the prime minister. We interviewed an Ontario contingent from Toronto who intended to join them. Taime Davis, Lil Himmelfarb Ilomaki, Alex McLennan, and Ernie Solwell, interview by Karen Teeple and Joan Sangster, January 30, 1983.

12. Elsa Dixler, "The Woman Question: Women and the American Communist Party, 1929–41" (PhD diss., Yale University, 1974).

13. Joan Sangster, *Dreams of Equality: Women on the Canadian Left, 1920s-1950s* (Toronto: McClelland and Stewart, 1989), 237.

14. Aldous Huxley, quoted in Bernard Ostry, "The Illusion of Understanding: Making the Ambiguous Intelligible," *Oral History Review* 5, 1 (1977): 7.

15. Paula Hamilton, "Edge: Debates about Memory and History," in *Memory and History in Twentieth-Century Australia*, eds. Kate Darion-Smith and Paula Hamilton (Melbourne: Oxford University Press, 1994), 13.

16. Ellen Kay Trimberger, "Women in the Old and New Left: The Evolution of a Politics of Personal Life," *Feminist Studies* 5, 3 (1979): 431–50; Peggy Dennis, "A Response to Ellen Kay Trimberger," *Feminist Studies* 5, 3 (1979): 451–61.

17. Sherna Berger Gluck, "From First Generation Oral Historians to Fourth and Beyond," *Oral History Review* 26, 2 (Summer 1999): 5.

18. Russell Hann, "Introduction," in Daphne Read and Russell Hann, eds., *The Great War and Canadian Society: An Oral History* (Toronto: New Hogtown Press, 1978), 10, 24, 30.

19. George Rosenwald and Richard Ochberg, "Introduction: Life Stories, Cultural politics, and Self-Understanding," in *Storied Lives: The Cultural Politics of Self-Understanding*, eds. George C. Rosenwald and Richard L. Ochberg (New Haven: Yale University Press, 1992), 2.

20. Alessandro Portelli, *The Death of Luigi Trastulli and Other Stories* (Albany: State University of New York Press, 1991), 50.

21. Michael Frisch, *A Shared Authority: Essays on the Craft and Meaning of Oral and Public Histories* (Albany: State University of New York Press); Linda Shopes, "Oral History and the Study of Communities: Problems, Paradoxes, and Possibilities," *The Journal of American History* 89, 2 (September 2002): 588–98.

22. Kerwin Lee Klein, "On the Emergence of Memory in Historical Discourse," *Representations* 69 (Winter 2000): 127–50.

23. Seyla Benhabib, "Epistemologies of Postmodernism: A Rejoinder to Jean-François Lyotard," in *Feminism/Postmodernism*, ed. Linda Nicolson (Routledge: New York, 1990), 125.

24. A few examples of many include Ruth Frager, *Sweatshop Strife; Class, Ethnicity, and Gender in the Jewish Labour Movement of Toronto, 1900–1939* (Toronto: University of Toronto Press, 1992); Dionne Brand, *No Burden to Carry: Narratives of Black Working Women in Ontario, 1920–1950s* (Toronto: Women's Press, 1991); Denyse Baillargeon, *Making Do: Women, Family and Home in Montreal During the Great Depression*, trans. Yvonne Klein (Waterloo: Wilfrid Laurier University Press, 1999).

25. Joan Sangster, "The Softball Solution: Women Workers and Male Managers in a Peterborough Clock Factory," *Labour/Le Travail* 32 (1993): 167–99; *Earning Respect: The Lives of Working Women in Small-town Ontario, 1920–50* (Toronto: University of Toronto Press, 1995).

26. Pamela Sugiman, "'These Feelings That Fill My Heart': Japanese Canadian Women's Memories of Internment," *Oral History* 34 (Autumn 2006): 722.

27. Anna Green, "Individual Remembering and 'Collective Memory': Theoretical Presuppositions and Contemporary Debates," *Oral History* 32, 2 (Autumn 2004): 36.

28. Corinne [pseudonym], interview by author, July 1991.

29. Rosenwald and Ochberg, "Introduction," 8.

30. Anna Green, "Individual Remembering," 41.

31. Craig Ireland, "The Appeal to Experience and Its Constituencies: Variations on a Persistent Thompsonian Theme," *Cultural Critique* 52 (Autumn 2002): 95.

32. Dorothy Smith, *Texts, Facts and Femininity: Exploring the Relations of Ruling* (London: Routledge, 990), 90.

33. Ibid; see also Marie Campbell and Ann Manicom, "Introduction," in *Knowledge, Experience, and Ruling Relations*, eds. Marie Campbell and Ann Manicom (Toronto: University of Toronto Press, 1995), 9.

34. Nancy Hartstock, "Postmodernism and Political Change: Issues for Feminist Theory," *Cultural Critique* 14 (1989/90): 24, 27.

35. Natalie Zemon Davis and Randolph Starn, "Introduction," *Representations* 26 (Spring 1989): 5.

36. V. N. Volosinov, *Marxism and the Philosophy of Language* (New York: Seminar Press, 1973), 86.

37. Ibid., 106.

38. Smith, *Writing the Social*, 120.

39. David McNally, "Language, History and Class Struggle," in *In Defense of History: Marxism and the Postmodern Agenda*, eds. Ellen Meiksins Wood and John Bellamy Foster (New York: Monthly Review Press, 1997), 29.

40. Michael Frisch and Dorothy Larson, "Oral History and the Presentation of Class Consciousness: The New York Times v. the Buffalo Unemployed," in *A Shared Authority: Essays on the Craft and Meaning of Oral and Public History* (Albany: State University of New York Press, 1990), 61.

41. Linda Shopes, "Oral History and the Study of Communities: Problems, Paradoxes, and Possibilities," *The Journal of American History* 89, 2 (September 2002): 597; Roger Horowitz and Rick Halpern, "Work, Race, and Identity: Self-Representation in the Narratives of Black Packinghouse Workers," *Oral History Review* 26, 1 (Winter/Spring 1999): 26. Yet, as Shopes notes elsewhere, "oral history material must be used in much the same way as intellectual historians use their documents–as clues into the mind of a person or group." Linda Shopes, "Oral History and Community Development," in *Presenting the Past: Essays on History and the Public*, eds. Susan Porter Benson, Stephen Brier, and Roy Rosenzweig (Philadelphia: Temple University Press, 1986), 256.

PART II

Encounters in Vulnerability, Familiarity, and Friendship

Hourig Attarian

Ruth Behar reminds us that "[to] write vulnerably is to open a Pandora's box."[1] Self-reflexivity brings to light the gray zones we encounter in our work.[2] In this often difficult and fragile process, we perform a balancing act between what becomes necessary to work through ourselves and what we select to present publicly.[3] This subtle process is also central to the connections that we negotiate and weave with "strangers," friends, or those who simply remain "familiar persons" in our projects. Regardless of the distinctions we make, these people always affect the course of our work and the many turns it takes. This balancing act is an exercise in trying to understand our own limits (choosing what and how to divulge), pushing our own boundaries, and assessing how each of these circumstances impacts our research. The Pandora's box is opened indeed. The self-reflexive journey has much in common with elements of wise folk tales. We experience impossible hurdles, try to find answers to riddles, make decisions at forked paths, descend into dark places, and eventually come up into light again. Negotiating the very challenging points of convergence between being both an agent and a locus of research is at the core of this journey. For all of these reasons, I view the stories we eventually tell as portraits that remain purposefully unfinished. This last point brings me to the stories told in the following chapters, three of which are situated in Montreal, Canada, and the dynamic *Montreal Life Stories* project[4] in particular.

Vulnerability is the main theme running through the four chapters in this section—vulnerable telling, vulnerable listening, vulnerable storying.[5] Vulnerability shapes every encounter. It pushes us tangibly to get in touch with our reflexivity as researchers and helps us understand our situatedness in the research processes. It follows naturally that this section is also about the place of emotion in the field. How do we cope with its effects? How do we negotiate it? What do we learn from it? While Martha Norkunas and Alan Wong ask the reader to delve deeper into the effects of listening vulnerably on both the researcher and the unfolding stories, Elizabeth Miller and Stacey Zembrzycki elucidate the transformative experiences for both researcher and narrator, demonstrating how the stories they hear and tell deepen as their relationships evolve over time.

Norkunas charts the emotional contours that shape listening in different situations. She constantly negotiates how she listens, what she can and cannot hear, what she hopes to know and also cannot bear to know. The emotional relationship that develops in the interview space has a lasting impact on both people involved. Most importantly, reflecting on a critical aspect of researcher situatedness, Norkunas argues that the stories the listener hears can change her sense of self. This understanding becomes an important anchor in her practice. As a listener, the cues that shape every interaction she has are the feelings she senses in the narrator and those she herself experiences. Emotions are no longer abstract observations of what a narrator goes through in her recountings—they are key players affecting narrator and listener alike. Moreover, when engaging in autobiographical inquiry through family interviews, vulnerability makes the listener aware of the limitations of immersing in the process. Taking the reflective gaze further, Norkunas argues that the courage to allow oneself to be vulnerable in painful listening experiences reveals ways for the listener/researcher to mend the fragmented self. In this paradigm, the researcher plays a central role in the meaning-making process, together with the narrator.

Wong reveals another dimension of researcher positioning in the listening process. For him, different ways of listening are contingent on the different ways he relates to his narrators. Mapping his various Montreal-based research endeavors, Wong explores how familiarity and feeling influence listening and storying when working with strangers, friends, and family members. Specifically, he finds interview encounters with strangers to be liberating, transforming the interview into a space of genuine curiosity and discovery. Interestingly, here he refers to the interview he conducted with me. Indeed that interview was also a significant experience for me—it was the first time that I, as an oral historian, was asked to be on the "other" side of the camera. Our conversation, over several encounters, enabled me to view the interview as a site of reflective vulnerability where I could gain a new perspective into my stories and my vulnerability as a narrator. Wong's sense of discovery made the interview experience authentic and enjoyable for both of us. As with Norkunas, the most challenging aspect for Wong was an interview he conducted with his father. Viewing it as "difficult listening," Wong realized that this emotionally difficult interview risked impacting their intimate familial relationship beyond the interview encounter. This is where the vulnerability of the researcher is laid bare. How much of the personal can the listener/researcher reveal in this instance? How much can he "bear to hear and know" as Norkunas points out? And how much of that gleaned knowledge can or should he bring into the interview space? Where does detachment begin and end in such an equation? And what of possible rifts that could result? These are some of the inevitable questions we have to reflect on as we come face to face with our own deep and very personal engagements in our research processes.

In her piece, Miller recounts how narrators engage listeners outside the interview circle, in going public with their stories through a participatory media project with refugee youth in Montreal. While describing the practical and ethical considerations of the project, she articulates the challenges and rewards of this methodological practice. For the youth participants, the most important part of the project was the bonds and relationships they created with each other because these sustained them through the difficult phases of storying and sharing. Creating such an environment required trust, the development of safe spaces, and, most importantly, time, so that all could feel comfortable letting their vulnerabilities shape their emerging stories. As Miller emphasizes, it is only when we allow ourselves (as participants and facilitators) to take time, sometimes beyond a project's initial framework, that we can hope to create the meaningful relationships required for stories (difficult or otherwise) to emerge.

Zembrzycki illustrates how narrator and researcher craft pockets of reflexivity together. Safe spaces cultivated within and outside of the interview, and the vulnerability that characterizes them, transform the nature of stories and their telling. To this end, experiences that occur "on" and "off the record" demand closer analysis. Zembrzycki argues that we must begin to pay more attention to the collaborative aspects of our practices. It is no longer acceptable to shy away from looking critically at the deep relationship bonds that we negotiate, construct, and weave together with our narrators. We cannot remain "outcome" and "product" driven without realizing that the product and outcome would not exist without the relationships we spend time nurturing. It is therefore imperative that we explore these relationships, using our reflective analyses to better understand what collaboration makes possible—how we listen, what we listen to, what we hear or cannot hear, what is recounted and what we retell. Zembrzycki and Montreal Holocaust survivor Rena Schondorf are committed to going where Schondorf's memories take them, while at the same time Zembrzycki always remains cognizant of the fine line she treads between researcher, friend, and granddaughter. This blurring of boundaries creates an ambiguous space for new possibilities, stimulating the telling of previously unheard stories. Navigating these spaces can be difficult, but when successful it can make the research more significant, transformative, and empowering.

Vulnerability within and outside of the interview is key in shaping researcher-narrator relationships, necessarily affecting the "what" and the "how" of the evolving stories. This implies the creation of a safe space where the researcher has empathy for the narrator, where the narrator feels safe enough to be vulnerable, and where the researcher allows herself to be vulnerable as well. Vulnerability is never a one-way street. It is only when both narrator and researcher allow it in equal measure that vulnerability can become the locus of writing and storying. In this regard, interviews become spaces where researcher and narrator can be themselves, with all their warts, bruises, and also hopes, open to each other and to the possibilities stories engender.

Notes

1. Ruth Behar, *The Vulnerable Observer: Anthropology That Breaks your Heart* (Boston: Beacon Press, 1996), 19.
2. See, for instance, Hourig Attarian, "Lifelines: Matrilineal Narratives, Memory and Identity" (PhD diss., McGill University, 2009); "Stories Fluttering in the Wind: How Clotheslines Tell our Lives," in *Was it Something I Wore? Dress, Identity, Materiality*, eds. R. Molestane, C. Mitchell, and A. Smith (Cape Town: HSRC Press, 2012), 41–56.
3. I am indebted to Roger Frie for his conceptualization of "the gray dividing line in autobiographical research" (personal communication, July 2012).
4. For more on this project go to: http://www.lifestoriesmontreal.ca/.
5. A common term used in educational research and narrative inquiry, "storying" speaks to the process of making a story and differentiates it from storytelling in general.

CHAPTER 4

The Vulnerable Listener

Martha Norkunas

In remembering and speaking, narrators reassess, relive, and sometimes pains-takingly reconstruct life experiences. What can be asked? The empathetic listener assesses the goals of the interview, the potential contribution the interview can make to social and cultural history, the emotional state of the narrator, the interactions between narrator and any other people present, what participants hope for in the narration, the political risks that may result when information is revealed, and whatever other concerns are salient in that con-text. The listener is keenly sensitive to the nonverbal communication from her narrator—gestures, voice intonation, pauses—in an effort to respect her narra-tor's emotional boundaries. Together narrator and listener negotiate what the narrator must tell, wants to tell, tries to shape into a coherent narrative, and cannot bear to tell.

What can be heard? The listener assumes sharply different roles in each interview: scholar, fellow survivor, a person with shared experiences, the Other, witness. She negotiates what she can hear, must hear, hopes to know, and cannot bear to know. She senses where the emotional boundaries are located for her, given her own complex memoryscape. She tries to shape the oral history interview so that it is intellectually honest, and historically relevant, yet does not draw her into painful waters she cannot navigate. She tries to assess how much emotional residue may remain after the interview ends, and what impact that will have on her. In Michael Riordon's interviews with oral historian Elizabeth Pozzi-Thanner she told him that while she may cry in her heart, she never openly cries during the interviews: "If I hear something that really cuts into my soul...sometimes the pain of it will only surface later...Then suddenly I will start to cry. It can overwhelm me for days."[1]

The listeners, those who bear witness, carry the stories. The listener notices the gestures, sees the tears begin to well up in the speaker's eyes, hears the abrupt halt. Empathetic listeners are ever sensitive to the nuances of trauma in the life story: long silences, detachment, a change in voice or body language.[2] Because neither the listener nor the narrator knows where the contours of traumatized memory lie, those who listen to these stories are fully exposed to the victims' pain and grief; the narrator and listener can be trapped in an interaction of emotions.[3] Others encounter emotionally painful narratives unexpectedly, in the context of life history interviews not ostensibly about genocide or violence. What does one do when the interview moves unexpectedly into pain or emotions so intense neither the narrator nor the listener knows where to take the interview or whether to question the narrator about the experience at all? What happens when family secrets are exposed? [4] Negotiations about the nature and depth of what can be revealed are always, to some greater or lesser extent, part of an oral history interview (unless the narrator is clearly revealing only "public" information about her or his life). The emotional relationship that the narrator and listener develop in the space of the interview may have a lasting impact on both people; the stories can change the listener's sense of self.

As is the case with many oral historians, I have often had the sensation that I am feeling the narrator's feelings. In the same way that one becomes emotionally involved in a film or a dream, I see the person's story unfold in visual terms. I understand that the narrator is experiencing a complex set of emotions and while I do not know if the feelings I am having precisely mirror those of the narrator, she seems to sense that I am deeply involved in her story.

Paul Stoller wrote that the anthropologist is in a between state much of the time: she is never of the people she studies, but she has been so changed by the experience of knowing them, or living with them that she is no longer what she was before. There is a sense of excitement in the possibility of personal transformation resulting from an intense engagement with others.[5] Stoller referenced the painter Andre Marchard: "To paint the forest...you have to open your body to it and let the trees flow through your being."[6] This between state, or embodied presence, that oral historians experience in the interview, carries over to the transformative process of letting the stories change them. All subsequent interviews are different because the listeners are different. One's life experience also changes the way an oral historian listens to narrators. She sees more in the next interview; she guides the narrator to explore his or her past in richer and deeper ways.

This process can be exhilarating as well as dangerous. I am aware of the power of the past to refragment or to make more whole a person's sense of self, and of the capacity of the past to dominate the present. I am careful not to transgress the narrator's boundaries, or lead them into territory I think might damage them. I am increasingly careful not to cross my own boundaries, but I do not always know where they are located, and what might be too painful for me to hear. The feelings that I sense in the person and the feelings that I experience are constantly shaping our interaction. The past is present in the interviews: their past, my past, the meanings we have assigned to our pasts, and the ways in which we have each struggled to make sense of our lives.

What I Can Hear

Some years ago I was asked to interview a woman who was dying of ovarian cancer.[7] I had taken care of my mother while she died of ovarian cancer. Those 14 months were profoundly moving. Later I did a series of interviews with other women whose mothers died of cancer. I thought these experiences would enable me to compassionately cocreate a life history interview with a dying woman. The woman, who I will call Lania, requested the interview through a hospice organization, so I assumed she had particular stories to tell. When I arrived at her house, she was in bed, on morphine, and her mother was in a chair at her bedside. A nurse was in the adjoining room. I expected the interview would be emotionally demanding, but I was unprepared for the radical refocusing it soon required:

> *MN*: I thought that you might have some ideas of what you wanted to say, and that I could just start with you telling me a little bit about why you wanted to do the tape.
> *Lania*: Well I haven't really had any thoughts about what I want to say.

I was completely taken aback. I could not imagine why she had requested an oral history interview. She seemed to be hoping I would help her express something important. It was up to me to ask her the kinds of questions that would allow her to say what she needed to say. What did she want to say? What did her family want to hear?

While I never forgot that I was not a therapist, it seemed impossible to conduct an ordinary life history interview in this context. Narrators have often wept as they recounted their life stories to me. In this case, the intimacy and emotional intensity of the interview was heightened by our awareness of the narrator's impending death. I had not been asked to cocreate a social history document that would be donated to an archive—I had been asked to do an oral history for a dying woman. I had to make a series of immediate decisions about what I thought the goals of the interview were for Lania and her family. What topics could I raise? I tried to closely listen to any cues she and her family members gave me. At each point in the process I tried to assess the emotional climate in the room, and the impact of the interview on the narrator, the family member present, and myself.

I thought about being in the room with my mother, as my siblings and I talked about some of our fondest memories with her, knowing she could hear us and would be pleased to be remembered so lovingly. I thought about allowing my mother the openness to express what she needed to say to each of us so that she could die more peacefully. I thought about what I might have wanted from an oral history if I had been so determined to create one on my deathbed. I had never met anyone in Lania's family before, so these were assumptions based on experiences in my life. I thought that the family might narrate memories of shared experiences and talk to each other about how important each had been to the other. I asked Lania to describe her son, Harry, whom she clearly loved. She had written a series of letters to him, so I thought she could talk about them.

> *MN*: When you were writing the Dear Harry letters, what did you want Harry to remember about you?
>
> *Lania*: I guess I want him to remember the truth about who I am. And you know, just as much of _____ (inaudible) (crying) you know can come out. My first priority has been to get everything organized so I can get these photographs in a box. So this [the interview] is wonderful because it gives me a break from doing other things and by, it gets me doing what I, my first priority is. Susan [the person who arranged the oral history] told you that this is very important to me. So I'm glad you are here.
>
> *MN*: When you say you want him to remember truth, tell me some stories about who you are as a person.

She asked me to come back the next day when her son was present so he could hear her stories. Her mother then described the five-year period when Lania had cancer as a time when Lania had forgiven people. I asked: "Forgiven you?" She said yes, and forgiven everybody. She went on to say that Lania had become an absolute joy. I hoped her mother's words would be healing to Lania.

I asked her if she was afraid of anything as she went through the dying process. Because of her profession she must have counseled dying people so I asked her what she said to them, thinking she might draw comfort from her own words. She was a spiritual person, so I asked her if God was with her in this process and she said yes.

> *Lania*: Well God is just with me in the way that people are surrounding me, you know and loving me. I'm really blessed with being able to have so much time here to have the people around that I love, because I know, you know that I'm clearly close to death, there's no doubt about it.

Her mother left and her former husband came into the room. Once again I was faced with decisions about how to guide the interview. I tried to follow any leads they offered. I asked Lania and her former husband to talk about when they first met, their decisions to return to school, and their early years in the city. They both spoke of their separation, and their mutual commitment to raise their son, which meant they had to be friends of a sort. They argued during the interview, and she talked about some of the difficult periods they had. I was surprised that he would not defer to her.

Later I asked her what she wanted for her son in his future. She talked about many of the things she wanted for him and then said:

> *Lania*: That's the thing that breaks my heart the most, is not to have grandchildren. Not that he has to have grandchildren or anything but I just really am sorry that I'm having to die here (crying) because I'm really going to miss that.

I tried to shape the interview around positive topics, thinking that would be a solace to all present, but Lania talked about some of the most painful periods in her life. I was not sure how fully to pursue these topics and did not follow-up on them as I did with the narratives that led to reflections on identity and life meaning. My experience with my mother's death led me to stories of resolution or affirmation. It may also have been my projection of myself on the deathbed that made me want her to avoid a despondent death. Whose boundary was I honoring? Looking back, I believe I encouraged the affirmation narratives because of my own emotional boundaries: I would not want my last hours to be spent on the pain of my life but instead on the most meaningful experiences and interactions. Redirecting to resolution narratives seemed to me an act of compassion and Lania willingly engaged with them, but I wonder what might have transpired if my boundaries had been different.

When I returned the next day, now familiar with the interview setting, I asked Lania and her son about shared positive memories. They talked about Christmas celebrations, his birthday, their dogs, trips they had taken, how they spent their evenings together. He also spoke about being depressed, and of challenges in his life. I asked him if he could always talk to his mother about things that were bothering him and they began to discuss their relationship. When I asked him what kind of vision he had for himself when he was in high school and he talked about how important writing was to him, Lania seemed pleased because she had always kept journals.

I asked Harry how old he was when his mother was diagnosed with cancer. He described how she had gone in for a hysterectomy when he was 14. When the doctors told him and his dad that they had found a large tumor on her ovaries he slowly realized how serious it was.

> *MN*: [To Lania] What were your thoughts when you recovered from the surgery and they told you what had happened?

Lania: Well the first thing I saw was Harry. And he was sitting at the edge of the bed and he said, "Mom...something terrible has happened." I said, "What did you say honey?" And he said, "You have ovarian cancer." And I thought to my[self], I mean I knew...that was like a killer disease. And so I said, "Well honey, that's awful."...Next thing I know...I'm crying or something. And but the main thing was that it was ovarian cancer...that that was a killer disease...I never even thought that Harry first of all would be the one to tell me, my God. You know, Lord have mercy. And then you know that Harry tells me and I'm in this hospital room and I don't even know who else is there, and then it's ovarian cancer. You know then it's like, my God, I'm going to die...And my boy is telling me this—it was just awful (cries).

MN: [To Harry] But that was very brave of you to be the person to tell her.

Harry: I think so, yeah. I think, definitely much less of day-to-day worries, that kind of thing. It was more of trying to prioritize what the real important things were. And in some ways that's like a, I guess a blessing, about the disease. Which is horrible, but you know...

MN: It's a strange thing because you have the time to think and do important things. And that's the wonderful part. The bad part is you know what's coming.

Harry: Right, it's like a real strange thing.

Lania: It's very strange.

MN: It's a weird mix to it...I was you [referring to Harry], watching my mother. You get really confused because you don't know whether to hope that they'll get better, or get ready to lose them.

Harry: Right.

MN: I don't know. Does that tension bother you?

Harry: Yeah, I think it has for a while, a long time. It's been a long process to be able to accept the reality of it. Like right now, the past few months I've come to accept the reality of it...It definitely was a difficult thing to get used to, those different extremes.

MN: What helped you the most in accepting?

Harry: I guess a lot of it was just time...That was a lot of it. And a lot of it was being able to talk about it with people and being able to know that things were okay, that this happened. Just being able to talk about what was going on.

I felt a deep empathy for Harry. I told him what I felt when my mother was diagnosed with ovarian cancer and asked if it was similar for him. I think he saw me, maybe for the first time, as a person whose experience was much like his.

I asked them to talk about Lania's dying process, what they would each miss, where they thought she was going, and if they thought they could communicate after she died. I realized these were questions I wish I had thought to ask my mother. I think I would also want to talk about them if I were dying and I was sure the listener could bear to hear them. I remember thinking that while my mother and I talked openly about many parts of our lives, I did not know how to broach these topics with her when she was dying. I thought that it might have eased her dying process if she had been able to speak about what she was experiencing. It might have enabled me to help her through it to an even greater extent, and it would have addressed my own questions about what it means to die. I also asked Lania what her hopes were for her son, and what kind of a person she wanted him to be. Because their experience together was to be so tragically abbreviated, I wanted to condense time for them so that she could share thoughts that normally would have been a part of a long mother-child relationship.

> *MN*: What do you think—where will you go after you die? What is your vision
> of where you're going to go?
> *Lania*: Well I don't really worry about it very much. But when I have time alone
> and have some quiet time... I kind of like to envision myself going to glory,
> (laughs) you know... So I really don't have to be afraid and that really gives
> me peace of mind... I don't know what Harry thinks about God. [To Harry]
> You want to say what you think about God?
> *Harry*: I'm really not sure either (laughs). I feel confident that when someone
> dies that they are able to join people that have also died, in some kind of
> spirit thing, spiritual awareness or whatever. I think it could be nothing but
> wonderful, so.
> *MN*: So you're not afraid for your mother?
> *Harry*: No, not at all.
> *Lania*: That's wonderful sweetie. Isn't that wonderful, that he is not afraid? Yeah,
> it's wonderful. I must have done something pretty good (laughs). My boy's
> not afraid.

I ended the interview by asking Harry to talk about the grandchildren Lania had mourned never seeing, thinking it would be comforting for her to hear how he would remember her with them.

> *MN*: If you have children someday, what are the things you will tell them about
> your mother?
> *Harry*: I don't know. [That she's] remarkable, amazing, just a beautiful person.
> *MN*: Will you raise them with certain values that she raised you?
> *Harry*: I think so. I'm sure similar to what she's taught me is just a part of me
> now. So if anything I would teach my children to come through that way.
> *MN*: To the person that you are.
> *Harry*: Yeah. And I'm glad I'll be able to do that someday.[8]

I cocreated the oral history through the interaction between Lania and the three people who came to sit by her bedside. I asked them to talk about very difficult subjects, knowing the normal boundaries of what is appropriate did not function in the same way in the presence of death. Yet I tried to ask the questions gently so as not to push them into territory that was too fragile. When I reread the transcript, I saw that I hoped the oral history process would release them from regret about unexpressed feelings or unresolved anger or guilt or any of the emotions that might haunt a person after someone close to them dies. Were my feelings dominating the interviews or did I read the family correctly?

I was exhausted after the interviews, but I did not feel conflicted. I had drawn on deep experiences in my past to raise issues that I thought were important to each person in the room. They had been reflecting on Lania's life for months before I arrived with my recorder. Yet something remained undone that prompted Lania to ask for an oral historian to come and listen to her. Something prompted her, after the first day, to ask me to return to record her conversations with her son. What did this mother want her son to know about her life that she had not already told him? Perhaps they wanted an empathetic listener to bear witness to their sense of loss, their affection, and their struggle to accept what they were going through. Perhaps they imagined, as a professional oral historian, I could reveal each person to the other, and most importantly, Lania to her son, in ways that she had not been able to do on her own.

I entered their between state as a vulnerable listener so they could speak to each other from their own states of raw emotion. While it was inevitable that we would approach our boundaries, the affirmation narratives may have prevented us from transgressing them, and may even have offered Lania and her son some of what they so deeply wanted.

What I Cannot Hear

As I became increasingly interested in the intersections of family stories, social memory, and history, I was drawn to family secrets and difficult, if not traumatic, memory.[9] Given my family's complex history, the secrets that haunt the present, and the wealth of material I had access to, I decided to use my family as a site of investigation.[10] In 2005 I began a series of interviews with my father, talking with him for the first time about his past.[11]

I was prepared for the intense emotions I expected the interviews would evoke, and completely unprepared for my response to them. Over the years I met with my father, he returned to the same stories repeatedly, telling them differently each time. The differences were not subtle: he radically changed either the chronology, or the nature of the relationships he had, or the context within which he knew someone, or how he felt about an experience in the past.

These interviews were different from any that I had previously done. I could not ask my father the questions that I most wanted answered. I was uncharacteristically indirect. I did not ask follow-up questions. When a painful topic was raised, I often changed the subject. The trope of the traumatized narrator being interviewed by the oral historian was reversed. I was the vulnerable party; the act of listening held the potential for disrupting the meanings I had ascribed to my family's difficult past. I had not lived with my father since I was five, but he played a large role in the life of our family. So much of his past was shrouded in silence; so much of what I knew about him and what I thought had happened to my family was unclear. A tension hung over this silence, as though the knowledge revealed or the process of seeking it would be dangerous.

I knew my father had spent several weeks in a psychiatric hospital when he was in his early fifties because I visited him there. I suspected his diagnosis was psychosis but I did not know for sure because he never told me, and the hospital never revealed this information. I knew that his reconstructions of the past were sometimes implausible, yet there often seemed to be some truth in them, as though he spoke in a coded language. So the process of listening for innuendo or indices of trauma, of hearing the stories emerge in fragments over a period of years, and of intuiting unspoken meanings became more complex.

As I transcribed the interviews I added other layers to the encounters. Like Art Spiegelman who wrote not only about his father's narratives, but also about how he felt when he heard the narratives, I was observing myself as much as I was observing my father.[12] Listening to passages multiple times and watching the videos of my father and myself evoked a range of emotions. I remembered how I felt when I was sitting at the table with him and how nervous I was talking with him about the past, the tremendous tension I felt that he would reveal something I did not want to know, or that he would denigrate my mother. I imagined how she would feel listening to my father's narrative, the corrections she would make, and the compassion or anger she might feel. I also occupied the subject position of the child and young adult who had experienced and remembered the events my father described.

The issue of what could and should be revealed was unclear. What question was I too terrified to ask? Why was I terrified? I pulled back from what I felt would be emotional landmines. There was no safe place. At times I asked my husband to pose the questions, and I stepped out of the room. I questioned if I wanted to hear what my father understood about his past. I wondered if I wanted him to bear witness to me, to construct a narrative of contrition. Internally, silently, I contested parts of his narrative. Yet I also wanted us to be honest and open to each other, to reveal ourselves.

Alisse Waterston and Barbara Rylko-Bauer call such interviews "intimate ethnography." They approached the life histories they did with their parents as daughters; as anthropologists, they posed broader questions beyond the personal story.[13] They entered a deeply private and interior place, searching for what was true for each of their parents.[14] They examined the role of emotion in ethnographic work and challenged their own positionality.[15] The emotions they confronted were "like a mound on a field that indicates something important lies beneath, needing to be excavated" but they understood it also involved risk.[16] "What negative impact might dredging up past history and reopening old wounds have on her mother? What might the ethnographer learn about her mother that could break the daughter's heart?"[17]

My father recounted a story several times about breaking a promise to his mother. Why did it pain him some 70 years later to remember this? This narrative, and other, darker stories led me to question if my father had been traumatized in his childhood. He only cried twice when talking about his mother: when he learned about her death, and when he told the story of the broken promise. Why was one of his two emotional memories of his mother in the context of a sexual experience? Why did my father so frequently sexualize his references to women so that not even his mother escaped the sexualized gaze? Were there other aspects of his childhood that were buried, kept secret? The 2005 interview took place with his wife (VC), and my husband (YE).

> SN: I made my mother a promise. She found a condom in my pants pocket and she said, "Stanley you're not going [unclear] now are you?" And I said, "No." I made a promise that I wouldn't have sex with a girl, intercourse, until I was 21. And I kept that promise and broke it four months before I was 21. And I had to go tell my mother. (He begins to cry.)
>
> MN: You had to go tell her? (gently) Why? So you could feel honest?
>
> SN: (He points to his head.) The brain. It would be a lie if I didn't tell her. (His voice is shaking.)
>
> MN: Well, you were so close though.
>
> SN: Right. (still crying)
>
> MN: You almost made it.
>
> SN: (Shakes his head yes) Almost made it. So that's it.

In a long and conflicted life, why did this instance stand out above other, more dramatic incidents? When I saw his tears I felt compassion for him, but later, in the transcription process I questioned his foregrounding of this particular narrative. I wondered if he used the language of a broken promise as a metaphor for other unresolved issues that continued to trouble him.

Another day my father spoke about the shoe business, and placing an order for shoes with a Japanese factory after World War II:

> SN: I was the one that gave the Japanese the first order for shoes in this country when everybody was against them. It was a big order for sneakers. They

had the best-made sneakers in the world. And Thom McCan was the first company that had a Japanese-made product in the United States...I gave them an order for a million pairs of sneakers...At that time nobody wanted to do a deal with a Japanese company. And they were very nice to me. They gave me $30,000 in cash to put into my pocket because I opened the market for them. I took it. Nobody knew it. This was the price that they, there was no other way that they could say thank you to me.

MN: Right.

SN: Okay? So I could use the money. I bought a car with it.

MN: Was, did you have a partner in that?

In interviews that were less emotionally laden, I would have asked the narrator about the bribe. What were the ethics of it? Why did he take a bribe? Later in the interview he returned to the topic of Japanese shoes:

YE: So because of your experience in Japan you were open to Japanese sneakers. Is that right?

SN: Well yeah. That's why I was not afraid to give them an order. When everybody in America was against doing business with Japan...I was criticized by my bosses...but I was in charge...And I felt I was right. In time it proved it, but not at that time. And that opened the door to other people going in there. The whole shoe industry started to accept Japanese shoes. But I had the balls to give them the first order.

Why? Because I knew the people. I had met them there when I was in Japan. They trusted me and I trusted them. And I was criticized severely by, oh, so many people that I had the balls to give Japan an order, the way they treated us. The way they raped the girls when they went into the Philippines. They should have seen how the American soldiers raped the Japanese girls when they went to Japan. But nobody's talked about that. They fucked everything that they could put their hands on. They're just as bad as the Japanese in the Philippines.

MN: Yeah.

SN: That they don't tell you.

MN: Daddy, when you came back, after, what I'd like to hear about is the designing of the shoes and the feel you had for it. Billy was trying to explain the other day what a last is.

SN: The last is what they make the shoe on.[18]

When my father retold the story of his initial foray into the Japanese shoe market, he omitted the bribe. Then he became angry, agitated. To my amazement, he cried out about the American soldiers raping Japanese women. I did not ask him anything about that explosive topic. I could not bear to hear any details of what may have happened. What did he see? How did this change him? He seemed too upset, and the memory, if it was a memory, was too painful for him and for me. I changed the topic to protect both of us.

The following year we again talked about the shoe order he placed with the Japanese.

> *MN*: Last time you told me about giving the first contract to the Japanese to make shoes, but when did the U.S. start regularly exporting out the factory production of things?
>
> *SN*: Well nobody would give Japan an order...Well why did I do that? Because I lived in Japan for nine months after the war. I ran a hotel for the US government in Japan.
>
> *MN*: I remember you told me a little bit about that.
>
> *SN*: Okay [he softens] and so I was familiar with the Japanese...I worked with them because I was in Japan. I was put there by the US government and I ran a hotel in Japan for the US government. And if I was a thief I could have walked away with a lot of money. I had a budget of $560,000 of American money that was available to me. But that money never does you any good.

I felt lost in the interview and in the transcription. Did he take money? Did he remember his story of the prior year about accepting a bribe from the Japanese for ordering shoes?

> *MN*: What do you mean that money never does you any good?
>
> *SN*: The greatest expression in the Lithuanian language from the people in Lithuania [he says it in Lithuania]. Don't you understand Lithuanian? How come? Your father's Lithuanian, isn't he?

He made a small joke on the divorce and his separation from our family. How come I did not know any Lithuanian when my father was Lithuanian? I did not speak Lithuanian because I rarely saw my father, but we did not say this. He employed gentle humor about a deeply difficult subject and relieved some of the tension around the divorce.

> *SN*: Was your mother Lithuanian? No? Okay. Translated in English it says, "Whoever does good, the good comes back to them, and whoever does bad the bad comes back to them." And that's true in life. Believe me it's true. So if you do good, the good is going to come back to you, so you do good.
>
> *MN*: Did that prove true do you think in your life?
>
> *SN*: Absolutely, 100 percent. So, you don't do things that you know are bad.
>
> *MN*: Did you ever do things that you knew were bad?

I could not ask the question I wanted to ask: did you do what was right for your family? I wanted to ask if he thought about the consequences of his actions. I could not confront him. I was indirect because I did not want him to cry or to become angry and I feared the effect his response would have on me.

When Alan Berliner produced *Nobody's Business*, a biographical film about his obstinate, opinionated father, he ultimately created a tender portrait.[19] Barbara Myerhoff wrote with compassion and affection for the elderly Jewish people she spent time with in *Number Our Days*, especially Shmuel Goldman, the learned man she came to admire.[20] I wanted to emerge with a portrait of my father that emulated the resolution present in Berliner's film or Myerhoff's book, yet our interviews were often dark.

Anna Sheftel and Stacey Zembrzycki wrote about their decision not to revisit a narrator whose life memoir included a racist perspective. They did not have the courage to ask the difficult questions and, as they never connected with the narrator, they dreaded the idea of going back.[21] Neither could I ask my father the most difficult questions. I explored the past with him while establishing emotional boundaries that at first glance seemed stricter than I would have maintained in interviews with a stranger. I do not think my father crossed his boundaries; he seemed instead to experience some relief to finally talk about his past.

I decided to be vulnerable in the act of listening, despite the difficult terrain, because I felt that was the only honest way that my father and I could try to cocreate the past together. I treated him with respect and compassion. I lifted parts of the veil of silence that clouded our past. I pushed my boundaries well beyond what I thought possible as I sought, and found, new ideas about the stories that shaped my family.

Final Thoughts

Those who listen to life histories seek to do no harm to their storytellers, their audiences, or themselves. The hope is that in the telling there is solace, and in the interpretation there is personal, social, or historical understanding. Because a genuine listening environment involves trust between the narrator and the listener, and trust entails some measure of vulnerability, shaping the direction of a difficult or potentially painful interview is based on the narrator and the listener judging their vulnerabilities, and negotiating emotional boundaries throughout the interview. There are emotional consequences for those who tell the stories and for those who listen to them.

In some instances, the listener can enter into the intimate space of a family and ask difficult questions that prompt honest and soul-searching dialogue. Drawing on experience and training in asking sensitive questions, oral historians cocreate narratives that offer a space for resolution or exploration of topics narrators may have been unable to pursue alone. When the oral historian is cocreating narratives in the intimate space of her own family, the vulnerability is deeper and the emotional risks are greater.

Subjectivity was heightened in each of the interviews I cocreated, due in part to the extraordinary contexts: a dying mother, and a father who had never spoken of his past to any of his children. I engaged in empathy and projection: how would I feel if I were that person? What would I want to talk about and to experience as a result of the interviews? I also looked outward: what did the narrators want, feel, and deem important? I was interested in the meanings Lania created in her narration and how she and her son constructed meaning together. I was interested in the events of my father's life but even more focused on the ways in which he made sense of his life.

I was vulnerable in both of these interviews yet they had unique emotional contours. While I knew in advance that they would be intellectually and emotionally demanding I did not know what my boundaries would be. I did not know what direction each interview would take, how the narrators would shape their stories, or what the nature of our cocreations would be. I encouraged Lania and my father to pursue difficult topics, yet I retreated when I sensed they were becoming painful to them. I also retreated when the topics were becoming too painful to me. Looking back I realize I found the notion of a deathbed reliving of some of the most disturbing moments in my life intolerable, so I shifted the questions to elicit more affirming stories. Lania's narrative also had the potential to alter my relationship to death and dying, to change an understanding that I had forged in the context of my mother's death. Lania and her son shifted direction with me. My father's stories carried the potential to alter my understandings of my family's past and impact my identity. The instability of my father's narrative made my vulnerability more difficult, as I was unsure if his stories were colored by age, memory, strong feelings, or mental illness. Yet I had to leave myself open to genuinely listening to them if I wanted to engage in the transformative processes of letting their stories change me.

Both narrative contexts involved an interaction between a parent and an adult child. In one case I was the third party to the narration, facilitating the cocreation of their story, imagining myself at once as the mother and as the son. In the second instance I was both the third party to the interview (the oral historian) and the adult child, asking the questions directly. I was vulnerable on behalf of Lania's son, but it was he who bore the responsibility of the relationship with his mother. In the case of my father I was both the vulnerable listener and the vulnerable daughter, and I bore the responsibility professionally and personally.

I think the most difficult oral histories are with the people whose lives have altered our own. Our vulnerability means that there are things we cannot ask and things we cannot hear. We try to listen nonetheless. I believe that we go to the places we fear the most because we hope to be brave, and use our courage to create public narrative spaces where these experiences will finally make sense, in concert with other, similar stories. I write about my father's life and my interviews with him so that I can explain these stories to the people whose family pasts were sites of pain. Oral historians and scholars speak for others who share our archive of feelings but have retreated into silence.[22] Given an intellectual, cultural, or social context, the stories that once haunted people's lives through the power of secrecy can no longer irreparably harm them, and may provide understanding about larger issues of history and memory. No one can ask the past not to intrude on the present, and no one can make whole the selves that were fragmented by experience. But if we are courageous enough to be vulnerable in potentially painful listening experiences, we can learn enough about the past so that it does not dominate the present, we can change the meanings assigned to it, and we can mend the many fragments of the self into something that is whole enough.

Notes

The title of this chapter is a reference to Ruth Behar's groundbreaking work on humanistic anthropology that discusses the vulnerability of the ethnographic field-worker. Ruth Behar, *The Vulnerable Observer: Anthropology That Breaks Your Heart* (Boston: Beacon Press, 1997).

1. Michael Riordon, *An Unauthorized Biography of the World* (Toronto: Between the Lines, 2004), 164.
2. Gadi BenEzer lists 13 signals that may indicate trauma in a person's life: "Trauma Signals in Life Stories," in *Trauma, Life Stories of Survivors*, eds. Kim Lacy Rogers and Selma Leydesdorff (New Brunswick: Transaction Publishers, 1999), 29–44, 34–36.
3. Nanci Adler, Selma Leydesdorff, Mary Chamberlain, and Leyla Neyzi, "Introduction," in *Memories of Mass Repression*, eds. Nanci Adler, Selma Leydesdorff, Mary Chamberlain, and Leyla Neyzi (New Brunswick: Transaction Publishers, 2009), ix–xxi, x–xii.
4. See Annette Kuhn, *Family Secrets, Acts of Memory and Imagination* (London: Verso, 1995).
5. Paul Stoller, *The Power of the Between* (Chicago: The University of Chicago Press, 2009), 33.
6. Ibid., 49.
7. I was asked by Hospice to do the pro bono interviews.
8. Narrator name withheld to protect privacy, interview by author, November 1999.
9. See Martha Norkunas, *Monuments and Memory, History and Representation in Lowell, Massachusetts* (Washington, DC: Smithsonian Institution Press, 2002; Rowman and Littlefield Publishers, 2006); "Narratives of Resistance and the Consequences of Resistance," *Journal of Folklore Research* 41, 2–3 (May–December 2004): 105–23.

10. This chapter stems from a book I am writing about difficult family memories. I reflect on my family story through the lens of four metaphors of postmodernity: the ruin, the fragment, the archive, and the sublime.

11. In this collection, Alan Wong also reflects on the "difficult listening" he experienced while interviewing his father.

12. Art Spiegelman, *Maus I, A Survivor's Tale: My Father Bleeds History* (New York: Pantheon Books, 1986); *Maus II, A Survivor's Tale: And Here My Troubles Began* (New York: Pantheon Books, 1992).

13. Alisse Waterston and Barbara Rylko-Bauer, "Out of the Shadows of History and Memory: Personal Family Narratives in Ethnographies of Rediscovery," *American Ethnologist* 33, 3 (2006): 397–412.

14. Ibid., 405, 408.

15. Ibid., 398.

16. Ibid., 402.

17. Ibid., 406.

18. Stanley Norkunas, interview by author, August 2005.

19. *Nobody's Business*, directed by Alan Berliner, 1996.

20. Barbara Meyerhoff, *Number Our Days* (New York: Simon and Schuster, 1978).

21. Anna Sheftel and Stacey Zembrzycki, "Only Human: A Reflection on the Ethical and Methodological Challenges of Working with 'Difficult' Stories," *The Oral History Review* 37, 3 (Summer/Fall 2010): 206, 208.

22. See Ann Cvetkovich, *An Archive of Feelings* (Duke University Press, 2003).

CHAPTER 5

Listen and Learn: Familiarity and Feeling in the Oral History Interview

Alan Wong

For several years now, I have been involved in a number of research projects that have employed, either in part or in full, an oral history approach to the sharing of personal stories. One of these projects, a five-year oral history endeavor based at Concordia University in Montreal, Canada, titled *Life Stories of Montrealers Displaced by War, Genocide, and Other Human Rights Violations*, required me, in both interview and interactive theatrical settings, to engage with participants who were often complete strangers to me prior to my initial encounter with them in these spaces.[1] Other projects, namely, my doctoral dissertation project, for which I collected and analyzed oral histories of racialized, ethnicized, and colonized (REC)[2] allosexual[3] activists in Montreal, as well as a more personal project involving an oral history interview with my father, saw me probing the lives of friends and family members. If I were to pinpoint a common theme running through all of these projects, it would be my interest in exploring how marginalized, disenfranchised, and oppressed individuals overcome adversity in the Canadian context. In pursuing this interest, however, I have also stumbled upon a rather intriguing methodological discovery: how I absorbed and responded to each narrative I heard depended on my relationship with the respective storyteller. Put another way, in an oral history interview context, familiarity often bred content.

Discussions on listening are by no means new to oral history. A plethora of foundational reflections on the topic have been anthologized in collections such as *The Oral History Reader*, and countless others have been published in scholarly journals and books since writings on oral history practice first emerged. Many of these have tended to be anthropological or sociological in nature or have focused on the technical and pragmatic aspects of the interview process, providing an instructive, but rather distant and clinical look at listening as both an art and a practice in oral history.[4] I have seen little in the way of how preexisting personal connections between the interviewer and interviewee can inject moments of expectation and affect into not only the offering of the narrative by the teller, but also its reception by the listener, complicating the latter's approach to the interview as it proceeds and progresses as well as beyond its completion. In my own multifaceted experiences as an oral historian, I have discovered that how I listen in the interview space is contingent on my relationship with the interviewee, with intimate knowledge and personal sentiment having an enormous impact on the ways that I function in that space as a collaborator in the endeavor.

If I take into account all of the various oral history projects I have been involved in over the years, four types of listening contexts emerge: interviews with individuals with whom I had no prior relationship; interactive performances of personal narratives wherein the personal relationship or lack thereof between myself as a performer and a narrator is inconsequential; interviews with friends; and interviews with family members. As a result of my experiences in these diverse settings, I have come to realize that the unique context in which the narrative exchange occurs has had a pronounced effect on both my engagement with the storyteller and my behavior in the narrative space. In other words, different ways of relating to the narrator and the narrative beget different ways of listening.

Listening to Strangers

When I began my journey as an oral historian, one of the first interviews I conducted was with Hourig Attarian, a Montreal-based scholar who also uses oral history methodology in her work. The purpose of the interview was to explore her life story as a Canadian of Armenian descent and its connection to her artistic and academic work on the Armenian genocide, which would then be included among the 500 narratives being collected for the *Montreal Life Stories* project. Prior to my session with Hourig, I had only conducted one other interview,[5] so I was rather green in comparison to other oral historians in the project.

I had never met Hourig before to my first interview with her, and thus she was a complete stranger to me. When I sat down with her for our initial session, I felt strangely calm. There was none of the angst that one usually has when meeting someone for the first time in what could be considered a formal situation. Usually, the unknown is a source of anxiety for me; the pressures of providing a good impression and representing the project in an appropriate way to someone whom I knew nothing about would have ordinarily had me fumbling for words and sweating buckets. Yet Hourig was beyond hospitable with my videographer, Elena and me, offering us a veritable feast of snacks and putting me at ease with her warm personality. This obviously helped in creating a sense of comfort as I asked the first question.

In terms of listening, however, what was most helpful as the interview progressed was the absence of any shared or common history between Hourig and me. With no wayward or distracting thoughts or assumptions arising from personal knowledge I might have had about Hourig or her community, such as information concerning specific dates or events in her life, I was able to give her my full, undivided attention. In effect, I was able to immerse myself in an act of "deep listening," which Anna Sheftel and Stacey Zembrzycki define as "listening for meanings, not just facts, and listening in such a way that prompts more profound reflection from the interviewee."[6] Because my mind was clear of epistemological clutter, I was able to think more profoundly about Hourig's reflections in process and, consequently, ask more contemplative questions in return.

This is not necessarily to say, however, that this ability to listen deeply has been consistent with other oral history interviews I have done with strangers since my sessions with Hourig; sometimes certain conditions, ranging from the banal to the complex, have affected the interview environment. An example of the former would be an interview I conducted with Iranian Canadian artist Khosro Berahmandi, part of whose interview was situated in his stifling, unair-conditioned studio on a hot summer's day, making maintaining focus a challenge for all parties concerned. On the other end of the spectrum was an interview with Tamil performer, writer, and painter Kamala Patpanathan that I had done in her apartment. While Kamala was certainly a warm and congenial interviewee, there was an issue with language between us that made it difficult not only to understand and communicate with each other with any sense of clarity, but also, more significantly, to ascertain the intent behind the words we were speaking. In the end, the interview was pleasant enough, but failed to move beyond surface details because I was unable to engage with her on a deeper level and, thus, explore the substance of her life story with her.

Disruptive as some of these circumstances may be, I have generally found them to be more the exception than the rule, irrespective of the fact that they are only external forces exerting pressure on the act of listening, rather than the problem emanating from a more rooted place within either my interviewees or myself. Another session I conducted with Khosro in his cool and airy apartment, for instance, was a much more focused affair, proceeding in the same way as had my interview with Hourig. Another stranger to me, gay Italian Canadian community organizer Gaspare Borsellino, whom I had recruited for my dissertation research, also provided me with a successful interview experience in this regard, with our sexual orientation the only truly common bond between us. As activists who had been prolific in the gay community during different eras—Gaspare's preceding my entrée into the scene—we had never encountered each other before the interviews took place, thereby making it much easier for me to listen for new information and come from a place of genuine curiosity about his experiences. This is where the pleasure of listening to strangers lies; every word uttered by them is a fresh discovery for interviewers such as me.

One could say, then, that listening to strangers is a very *organic* process. In some ways, it requires very little effort on the part of the interviewer, as there are few barriers beyond surface conditions to obstruct his or her engagement with the narrator. Of course, this does not discount the fact that interviewees may offer traumatic stories from their lives that can affect the oral historian emotionally and psychologically; from the standpoint of interpersonal relationships with the tellers, however, the pure act of listening is a relatively unencumbered endeavor.

Performing Personal Narratives

In addition to the interview component of the *Montreal Life Stories* project, I was also involved in research creation through a Playback Theatre (PT) troupe called the Living Histories Ensemble (LHE) (see figure 5.1), which was founded to explore, through performance, specific moments in the lives of those involved in the project. Thus, we collaborated with each of the working groups[7] that

Figure 5.1   LHE rehearsal, from left to right, Alan Wong, Lucy Lu, and Lisa Ndejuru. Photograph by David Ward.

comprised the project, including those focused on mass atrocities such as the Holocaust as well as those perpetrated in places such as Rwanda, Cambodia, and Haiti, sharing performances that have been devoted to representing their realities as they have experienced them.

Playback Theatre, which was conceived by Jonathan Fox and developed by Fox and Jo Salas in the United States in 1975,[8] is an improvisational form of community-engaged theater that solicits stories related to specific topics from audience members; these are then immediately "played back" by troupe members using different performative forms and techniques that are determined by the "Conductor," an individual who functions as an emcee or facilitator between the audience and the actors. These stories are always performed from the perspective of the storyteller, and the performances are grounded in metaphor rather than a literal retelling. My initiation into PT occurred in 2006, when I was recruited by a friend to perform in an ad hoc Playback troupe that was assembled for the opening of the *Accès Asie* Festival, which marks Asian Heritage Month in Montreal. Since then, I have performed in countless shows that have addressed a wide array of issues, including literacy, leadership, and women's rights as well as the diverse concerns of the *Montreal Life Stories* working groups.

Having been a practitioner of PT for several years now, I have developed a way of listening that, while often as free of constraints as my approach to oral history interviews with strangers, has some distinct qualities of its own, as well. One significant difference is that the stories audience members tell in a theatrical context tend to be brief and anecdotal in nature, rather than drawn out over several hours like a life story interview. For example, usually the Conductor will begin a show by asking the audience what has drawn them to attend that particular performance, and the response is generally short, such as: "I wanted to discover a new form of theatre" or "I wanted to explore different ways of storytelling." The Conductor may try to coax more details from a given audience member, but often a short, one-sentence answer is enough around which the group can build a performance. Thus, to "play back" the story, we will pick a short form such as a fluid sculpture, whereby the actors use sound and movement to create a visual and aural sculpture composed of their bodies and voices that metaphorically reflects the teller's story. For us as actors, such one-liners or brief anecdotes are easy both to listen to and to interpret performatively, since they are broad enough for us to find our own respective narrative openings.

A second difference is that because the telling is moderated by the Conductor, I have no control as an actor over the questions being asked in the moment, though during rehearsals before a given performance we, as a troupe, usually discuss the theme of the event to which we have been invited and contribute questions that may potentially be used during the show. Oftentimes, we will even invite a "consultant" from the community for which we will be performing to come to our rehearsal and provide us with some insight into and context around his or her community and the issues that affect it. For one show that was aimed at allosexual refugees and immigrants in Montreal, we invited several members from Agir, a local organization focusing on matters of concern to allosexual asylum seekers and "New Canadians," to a rehearsal. We asked them to tell us some stories, which we then played back using a few different forms so that they could have an understanding of the kind of theater we do. Many of the narratives that they shared conveyed their feelings of loneliness and isolation in Montreal. If we had listened properly in that space, we would have understood that the stories that were relevant to them were those about their life in their new land; however, when it was time to perform for the community in a formal show setting, the questions we asked ultimately revolved around their histories prior to coming to Canada. As a consequence, few people were willing to offer their stories, and the show felt rather flat to me in the end. Halfway through the performance I realized why we were not connecting with the audience, but there was nothing I could do at that point, lest I disrupt the show. It was important not to distract myself with my epiphany, and so I simply continued with the show and followed whatever directions— both expected and unexpected—the Conductor was taking it. I would describe the kind of listening we do in this particular type of situation, then, as having two dimensions: the first revolves around the development of a listening relationship between the theater troupe and the community for which we are performing, wherein we, as the former, must grasp, as strongly as possible, the messages that members of the latter are trying to convey to and through us in order to serve them honorably and well; and the second can be understood as a listening relationship that develops between the Conductor and the actors, wherein the latter must stay focused on, pay attention to, and be ready for the former's instructions at all times, regardless of what other thoughts may intrude because, as the cliché reminds us, "the show must go on."

The most significant distinction in how I listen as a Playback actor, however, is that as the story is being told, I am not only paying attention to its content, but also searching for specific narrative moments that inspire metaphors that I can bring to life through performance while staying true to the essence of the narrator's experience. For example, in a show for racialized allosexuels that I performed in with the Montreal Third Space Playback, a troupe I belonged to and that preceded the LHE, a woman told a story that expressed her difficulty in figuring out how to support a Moroccan friend of hers who was facing problems with his family because of his transsexuality. The Conductor decided that this story would be better reflected in a longer form, so she asked the teller to assign actors specific roles for the playback; to my own surprise, she chose me to play her friend. Having listened attentively to her story, however, I was able to find a suitable impulse within me that translated into an appropriate metaphor, despite my lack of connection to experiences of transsexuality. I selected a lilac-colored scarf from the rack of scarves we keep at the side of the stage for use as props and slowly pulled it over, under, and around different parts of my body in a flowing, constant motion while standing in place throughout the whole narrative while the other actors performed their roles around me in response to the performative choice I made. To me, the scarf and the way I used it symbolized the fluidity of the subject's sexuality as well as the notion that it was an inseparable part of his identity, while the stillness of my feet signified his inability to escape the turmoil around him. Here, again, I can point to two dimensions of listening at work: the first is listening for elements in the teller's story that I, as an actor, can convert into performance through metaphor, whether it be materially in the form of a prop, physically through movement, verbally through voice, or all of the above mixed together; and the second is listening to the other actors and vice versa so that we are attuned to what each one is doing and to the choices each one is making so that we all may respond in an appropriately performative way—which is the essence of all improvisation, ultimately. In this context, the relationship between the storyteller and myself and that between the other actors and myself only exists in the time and space of the story's telling; whether the teller and I and the other actors are strangers or familiars outside of this spatial and temporal frame is irrelevant. Only the here and now of the words being spoken matter; we, as Playback actors, accept them as an offering or a gift, embodying them in a way that respects the teller and his or her history and identity—an act of performative listening.

Interviews with Friends

For the better part of a decade, I have been an activist in Montreal, focusing on issues of concern to those who situate their identities at the intersections of racial, ethnic, sexual, and gender diversity. Throughout this time, I have been struck by the absence of racialized, ethnicized, and colonized (REC) voices in historical accounts of the local gay and lesbian[9] community at-large, and likewise the lack of allosexual representation in the narratives of the city's various ethnocultural communities. To help remedy this, I decided that for my doctoral dissertation project, I would collect the life stories of friends of mine in Montreal who, like me, were also REC allosexual activists. In so doing, I hoped to not only fill this gap in history, but also show the contributions we have made toward fighting racism and heterosexism and the various phobias associated with these discourses. At the outset, I assumed that this would be a relatively straightforward endeavor, as there were not many individuals who "fit" the criteria for my project, and I already had relatively trusting relationships with most if not all of them as well as varying degrees of background knowledge about them, not to mention the fact that I was also "one of them." However, as I soon discovered, the privileges of friendship and insider-ness did not necessarily lead to an easier path in the research process, particularly where listening was concerned.

To call REC allosexual activists in Montreal a "community" is a bit of a misnomer. Even if one understands the idea of community in the political sense as "imagined," as Benedict Anderson famously did, it would be difficult to apply this notion to this particular group.[10] While we have, to a certain degree, created "a collective identity out of the myriad [sic] collage-like fragments of the mind," the notion of us as a community might only rest in my mind, as I am not sure if other activists would view "us" in the same way.[11] Still, it is difficult for me to come to any set of conclusions about this, since, as with any concept grounded in subjectivity, the construction of a given "community" can shift and mutate from moment to moment, location to location, and person to person. At the very least, I can say that from my own vantage point, what binds these individuals to me and me to them are my personal relationships with them.

In her theorization of "friendship as method," Lisa M. Tillmann-Healy states that "friendship and fieldwork are similar endeavors" in that both of them "involve being in the world with others" and "[gaining] entrée" into communities.[12] An amalgam of interpretivism,[13] feminist standpoint theory, queer methodologies, and participatory action research,[14] friendship as method answers the call "for inquiry that is open, multivoiced, and emotionally rich."[15] When fused with an "insider identity," those who engage in friendship as method become, in Jody Taylor's words, "intimate insiders," since

> the researcher is working, at the deepest level, within their [sic] own "back-yard": that is, a contemporary cultural space with which the researcher has regular and ongoing contact; where the researcher's personal relationships are deeply embedded in the field; where one's quotidian interactions and performances of identity are made visible; where the researcher has been and remains a key social actor within the field and thus becomes engaged in a process of self-interpretation to some degree; and where the researcher is privy to undocumented historical knowledge of the people and cultural phenomenon being studied.[16]

Taylor's paradigm fits aptly with my own situation. Since I have been deeply entrenched in the REC allosexual activist scene for almost ten years, it became not only part of my political world, but also my social world. I have attended parties thrown by other activists and invited them to my parties, met them for coffee or a meal or a movie, and have gone dancing with them at nightclubs. Though such socializing preceded my dissertation studies, it has also continued during them. People know me in the community; they turn to me for advice, and I to them. We confide in each other, tell each other our secrets, embrace each other in times of happiness and sorrow, and laugh together. We also fight in solidarity alongside each other through common struggles, lend our support to each other's causes, and share resources and ideas. We can express both empathy with and sympathy for each other as friends, activists, and REC allosexual people.

Being an intimate insider is not without its challenges, however. I, like Taylor, have worried that the "[empathy] and affection" between myself and my friend-participants might have contributed to their participation in my project, in that they may only have agreed to be interviewed by me because they wanted to "please" me.[17] Among other potential obstacles, Taylor also lists: tensions arising from identity politics; perceptions of favoritism in approaching some friends for interviews and not others[18]; and distinguishing in memory what friends may have said during "the designated time" of the research process from what was known of them already outside of that time.[19] To these I would add difficulties with listening as another challenge that is unique to the intimate insider, particularly in life story interviewing, as my experience with my dissertation research demonstrates.

As an intimate insider, I took part in many of the same activist activities, attended many of the same events, and worked on many of the same ventures as my friend-participants. Thus, during our interview sessions, I found myself listening for and anticipating stories about some of those activities, events, and ventures at which I was also present. These were memories that I thought were quite critical to the history of the community not because I was there, but because they were moments that demonstrated our solidarity with each other as a community. For example, I expected to hear personal perspectives on the formation of Coalition MultiMundo,[20] which I felt was an important event for all of us. However, when I asked some of the key players in the creation of the coalition to recount the most significant events in REC allosexual activism, they neglected to mention this episode from our collective past. Since I did not want to affect the course of their interviews by steering them directly to that story, I asked questions such as "Anything else?" in the hope that they would bring it up on their own. As a result, I distracted myself from listening deeply to their interviews from beginning to end, my intimate insider knowledge frequently getting the better of me by filling my head with self-designated historical priorities that may not have been shared by my friend-participants. In a negative sense, one could dub this as a form of "intimate listening"—a way of listening so closely for one's own story or interests to be reflected that one risks overlooking the *teller's* truth as it is being conveyed or even an advantageous opening to further investigation of the topics that interest the interviewer. For my own research, such listening resulted in missed opportunities not only to inquire into other forms of my interviewees' engagement with activism and community, but also to delve further into those areas that I had a personal investment in—simply because I adhered too rigidly to some methodological rules of oral history interviewing rather than giving myself the flexibility to explore certain shared areas of history. I was so concerned with my friendships "tainting" my interviews that, in some cases, I neglected the historical significance of those friendships altogether. In other words, I forgot that my relationships with my interviewees were just as important to the narratives as any other element of their histories. Thus, some of the interviews I collected now feel less *complete*—at least insofar as the depth of perspectives I was hoping to gather— than they could and should have been.

Interviews with Family

The story of my coming out as a gay man to my parents is not a typical one. It was October 1995, and I was pursuing a master's degree in creative writing at the University of New Brunswick in Fredericton, New Brunswick. I had been suffering through some particularly strong bouts of depression, brought on in part by my parents' relentless queries about whether I had found myself a girlfriend. When I expressed my emotional state on the telephone to my sister in Toronto, she gently suggested that perhaps it was time to divulge my secret to them. I reluctantly agreed; however, because my parents were living in Mississauga, a suburban city adjacent to Toronto, I would either have to tell them over the telephone or wait until my next trip home to visit them at Christmas. Neither of these was an appropriate option to me. My sister then asked me if I wanted her to do it for me. After some hesitation, I said yes. Thus, the following Saturday, I found myself waiting by the telephone for the call that I knew would inevitably come after my sister told my father the news earlier that day, as we had arranged it. When the telephone finally did ring, I was prepared; my father had a volatile temper in those days, and was given to yelling loudly and harshly when he was angry, so I was ready to yell back. When I picked up the receiver, however, the voice I heard on the other end was not angry, but rather somber and melancholic in tone. In that tone, my father expressed his heartache at the news, telling me that it was the darkest day in his life, that all he could see was a black hole in front of him. The worst thing he said to me was that he wished I had told him earlier so that he would not have invested so much money in me. I was taken aback by the entire conversation, paralyzed with uncertainty as to how to respond. It was a trying moment in my life, one that I hoped never to go through again. In the 14 years since my coming out, I felt that my father's mood had mellowed. Still, I knew that he, as an ardent Confucianist, continued to hold firmly to his conservative beliefs about homosexuality.[21] Although he may not have accepted my gay identity, however, it seemed to me that he had reached a point of tolerance, or, at the very least, resignation. Then in 2009, I recorded my father's life story.

This was a personal project of mine, as I had just found out that my uncle was dying of cancer. So, faced with my aging father's own mortality, I thought it was time to preserve his life story for my family—family as method, one could say. The first sessions focused on his early years, including his birth and upbringing in China and his first couple of decades in Canada. During these initial interviews, I was completely immersed in his story. While I had heard some of his anecdotes before, new pieces of information were being offered that helped expand on some stories while also creating entirely new narratives. In the third session, my own birth entered my father's story, and it was then that I started to become anxious. I began to zero in on the ways in which my father spoke about me, listening for specific comments that would give me hints about how he perceived me or what he thought of me. As we neared the 1990s and the disclosure of my sexuality in his narrative, a feeling of dread began to wash over me; the uncertainty of what he was about to say was unnerving. I tried to convince myself that I had nothing to worry about. When we reached the coming out event in his story, however, my worst fears were realized. All of his negative sentiments about this episode in his—our—life still remained after all of these years and now came pouring out of his mouth for me to hear. What made the situation worse was that he was referring to me in the third person as he spoke, even though I was right there in front of him. Through all of this, I chose to remain silent; I saw myself as the family oral historian during this process, and to interject or try to discuss the matter with my father would have been intrusive and disruptive to the project at hand. I wanted to be, in a word, professional. Thus, I continued to listen to him as all of his hurt and anger filled the air, while my own feelings remained bottled up inside of me. It was an endurance test, one that tied my stomach in knots and constricted all of my nerves. To me, this was no longer a matter of deep listening; it had become, in effect, difficult listening.

Difficult listening occurs when the interviewer is not merely implicated in the story the interviewee is telling, but is implicated in such a way that it has ramifications for the relationship between the oral historian and the teller outside of the interview. It can lead to the development of a new and unexpected fissure between, for example, a father and son. In that moment, it can make the rest of the interview seem irrelevant, unimportant, and frivolous. When emotion, in a negative and personalized form, rises to the surface, it can bring the entire interview to a halt, at least in a metaphysical sense; the questions may continue to be asked, but the ensuing stories may not be heard. I cannot say if this moment between my father and me marked the limit of my listening; my despair was not such that it debilitated or destroyed me. I am sure that it is possible for me to hear much worse things that can cause irrevocable damage to the heart and soul. That does not mean, however, that what my father said in those few achingly long minutes did not come as a blow to my spirit. As oral historians, we always strive for depth during our interviews, often forgetting that the waters can become difficult—treacherous—and we risk drowning.[22]

Since that interview, my father and I have repaired our relationship to the extent that the wounds have healed. However, my experience of that event has taught me that in certain situations, where there is a shared history of explosively emotional events, where there is a dynamic between the interviewer and interviewee that goes beyond even intimacy, it is important to proceed with caution and also anticipate the potential dangers that lie ahead. In the end, an interview is only an interview; it should not take priority over our own well-being.

Conclusion

The four types of listening detailed here—with strangers, in interactive performance, with friends, and with family—demonstrate that just as our relationships with individuals influence what we say to each other, so too do they affect how we listen to each other. In the context of oral history, this can have an enormous impact on how the oral historian (or performer) approaches the interview and functions in the interview space. Often, the closer the connection to the storyteller, the more complicated the emotions for the interviewer. In my own work as an oral historian, this has made for some very intense battles with my own mental capacities, especially in sessions with my father. I do not mean to suggest here that one should not engage in oral history endeavors involving friends or family members or other people who can be classified as "intimates"; while interviewing strangers certainly has its rewards, so too does collaborating with the ones we know and love (or like) to make sense of the moments in our histories that we both do and do not share. What I mean to impart, rather, is that it is important to be clear about our goals and intentions as oral historians when we enter the interview space. We should not only look forward to the potential discoveries to be made, but also remind ourselves that we are human beings who are often burdened with heavy baggage. In this sense, oral history projects are serious endeavors, and must be treated as such. The better prepared we are to interact on such a level with another human being, no matter who he, she, or they[23] might be, the more positive the experience is likely to be for all parties concerned. One cannot account for all situations, of course; but a negative can always be turned into a positive if one chooses to make it so. After all, every listening experience is a learning experience.

Ultimately, oral historians need to pay attention to listening as a critical aspect of the practice and discipline. It is something we often take for granted, and if we are not careful, it can roll right over us like a steam shovel, ruining not only our interviews, but also our psyches. Care for the self is just as important as care for the interviewee in oral history projects, and understanding the multifacetedness of listening is a part of that self-care. That qualitative researchers must never be disentangled from their humanity goes without saying; for oral historians, I would argue, that goes double, especially given that in what we do, we are not only sharing authority—we are also sharing ourselves.

Notes

1. For more on this project, go to http://www.lifestoriesmontreal.ca/. Note that the project recently ended, in July 2012.
2. "Ethnicized" and "colonized" are employed here in the same sense as "racialized," given that "racialization [sic] refers to the process whereby groups are marked on the basis of some kind of real or putative difference." See Yasmin Jiwani, *Discourses of Denial: Mediations of Race, Gender, and Violence* (Vancouver: University of British Columbia Press, 2006), 6. Thus, ethnicization and colonization suggest similar processes that actively impose certain putatively identificatory qualities on individuals that differentiate them from majoritarian populations based on ethnicity in the former case and aboriginality in the latter instance. This is not to suggest, however, that such marked individuals are not engaged in their own processes of resistance and decolonization.
3. [A] Office québécois de la langue française, "Le grand dictionnaire terminologique," http://www.granddictionnaire.com (accessed April 22, 2012); [B] UC Berkeley Gender Equity Resource Center, "LGBT Resources—Definition of Terms," http://geneq.berkeley.edu/lgbt_resources_definiton_of_terms (accessed April 22, 2012). "Allosexual" is an Anglicization of the French Canadian term "allosexuel," which itself was coined as a French response to the English term "queer," though the translation is not quite as tidy as one might expect. "Allosexuel" [A] refers to "a person whose sexual orientation is not heterosexual" (it may also function as an adjective), and while "queer" has also been used similarly as an umbrella term for nonheterosexual orientations and identities, among activist and academic circles in the Montreal Anglophone community it is contextualized more as "[a] political statement, as well as a sexual orientation, which advocates breaking binary thinking and seeing both sexual orientation and gender identity as potentially fluid" [B]. Thus, I use "allosexual" in the same spirit as "allosexuel," and also to recognize the specific local context in which my research was conducted.
4. See, among others, Hugo Slim and Paul Thompson, with Olivia Bennett and Nigel Cross, "Ways of Listening," in *Listening for Change: Oral Testimony and Development*, eds. Hugo Slim, Paul Thompson, Olivia Bennett, and Nigel Cross (London: Panos, 1993), 61–94; Kathryn Anderson and Dana C. Jack, "Learning to Listen," in *Women's Words: The Feminist Practice of Oral History*, eds. Sherna Berger Gluck and Daphne Patai (London: Routledge, 1991), 11–26; Henry Greenspan, *On Listening to Holocaust Survivors: Recounting and Life History* (Westport, CT: Praeger, 1998).

5. For an analysis of that interview experience, see Alan Wong, "Conversations for the Real World: Shared Authority, Self-Reflexivity, and Process in the Oral History Interview," *Journal of Canadian Studies* 43, 1 (2009): 239–58.

6. Anna Sheftel and Stacey Zembrzycki, "Only Human: A Reflection on the Ethical and Methodological Challenges of Working with 'Difficult' Stories," *The Oral History Review* 37, 2 (2010): 199.

7. The *Montreal Life Stories* project was organized around seven distinct working groups. Four of these groups were grounded in a specific geographic or historic context: Haiti; the Shoah/Holocaust; Cambodia; and Rwanda. Two others were more discipline-based: Education; and Oral History and Performance. The final group, Refugee Youth, was age-focused. The Living Histories Ensemble was involved with the Oral History and Performance working group.

8. Jonathan Fox, *Acts of Service: Spontaneity, Commitment, Tradition in the Nonscripted Theatre* (New Paltz, NY: Tusitala Publications, 1994).

9. I use "gay and lesbian" here instead of the more inclusive and commonly used adjectival clump "lesbian, gay, bisexual, transsexual, transgendered, and queer" (LGBTTQ) to highlight the hegemonic structures that privilege gay and lesbian voices above all others in Montreal.

10. Benedict Anderson, *Imagined Communities: Reflections on the Origin and Spread of Nationalism* (London and New York: Verso, 1983).

11. Avtar Brah, *Cartographies of Diaspora* (London and New York: Routledge, 1997), 124.

12. Lisa M. Tillmann-Healy, "Friendship as Method," *Qualitative Inquiry* 9, 5 (2003): 732.

13. Ibid.

14. Ibid., 733.

15. Ibid., 734.

16. Jodie Taylor, "The Intimate Insider: Negotiating the Ethics of Friendship When Doing Insider Research," *Qualitative Research* 11, 1 (2011): 9.

17. Ibid., 15. For similar reflections, see chapter 14 in this collection.

18. Taylor, "The Intimate Insider," 17.

19. Ibid., 18.

20. Established in 2006, Coalition MultiMundo brought together allosexual ethnicized and racialized organizations and their allies in Montreal under one umbrella group as a means of providing a more unified political voice. LGBTQ Asians of Montreal (formerly Gays and Lesbians of Montreal, though still using the acronym GLAM), of which I was one of the coordinators at that time, was one of the coalition's founding members. The coalition has since disbanded, and a new coalition is currently in the process of being formed.

21. "Confucian doctrines do not speak directly on the subject of same-sex love. Instead, Confucian teachings were focused on the family as the basic unit of the state. The emphasis of 'self' was placed on the kin-family relationship an individual held, not on the individual being. Marriages were formed in a way to strengthen these kinship ties amongst different groups [and were] not particularly focused on individual desire. The offspring's primary responsibility was to respect their elders and continue these lineage lines, the concept of marriage correlated with reproduction[,] not sexuality." Jennifer Q. Zhang, "Tongzhi Today,

Tomorrow," *Senior Theses* (Hartford, CT: Trinity College Digital Repository, 2011), http://digitalrepository.trincoll.edu/theses/8. See also Yanqui Rachel Zhou, "Homosexuality, Seropositivity, and Family Obligations: Perspectives of HIV-infected Men Who Have Sex with Men in China," *Culture, Health & Sexuality* 8, 6 (2006): 489–90.

22. For a related discussion, see chapter 4 in this collection.

23. Many transgender, genderqueer, and queer individuals prefer the pronoun "they" in the singular sense when being referred to by others; my use of it here is therefore an acknowledgment of that desire.

CHAPTER 6

Going Places: Helping Youth with Refugee Experiences Take Their Stories Public

Elizabeth Miller

Leontine Uwababyeyi approaches the front of the bus as it pulls into St. Joseph's Oratory, a spiritual landmark in Montreal, Canada. This is the place she has chosen to share her story of losing her entire family during the Rwandan genocide. The passengers on this youth-led, alternative bus tour are completely still as her recorded story begins:

> I want to tell you a story, a true story, my story. It's about how quickly your life can change in just three days, and then three months...In the morning we return home...windows and doors are broken. There are many people around talking to each other. I am eight years old, and for me it is exciting. Everyone is wondering what happened. A lady comes running towards us. She seems crazy. She tells us that they are killing people. We start running. I follow my brother. We go into the woods. We stay there for hours.[1]

Leontine stares out the window as the story plays, and it seems that, for both her and everyone on this crowded bus, time stands still.

Leontine was one of many youth who became involved with *Mapping Memories*, a Montreal-based participatory research-creation project. Her ongoing involvement over several years actively shaped the direction of the project and my own understanding of working with sensitive stories. As a documentary filmmaker and the project coordinator, I brought together media artists, policy advocates, service providers, and youth with refugee experiences to collaborate on media projects. Through workshops, we offered youth participants a chance to learn new media skills, reflect on their past experiences, work in a collaborative context, and express themselves creatively as they shaped their experiences into compelling stories. Each project resulted in public presentations so that participants had a chance to witness the impact of their stories on diverse audiences. Over the course of four years, we developed ten media projects that involved over one hundred newcomers. One of the most complex and rewarding projects was a ten-week workshop that resulted in the aforementioned bus tour, *Going Places*.

One way to launch a participatory media project is with a specific final event in mind. This is how the *Going Places* course and bus tour took shape. Nine thousand academics from across Canada would be visiting Concordia University to participate in the 2010 Congress of the Humanities and Social Sciences, and the university wanted to showcase research initiatives. I proposed a mobile memoryscape in the form of an alternative city bus tour, created by youth with refugee experiences. A memoryscape is a method, used by artists and historians, that combines personal narratives, interviews, and ambient sounds to help audiences experience places in new ways.[2] By connecting personal stories to significant places throughout Montreal, this tour would not only heighten awareness of both the stories and the locations, but also sensitize visitors to what it is like to be a youth refugee in Montreal. Seven young participants from Zimbabwe, Palestine, the Congo, and Rwanda signed up for the ten-week course to develop their stories and plan a tour itinerary. Several Concordia Communication Studies students helped with hands-on media training in photography, sound recording, and editing at the Centre for Oral History and Digital Storytelling (COHDS). Having a concrete objective and a "finish line" was an exciting parameter. At the same time, planning such a high-profile event meant that we would have to ensure that the end goal did not overshadow either the process or the individual objectives of the workshop participants who were involved in planning the tour. We were walking a fine line between a rewarding experience and something akin to "dark tourism."[3] The challenge was how to avoid a voyeuristic experience that would reinforce stereotypes rather than unsettle them. For me, the way to avoid an exploitative scenario was through a process-based participatory approach. Inspired by Julie Salverson's thoughts on what it means to have a meaningful *encounter* with difficult stories, I hoped to create an environment where the youth involved would have room for reflection and audiences would be encouraged to challenge their assumptions and feel implicated in the process.[4] In this chapter, I discuss our methodology as well as the challenges and insights I gained in developing *Going Places*. While there were seven youth involved, I have chosen to focus on Leontine's experience to help illustrate the complexity, risks, and benefits involved in taking very personal stories public.

Why Use a Participatory Media Method?

Participatory media has become a bit of a catch-all phrase for media creation and exchanges that challenge divisions between audiences and creators, such as video mashups, digital cartography, wikis, and more.[5] In using this term, I am referring to a method where individuals frame their own experiences and then explore how their stories are connected to others and larger social concerns.[6] This method is guided by what Marit Corneil calls an "ethics of access," whereby documentary filmmakers are more reflexive in their approach and individuals have better access to technology and control over both the production and the dissemination of their work.[7] An "ethics of access" requires grappling with larger representational questions as well as practical concerns. For example, when selecting media tools for *Going Places*, one of my priorities was to ensure that at least some of the software programs we used would be available to participants after the workshop. For this reason, I chose to use the free open-source sound-editing program Audacity. When planning the workshop I also wanted to be sure that the challenges of learning new tools did not overshadow the process and the opportunity to share experiences. While trained in video, I put the camera aside and instead facilitated workshops in writing, sound recording, and still photography so that students could grasp the technical tools quickly and focus on their stories.

Participatory video practices date back to the National Film Board of Canada's *Challenge for Change* program of the 1960s, and are increasingly used by media practitioners, researchers, and individuals hoping to challenge power dynamics in research and representation.[8] *PhotoVoice*, a method developed in England that involves writing and photography, is now practiced worldwide. Technologies of mobility, such as cell phones and global positioning system (GPS) mapping devices, have presented new opportunities for participatory projects, permitting groups to use location as a prompt for sharing stories and addressing issues connected to a specific site or place.[9] While the tools and forms of participation continue to develop and vary from project to project, for *Mapping Memories*, our method was grounded in mutual respect and shared authority.[10] This meant helping participants articulate personal goals, teaching them media and presentation skills, and involving them in key decisions. In her articulation of "citizens' media," Clemencia Rodriguez describes how collaborative media projects can influence both identity construction as well as positions of power or personal agency. She explains that "[alternative] media spin transformative processes that alter people's sense of self, their subjective positionings, and therefore their access to power."[11] Implementing a participatory method was particularly important in a project involving youth with refugee experience, who often have little control over how they are represented and struggle with confining identifications. For those who have gone through the arduous process of developing an official refugee narrative to gain entry into a country, a creative workshop presented opportunities to reframe this initial self-representation and move beyond a narrative that essentialized their notion of self.[12]

A memoryscape seemed like an ideal means to explore the significance of identity, place, and memory with youth whose lives had been dramatically impacted by physical displacement. Coined by Toby Butler, a cultural geographer who has organized audio walks around various oral histories of the city of London, memoryscapes enable people to explore how mobile technologies (smart phones, music players) help illuminate connections between history, memory, and place: "Place, home and 'roots' are a fundamental human need and they shape our cultural identity."[13] Our intention for the bus tour was to explore the significance of places and stories while moving through the city. As we passed the locations evoked in the stories, the bus stopped for the youth tour guides so that they could introduce and then play their recorded stories. At certain stops, we asked passengers to get off the bus and explore some of the places with the guides. By staging a literal enactment of *walking in their footsteps*, we wanted to immerse the audience in the lived realities of the youth, encouraging reflection, interaction, and discussion. We were eager to explore how place-based media might offer new ways of building understanding of the refugee experience and we also hoped that experiencing a familiar landmark from a new perspective would generate a heightened sensitivity of the specific challenges refugee youth face when navigating a city for the first time.

Partners and Goals

To develop this project and recruit participants, we collaborated with two groups. The first was with *Life Stories of Montrealers Displaced by War, Genocide and Other Human Rights Violations*, a Concordia University and community-based oral history initiative working with refugee communities to record their own life stories and share them with the larger public.[14] *Mapping Memories* had initiated a refugee youth working group within this unique community-university collaboration to ensure a youth perspective and to adapt the life story method so that young people would be inclined to participate. Our approach was to develop life stories through media workshops, enabling youth to work together in a supportive environment to engage with the complexity of sharing and representing difficult personal stories on their own terms. Enrollment for the workshop was open to any young person, aged 20–30 years, who had been *impacted by a refugee experience*. This might include a sister, brother, daughter, or another family member of a refugee. By broadening enrollment, we hoped the course would facilitate informal intergenerational exchanges between participants and their families in the creation of their personal memoryscapes.

According to education theorist Geraldo Campano, there are great benefits when it comes to intergenerational storytelling:

> Often immigrant, migrant, and refugee children bear witness to the suffering of their parents, as well as their own suffering. It is difficult to isolate hardship to any individual psyche; it spills, so to speak, onto the fabric of the diaspora. A child, being at once removed and part of what his or her family has endured, may be in a unique position to make new sense out of what has happened. The passage from silence to voice may be achieved through intergenerational storytelling.[15]

We also hoped that a range of experiences would deepen exchanges among participants and, as a group, permit us to explore questions such as: What is the role of storytelling in keeping family histories alive?

Our second group partner was the Young Women's Christian Association (YWCA) of Montreal, an organization dedicated to improving the lives of women and girls by reinforcing their self-esteem and autonomy.[16] Together, we wanted to explore ways of using a media project to foster leadership skills and create safe spaces where young women with refugee experiences could express themselves. It had been easier to recruit young men into our previous workshops and I wanted to use this opportunity to involve young women. Rania Arabi of the YWCA of Montreal helped to identify participants and coordinate the course. She also chose to develop her own story about her family's refugee experience alongside the other participants. Describing her role as participant-observer, she explained:

> Our intention was to establish a context of trust and safety, which are integral for the participants who come from vulnerable backgrounds. This intention fed all the sessions and the bus tour (even when things appeared not to go smoothly). I believe that my presence, though I was learning at the same time, gave credibility, as I have lived that experience myself, and it helped in creating a safe place. Co-facilitating a group is a delicate matter, and the details of how it is done and who assumes what responsibilities need to be clear from the start.[17]

Participatory projects often require more than one facilitator to play different but complementary roles. My primary role was as a media trainer and a producer who kept track of production timelines and stories. Rania used her personal experience and strong facilitation skills to maintain our group dynamic. Her willingness and enthusiasm to explore the impact of her parent's experiences in a collective context helped other participants gain confidence in exploring their own stories in the presence of others.

Building Trust and Ensuring a Safe Space

For Leontine and other group members this was the first time they would be sharing their personal stories with a wider public and, as a result, our group grappled with complex questions around revisiting and representing traumatic events: When is someone ready to take a personal story public? How do you decide how much of a story to share? Is there a message and who should hear it? To address these questions we had to establish trust and build relationships. One very practical way we did this was to begin the workshops with a shared meal. Each week, a different participant prepared a dish that reminded them of home. By preparing the meals, participants contributed to the course in concrete ways. We also asked them to tell a story that was connected to the dish and we recorded them on a digital audio recorder. The cook of the day might describe the person who shared the recipe with them, the origins of the dish, or the challenges of making it here in Montreal. Recording these food stories was a practical decision that was intended to develop technical skills and foster confidence in working with recorders and other equipment. Additionally, it was a way to create an initial set of stories for the tour. Since participants were simultaneously developing very sensitive personal stories, we wanted them to have a back-up story in case they felt too vulnerable sharing these with a larger public. Of course, the flip side of this safety net was that producing digital versions of our food stories involved more work and required more technology for all of us. It would also have made sense to simply share a meal together. The challenge of balancing a meaningful *process* with the practical need to *produce* public stories is often present in participatory media projects. The difficult nature of the stories, coupled with the big public event we were planning, made this challenge especially daunting, and we proceeded cautiously to ensure that the benefits of the experience outweighed any risks or discomfort.

As facilitators working with difficult stories, it was especially important to understand each participant's motivations for being involved in the course. To do this, we first asked everyone to draw a "map" of his or her new "home community" in Montreal. We asked them to draw places that made them feel at home; these could include a store, a community center, a community garden, a café, or a place of worship. On the back of the drawing, we asked them to write their motivation for sharing a story and joining the course. This exercise helped participants identify personal goals and gave them ideas for stories. We viewed these exercises as a form of *mutual* exploration. Everyone, including the facilitators, took part in the introductory mapping/goal exercise and this was the first of many steps in clarifying our individual and collective goals.

The objectives that had shaped the formation of the course included teaching media and presentation skills and raising awareness around youth refugee experiences with the general public. While individual and collective goals may change over time or differ somewhat, we wanted to respect both sets of objectives and explore creative ways of bringing them together throughout the process. For example, Leontine planned to share her story of losing her family during the Rwandan genocide. Her personal goal in telling the story was to honor her family and ensure her experience was part of a historical record. It was important to understand Leontine's personal motivation and support her throughout the creative process of telling this story for the first time.

Being Sensitive to Difficult Stories

Three days, three months, three weeks. So much has changed. I have found myself alone. I am the only survivor of my family...but I am a survivor and today am 22 years old and I am no longer alone. I have a new family. I am the mother of this family, and I have 16 children—girls and boys. Some of my children are older than me. You may ask yourself how is this possible?...My family is made up of orphans, of students at my school who are also trying to fight loneliness.[18]

Writing was the starting point for shaping the stories in the "Memoryscape Course." We led writing exercises and allocated time for individuals to work on their stories individually and with the support of a facilitator over an eight-week period. Our role as facilitators was to respond to the work as outside readers and help participants identify what details were clear or what additional details could make a story come alive. We encouraged participants to experiment with a variety of styles and genres when telling their stories, including a letter, a poem, a list, an interview, or a series of questions. Because our group was small and we had several facilitators, we were flexible and could accommodate diverse approaches to the project. The one parameter was that they tell their own story. This was not easy and for several participants their first inclination was to tell someone else's story. Leontine explains: "At the beginning, it wasn't easy to tell a story, I had many stories in mind, I wanted to tell other people's stories, not my story. But then I wrote *once upon a time there was a little girl she was eight years old, she lived happily...until everything changed*." And I thought if she wasn't alive who could tell this story, who could remember her family?[19]

By asking participants to tell their own stories we also had to be sensitive of the personal and creative risks involved. We explained that sharing personal stories means revisiting past events and, as a result, they may trigger difficult emotions. Stories emerge when an individual is ready, and we reinforced our belief that whatever story each participant was ready to tell was valuable. To this end, we offered a range of exercises and themes to explore. Dealing with difficult stories was challenging for the participants, as well as for the facilitators.

For example, when I first read Leontine's account of losing her family in the genocide, I was immediately struck by the intensity of the story. I noticed her calm demeanor while sharing, but was not sure if I should address how she felt about her experience or focus on providing feedback about the story's structure. I asked her how I could help, and she replied: "I need you to help me to correct the English," and so that is where we began.

Early on, Leontine did not know me well enough to ask for more, and as a creative facilitator, I could not assume to know what she needed. The context of our media workshops was self-expression, not therapy, and I needed to follow her lead. As she came to know me better, we were able to discuss the context, content, and structure of her story. For instance, Leontine initially sought to write about the family she lost to the genocide. During a writing session she mentioned her second family, made up of students who were also survivors of the genocide. We began to discuss how her story would change if she brought the two families together in one story. In this way she could honor both families and also offer audiences an opportunity to see her as more than a victim of this horrific event. By slightly changing the structure and adding other details, Leontine's story acknowledged her loss as well as how she coped afterward.

As facilitators, we also took into account the cultural, social, and political backgrounds of each participant. For example, as Leontine and I came to know each other, she took time to make sure I understood the nuances of what had taken place in Rwanda. For her, it was important that I knew both her personal story and the historical factors that led to the Rwandan genocide. That context was important for me as well as for anyone else reading her story and would present an ongoing challenge for the group when sharing their stories with diverse audiences. We knew that the story was an invitation to learn more but in itself it could not present the complexity of what had taken place.

It was important to be observant during sessions and inquire about participants' support networks outside of the class. We also provided the group with a list of psychological services developed by the *Montreal Life Stories* project, in case a participant needed professional support. There was always a possibility that a participant would drop out for emotional or practical reasons as they were juggling jobs, studies, and other responsibilities. It was especially rewarding to watch the network that developed among the participants themselves. Perhaps one of the biggest motivations for staying involved in the project were the friendships that developed and the support that participants gave each other. For many of them, this was the most valuable aspect of the project. Sharing personal stories offered them the opportunity to reflect upon a past event in the context of a supportive group. At the same time, sharing a story in the closed environment of the workshop as opposed to on a bus tour or the Internet implied different degrees of exposure.

Personal and Public Stories

Throughout the course, it was essential to create opportunities for participants to consider any potential privacy or security risks incurred by going public with their stories. One way we ensured they were comfortable was to have ongoing discussions about the difference between *private* and *public* stories. Early on we agreed that private stories originated from a personal memory or lived experience, and that these could take shape when participants recorded conversations with a family member, wrote down memories or past dialogues, or recalled a pivotal moment in their lives. With private stories, we emphasized that it was important to consider if any personal details might make a participant feel vulnerable at a later date, especially those that could compromise their safety or asylum application.

Public stories, on the other hand, were focused on collective memories, public events, or places important to a larger community. One example of a public story developed in the course was the Rwandan Commemorative Walk to the St. Lawrence River in Montreal's Old Port to remember the Tutsis who were murdered during the 1994 genocide.[20] Leontine and participant Stephanie Gasana, also from Rwanda, worked together on this public story. On the bus tour, they led passengers on a re-creation of the walk and asked passengers to throw petals into the harbor to honor those who had died. By introducing the notion of public and private stories, we wanted to reiterate that all of their stories mattered and that ultimately, they were in charge of which ones they would share with a general public.

We had to make sure there was time and space for participants to process difficult emotions as they arose. For example, as part of the larger *Montreal Life Stories* project, Leontine also conducted a life story interview with the Rwandan Working Group. For her it was a necessary but difficult experience. Following the interview she debated quitting the memoryscape course, feeling emptied and as if she had nothing left to share. After further reflection, however, she decided to continue with the course. She later explained to me how doing an interview was different than shaping a digital story, articulating the challenges and benefits each form offered. The video interview was conducted in Kinyarwanda with someone she knew and trusted, and Leontine was given a copy to make sure she was comfortable with what she had shared. Watching the video interview was very difficult but it also permitted her to experience her story in a new way, as both an insider and outsider to her life experiences. Furthermore, she could watch this interview with her aunt who had raised her, but with whom she had never been able to fully explain the details of her past. With the digital story, Leontine had the ability to shape her narrative over time and in a supportive context with facilitators and peers. The well-structured story offered some distance and relief from the messiness of the raw interview and was the version she felt comfortable revealing to a more general, unknown public. For me, Leontine's experience demonstrated the ways in which the process of sharing a sensitive story, in either an interview or digital story format, is full of contradictory feelings, of being both in and out of control at various stages.

A Collective Experience

After writing, recording, and editing the stories, the final step was to link the stories to locations around the city and plan our bus route. Place was the inspiration for a few stories, but in most cases connecting the story to a place was determined after the story was written. Leontine's narrative about her two families had no obvious Montreal marker but she decided to make St. Joseph's Oratory her place, because this is where she found solace when she first arrived in Montreal. Once we chose sites and planned the route, we determined what would happen before and after the recorded stories. We decided that after each story, the tour guide would play a song from home. The music choice was a form of self-expression and also provided a break from the intensity of the stories. We also helped the guides prepare introductions and anecdotes for their stories to share along the route.

Two weeks before the tour, we planned a dress rehearsal on the same university shuttle bus that we would use for the tour. We were moving beyond the safe confines of our workshop space and the dress rehearsal was essential for building confidence. Leontine explained: "In the beginning, I couldn't look people in the eye, I was so shy, I had never stood in front of more than three people, practice helped me, and working with others. They help you to do something you can not do alone."[21] Our rehearsal was also the first time we had a chance to understand the power of the stories as a collection and the experience forged a new intimacy among group members. Our emphasis shifted from individual process to collective experience, giving us a chance to explore our mutual goals for the tour. According to Rania, "[what] was shared was the desire to create a deeper understanding of the refugee experience—of exile, of home, of finding home. We wanted to build compassion around a human experience that is many times marginalized, forgotten, judged, or avoided."[22]

Organizing a public event is an essential part of a participatory project, regardless of the scale, because it offers a chance for individuals to experience the collective impact of their work. To this end, Gerald Campano states that "stories may be personal but the emotions they convey have social import, reflecting readings of the world that are embedded in collective history, and group experience."[23] During the rehearsal we reiterated our shared goal of using personal stories to get past limiting stereotypes about refugee experiences that focus primarily on tragedy, victimization, and sensation. We wanted audiences to also witness the joys, talents, strengths, and achievements that are a big part of their lives. Furthermore, instead of focusing on the story of any one individual, we wanted to emphasize that while every refugees' lived experience is unique, it is also broad and far-reaching, impacting families, classrooms, communities, and society. We kept these goals in mind when dealing with the media.

Negotiating Exposure

Because the stories were produced in a supportive group context, the challenge was to bring that approach into our dealings with the press. Our tour captured a great deal of attention and was featured in several newspapers, radio programs, and on television. The attention we received was, in part, due to the immersive and engaging approach of a bus tour. It was also a result of our connection to a "big event" (the Congress) and the support offered by Concordia University, which dedicated media-relations staff to the project.

To prepare ourselves for the challenge of negotiating press coverage, we started local and then moved outward, speaking first to the Concordia University media representatives, then to local radio stations, and finally to television and larger press outlets. Members of the group who wanted public speaking experience represented the rest of the group. Before agreeing to a press interview, we did research to see if and how each journalist had covered this issue in the past and we also asked about the length of the segment to discern if they were looking for either a sound byte or a more in-depth story. We wanted, whenever possible, to avoid having one of our participants framed in a sensationalist way.

We made sure to rotate speakers and often worked in groups of two or three to present ourselves as a collective, which also served to avoid placing too much of a spotlight on any one individual. When questions became too personal and participants did not want to answer directly, we encouraged our press representatives to prepare nonspecific answers such as: "The refugee experience impacts all of us in different ways" or "That is a story for another time." For those participants who were hesitant, we reiterated that saying no to the press was also a form of empowerment. One reporter was quite keen to interview Leontine, who had decided that she did not want to be interviewed. The reporter was persistent, but we held firm, and insisted that the journalist respect her decision.

Despite our best intentions to prepare for press interviews in advance, the real learning happened on the spot and the process was largely out of our control. The experience did get easier over time but we remained ambivalent about how much press exposure we wanted. We made sure to check in with participants before and after any press interviews, to ensure that their experiences remained positive. Although this element of the workshop offered participants further insights into how to balance privacy with media exposure, it was time consuming and risky. Working with the mainstream media in a participatory project is a complex challenge. While it has the potential to raise the profile of a project, help build awareness, and offer training opportunities for participants, it can just as easily reinforce stereotypes or alienate those involved.

A Live Performance

One of the most satisfying aspects of the tour was the interplay of the pre-recorded audio stories with the live presentations of the guides. Crammed into a bus, there was an unexpected intimacy between audience members. As we traveled through the city, we journeyed through a range of emotions. People cried during Leontine's story and then clapped and laughed when Rania spontaneously invited her 70-year-old father to dance with her as a Palestinian song played over the loud speaker. Rania explained that "[when] something is shared out loud, when people are heard by an audience, when a group is formed to go beyond individuals' stories, this is where the trans-formative work takes place."[24] The prerecorded stories permitted the youth guides to share their intimate experiences without having to retell them in person. Instead, as their stories played, the youth were also able to listen to them and observe how the audience reacted. The distance the recorded story provided helped the youth feel less vulnerable, directing attention beyond the specifics of a single story to a deeper reflection about integration and belong-ing in Montreal. The live component of the tour presented an opportunity to connect the stories to the larger context of immigration rights and address legislation that was under debate at the time. Bringing to light the broader context of immigration policy was an important part of the tour and was "the story" that I, as a facilitator, could help convey. By explaining legisla-tive changes, we made personal what would have otherwise been a dry and abstract shift in federal immigration policy. At the time, Bill C-11 was under consideration and threatened to change Canada's refugee determination pro-cess for individuals from certain countries.[25] We used the tour to reinforce the important message framed by the Canadian Council for Refugees and other concerned advocates: that decisions need to be based on an individual's story regardless of where they are from.

Final Reflections

Through this experience, I learned a great deal about the value of creating safe and supportive environments in collaborative oral history projects. Incorporating meals into our workshops, letting technology play a valuable but secondary role, offering a range of creative exercises to participants, and giving space for the youth to develop relationships with each other was essential to establishing the intimacy we developed as a group. Rehearsals were key in building confidence and group dialogue helped us identify our goals. Perhaps most important to the process was structuring time for reflection, which offered members the clarity and courage they needed to take their stories public.

The response to the tour was overwhelmingly positive but we also recognized that it was just a first step in a longer process—our next challenge was to find ways to continue sharing these important stories with more people. Inspired by the stories produced for the bus tour, a member of the *Montreal Life Stories* team aired them on community radio and then ran a follow-up workshop in radio production. To share with educators what we learned about dealing with sensitive issues, we created a book/DVD/website (www.mappingmemories.ca) that includes the stories as well as methods and insights on how to conduct a similar project. To reach out to high school students we organized classroom visits and used the stories to facilitate dialogue about safe spaces in schools for refugees and all newcomers. Involving the youth in different forms of outreach helped them better understand how their stories resonated with different audiences. It also offered them an opportunity to gain perspective on their stories and see themselves as educators and their stories as educational tools. In speaking about his work with Holocaust survivors, Henry Greenspan emphasizes the value of sustained acquaintance, explaining how new discoveries and understandings surface over time.[26] Sustained involvement in a participatory media project is equally rewarding. We were able to observe how the project impacted the youth over time and likewise appreciate the ways in which they shaped and informed the direction of the project.

Most participants, including Leontine, assumed that once the tour was over their involvement with *Mapping Memories* would end (see figure 6.1). But a few months quickly turned into a few years and, not surprisingly, we continue to work together. We all acknowledge the invaluable ingredient of time in developing trust and understanding between facilitators and participants. Leontine explained: "Not everybody is ready to share, it takes time. It took me fifteen years to share my story."[27] In describing the personal benefits of taking part in a project like this, she went on to state: "Difficult stories, they are not easy. But after sharing it, you feel free, you can see what the future would be. But when you don't tell your story, you only stay in a circle, you don't move, you only see the past, and you don't see the present or the future."[28] Leontine's next goal is to lead workshops for Rwandan youth in Montreal because she firmly believes that they too may benefit from this method. As for me, I can see that our investment in building relationships over time was a rewarding and effective means of creating continuity in using stories to build awareness around refugee experiences.

Figure 6.1 Participants and facilitators involved in the *Going Places* bus tour. Credit: *Mapping Memories.*

Notes

1. This is an excerpt from Leontine Uwababyeyi's story. See Elizabeth Miller, "Creating A Memoryscape of Montreal," in *Mapping Memories: Participatory Media, Place-Based Stories & Refugee Youth, Montreal*, eds. Michelle Luchs and Elizabeth Miller (Montreal: Self Published, 2011), 53. Also see www.mapping-memories.ca.

2. Steven High, "Telling Stories: A Reflection on Oral History and New Media," *Oral History* (Spring 2010): 101–12; Toby Butler, "Memoryscape: How Audio Walks Can Deepen Our Sense of Place by Integrating Art, Oral History and Cultural Geography," *Geography Compass* 1, 3 (2007): 360–72.

3. Steven High, *Corporate Wasteland: The Landscape and Memory of Deindustrialization* (Toronto: Between the Lines Press, 2007); Richard Sharpley and Philip R. Stone, eds., *The Darker Side of Travel: The Theory and Practice of Dark Tourism* (Bristol: Channel View Publications, 2009); Erica Lehrer, Cynthia Milton, and Monica Eileen Patterson, eds., *Curating Difficult Knowledge: Violent Pasts in Public Places* (New York: Palgrave Macmillan, 2011); John Lennon and Malcolm Foley, *Dark Tourism* (London: Continuum, 2000).

4. Julie Salverson, "Anxiety and Contact in Attending to a Play About Land Mines," in *Between Hope and Despair: Pedagogy and the Remembrance of Historical Trauma*, eds. Roger I. Simon, Sharon Rosenberg, and Claudia Eppert (Maryland: Rowmand & Littlefield Publishers, 2000), 77.

5. Henry Jenkins, *Convergence Culture: Where Old and New Media Collide* (New York: New York University Press, 2006).

6. Elizabeth Miller, "Queer Is In the Eye of the Newcomer: Mapping Performances of Place," *InTensions* 4 (Fall 2010): 2.

7. Marit Kathryn Corneil, "Citizenship and Participatory Video," in *Handbook of Participatory Video*, eds. E.-J. Milne, Claudia Mitchell, and Naydene de Lange (New York: Rowman & Littlefielf Publishers, 2012), 20.

8. Ibid.

9. High, "Telling Stories," 105.

10. Shared authority is an approach, first termed by Michael Frisch, that encourages historians to challenge the more traditional power relations between historians and narrators in oral history research: Frisch, *A Shared Authority: Essays on the Craft and Meaning of Oral and Public History* (Albany: State University of New York Press, 1990); Alistair Thomson, "Introduction–Sharing Authority: Oral History and the Collaborative Process," *Oral History Review* 30, 1 (2003): 23.

11. Clemencia Rodríguez, *Fissures in the Mediascape: An International Study of Citizens' Media* (New Jersey: Hampton Press, 2001), 18.

12. Miller, "Queer Is In the Eye of the Newcomer," 10.

13. Butler, "Memoryscape," 366. Also see Edward Relph, *Place and Placelessness* (London: Pion, 1976).

14. For more on this project, go to: http://www.lifestoriesmontreal.ca/.

15. Gerald Campano, *Immigrant Students and Literacy: Reading, Writing and Remembering* (New York: Teachers College Press, 2007), 56.

16. For more information about this organization, see www.ydesfemmesmtl.org.

17. Miller, "Creating A Memoryscape of Montreal," 53.

18. This is another excerpt from Leontine's story. See ibid., 70.

19. Leontine Uwababyeyi, interview by Elizabeth Miller and Michele Luchs, Montreal, Quebec, March 3, 2012.

20. The event is organized every year by Page-Rwanda, a group formed by the parents, family, and friends of the victims of the genocide now living in Montreal.

21. Elizabeth Miller, *All I Remember* (documentary film, 2013).

22. Miller, "Creating A Memoryscape of Montreal," 65.

23. Campano, *Immigrant Students and Literacy*, 60.

24. Rania Arabi, email message to author, April 11, 2011.

25. For more information on Bill C-11, the Canadian Council for Refugees publishes reports on all policies that impact refugees: http://ccrweb.ca/en/bulletin/10/04/27.

26. See, for instance, Henry Greenspan, *On Listening to Holocaust Survivors: Recounting and Life History* (Westport: Praeger Press, 1998).

27. Miller, *All I Remember*.

28. Ibid.

CHAPTER 7

Not Just Another Interviewee:
Befriending a Holocaust Survivor

Stacey Zembrzycki

On a damp, grey day in April 2010 I found myself in a suburb of Krakow, Poland, on a grassy and wet plot of land that once housed Plaszow, a German forced labor and concentration camp during World War II. Now a park, visitors must imagine what this place looked like, since the rugged landscape of this former Jewish cemetery turned granite quarry is all that remains. On one side of me stood an imposing, communist-era stone memorial that pays tribute to those who died in this place. On the other, there was a line of roaring chartered buses filled to capacity with hundreds of chatty Jewish high school students, there to participate in the annual international March of the Living educational program. Tired and overcome with emotion, I struggled to find a silent space where I could pull myself together and reflect upon the touching and difficult stories that Rena Schondorf, a Holocaust survivor that I had begun interviewing almost two years before, shared with me. This was the first time she had come back to this site without her husband, Mayer, her rock of 57 years; he passed away four months before the trip. As we mourned his loss, she told me stories— about the sadistic commandant and his vicious dogs; the unspeakable jobs she did as a prisoner here; and the last time she saw her father—that deepened our conversation about the past.[1] Although this was not the first time I heard most of these memories, I came to understand them in new ways on this particular day. Being in the place where they occurred was important but so too was the relationship that Rena and I had developed over our many exchanges. She was no longer simply an interviewee but a friend. This chapter offers a close reading on the evolution of our relationship, arguing that the stories we hear "on the record" depend on everything that happens "off the record." If we are to understand the memories that emerge within our interview spaces, then we must acknowledge the processes through which they are cocreated.[2]

Beginning a new oral history project is always a daunting but exhilarating task. As oral historians, we spend countless hours researching the communities with which we intend to work, revising our interview guides so that they are composed of thoughtful and balanced questions, going through the rigors of satisfying ethics committees, and devising strategies for gaining access to interviewees. Upon entering the field, however, our carefully crafted methodologies quickly fall by the wayside, evolving as the people we meet bring our projects to life and make them their own. This collaborative and highly organic journey into the past is oral history's greatest appeal. If dusty documents about dead people draw some to the archive, it is the rich and deeply textured stories told by the living that lead oral historians to continue knocking on the doors of strangers.

Every encounter we have with our interviewees is unpredictable because we tend to know little to nothing about them until we sit face to face and strike up a conversation. Sometimes we connect immediately, bonding midway through a good story.[3] In other instances, building trust takes time and occurs over a series of meetings. We have to get to know each other before they feel comfortable sharing their memories with us. The potential for outright failure also looms large in these spaces. On occasion, it is difficult to find common ground with an interviewee. Rather than listening to one another we speak past and over top of each other, accomplishing very little.[4] Although it is next to impossible to forget these moments, when there are breakdowns in communication, most of us tend to focus on the colorful characters that come to dominate our projects. Their stories, for one reason or another, linger with us and we become emotionally invested in the meaningful and lasting relationships that develop as a result. These relationships are incredibly important because they have the ability to change them and us. While we bring new perspectives to their tales, they shape and reshape our research questions and alter how we understand our projects and, ultimately, ourselves.[5]

Nearly 15 years ago, Valerie Yow asked us to make a conceptual shift toward the subjective—to acknowledge the "complex web" of interpersonal relations that develops during an interview and explore how these dynamics "prevent us from sorting things out in discrete boxes."[6] We can be both researchers and friends in these spaces. To complicate matters further, when friendships develop they are atypical because of their asymmetrical nature. We ask a great deal of our interviewees and few, if any, ever do the same of us. These are important dynamics that are worthy of exploration and yet few have taken up Yow's challenge.[7] We are very good at writing about the powerful stories that our remarkable interviewees share with us, but the circumstances that led to their telling rarely appear in our work. This is unfortunate given that all of our projects are contingent upon the kinds of relationships we form with our interviewees. Tracing their evolution reveals how we build trust, establish limits, ask questions, and, ultimately, listen.

My relationship with Rena is a case in point.[8] Over the past four years, we have cultivated a connection that is premised upon our identities—she is an elderly Jewish Holocaust survivor from Poland who gives testimony regularly and prides herself on being a good mother, grandmother, and great grandmother, and I am a young Roman Catholic woman of Eastern European descent who is interested in learning more about her wartime experiences and how she communicates them to others. Our initial exchanges were professional and, by extension, asymmetrical, but they are now rooted in a close and continually evolving friendship that has sparked a sustained conversation. Our relationship has taken us beyond the interview space, chipping away at the power imbalance that initially structured our interactions. Together we are committed to not only going where Rena's memories take us, but also discussing the monotony of our daily lives—we ask a great deal of each other, as most friends do. Since our conversations are no longer limited to the past, I always walk a fine line between researcher, friend, and granddaughter when we chat. Conducting humanistic research forces us to recognize that our boundaries, as well as those of our interviewees, are never clear-cut. Oral history projects are always deeply personal and this level of investment puts our fieldwork relationships on par with our projects themselves.[9] If we are willing to adopt an ethnographic approach, what can we learn from reflecting on these relationships and the directions in which they take us? These types of "off the record" stories must be included in our accounts because they have significant implications for our work. In this instance, Rena and I bonded on a variety levels—I have come to know her through her stories about the Holocaust as well as those that speak to her experiences as a woman, mother, and prominent figure in Montreal's Jewish community. Getting to know Rena better has enabled me to access the meanings implicit in the stories she tells.[10] Moreover, she has shaped my project in a variety of ways: helping me gain access to Montreal's Jewish community; briefing me on its politics; and continually acting as a cultural translator. The road that I have traveled throughout this project would look very different without Rena.[11]

Meeting Rena

In September 2008 I became an interview coordinator for the *Montreal Life Stories* project (http://www.lifestoriesmontreal.ca/). Rooted in a collaborative, humanistic interviewing methodology, this community-university initiative aimed to interview five hundred people who came to Montreal from situations of large-scale violence and then disseminate their stories through a variety of academic, new media, and artistic channels.[12] My job was to connect with local Holocaust survivors who frequently give testimony and then coordinate and conduct multiple, life story interviews with them to understand the roles they play in Holocaust education. When I began this project, I had absolutely no connection to this community. Raised as a Roman Catholic in a small city in northern Ontario, I was a newcomer to Montreal who knew little about Jewish culture. I had also never met a Holocaust survivor, let alone interviewed one. I felt unprepared but forged on nevertheless. I distributed a call for interviewees through the Montreal Holocaust Memorial Centre's (MHMC) network and began to frequent some of the events it organizes so that I could familiarize myself with the community. My relationship with Rena started with a chance encounter at a public testimony.

I arrived at McGill University's Newman Centre on November 3, 2008, about 15 minutes before Mayer Schondorf, Rena's husband, was scheduled to bear witness to a mixed crowd. A cool, crisp autumn evening, I climbed a flight of stairs and found myself alone in a small, dimly lit room where 40 chairs were assembled for the event. The nineteenth-century building was eerily silent for a few moments and then, suddenly, voices began to travel up the stairwell. Turning, I saw an elderly man and woman and a young boy. The man had white hair, wore a kippah and glasses, and was well over six feet tall. The woman beside him, arms linked, was nearly a foot shorter. They spoke in hushed tones and then turned to the boy, who could not have been more than ten years old. The man continued to stand in the hallway and the woman made her way to the seats in front of me and introduced herself: "Hi, I'm Rena, Mayer's wife." A friendly but serious woman, Rena began to tell me about her husband and, in the course of our conversation, also mentioned that she too was a Holocaust survivor. Pointing to the young boy, she introduced him as her youngest grandson and declared that this was the first time he would be hearing his grandfather's story rather than "just snippets" of it. Before I could get a word in, Rena asked me why I had come to Mayer's testimony. In my mind, this was a perfect opportunity to introduce my project and ask her if she would participate in it: "Maybe we could sit down to talk about your work. I am interested in hearing about why you tell your story and what you say." Rena looked me straight in the eye and simply said: "No. Interviews are too painful." In her next breath, she answered some of my questions, explaining: "If I am speaking to young children, for example, I always leave out the traumatic parts." By this point, the room had begun to fill up around us. Rena invited me to attend her public testimony the following day, and then she turned around in her chair and began to speak with her grandson. Discouraged, I sat and listened to Mayer tell his compelling story. When he finished, and the crowd around him dispersed, I introduced myself and thanked him for sharing his experiences. By this time, Rena and her grandson were at his side and he encouraged me to tell him a little bit about myself. Although I could not put my finger on it, there was something special about Mayer and Rena—their warmth and sincerity as well as how they interacted with each other made me want to learn more about them. I once again brought up my project and asked whether they would meet with me to discuss it. To my surprise, they agreed. Little did I know that Mayer and Rena were major figures in Montreal's Jewish community, interacting with hundreds of children each year by giving testimony in classrooms and participating in the annual March of the Living.

Building Trust

The *Montreal Life Stories* project required all of its interviewers to write short blogs after every interview. Mayer's testimony did not constitute an interview but I reflected upon it nevertheless. He was a skilled storyteller and I was impressed by how he repeatedly used luck to communicate why he thought he survived Auschwitz, Buchenwald, and a death march.[13] My blog was honest and thoughtful and upon completing it, I posted it to the *Montreal Life Stories'* password-protected website, an exclusive space for project members.

The following day I went to Marianopolis College to listen to Rena bear witness to 150 students. Unlike the intimate space in which Mayer told his story, this event occurred in a large and noisy auditorium. The room quickly fell silent, however, when Rena uttered her first words: "I am telling you the story of a little girl." Like Mayer, she captivated her listeners and took them on a personal journey that began with the cessation of her studies and her family's move to the ghetto in Krakow. It was here, Rena declared, that her world collapsed. After a heartbreaking encounter with an SS officer she realized that her father, a strong and determined man, could no longer protect her or her family. Rena focused on this realization and the childhood she lost as a result of it. For her, under-standing survival was tied to her ability to pretend that she was older than her actual age: to make it through selections, she constantly lied about her age and wore high heels, sophisticated clothing, and makeup to look like a young adult. This was how she communicated the loss of her innocence. Rena went on to speak broadly about her experiences in a number of camps, including Plaszov, Auschwitz, Birkenau, and Bergen Belsen.[14] I was intrigued by the different and highly gendered ways that Rena and Mayer made sense of their experiences and looked forward to discussing their narratives in more depth.[15]

Upon arriving home after listening to Rena bear witness, I received an email from Mayer telling me that he had read the blog I wrote about his testimony. I was horrified. I was stunned by the fact that a man his age used email—I soon learned that he was virtually connected to family members scattered throughout the globe, a researcher in his hometown in Slovakia, and an international network of Buchenwald survivors. As I threw myself into damage control mode, I worried about the impact my words would have on building trust with the Schondorfs, especially since Rena was not particularly keen on being interviewed. Thankfully, this experience worked in my favor, showing Rena and Mayer the seriousness with which I approached this project and my commitment to listening to their stories.

About two weeks later, Rena and Mayer warmly welcomed my cointerviewer, Steven High, and me into their Côte Saint-Luc condominium. Contrary to our initial encounter, Rena was forthcoming and open to discussing the past; I am convinced that my email exchange with the Schondorfs was an exercise in building trust. Since this was our first meeting with any survivors, Steven and I initiated an informal (and unrecorded) conversation to get a sense of their experiences so that we could tailor our questions to them. We were not the only ones with an agenda. Rena and Mayer had been interviewed before and so they began by asking us about our project.[16] Why should they do another interview? How would it be different from the others? As we explained our purpose, Rena interjected, asking personal questions to connect with us. Were we married? Did we have children? Was I Polish? Whereas Mayer focused on the Holocaust, Rena constantly veered in different directions, emphasizing the issues that mattered to her: family, children, and relationships. For her, the Holocaust was just one chapter in her life and so we tried to give her the space she needed to explore these other dimensions of her story. The more we spoke to one another, the more gendered the room became—Steven gravitated toward Mayer and I was drawn to Rena. These dynamics felt as organic as Rena's and Mayer's ability to seamlessly weave their different experiences and perspectives into one coherent narrative. Unlike the interviews they had done before, which began with their first memories and finished with liberation, Steven and I encouraged Mayer and Rena to speak about their postwar experiences, the place of the Holocaust in their home, their trips to Poland, and how they came to tell their stories in public. Our conversation was relaxed and naturally flowed from one topic to the next.[17] Their fragmentary stories raised many questions for Steven and me and laid the groundwork for our subsequent exchanges with this couple. In this instance, however, we had to feel each other out and get to know each other better before we could begin to understand who Mayer and Rena were and why they told the stories they did. All of us were simultaneously pushing and pulling at the power dynamics that typically characterize these sorts of encounters.

Steven and I returned to Mayer's and Rena's home about two weeks later to conduct our first recorded interview with them. While they favored a structured approach, we tried to recreate the informal, conversational setting that characterized our previous encounter. We settled somewhere in the middle and I asked

Rena to explain a comment she made in our last meeting, about the "different kind of hell" she experienced in 1945. Jumping right in, she spoke movingly and in depth for about half an hour, telling us about her inability to understand freedom, her job as a nurse in a displaced persons camp, her return to Krakow, and her struggle to get out of Europe. Ultimately her "different kind of hell" was tied to her inability to feel safe. With liberation came a new set of dangers: drunken and dangerous Russian soldiers, mob violence, and the threat of pogroms. Arriving in Montreal in 1948 created another set of challenges. Similar to her testimony, she stressed the loss of her childhood and spoke about the disconnect she felt between herself and the Canadians she encountered: "I was an eighteen year old with a memory of a hundred years." Rena remembered one woman in particular who commented on her small stature and asked her what she had done to survive. This remark, she declared, silenced her for the next 40 years. Rena had survived the Holocaust, but she continued to experience "a different kind of hell" for many years afterward.

Mayer sat patiently and listened to Rena's tale, but jumped in at this point to speak about his journey from Buchenwald, to his hometown in Slovakia, and then to Canada as a war orphan. As he shared his memories, Rena interjected from time to time, adding a missing detail or a short story. Sometimes the two even spoke over top of one another, trying to convey their different points of view. The Holocaust was never far from their minds, a defining feature in every one of their stories. A memory about a set of candlesticks that was given to them by a couple who did not make it out of the camps led to a comment about the tendency of survivors to marry other survivors. It was important to have a spouse who could relate to them, because, as Rena stated: "[there] are days where you keep quiet and there are days when you can talk." Neither one had to say anything more. If there was one thing that became abundantly clear that day, it was this couple's special bond and deep connection. Although they shared different experiences, we were, in many respects, listening to one story about two people. Their comments became more intertwined as we asked them about giving testimony, an act they had done together until fairly recently. Steven and I quickly realized that understanding the stories we heard on this occasion, and the meanings implicit in them, would take many more exchanges. We had only just begun to scratch the surface.[18]

Accessing Montreal's Survivor Community

About a month after this interview with Mayer and Rena, I was invited to speak about the *Montreal Life Stories* project at an MHMC meeting of Holocaust survivors who frequently give testimony. For the most part, the project was going well. A handful of interviewees had responded to my initial call and interviewing was under way. Although I hoped to recruit more interviewees, my main purpose was to ask those in attendance for permission to conduct walking interviews in the exhibition space. I was pleasantly surprised to see many familiar faces as I entered the room. Rena and Mayer were among those who warmly greeted me at the door. The audience was receptive to the ideas I put forth, but I got a considerable boost when Mayer and Rena stood up and stressed how attentive we had been in listening to their stories and then proceeded to encourage those in the room to participate. When I finished speaking, I was encircled by a large group of survivors who were all trying to give me their telephone numbers at once. My telephone rang off the hook for weeks afterward. Mayer's and Rena's remarks were crucial to gaining credibility within this community.[19]

The Conversation Continues

In addition to seeing Mayer and Rena at MHMC events, I interviewed them two more times in January and June 2009, with Steven High and Anna Sheftel. The March of the Living and the postwar period dominated our conversations. The March of the Living is an international educational program that brings thousands of Jewish teenagers (250 Montrealers) to Poland and Israel every spring for a "once-in-a-lifetime" experience.[20] This two-week trip induces "powerful emotions such as pride, religious awe, anger at the historical persecution of Jews, camaraderie, a sense of entitlement toward the 'land of Israel,' nostalgia, and a longing for a return to Zion."[21] The trip helps those who lack a connection to Eastern Europe to "[invent] the link between the destruction of the past and the possibility of their own Jewish futures."[22] Mayer and Rena had just returned from a retreat to prepare students and chaperones for this trip and so it was fresh in their minds when Steven and I arrived at their home on a cold January day. They gave us a history of the program and their involvement in it and then explained the important cultural role it plays in the Jewish community: "It has become a rite of passage," Mayer emphasized. Rena then spoke about the first time she went back to Poland, before going on her first "March." "I was an impossible person, I was angry," she declared. Auschwitz did not look as it should—it had trees and she had to pay a dollar to use the washroom. It had, in her opinion, become even more demeaning than before. She refused to speak Polish and she continually fought with her tour guides throughout this trip. She had no intention of ever returning, but then March of the Living organizers approached her and Mayer and asked whether they would participate. Aware of the impact she was making in Montreal classrooms, she decided that this would be another way for her to "pass on the history." This interview piqued my interest. If I was going to understand the important work that Mayer and Rena do, then I would have to go on the March of the Living myself. I floated the idea past them and we left it at that, agreeing to discuss it later in the year. Steven and I left this session with a good sense of how this couple publicly and privately remembers the Holocaust, the main goal of our project.[23]

Anna and I returned to the Schondorf's home in June, to ask them about their postwar experiences. We were writing an article about the social worlds that survivors created in Montreal during this period and we wanted to hear more about the circumstances that led to Mayer's and Rena's 57-year marriage.[24] How did they meet? How did the Jewish community treat them? And, what were their first impressions of Canada? Over the course of that afternoon, we focused on a short period of time in their lives (1948–1952), zooming in on the moments and stories they thought were important in conveying their experiences. They told us that the Jewish community helped them but there were social barriers that could not be overcome. They had been through something that Canadians, Jews and Gentiles, could not understand and so survivors formed their own communities and as Mayer put it: "We created our own social." Mayer and Rena met and eventually married in one of these settings, the New World Club. How they went on with their lives and recreated their family was central to our conversation. I gained new insight into the roots of this couple's deep connection but again I just felt like I was scratching the surface of a whole range of issues.[25]

Becoming Friends

My conversation with Mayer and Rena continued off camera for the next couple of months. In autumn 2009, we began to seriously discuss the possibility of me going on the March of the Living. According to the organizers, however, I was not Jewish so I could not go on the trip. Mayer and Rena thought that this was ridiculous, especially given my commitment to interviewing survivors, and they proceeded to lobby on my behalf, getting me a meeting with the head of the Montreal division of the program, Josh Pepin. Again, they were instrumental in breaking down barriers and helping me gain access to Montreal's Jewish community. Unfortunately, before I was able to meet with Josh, Mayer passed away suddenly in December 2009. I was devastated. How could this happen? I had just exchanged emails with him a few days before.

Mayer was an incredible person, not just one of my most memorable interviewees but a devoted husband, father, grandfather, great grandfather, and community leader. I was lucky to have known him. Death is always hard, but what affected me the most was thinking about Rena. What would she do without him? I had grown very fond of this couple and as I sat in a back pew at a service for Mayer a couple of days later, standing room only, I heard new stories about him and his relationship with Rena. These were tales that we never had a chance to explore in our meetings. It really drove home the importance of recognizing the kinds of relationships we have with our interviewees, reminding me of the limits of conducting life story interviews in asymmetrical settings. Since Holocaust education was central to our exchanges, I knew little about Mayer's particular Holocaust experiences as well as many of the other issues that were central to his identity: religion, Israel, and family, to name just a few. I came to know one dimension of Mayer's complicated, layered, and deeply textured life and even then, I still question what I think I know about it.

About a month after Mayer's death, I was granted permission to go on the March of the Living. I would act as a "survivor chaperone," attending to the needs of the trip's five survivors and helping them get around Poland. Ironically, all but one survivor had been on the trip many times before and two were fluent in Polish. I did not know what kind of a role I would play but I was prepared to listen to their needs, and mostly their stories, nevertheless. I was quite torn about going to Poland.[26] Part of me did not want to go because Mayer and Rena would not be there. I assumed Rena would back out of the trip, finding it too difficult to be there without her late husband. On the other hand, I also knew what the trip meant to this couple and how badly they had wanted to share it with me. In the end, I decided to go on the March of the Living because Mayer and Rena had fought for me to be on it. I could not back out now. A couple of weeks before I was scheduled to fly to Warsaw, I found out that Rena planned to go on the trip after all. She had made a commitment and she wanted to see it through to the end. I had not spoken to Rena since Mayer's death, but I saw this as a good opportunity to get in touch with her. She was, naturally, still mourning but seemed to look forward to the trip. "Mayer would have wanted me to go," she told me. The staff and students who participate in the March of the Living are like a family, Rena explained, and she wanted to be there with them, no matter how difficult it was going to be.

The March of the Living pushed my relationship with Rena to a new level. No longer just an interviewee, she became my friend during the week I spent with her in Poland.[27] This trip was a bonding experience that enabled us to level out the power differential of our earlier exchanges. As we spent time together, on long bus rides through the Polish countryside, sitting across from each other at the dinner table, or walking arm in arm through the dark sites on our itinerary, we spoke as friends do (figure 7.1). My research agenda was no longer as clear as it had once been. My conversations with Rena were suddenly about much more than the Holocaust. In addition to being a friend, Rena acted like a grandmother, guiding me through Poland: physically, she led me through some of the places that featured prominently in her story; mentally, her memories took me on an imagined journey into the past; and emotionally, she was always there to give me a hug or offer words of encouragement. In return, I walked a fine line between

Figure 7.1 Rena Schondorf and Stacey Zembrzycki walk through the monuments at Treblinka. Photography by Ryan Blau, PBL Photography.

researcher, friend, and granddaughter, listening to her and offering support when I thought she needed it. I never thought twice about juggling these roles. This is just what friends and family do for each other.

Some of the stories that Rena recalled while we were in Poland were new to me, and others were part of her rehearsed narrative. Trust was one reason why I had not heard some of them before. The intimate moments we shared, as a result of the bond we developed on this trip, led her to tell me about experiences that never would have come up in an interview. As she shared deeply personal stories about her family, for instance, I came to understand her memories better. The nature of my interviews with Rena also explains why I heard new stories on this occasion. As we spoke in depth about her work as an educator, we often got farther away from her actual Holocaust experiences. Since bearing witness to these experiences is central to the March of the Living, being on this trip allowed me to hear new parts of Rena's stories.

Regardless, the point that I am trying to make is this: I came to understand all of Rena's stories, new and old, differently as we got to know each other better. When I think about this transition to "knowing with" Rena rather than "knowing about" her, I associate it with the deeply troubling morning we spent at Plaszov.[28] Every year, those who organize the itinerary for the Montreal section of the March of the Living ensure that students spend some time at Plaszov. It is an interesting choice given that visitors must rely on their imaginations to envision what happened there. Organizers, however, see this as an important stop because it is a major part of Rena's story. She is always asked to give testimony at this site. This year, 2010, would be different. Everyone knew it would be hard for Rena to speak because this was the first time Mayer would not be by her side. As my group, which included students, a guide, some chaperones, and Rena, made its way through the site, listening to its history and Rena's memories about it, nothing seemed out of the ordinary. As Rena negotiated the uneven terrain, she happily answered students' questions, just as she had done throughout the trip. I was therefore able to see her in action. She and Mayer had gone to great lengths to explain their role on the March of the Living and it was here that I saw their words playing out before my eyes. It was impressive: she was good at opening herself up and making the students comfortable. When we got to the top of the site, a hill that now overlooks the city of Krakow, the atmosphere started to change. Rena went in one direction to prepare herself to speak and March of the Living staff members and chaperones began to flurry about, ensuring that the ensuing moments would go off without a hitch. Soon Rena was standing before the crowd declaring: "What we are seeing right now is the camp where I was for more than a year." Just as she had before, she stressed that she was fortunate to spend time here because she succeeded at passing as a young woman. Children, she made clear, did not live to make it to places like this. She then called on listeners to use their imaginations as she described what Plaszow looked like. She pointed to where the barracks had been, explained what a typical day was like here, and mentioned the heartless commandant who took "pot shots" at passing prisoners. Rena was doing well until she began to tell a story about a group of men who were hung for hiding in the camp. One of these men had been her sister's friend. "The rope broke," her voice wavered and she paused for a moment, "he begged for his life and yet it was not meant to be." She collected herself and remembered how she and others had to walk around the bodies of these men. "They were hanging there like marionettes," she stated, serving as a warning to others. Rena went on to recall another difficult moment, when all of the children and adults who could not work were put on trucks and sent to their deaths at Birkenau. A lullaby played over a loudspeaker as this took place, she explained. The soldiers who ran this camp "did not have a shred of humanity" left in them. As the camp was liquidated, Rena remained behind and became part of the cleaning crew: "Cleaning the camp did not mean cleaning away the barracks...there were two major graves...we had to dig up the bodies, put them on a pile, and light the fire...if I have a nightmare that's part of it." Eventually, in 1945, Rena was taken from "this hell hole" to another one, Birkenau. Following this statement, Rena turned to Josh Pepin, the March organizer, and collapsed into his arms. A group of students rose from the crowd, gathered beside Rena and began to sing. Another student came forward and read a letter written by one of Rena's and Mayer's granddaughters. It told listeners a little bit about Mayer and stressed his dedication to Holocaust education: "He would like nothing more than to be here with you." An explicitly orchestrated part of the visit to this site, the letter was too much to bear. There was not a dry eye in the crowd. After saying Kaddish to honor Mayer and another memorial prayer for those who died at Plaszov, I walked over to Rena and put my arm around her. As we walked toward the bus, she added more to the testimony she had just given, telling me that the only detail she left out was that the transport she spoke about included her father. She never tells that part of her story in public, she explained, it is her breaking point. Rena went on to recall the first time she came back to Poland and specifically her anger. Although she vowed never to return, she looked at me and simply said: "This is why I come back, to teach the kids. If I don't do it, no one else will." This difficult day marked a turning point for Rena and me—we had finally gotten to a place in our relationship where I could truly begin to understand her stories. She, clearly, also felt comfortable going "deeper" with me.

Conclusion

Since returning from the March of the Living, Rena and I have met many times and we often speak on the telephone. When we see each other there are no cameras. We sit at her dining room table, share a cup of tea, and chat "off the record." I know a lot about Rena and she knows a great deal about me—more than any other person I have interviewed. The asymmetry that once structured our interactions has all but vanished. Yet the more I "know" Rena, the less it seems that I do in fact "know" about her. I am constantly awed by the complicated ways that her stories shift over time and through experience—she is different now that Mayer is gone, more outspoken and opinionated than before. Life stories are complex and perhaps, as oral historians, we can only scratch the surface, no matter what kind of relationships we form with our interviewees. Regardless of the limits, Rena and I continue our conversation. Poland always comes up, at one point or another. As a shared experience that connects us in significant ways, it now serves as a starting point that allows us to plunge deeper into the past.

The relationships we forge with our interviewees matter. How we build them and the directions in which they take us inform our practice as oral historians. We must get better at reflecting on this process because it is central to the stories we hear and the meanings we extract from them. The first time that Rena told me about being in Plaszov was very different from when we were standing in that place together. Being at this site was important, but so too was our friendship. It took nearly two years of conversations for Rena and me to get to this place in our relationship. Although this particular case is special—not everyone can travel with their interviewees and return to the places that are at the heart of their stories—it is instructive nonetheless. Tracing the evolution of my relationship with Rena, through all the ups and downs that life thrusts upon us, reminds us of oral history's staggering limits and its great potential. It also demonstrates how quickly we become deeply invested in our projects. Our interviewees are human beings after all, and we would do well to discuss the complicated nature of our research more often.

Notes

I would like to thank Rena Schondorf for her friendship. The Social Sciences and Humanities Research Council of Canada (SSHRC) funded the research for this work and the *Montreal Life Stories* project also provided substantial assistance.

1. These reflections come from the field notes I wrote and the informal conversations I recorded with Rena on the 2010 March of the Living; they are in my possession. See, in particular, Rena Schondorf, informal conversation with author, Krakow, Poland, April 13, 2010.
2. Regarding relationships, also see the chapters written by Pamela Sugiman, Martha Norkunas, Sherna Berger Gluck, and Julie Cruikshank and Tatiana Argounova-Low in this volume.
3. To this end, see Henry Greenspan, *On Listening to Holocaust Survivors: Beyond Testimony*, second edition (St. Paul: Paragon House, 2010), 219.
4. For thoughtful discussions about this dilemma, see Anna Sheftel and Stacey Zembrzycki, "Only Human: A Reflection on the Ethical and Methodological Challenges of Working with 'Difficult' Stories," *Oral History Review* 37, 2 (Summer–Fall 2010): 191–241; Tracy E. K'Meyer and A. Glenn Crothers, "'If I see some of this in writing, I'm going to shoot you': Reluctant Narrators, Taboo Topics, and the Ethical Dilemmas of the Oral Historian," *Oral History Review* 34 (2007): 71–93; Katherine Borland, "'That's not what I said': Interpretive Conflict in Oral Narrative Research, " in *Women's Words: The Feminist Practice of Oral History*, eds. Sherna Berger Gluck and Daphne Patai (New York: Routledge, 1991), 63–75.
5. See Lorraine Sitzia, "A Shared Authority: An Impossible Goal," *Oral History Review* 30, 1 (Winter–Spring 2003): 87–101.
6. Valerie Yow, "'Do I Like Them Too Much': Effects of the Oral History Interview on the Interviewer and Vice Versa," *Oral History Review* 24 (Summer 1997): 71. This call to arms was also rooted in the feminist oral history movement: Gluck and Patai, *Women's Words*.
7. Daniel James's discussion about his relationship with Doña María Roldán and the fascinating exchanges they had over a 13-year period remains one of the most thoughtful and theoretically sophisticated analyses to grapple with the discipline's messiness: *Doña María's Story: Life History, Memory, and Political Identity* (Durham: Duke University Press, 2000). Also see Alessandro Portelli's afterword in this collection.

8. For a related discussion, see Jürgen Matthäus, ed., *Approaching an Auschwitz Survivor: Holocaust Testimony and Its Transformations* (Oxford: Oxford University Press, 2009).

9. Lisa M. Tillmann-Healy, "Friendship as Method," *Qualitative Inquiry* 9, 5 (2003): 735.

10. I reject Lawrence Langer's notion of "deep memory." While I agree with his understanding of "common memory," which recognizes the important interplay between past and present, I do not believe that "deep memory" exists and is accessible to researchers. For me, it has never been about accessing Rena's "Auschwitz self as it was then." See Langer, *Holocaust Testimonies: The Ruins of Memory* (New Haven: Yale University Press, 1991).

11. Rena has played a role that has much in common with the one my grandmother assumed in my first oral history project about the Ukrainian community in Sudbury, Canada: Zembrzycki, "Sharing Authority with Baba," *The Journal of Canadian Studies* 43, 1 (Winter 2009): 219–38.

12. Some of the texts that inspired this methodology include: Michael Frisch, *A Shared Authority: Essays on the Craft and Meaning of Oral and Public History* (Albany: State University of New York Press, 1990); Greenspan, *On Listening to Holocaust Survivors*; Special Issue on "Sharing/Shared Authority," *Oral History Review* 30, 1 (Winter–Spring 2003).

13. Stacey Zembrzycki, "Reflections on Mayer Schondorf's Testimony," November 4, 2008, *Montreal Life Stories'* Archive.

14. Stacey Zembrzycki, "Reflections on Rena Schondorf's Testimony," November 5, 2008, *Montreal Life Stories'* Archive.

15. Many survivors and scholars have written about the impossibility of understanding Holocaust experiences: Primo Levi, *Survival in Auschwitz: The Nazi Assault on Humanity* (New York: Simon and Schuster, 1996); Charlotte Delbo, *Aucun de nous ne reviendra* (Paris: Editions de Minuit, 1965); Giorgio Agamben, *Remnants of Auschwitz: The Witness and the Archive* (New York: Zone Books, 1999); Cathy Caruth, *Unclaimed Experience: Trauma, Narrative and History* (Baltimore: Johns Hopkins University Press, 1996); Dominick La Capra, *Writing History: Writing Trauma* (Baltimore: Johns Hopkins University Press, 2000).

16. The Shoah Visual History Foundation, the MHMC, and McGill University's Living Testimonies Project interviewed Mayer and Rena separately.

17. See Stacey Zembrzycki, "Reflections on Our Pre-Interview with the Schondorfs," November 18, 2008, *Montreal Life Stories'* Archive; Steven High, "Mayer and Rena Schondorf," November 18, 2008, *Montreal Life Stories'* Archive.

18. Mayer and Rena Schondorf, interview by Steven High and Stacey Zembrzycki, Montreal, Quebec, November 26, 2008.

19. Stacey Zembrzycki, "Meeting with MHMC Speakers," December 15, 2008, *Montreal Life Stories'* Archive. Since Montreal has a small community of about 40 survivors who give testimony, gaining multiple points of access was not a major concern for me in this project. That said, this limitation has determined the type of story I can tell about testimony and Holocaust education.

20. March of the Living International Homepage, http://motl.org/?page_id=160 (accessed on January 16, 2013).

21. Caryn Aviv and David Shneer, "Travelling Jews, Creating Memory: Eastern Europe, Israel, and the Diaspora Business," in *Sociology Confronts the Holocaust: Memories and Identities in Jewish Diasporas*, eds. Judith Gerson and Diane L. Wolf (Durham: Duke University Press, 2007), 71. Also see Rona Sheramy, "From Auschwitz to Jerusalem: Re-enacting Jewish History on the March of the Living," *Polin: Studies in Polish Jewry* 19 (2007): 307–26; Oren Baruch Stier, *Committed to Memory: Cultural Mediations of the Holocaust* (Amherst: University of Massachusetts Press, 2003), 150–90.

22. Aviv and Shneer, "Travelling Jews," 74.

23. Mayer and Rena Schondorf, interview by Steven High and Stacey Zembrzycki, Montreal, Quebec, January 28, 2009.

24. See Anna Sheftel and Stacey Zembrzycki, "'We started over again, we were young': Postwar Social Worlds of Child Holocaust Survivors in Montreal," *Urban History Review* 39, 1 (Fall 2010): 20–30.

25. Mayer and Rena Schondorf, interview by Anna Sheftel and Stacey Zembrzycki, Montreal, Quebec, June 11, 2009.

26. Having just returned from Israel, I decided to participate in the Poland leg of the trip only.

27. Tillman-Healy, "Friendship as Method," 734.

28. Greenspan's *On Listening to Holocaust Survivors* has led me to conceptualize interviews in this manner.

PART III

The Intersection of Ethics and Politics

Leyla Neyzi

As oral historians, it is perhaps what we most need to write about that we have tended to be most reticent about. Why is this the case? As the chapters in this section demonstrate, it is due to "ethical murk," which, as Monica Eileen Patterson points out, we are not always able to resolve. In the early days of oral history, researchers were relatively sanguine about the benefits of what they termed "giving voice to the voiceless." As pioneers, they believed their work would be of use to their interviewees while contributing to the academic literature. Today, with the benefit of hindsight, we have become more skeptical, albeit probably more realistic, about the achievements and possibilities of oral history. Dealing squarely with the ethics and politics of practice will undoubtedly make for better research and more sophisticated methodological and theoretical analyses. For, as Patterson argues later, it is no longer simply the past, but what *engaging with the past entails*, that matters for oral historians.

All of the authors in this section address the ways in which the positionality and politics of the researcher affect our interviewees' stories and our own representations of them. For example, in "I Can Hear Lois Now," Pamela Sugiman faces up to a challenge she avoided earlier while doing research on the internment of Japanese Canadians during World War II: a naysayer from within the community. As an insider, it was particularly difficult for Sugiman to deal with Lois Hashimoto, who, on the basis of her own experience, claimed that Sugiman misrepresented the internment in her work. Hashimoto spoke with authority, conferred by both her experience and age, a fact of some importance in the Japanese Canadian community. Sugiman admits that it was difficult to deal with this criticism at a time when political activists, such as herself, were attempting to gain redress. An important point here is that as oral historians, we tend to take a critical stance, identifying with those we view as underdogs. But what happens when our interlocutors defend the powers that be? By telling the story of Lois, and of their relationship, Sugiman gives credence to the diversity of individual experiences and interpretations, which may or may not jive with our own analyses.

While Pamela Sugiman is an insider, albeit an educated and privileged one, Nadia Jones-Gailani is both an insider and an outsider with a complicated relationship with the Iraqi women she interviewed with the aid of her Arabic-speaking stepmother. As a young woman of mixed Iraqi upper-class Sunni and Welsh parentage, she conducted her interviews with Iraqi transnational migrants in English. She claims that since her interviewees viewed her as a representative of an international audience, they reproduced hegemonic, Arab nationalist narratives in English. However, speaking informally in Arabic to her stepmother—who acted as a local gatekeeper and translator outside of the discursive interview space—they belied their formal narratives, reflecting everyday divisions among Iraqis based on ethnicity, religion, class, and gender. She suggests that her stepmother shaped interviewees' narratives so as to protect them from various forms of criticism. Jones-Gailani also hints at how emotionally difficult it is to use a translator and thereby a third person in an oral history interview. Yet bravely writing about the methodological and ethical issues that she faced allows her to deeply delve into the understudied issue of cultural and linguistic translation in oral history practice. Jones-Gailani and her stepmother's joint experience shows quite transparently the degree to which our interviewees' perception of us (and the audience we represent) and the relationship we establish with them shape their stories.

Nancy Janovicek, using the case of her research on the back-to-the-land movement in Canada, notes that recent historical work on (and the politics of) the 1960s, as well as popular writing on the period, predisposed her to expect nostalgic narratives from her interviewees. In speaking about how we situate our research, Janovicek shows how these factors shape our expectations of this decade and ultimately determine what we can and want to hear from our interviewees. On the other hand, as she also argues, our interlocutors may have their own expectations of what to expect from us and often, as a result, develop their own strategies for telling (or silencing) their stories. In cases where informants were unwilling to openly discuss the past, Janovick found that focusing on their preoccupations in the present and building a personal link helped create a climate of trust. By mentioning her own experience growing up in an agricultural community and asking about narrators' current involvement in local environmental issues, Janovicek was able to access unexpected and diverse stories.

In her discussion of the Truth and Reconciliation Commission (TRC) in South Africa, Monica Eileen Patterson suggests that the approach, methods, and expectations of the TRC shaped both the stories produced and the stories it selected to be both told and publicized. Using the concept of intermediation, she argues that the increased circulation of oral histories, like those gathered by the TRC, through various media poses ethical dangers to interviewees and their communities—I would also add, to the researchers themselves. Furthermore, Patterson critiques the "perpetrator" versus "victim" binary, which, in her view, reduces the complexity of experience in cases of intrasocietal conflict. This view certainly jives with my understanding of the yet understudied memory of violence in Turkey in the twentieth century, a focus of my work.[1] As Patterson shows, we tend to select iconic stories from among the many we hear, and though selection is inevitable, I believe that we might make use of new media technologies by sharing our archives more widely within necessary ethical constraints. For example, if Sugiman's work had not been widely circulated, it might not have reached someone like Lois Hoshimoto.

An important issue raised in the contributions in this section is affect. Sugiman, Jones-Gailani, and Janovicek discuss their complicated feelings vis-à-vis their interviewees as well as community members and the various groups to which they belong or with which they attempt to build relationships. Lois's email has Pamela Sugiman in tears; Nadia Jones-Gailani is frustrated and angry with her stepmother/translator's role in her interviews; and Janovicek tries to find common ground with those she feels connected to through her own agrarian past. On the other hand, Patterson shows how the TRC regulates affect: black South Africans giving testimony were expected to express forgiveness while holding their anger in check. Oral historians could usefully mine the theoretical literature on affect that anthropologists in particular have used to get beyond discussing emotion only in terms of methodology and reflexivity.[2]

There are no simple answers to "ethical murk." Patterson provocatively argues that the TRC may have raised more expectations than it was able to fulfill, possibly resulting in more, rather than less, conflict. We can no longer assume that telling one's story is healing, particularly in the case of traumatized individuals.[3] Jones-Gailani tells us that some of her interviewees were in mortal danger for choosing to speak to her. Both Sugiman's and Janovicek's interviewees were rightfully concerned about how they would be represented in their work. Nevertheless, interviewees continue to tell us their stories, and we as oral historians continue to listen. Why, how, with whom, and for whom are those provocative questions that will continue, I am sure, to disturb us in the near future?

Notes

1. See, for instance, Leyla Neyzi, "Remembering Smyrna/Izmir: Shared History, Shared Trauma," *History and Memory* 20, 2 (Fall/Winter 2008): 106–27; Leyla Neyzi and Hranush Kharatyan-Araqelyan, *Speaking to One Another: Personal Memories of the Past in Armenia and Turkey* (Bonn, Germany: DVV International 2010).
2. Yael Navaro-Yashin, "Affective Spaces, Melancholic Objects: Ruination and the Production of Anthropological Knowledge," *Journal of the Royal Anthropological Institute* 15, 1 (2009): 1–18.
3. Susannah Radstone, "Trauma Theory: Contexts, Politics, Ethics," *Paragraph* 30, 1 (2007): 9–29.

CHAPTER 8

I Can Hear Lois Now: Corrections to My Story of the Internment of Japanese Canadians—"For the Record"

Pamela Sugiman

Until recently, the World War II internment of Japanese Canadians was one of many stories hidden from public history. Scarcely heard were the voices of the 22,000 women, men, and children who were removed from their homes, labeled enemy aliens, dispossessed of property and personal belongings, and relocated by the Canadian government.[1] Of the interned 75 percent were Naturalized or Canadian-born citizens. "Framed by race," Canadians of Japanese descent were "produced as outsiders" in their own country.[2]

Over the past two decades, however, this collective amnesia has been partially remedied. In 1988, the National Association of Japanese Canadians (NAJC) reached a Redress Agreement with the government of Canada. The details of the agreement included: an official acknowledgment of the wartime injustices, compensation payments to eligible surviving persons of Japanese ancestry, payment to the Japanese Canadian community to support the community's well-being or to promote human rights, and funding for the establishment of a Canadian Race Relations Foundation. In so far as Redress lent legitimacy to people's wartime memories, the years following the settlement witnessed an outpouring of films, memoirs, and scholarly studies, all of which document the racial politics and personal impact of the internment on the *Issei* (first-generation pioneers), *Nisei* (second-generation, Canadian born), *Sansei* (third-generation), and *Yonsei* (fourth-generation).

My own research of well over a decade has been a part of this liberation of memories and reconstruction of history. Though I was not an eyewitness to the war, as a child, I gathered fragmented memories of the internment vicariously through my family.[3] My father was in his early twenties when Japan bombed Pearl Harbor in 1941. A rebellious young man who was born and raised in Vancouver, he resisted the orders of the RCMP to leave his hometown. For this, he was picked up, detained in the city's Immigration Building, and subsequently incarcerated in a prisoner of war camp in Petawawa, Ontario. My mother was a young woman when the government confiscated and soon after sold her family's ten-acre berry farm in Haney, British Columbia (BC). After being held for several months in Hastings Park, in the former livestock building in the Pacific National Exhibition fair grounds, the Matsuoka family was sent to live for four years in Rosebery, one of the smallest and most northerly sites of internment. As an adult, educated and politicized by the literature that grew out of the Redress struggle, I attempted to situate my family's memories in a wider social and political framework. With my daughter in tow, I embarked on a pilgrimage to the sites of internment. In addition, I poured over thousands of old letters and government reports housed in government archives and I conducted oral history interviews with 75 *Nisei* women and men.

Needless to say, this project is close to my heart. My efforts to give "voice to the voiceless" were motivated in part by an affinity toward, and feelings of empathy for the *subjects* of my study.[4] My research has, without question, also been guided by social justice. Fortuitously, while in the final stages of my fieldwork, I was approached by the NAJC. When asked to join its National Executive Board, I eagerly accepted the appointment, feeling that it was time to give back to a community that had so generously opened up to me. The role of advocate, I believed, would complement that of scholar.

Over time, one of the harsh lessons that I have learned, however, is that when we combine personal and academic motives in research on living communities we sometimes run into complications.[5] In the process of collaboration and in trying to fairly represent a community of people, we must also be prepared to listen to voices that are dissenting, words that are cutting, and the expression of ideas that we may view as damaging to our own political projects. As discussed by many oral historians,[6] we need to consider how ideological clashes may affect the relationship between interviewer and narrator, the conversational narrative, and our vision of history.[7]

In her study of women of the Ku Klux Klan, Kathleen Blee specifically raises questions about how we can establish rapport with "politically abhorrent informants," interpret accounts that are "distorted," and present benign memories that mute "past atrocities."[8] Such dilemmas, as Antoinette Errante states, may also have implications for our selection of informants and our use of their memories.[9] These challenges have also led me to reflect on the emotional impact that the interview and respondents may have on the researcher herself. As noted by Ruth Behar, when we write about an emotional connection to our academic research, this emotional investment becomes part of the public domain, leaving the researcher vulnerable to charges and attacks from unsympathetic subjects and bystanders.[10]

A Message from Lois

These are issues that I was forced to confront several years ago when I received an angry email message from a stranger, a *Nisei* woman named Lois Hashimoto, who had read one of my articles on the internment. At the time, Lois resided with her husband in Laval, Quebec. Like many other *Nisei*, when Japan attacked Pearl Harbor, Lois (then a teen) and her family were forced, by the government under the War Measures Act, to leave their home in BC. She was then housed temporarily in Hastings Park in Vancouver before being transported to an internment site in the Slocan Valley. After spending four years in Slocan, she headed east of the Rockies to build a new home in the province of Quebec. The only alternative to resettlement outside of BC was deportation to Japan. Her letter to me began:

> I am a 77-year old who spent four years in Slocan. There is a serious flaw in your study in that you based your study on false premises. What, exactly, do you mean when you say, "[though] many decades have since gone by, Japanese Canadians continue to live with the injustices of the past?" What examples do you have to justify such a sweeping statement about thousands of us whom you have never met, let alone known.

Lois directly laid her charge. Much of my writing about the internment has highlighted the emptiness of life, confiscation of property, denial of opportunity, violation of rights, and enduring losses. Lois remembered these times differently. About her years in Slocan, she wrote: "It was truly an exciting time, even if you think you know better than someone who actually lived it." She further accused me of constructing a one-dimensional, oppressed "internee" and referred to my statement about the silences of the past as "utter nonsense." Lois ended her letter on a sarcastic note, writing, "[Thought] you might be interested in the thoughts of one not so silent 'victim' of the 'most devastating event' in JC lives." [11]

My initial reaction to this message was one of hurt and dismay. I felt crushed. After all, I had a strong investment in my project, as a scholar, advocate, and most importantly, bearer of memories of the wartime injustices. Furthermore, since my days as a young academic, I have been steeped in the literature on feminist process and have long believed in the democratizing potential of the oral history interview.[12] In my internment study, I thereby sought to establish a unity with my interviewees. At the outset, all of them were women of my mother's generation, then in their eighties and nineties, and so I felt a sense of kinship. In some, I even observed gestures, expressions, and cultural idiosyncrasies that were reminiscent of my mother, grandmother, and the many female relatives and family friends that I encountered as a child. With both *Nisei* women and men, I also assumed bonds based on a shared racial identity and community history. As a *Sansei*, I lacked experiential authority but I was not simply a bystander either.

My childhood memories informed these interviews, and they became even more potent as I framed them in a political critique of racism in Canadian history and the internment in particular. I thus broke down in tears as I read Lois's harsh assessment of me and her invalidation of my work. Lois's message threw me off balance. Her accusations made me question my skills as an oral historian, my ethical obligations as a researcher, and the value of my research to a community about which I cared deeply. Her indictment placed me in a category that I had emphatically sought to avoid: that of a detached academic who, in the interests of furthering my own political or professional objectives, not only spoke for, but also misrepresented the subjects of my study. Early in this project, I foresaw a need to address an asymmetry of power between academic interviewer and working-class narrator. I was prepared for criticism or disinterest on the part of *Hakujin* (non-Japanese) audiences, but I did not anticipate receiving such disparaging words from someone within my own cultural community. I was caught off guard by such an unequivocal assertion of authorial control from an elderly woman whom I had never met.[13]

At first, I was tempted to fire off a defensive reply, informing this stranger that my analysis was an academically rigorous one based on in-depth interviews with dozens of *Nisei* with whom she had never spoken, and that although she herself had been interned, she did not have the perspective that I had developed as a scholar. It would be easy to pathologize Mrs. Hashimoto, dismiss her as a cranky, ignorant old woman, or demonize her as a right-wing fanatic. But upon rereading her message, the ethical and professional dilemmas it raised made me pause. Lois's letter spoke to questions about sharing authority,[14] highlighted the importance of self-reflexivity on the part of the researcher, and it prompted me to contemplate the analytical value of personal memory.[15] Rather than simply defend my work, I tried to better understand her perspective. I invited Lois to say more.

She quickly responded to my invitation and her second message was written in a different tone than the first: "Thank you for replying so courteously and thoughtfully to my ill-tempered email. I confess that I was happily surprised to hear from you—I am more accustomed to being ignored, or being written off by earnest sansei Redress activists as someone in denial of my internment pain:-)!!" Lois's reply made me realize that she passionately wanted to comment on the public representation of her generation. How could I write about giving voice and sharing authority but proceed to marginalize, censor, or dismiss a woman who wanted to engage me, even if I regarded her views as misguided, heretical, and dangerous to my larger political objectives? If I viewed her interpretation of the past with such skepticism, how could I highlight the concept of personal memory as fluid, subjective, interpretive—as being at the heart of oral history? In writing a comprehensive analysis of *Nisei* memories, did I not have a responsibility to listen to this woman? And if so, in what ways would her story shape my interpretation of the memories of others that I had interviewed? What is the relationship between one woman's memories and a community's collective memory? Could or should I keep Lois Hashimoto "off the record?"

Lois and I corresponded for the next three and a half years. In the first two years, she sporadically sent email messages, mailed me a couple of books, and copied me on various items of correspondence. She voiced her political opinions and promoted her causes, but we also complained about the weather, shared health concerns, and spoke of family vacations and celebrations. Several winters ago, I visited Lois at her home in Quebec. Here, I gathered six hours of oral testimony, and conversed with her (and her husband) for many more hours, over lunch and dinner.[16]

Voice and Truth

Lois was a working-class woman. She described herself as an "underachiever" partly because she was forced to leave school suddenly with the outbreak of war, when her formal education was limited. Her first job was as a seamstress in Morgan's department store. Before retiring, she worked in customer service at the Hudson's Bay Company. Over the course of more than a decade, Lois gained some visibility, if not notoriety, within the Japanese Canadian community and in the wider Montreal area because she expressed her views publicly, often in the form of letters to the editors of newspapers and to local and national-level politicians. Lois was especially critical of some prominent community members who played leading roles in the struggle for Redress, notably the nationally acclaimed novelist Joy Kogawa, author of the classic work *Obasan*, Audrey Kobayashi, a highly regarded and outspoken antiracist academic, and the Miki brothers, Art (former NAJC president) and Roy (professor emeritus of literary studies).

As Karen Olsen and Linda Shopes note, in our sensitivities to inequalities, academics may "overestimate our own privilege, even our own importance, in the eyes of the people we interview." But in fact, most interviewees, they observe, "seem not especially overwhelmed, intimidated, or impressed with us at all."[17] Although she was a working-class woman with limited formal schooling, Lois was by no means intimidated by me. She contested my authority from the outset. While Lois frequently mentioned her failing memory, and expressed frustration in being unable to find the right words to articulate her views, she never threw into question the veracity of her memories. Likewise, her sense of efficacy did not wane. Lois's authority was rooted in her direct experience of the war. She was an eyewitness and I was not. Likewise, I deferred to her age (she was my elder) and generational status (she was a *Nisei* and I a *Sansei*). Given that she had shared her thoughts with me (via the Internet) for years, by the time we sat down for a face-to-face interview, I was prepared for her rehearsed narrative.[18] Indeed, at times, I wondered if she approached the life story interview as simply another opportunity to step onto her political platform.[19]

In both her spoken narrative and written correspondence, Lois drew on the concepts of voice and representation. She claimed that the hegemonic voices of the Redress activists, human rights advocates in the NAJC, and *Sansei* academics (such as myself) now dominate the public discourse. In her view, the Redress activists, in particular, were responsible for authoring and promoting our history as one of suffering, hardship, and injustice. Indeed, critical remarks about the activists are woven throughout her narrative. While Lois admitted that the government's decision to intern Japanese Canadians was unfair, she believed that the costs of our wartime treatment have been greatly exaggerated by a generation that was born after the war. Lois reiterated these views in many email messages: "A phenomenon that intrigues me is the tendency of *Sansei* activists ... to assume they know more about the nature of racism than we who experienced, and overcame the most overt case of racism in Canadian history. I mean, that's pretty funny, don't you think?"[20]

Epitomizing Personal Memories[21]

Lois was a bright and knowledgeable woman. She had done some reading on Japanese Canadian history, perhaps more than most, and she was therefore aware of the range of internment experiences. One's placement during the war depended largely on age, sex, socioeconomic position, religion, and family status. Lois was among the majority of Japanese Canadians who were interned in a ghost town in the BC Interior. A smaller number of families that had sufficient economic resources relocated to the so-called self-supporting camps and, in effect, assumed the costs of their own internment. As compared to the ghost town internees, the "self-supporting" groups had fewer government-imposed restrictions. However, they were more isolated, without a community of Japanese

Canadians, and lacking even in a rudimentary infrastructure. Those who spent the war years on sugar beet farms in Manitoba and Alberta likewise faced physical and social isolation and harsh living conditions. In addition, they had to perform back-breaking labor in exchange for keeping their families intact. Reinforcing existing sex- and age-based divisions, the British Columbia Security Commission (BCSC) separated many young and middle-aged men from their families and exploited their labor in road or lumber camps. Men who displayed even mild resistance were incarcerated as prisoners of war (POWs). POWs spoke of poor nutrition, hard labor, harsh weather, loneliness, and occasional acts of rebellion. Some *Nisei* men, in an attempt to assert their national loyalty, also had unique and complex memories of war as soldiers in the Canadian Army.

Lois recognized that these varied experiences of internment produced a multiplicity of memories and it was important to her that these voices be evenly represented in public history. Yet, at the same time, she confessed: "I'm not a historian...I could just write about *my* personal experience of internment." Throughout her interview and in all of her writings, she prioritized her personal memories, highlighting fun, carefree days, friendship, and opportunity.

Indeed, Lois's memories of fun and frivolity took on a symbolic meaning in her life story narrative. They epitomized her experiences during the war and resettlement years and were so powerful in personal memory that they shaped her interpretation of history.[22] The hardship stories that were voiced during and after the Redress campaign, she believed, were therefore a gross distortion of historical truth. She commented: "Slocan was fun. Right from the get go, it was fun! We got there and there were people meeting us." Lois attributed these happy times in part to youth. As a girl during the war, she did not shoulder the worries and responsibilities of her elders. Lois readily admitted that the experiences of her mother and father must have been different than hers, but added that, as a 14-year-old, she was pretty "self-centered" and unaware of what her parents (and other *Issei*) were going through. For instance, she explained: "My husband's father lost his logging camp...But people like me, I didn't lose anything. I mean I was fourteen years old. What did I lose that's of monetary value?" She articulated these same sentiments more fully in her written essay "Go East, Young Ladies!" In this composition, she responded to ideas that had been expressed by a *Sansei* human rights activist: "I DID experience the forced assimilation of Japanese Canadians into mainstream Canada and can assure her [a *Sansei* activist] that far from being the humiliating and traumatizing event that she imagines, it was for me and I'm sure for many other Nisei, an exhilarating and liberating experience." She continued:

> I knew that not being allowed to finish my school year in 1942, and being forced out of our home in Queensborough, and having to live for two months in a converted horse stall in the Hastings Park livestock exhibition hall was

not exactly experiencing Democracy's finest hour. But after our arrival in the internment camp of Slocan, it was impossible to maintain any sense of outrage, because quite simply, I was enjoying myself too much.

"I was enjoying myself." This was Lois's defining statement about the internment. As her narrative unfolded, I could see that this epitomizing memory was the foundation for her vision of the history of her generation.[23]

Visions of History

In my second meeting with Lois I detected that she was trying to move me from the position of passive listener to that of active participant. As a result, in spite of my efforts to minimize my role in shaping the conversational narrative, our format shifted at points from monologue to dialogue. Posing direct questions, Lois left me little choice but to share my opinions, if only coyly. Yet the more Lois proclaimed her conservative anti-NAJC views, the more difficult it became for me to fully express my own; and my level of discomfort became heightened as did feelings of ambivalence about my growing involvement with this woman. I dreaded to imagine what my fellow NAJC board members would think about our relationship and I wondered if our association would throw into question my credibility with the critical factions of our small ethnic community.

As our conversational narrative progressed, Lois persisted in her efforts to minimize internees' "suffering" and downplay the long-term damages of the government's wartime policy. She did this in part by prioritizing historical acts of injustice and experiences of suffering. For example, she sought my reaction after comparing the millions of fatalities during the war to the property losses and uprooting of Japanese Canadians:

> *Lois*: They [Redress activists] just talk about the internment. The injustice that was done to our, you know, they just talk as though it was separate from the war. I mean, over fifty million people were killed and died in horrible ways. What was our suffering compared to that? *I mean, don't you see that, Pam?*
>
> *Pam*: Do you think that the internment was necessary, a necessary part of the war?
>
> *Lois*: Well, of course not! But it was still part of the war. It would not have happened if Japan hadn't bombed Pearl Harbor. How many innocent people died in Pearl Harbor? Where's the anguish over that? You know, why don't these people ever feel bad about that?

Lois further argued that the Redress campaign was redundant because Japanese Canadians had already won back their citizenship rights by 1949, when they secured the federal franchise and were permitted to return to the west coast.

Again, weighing the suffering of internees and struggles of the Redress activists against the military casualties of World War II, and in defense of "democracy," she argued:

> [It's] not because of the Redress that you and I have done all the right things, freedom of Canadian citizenship. It's the fact that, I mean, what if Japan and Germany had won the war? What more racist countries were there than Japan and Germany? And how many, 40,000 Canadians died to grant us, to make sure we had our rights and freedoms. And we got all the rights and freedoms. By 1949...we had a right to move back to the Coast. It wasn't the Redress that got us that...It's not the Redress that brought us the democratic rights.

Echoing one of the myths that had been promoted by BC politicians in their attempts to justify the uprooting, Lois maintained that Japanese Canadians were interned for their own protection—protection against racism in the wider society: "Well, with Slocan there was no hardship...It was like a, never-never...because we were taken out of the real world. The rest of Canada was fighting a war. We were kind of secluded. We were separated from the racism that was...outside the camps."

Another theme that emerged in Lois's life story was that of redemption. Echoing the long-standing "blessing in disguise" aphorism, Lois presented evidence not only of the survival of Japanese Canadians, but also of their educational and material successes in the postwar years, outcomes that she attributed to the wartime uprooting and dispersal. The view that past adversities (such as the internment) are ultimately for the good of a community serves different functions. It may help people define themselves in the present period, with dignity, as individuals who have triumphed in the face of adversity.[24] It is also a way of bringing "coherence" to a life story.[25] Lois admitted that, for some, there had been injustice and hardship but with more conviction, she spoke of the triumph of the *Nisei* and their *Sansei* offspring. In doing so, she also vehemently rejected the label of victim, declaring: "[The] internment, it didn't crush me. It didn't make me feel ashamed...It was just part of my life experience and I know it was wrong and I know it hurt a lot of people. But this was a fact." About the community as a whole, she similarly stated: "[We] were treated so unjustly but we didn't let it crush us. We persevered and we didn't just survive, you know, we flourished." And in one of only a few references that she made to the *Nisei* who were interned as agricultural laborers, Lois commented: "[People] that went through, sugar beet farms, well, they did backbreaking work...They went all through that and they weren't crushed by it. They won't become alcoholics and they persevered and they survived. I mean, I'm awfully proud of that...The fact that they went on to be doctors and Sociology professors." The reference to sociology professors was, of course, aimed specifically at me.

In extending the blessing in disguise argument, Lois also spoke of the assimilation of Japanese Canadians. Proudly, she observed that we are now among the most assimilated groups in this country. In her view, this is precisely because of the government's wartime policy. In 1944, after declaring the innocence of Japanese Canadians, Prime Minister Mackenzie King announced the government's decision to disperse them throughout the country. According to King, dispersal was in the community's best interest: "The sound policy and the best policy for the Japanese Canadians themselves is to distribute their numbers as widely as possible throughout the country where they will not create feelings of hostility."[26]

This policy of dispersal was effective. Prior to the war, 95 percent of Japanese Canadians (22,096) resided in the province of British Columbia. By 1947, this figure dropped to 6,776. Not long after the war's end, the community was scattered throughout Canada.[27] Lois's views of these demographic shifts were far more sanguine: the assimilation of Japanese Canadians was another positive outcome of the internment. She stated: "Most of my friends, the friends that I've talked with, they say, looking back they say, 'It was the best thing that happened to us, that we were assimilated into the nation.' Without exception, my friends say that." While she recognized that their assimilation was "forced," Lois also saw it as a unique opportunity for Japanese Canadians to become rapidly integrated into the dominant society. Restating her argument, she remarked: "[In] the final analysis, it [internment] was the best thing that could have happened to us. I mean would you really like to live the way we did in, all those completely Japanese communities? *Is that what you would like for yourself?*"

Lois's reasoning was tautological, though. Her analysis of the internment was based on her retrospective knowledge of the postwar educational and material gains of many members of the community. In her view, because the *Nisei* not only "survived," but "flourished" in the face of unjust treatment, the latter facilitated their present-day success. In telling her life story, she repeatedly zigzagged between past and present, and she was most loquacious when she situated herself in contemporary political debates.

Not surprisingly, Lois was unmoved by my suggestion that subsequent generations have felt the injustices of the past and they have since left psychic scars on some *Nisei*. She rejected this interpretation for it was inconsistent with her blessing-in-disguise conclusion. When I introduced the idea, she retorted: "I don't buy that!" Shifting the focus from subjective experience to socioeconomic outcomes, she reminded me that:

Japanese Canadians of all the ethnic groups have the highest average income...They've done well! I mean, no, I don't buy that. I don't. No. That's not true...I just don't buy that. To me, it doesn't make sense. I mean we left the camps and we didn't dwell on that. Internment, you know? We just got on with life. And we overcame. Japanese Canadians are the most successful visible minority group. I mean, I think everyone has accepted us. I think Statistics Canada has proved that, you know. So, so, no.

Lois was speaking to an audience of more than one. Her views were not just intended for me. Rather, she was making a case for the respectability and redemption of Japanese Canadians to the public, at large—for the record.

Framing Personal Memories in Contemporary Political Discourse

Lois was not the first nor was she the only *Nisei* to talk about having fun at an internment site or to speak of the uprooting as a blessing in disguise. Prior to meeting her, I interviewed several other women who had also spent their teen years in Slocan. Some of these women offered similarly nostalgic memories of friends, flirtations, and dancing to the music of the Big Bands. The difference between their narratives and the one articulated by Lois, however, was in how they framed and interpreted their personal memories. While Polly Shimizu, for instance, remembered good times, she balanced these memories with richly detailed descriptions of terrible living conditions, cruel acts of racism, and the violation of her citizenship rights. Kay Honda likewise contextualized her fond memories in a poignant discussion of the suffering that she felt all around her.[28] While Lois recognized the suffering of others, this was not expressed as part of her personal memory, nor did this knowledge inform her sense of a collective memory, her interpretation of the internment, or her vision of history.

What is also unique about Lois's life story is that it is densely woven into a contemporary public debate about racism and racialization. As she related her wartime experiences, she presented a counternarrative to that which has been popularized by the Redress activists. Lois drew on her personal memories to legitimate two related beliefs. One, she believed that although some groups have experienced racism, many others have exaggerated its effects. Two, racism, in Lois's view, is something that we as individuals can overcome. The conclusion she drew is that collective efforts to fight against racism are thereby unwarranted. Many of Lois's personal memories served to legitimate these beliefs. For example, she asserted: "I never had problems with race, I don't know. Oh, when my kids were little...in grade one, and on the way to school, some little French boy would say, '*Chin, chin, macarine*,' but her reaction was to just whirl around and yell at him, yell right back at him. And they stopped [*laughing*]." Again distancing herself from the subjects of racism, she stated: "I didn't have the experience of being called 'Jap' I was sure others did but I didn't. I mean, we'd go shopping.

We went to a movie several times. But it was just kind of normal. That was *my* experience."

Consistent with these views, Lois proceeded to express her opposition to various struggles to challenge racial discrimination in Canada, past and present. She was critical of, for example, employment equity measures, the contemporary redress campaigns of Aboriginal groups (around residential schools), and the Chinese Canadian campaign to seek reparations for the Head Tax. About the latter, she stated:

> I don't think they [Chinese Canadians] should have got redress because at that time...we were still evolving...At that time, when the Chinese were coming [into Canada]...we didn't have this...anti-racism. But the important thing is that these Chinese people came anyways, and they paid the exorbitant head tax. And despite that racism, they still came. Why? Why did they do that?...They felt that despite all that hardship and the racism...their hopes for a happier future for their kids here in Canada. And so you've got to admire their tenacity, you know, the fact they took it and they worked hard...and managed to survive and just persevere. But look where they are now. I mean, their hopes were realized.

The more Lois moved from personal memory to direct assertions of her political position on current issues, the more I squirmed.[29]

There is a striking consistency in Lois's narrative from beginning to end. Her memories of life as a 14-year-old during the war, as a young woman in the postwar period, and later as a mother and grandmother all supported her ideological position. While she did not deny the existence of racism in Canada generally, she claimed that personally, she never experienced it. Furthermore, Lois maintained that like Japanese Canadians, other racialized or colonized groups, whether Chinese Canadians or Aboriginal, had to find ways of stoically coping on an individual basis. Her life story from childhood to old age was a coherent one. There were no victims in her narrative, and everyone was or could be an agent of their own fate. These arguments are consistent with a wider, neoliberal politics, of which meritocracy and the myth of individualism explain away racism as a purely personal outcome, the result of individual failure or inadequacy.[30]

Conclusion: One Voice among Many

Why did I want to hear Lois's life story? Was I attempting to assert my authorial control in response to her attacks on my published work? Did I set her up, in an attempt to use her memories as an example of a counternarrative to that made public by the Redress Committee? Was I prepared to listen to her with a smile and seeming neutrality, only to critically dissect her life story later, in the privacy and safety of my own study? Was I simply assuaging my feminist conscience and proving my commitment to democratic process by *giving* her voice?

In part, I wished to hear and understand Lois precisely because we were in such fundamental disagreement. Years ago, E. P. Thompson wrote: "It is only by facing into opposition that I am able to define my thought at all."[31] Like Thompson, I believed that Lois's contrary views would help me to sharpen my own. More importantly, I felt an ethical and professional responsibility to listen to this woman. Lois took the initiative not only in composing that first email message to me, but also in maintaining communication over the years. And, for well over a decade, she generated binders and file folders of written memoirs, letters, and statements of opinion. These efforts demonstrated a deep-felt concern about the representation of her community.

What did I learn from Lois? My exchanges with this woman taught me lessons about the relationship between researcher and narrator, as well as the interview frame itself. As Blee found, it can be fairly easy to establish rapport, even with a narrator whose views are "politically abhorrent."[32] I would not describe Lois's views as "abhorrent." However, I did find her opinions highly objectionable. Not only had I devoted most of my academic career to the kind of antiracist work of which she spoke so disparagingly, but many of the targets of her criticism were people whom I have long regarded as icons in the community.

Yet, as Olsen and Shopes note, oral history interviews are "highly framed encounters" that are "not governed by the rules of ordinary interaction."[33] The interview presents us with a "social space where normal power relationships get blunted."[34] In such a context, the "power of the personal interaction" can override the "critical judgment" of the oral historian. In addition to our political differences, my relationship with Lois was shaped by my concerns about the practice of oral history (letting the narrator construct her or his own narrative), her status as an eyewitness and my senior, as well as the generosity and openness that she displayed in our interpersonal exchanges. After all, she not only gave me access to all of her private papers, but also welcomed me into her home, fed me, baked me cookies, and treated me to dinner at a local restaurant.

In turn, I remained empathetic throughout our interviews. Never did I suggest that she was wrong; though in the hope of avoiding misrepresentation or deception, I did mention at the outset that I disagreed with her interpretation. But in fact, so subtle was I in expressing my dissenting views that after many exchanges, Lois asked me what exactly we disagreed about? After visiting her in Laval, I was convinced more than ever of the value of the face-to-face interview. Hearing Lois's voice, observing her mannerisms and facial expressions, and noting when she would get up to eagerly retrieve her scrapbook of photos gave me a fuller sense of who she was as a human being. Meeting her in person enabled me to detect her ardency, frustrations, limitations, and vulnerabilities, and this understanding has helped me become a more empathetic researcher.[35]

Should Lois's story remain "off the record?" Clearly, her narrative raises tensions that many of us do not wish to air in public. She exposed political differences within our community: the conservative voices in conflict with progressive ones, those who wish to narrow the NAJC's mandate to community development (sushi-making, *taiko* drumming, and flower arranging) as opposed to advocates of a human rights agenda. Her narrative further reveals the unsavory reality that even people who have been racially oppressed may be critical of antiracist activism, and may themselves promote or perpetuate racist thinking.[36] Lois chose to highlight her positive, uncomplicated memories of internment and resettlement in postwar Canada. These memories give credence to a neoliberal agenda that highlights an ethic of individualism and downplays the role of systemic discrimination and structural inequalities in shaping people's life choices. In doing so, she minimized the negative and enduring impact of the wartime events and trivialized the efforts of some *Nisei* and many *Sansei* to challenge the government's actions.

Lois passed away unexpectedly in January 2010. I learned about her death weeks later. I could have dropped this project with Lois, kept her interviews locked away, or simply treated her as an informant, thereby selectively drawing on her memories. But rather than dismiss or diminish this woman, I wish to put her memories on record. Lois's story has enhanced my analytical understanding of Japanese Canadian history and deepened my reflections on the practice of oral history. Lois forced me to listen deeply, and to consider an interpretation of history that was inconsistent with my own. And these practices—deep listening and inclusiveness—are at the heart of oral history. Granted, all research, oral history included, is built on bias and selectivity. But when we select or omit participants and stories for purely ideological reasons, then our practices become dubious and our analyses ultimately limited.

If we wish to uphold the value of personal memory, we cannot exclude memories from our accounts because they are inconsistent with public memory or from what we view as historical truth. If a stranger presents us with her personal truths, with memories that are sincere, we cannot look away. Rather, we must take up the challenge and consider how they bear on our interpretation of history and how they stand up to the memories of others. My writing is inspired by my advocacy, but, as an oral historian, I must allow the personal narrative to unfold under the direction of the narrator. If I view memory as being at the heart of oral history, then I must be prepared to learn from an old woman's memories, even if they do not cohere with my own.

This is not to say, however, that researcher/advocates never make strategic choices. As Julie Cruikshank and Tatiana Argounova-Low observe, the temporal frame of each project plays a role in shaping our decisions about what to put on or leave off the record.[37] Twenty-odd years ago, in the heat of the campaign for Redress, I may have decided to keep Lois's memories off the record. Back then her words could have been more damaging to the political cause; more persuasive in the absence of a strong critical discourse. However, it now seems time to air the divisions within our community, to offer accounts that reveal the nuances of the war and resettlement years, and the complex ways in which racism has impacted the second generation. It is time to enrich the story of internment. Lois agreed, pleading with me to write a complex history. Paradoxically, *she* urged *me* to be more than a conduit for a political cause: "You have a wealth of real memories narrated to you by people who generously shared their experiences with you—and they are far more valuabe [*sic*] and real than the vicariously felt emotions of sansei Redress activists. You have the ingredients for an interesting and enlightening book."[38]

After listening to Lois, in seriously considering this woman's perspective on her own life, I listened somewhat differently to the narratives of the 74 other *Nisei* women and men I interviewed. And "off the record," when I now read overly theorized, polemical writings authored by those whom Lois would call "earnest Sansei," I say to myself, "I can hear Lois now!" In a way, Lois acts as my conscience in the practice of oral history. She reminds me to consider all voices of the past. She taps me on the shoulder when I am swayed by deterministic accounts that lack empirical grounding, and when I romantically envision historical victims that are without human dimension. Lois has given me a heightened sense of nuance in oral history practice. And her death does not exempt me because her voice is not an isolated one. While the details of her life story, the idiosyncratic nature of its telling, and the form and development of her narrative are particular, Lois's repertoire of memories and interpretation of history may be understood as part of a larger political analysis.

Over time, I grew to like and respect this somewhat irascible woman. But do I agree with her description of the past? As noted earlier, my objective is not to establish the veracity of any individual's memories of her or his own life. I do, however, believe that if we wish to escape the postmodernist trap of positing ever-shifting realities, we need to make some claims about history.[39] As Iwona Irwin-Zarecka writes, there is a "baseline historical reality."[40] Lois's memories are meaningful, without doubt. But when she extrapolated from her personal memories to make statements about the community as a whole, I believe that she was on shakier ground. The memories of my many *Nisei* interviewees, in addition to my reading of thousands of censored letters that were written by Japanese Canadians in the 1940s, have led me to a starkly different understanding of the war years—it was a time that was sometimes marked by fun and frivolity but also by deep suffering, loss, pain, anger, and wounds that have never fully healed.

I am not arguing that Lois's memories are inaccurate or that she is a *Nisei* "in denial." I am saying that memory is selective, partial, and shifting. Oral history can be both unreliable and revelatory. According to Blee, it is unreliable because of the subjectivity of personal memory, because of its gaps, its faultiness, its lapses.[41] But at the same time, as Alessandro Portelli notes, it is revelatory because "[what] informants believe is indeed a historical *fact* (that is, the fact that they believe it), as much as what really happened."[42] What does Lois's narrative reveal? I cannot nor do I wish to psychologize Lois. As a sociologist, however, I can attempt to situate her memories. Lois's narrative tells us about the relationship between personal memory and a wider public discourse. As Ronald Grele states, personal memories are neither static nor spontaneous. Memories of the past are situated in contemporary ideological beliefs and cultures and they are crafted over time.[43] I can only speculate on the extent to which Lois's present-day political agenda shaped her personal wartime memories, and on the ways in which her position on current political debates, in turn, was a product of her early experiences as a Japanese Canadian internee. However, Lois, unlike most narrators, demanded interpretive authority of her life story, and with authorial voice, she framed her personal memories in contemporary ideological debates around racism, human rights, and political redress. In the words of Gary Y. Okihiro, oral history offers ordinary individuals a way of evaluating their lives in relation to the historical metanarrative.[44] Lois's narrative then is as much a comment on the social conflicts that have marked Canadian history, as it is a definition of her individual self. It is not only a description of the past, but also an ideological statement on the contemporary world in which she lived. Lois attempted to immortalize her personal memories, carve out her identity, and define a new social identity for the women and men of her generation[45] and, in her narrative, this is a world in which structure does not set limits, "race" no longer matters, and the individual is triumphant.

Notes

1. At the beginning of the war, the government passed Order in Council PC 365, which designated an area one hundred miles inland from the west coast a "protected area." On March 4, 1942, the government formed the British Columbia Security Commission (BCSC), a civilian body that was given the power to execute a "systematic expulsion" of all persons of Japanese origin from the area that lay within this zone. See Roy Miki and Cassandra Kobayashi, *Justice in Our Time: The Canadian Redress Settlement* (Vancouver/Winnipeg: Talonbooks/National Association of Japanese Canadians, 1991), 20–24.

2. Roy Miki coined the term "framed by race" in *Redress: Inside the Japanese Canadian Call for Justice* (Vancouver: Raincoast Books, 2005), 13–37.

3. See Antoinette Errante, "But Sometimes You're Not Part of the Story: Oral Histories and Ways of Remembering and Telling," in *Feminist Perspectives on Social Research*, eds. Sharlene Nagy Hesse-Biber and Michelle L. Yaiser (Oxford University Press, 2003), 411–37.

4. Daniel James, *Doña María's Story: Life, History, Memory, and Political Identity* (Durham: Duke University Press, 2000), 138.

5. Sherna Berger Gluck, "Advocacy Oral History: Palestinian Women in Resistance," in *Women's Words: The Feminist Practice of Oral History*, eds. Sherna Berger Gluck and Daphne Patai (New York: Routledge, 1991), 214.

6. Kathleen Blee, "Evidence, Empathy and Ethics: Lessons from Oral Histories of the Klan," in *The Oral History Reader*, second edition, eds. Robert Perks and Alistair Thomson (London: Routledge, 2006), 322–31; Katharine Borland, "'That's Not What I Said': Interpretive Conflict in Oral Narrative Research," in Perks and Thomson, *The Oral History Reader*, second edition, 310–21; Gluck, "Advocacy Oral History," 205–19; Tracy E. K'Meyer and A. Glenn Crothers, "'If I see some of this in writing, I'm going to shoot you': Reluctant Narrators, Taboo Topics, and the Ethical Dilemmas of the Oral Historian," *The Oral History Review* 34, 1 (2007): 71–93; Valerie Yow, "Do I Like Them Too Much? Effects of the Oral History Interview on the Interviewer and Vice-Versa," *The Oral History Review* 21, 1 (1997): 55–79.

7. On the conversational narrative, see Ronald Grele, "History and the Languages of History in the Oral History Interview: Who Answers Whose Questions and Why," in *Interactive Oral History Interviewing*, eds. Eva M. McMahan and Kim Lacy Rogers (New York: Routledge, 1994), 2.

8. Blee, "Evidence, Empathy and Ethics," 324, 328.

9. Errante, "But Sometimes You're Not Part of the Story," 2000.

10. Ruth Behar, *The Vulnerable Observer: Anthropology That Breaks Your Heart* (Boston: Beacon Press, 1996). Also see chapter 4 in this volume.

11. Personal correspondence between Lois Hashimoto and the author, May 3, 2006.

12. See Susan Geiger, "What's So Feminist About Women's Oral History? *Journal of Women's History* 21, 1 (1990): 169–82; Judith Stacey, "Can There Be a Feminist Ethnography?" in Gluck and Patai, *Women's Words*, 111–19; Joan Sangster, "Telling Our Stories: Feminist Debates and the Use of Oral History," in *The Oral History Reader*, first edition, eds. Robert Perks and Alistair Thomson (London: Routledge, 1998), 87–100.

13. For a related discussion, see: Kathryn Anderson and Dana C. Jack, "Learning to Listen: Interview Techniques and Analyses," in Gluck and Patai, *Women's Words*, 19.

14. See Michael Frisch, *A Shared Authority. Essays on the Craft and Meaning of Oral History* (University of New York, 1990; Kathleen M. Ryan, "'I Didn't Do Anything Important': A Pragmatist Analysis of the Oral History Interview," *The Oral History Review* 36, 1 (2009): 25–44; Lorraine Sitzia, "A Shared Authority: An Impossible Goal?" *The Oral History Review* 30, 1 (2003): 87–101; Special Issue of the *Journal of Canadian Studies* 43, 1 (Spring 2009).

15. See Andrea Doucet, "'From Her Side of the Gossamer Wall(s)': Reflexivity and Relational Knowing," *Qualitative Sociology* 31, 1 (2008): 73–87.
16. Lois Hashimoto, interview by author, Laval, Quebec, December 16–17, 2008.
17. Karen Olsen and Linda Shopes, "Crossing Boundaries, Building Bridges: Doing Oral History among Working-Class Women and Men," in Gluck and Patai, *Women's Words*, 196–97.
18. See James's discussion of the "performative" aspects of a narrative" in *Doña María's Story*, 183–85.
19. Gluck notes that individual consciousness is rarely revealed through the recitation of a political platform. Gluck, "Advocacy Oral History," 209.
20. Personal correspondence between Lois Hashimoto and the author, May 6, 2006.
21. E. Culpepper Clark, "Reconstructing History: The Epitomizing Image," in McMahan and Rogers, *Interactive Oral History Interviewing*, 20, 26. Writing in 1969, K. Burke (cited in Clark) introduced the concept of an "epitomizing image" to describe an episode that symbolically represents the "course of the plot." Certain anecdotes, says Clark, are so "salient" that the researcher cannot dismiss them. To this end, Linda Shopes states that "iconic stories" are "concrete, specific accounts that 'stand for' or sum up something the narrator reckons of particular importance." See Shopes, "Making Sense of Oral History," http://historymatters. gmu.edu.
22. See Marigold Linton, "Phoenix and Chimera: The Changing Faces of Memory," in *Memory and History: Essays on Recalling and Interpreting Experience*, eds. Jaclyn Jeffrey and Glenace Edwall (Lanham: University Press of America, 1994), 81.
23. In turn, her personal narrative is governed by a particular vision of history. See Marie-Francoise Chanfrault-Duchet, "Narrative Structures, Social Models, and Symbolic Representation in the Life Story," in Gluck and Patai, *Women's Words*, 77–92.
24. See Kim Lacy Rogers, *Life and Death in the Delta: African-American Narratives of Violence, Resilience, and Social Change* (New York: Palgrave, 2006).
25. Charlotte Linde, *Life Stories: The Creation of Coherence* (New York: Oxford University Press, 1993).
26. *Debates*, House of Commons, August 4, 1944, as cited in Miki and Kobayashi, *Justice in Our Time*, 50.
27. Audrey Kobayashi, *A Demographic Profile of Japanese Canadians and Social Implications for the Future* (Ottawa: Department of the Secretary of State, 1989), 6; Miki and Kobayashi, *Justice in Our Time*, 105.
28. Both Polly Shimizu and Kay Honda were outspoken advocates of Redress. See Pamela Sugiman, "Memories of Internment: Narrating Japanese Canadian Women's Life Stories," *Canadian Journal of Sociology* 29, 3 (2004): 359–88.
29. In their study of second-generation, grown children of Korean and Vietnamese immigrants in the United States, Karen Pyke and Tran Dang argue that "by accepting and internalizing mainstream racist values and rationales," the second-generation often ends up justifying the oppression of their own ethnic group, albeit often unintentionally. Pyke and Dang, "'FOB' and 'Whitewashed': Identity and Internalized Racism Among Second Generation Asian Americans," *Qualitative Sociology* 26, 2 (Summer 2003): 151.

30. See Christopher Robbins, "Racism and the Authority of Neoliberalism: A Review of Three Books on the Persistence of Racial Equality in a Color-blind Era," *Journal for Critical Education Policy Studies* 2, 2 (2004), available at: http://www.jceps.com.

31. E. P. Thompson, "An Open Letter to Leszek Kolakowski," in *The Poverty of Theory* (New York: Monthly Review Press, 1978), 186.

32. Blee, "Evidence, Empathy and Ethics," 328.

33. Olsen and Shopes, "Crossing Boundaries," 195–96.

34. Ibid., 196.

35. Lois was deeply embarrassed when she read the transcripts of our interviews. She felt that she had been incoherent, never finishing a sentence or thought, and failing to find the correct words to express her ideas. Despite my insistence that she had been lucid, Lois spent days writing out fuller explanations of her spoken words.

36. See Gluck, "Advocacy Oral History," 205–19; Claudia Koonz, *Mothers in the Fatherland. Women, the Family, and Nazi Politics* (New York: St. Martin's Griffin, 1988); Anna Sheftel and Stacey Zembrzycki, "Only Human: A Reflection on the Ethical and Methodological Challenges of Working with 'Difficult' Stories," *The Oral History Review* 37, 3 (Summer/Fall 2010): 191–214.

37. See chapter 2 in this collection.

38. Personal correspondence between Lois Hashimoto and the author, May 6, 2006.

39. For a persuasive discussion of oral history, feminism, and material analysis, see chapter 3 in this collection.

40. Iwona Irwin-Zarecka, *Frames of Remembrance: The Dynamics of Collective Memory* (New Brunswick, New Jersey, 1994), 102.

41. Blee, "Evidence, Empathy and Ethics," 324.

42. Alessandro Portelli, "What Makes Oral History Different," in Perks and Thomson, *The Oral History Reader*, second edition, 36.

43. Ronald Grele, "Movement Without Aim: Methodological and Theoretical Problems in Oral History," in Perks and Thomson, *The Oral History Reader*, first edition, 38–52.

44. See Gary Okihiro, *Whispered Silences: Japanese Americans and World War II* (Seattle: University of Washington Press, 1996).

45. Claudia Salazar, "A Third World Women's Text: Between the Politics of Criticism and Cultural Politics" in Gluck and Patai, *Women's Words*, 93–106.

CHAPTER 9

Third Parties in "Third Spaces": Reflecting on the Role of the Translator in Oral History Interviews with Iraqi Diasporic Women

Nadia Jones-Gailani

In the heat of an Amman summer with the smell of jasmine thick in the air, I sat back and surveyed the porch cluttered with *hookah* pipes and the branches of ripe figs overhead, while my stepmother, Om-Yasameen,[1] argued in Arabic with the fortune-teller. We were in the midst of an interview, when the participant, the fortune-teller, abruptly turned to me and, with my coffee cup in hand, began to tell me my fortune. As she delivered promises of future wealth and happiness, she also carefully, even cunningly, wove into the "reading" threads of her personal experiences and memories of Iraq, uncovering a very painful past. Her revelations about the persecution of the Armenian minority in Iraq became a narrative in defense of her people's suffering and a testament to her own experiences of displacement, loss, and trauma. My stepmother, a Sunni Muslim of elite background, did not agree with her, prompting a heated exchange. I listened carefully as the two women went back and forth, fighting over competing versions of Iraq's national history and making their respective claims to indigeneity, an old debate that has acquired new meaning in the aftermath of the Saddam Ba'th regime.[2] As with many of the oral histories conducted for my research, these negotiations between Arabic and English, past and present, and collective and counternarratives of national memory, resulted in women's life histories being formed within this symbiotic exchange of views and experiences. These complicated negotiations between participant and translator in the interview space are the focus of this chapter.

More broadly, my dissertation research explores how ethnoreligious difference, an important part of modern "national" historical memory, is transported from the homeland, informing how Iraqi communities in diaspora settle, organize, and construct identity in North America. With a view to exploring how women's national and ethnoreligious identities, as well as socioreligious hierarchies, are contested and reconceived in the diaspora, I conducted interviews with over one hundred Iraqi women; their narratives shed light on the interactions between recent refugees and settled Iraqi communities in North American. From my position as a historian of mixed Iraqi heritage, Om-Yasameen's role as facilitator was essential to brokering contacts in communities of Iraqi refugees awaiting exit visas in Amman, and in communities of recently settled Iraqis in Toronto. The biggest challenge I faced when I began the research was in convincing recent victims of disruption, loss, repression, and violence to trust me enough to bring me into their homes and record their narratives. My stepmother's reputation in Iraqi society was an important source of legitimization for my research agenda; her social status and mine were an essential bridge for my initiation into communities of diasporic Iraqis.

As translator, Om-Yasameen as a refugee first in Jordan and more recently in Canada found ways to mediate the intersections of ethnoreligious and class divides, thereby informing how women shaped their narratives. An upper-middle-class Sunni Muslim (Iraq's elite, championed by the Ba'th), she became both a linguistic and cultural translator, the third person in interviews with Iraqi women of differing class, religious, and ethnic backgrounds. She translated across cultures to initiate intimate connections within the interview space, facilitating provocative exchanges with women from diverse ethnoreligious and class backgrounds. Here, I explore how the presence of a translator in the interview space informs the construction of participant narratives as well as the process of remembering and retelling past traumas and life histories.

As feminist oral historian Franca Iacovetta and others have noted, even when our project is to recover and center the voices of marginalized women, we cannot either assume to be collecting unmediated voices, or simply ignore the power dynamics of the interview, or suppose we have democratized it sufficiently.[3] The extensive literature and guidebooks on conducting oral histories pay very little attention to how the already complex power dynamics of the interview space are further complicated by the introduction of a translator, forcing the interviewer to share authority and listen vulnerably to her subjects, cede control, and enable discussions to develop organically.[4] Situated within the diaspora, and particularly within feminist scholarship on non-Western religious women,[5] my work reconfigures Homi Bhabha's hybridized "third space" as a feminine safe space within which female subjectivities and diasporic identities are negotiated.[6] For women, masculine collective identities transposed from the homeland continue to shape how they remember and reconstruct trauma and loss in their oral histories. Complicated by hierarchies of gender, class, and religious difference, narratives of Iraqi diasporic women conform to dual, and often dueling, versions of the past: the official "myth of nation" of Iraq's Arab collective and harmonious past,[7] and the unofficial (and often unrecorded) counternarrative of subjective female life experiences, which reveals a long history of interethnic conflict and violence.[8]

Feminist discourses of subjectivities claim to correct the power imbalance and give equal weight to women's experiences and their interpretations.[9] These research methods, designed to include women in the historical narrative, often exclude religious women of color and cast them as victims in their colonial histories.[10] As a female researcher, access to Iraqi women in the private sphere is a privilege, but this alone cannot correct the imbalance of authority and power. As this chapter demonstrates, in order to overcome the power imbalance and unsilence their subjective memories, Iraqi women created a "third space," a safe space for feminine exchanges about personal experiences. This occurred in a variety ways, the most prevalent of which was the use of language during the taped interview and in informal and intimate discussions following the formal interview. This "third space" became the safe area within which women disrupted the national imposed narrative and shared subjective female lived experiences of trauma, exile, and violence.

The Ties That Bind: Family Lineage and Class Status in the Interview

In order to bridge the divide between public and private and official and informal memory, gaining the women's trust was critical. In this regard, Om-Yasameen's role was invaluable. When I first began the process of conducting life histories, Om-Yasameen's primary role in the interview space was to help me navigate between Arabic and English parts of the interview and to clarify parts of the English dialogue for participants. The participants were generally fluent if not proficient in English and did not require a translator to interpret the conversation, but they often benefited from clarifications in Arabic of certain elements of the discussion. My own basic comprehension and ability to converse in Arabic made it impossible for me to help with these clarifications, which is why interviews in Amman were conducted with a translator present. For her part in the interview, Om-Yasameen demanded to be allowed to chaperone me to and from the interviews, with the cultural understanding that she was protecting my reputation and that of the family as I traveled around the city of Amman as a single woman. She viewed these interviews as social calls, and when we first began this series of interviews, I was constantly frustrated by the amount of time and energy that was wasted on the social portion of our visits with Iraqi women. It was only later in the process, when I began to make contacts and conduct interviews in Canada and the United States without her help, that I realized the importance of these social rituals.

Om-Yasameen's presence enabled the dialogue to move easily between English and Arabic, and unless the interviewee requested a translation, I tried not to interrupt the flow of conversation. Most of the dialogue was in English, but the women often used the presence of another Arabic speaker, Om-Yasameen, to either divert the conversation away from sensitive questions posed in English or simply lighten the tone of the exchange. The latter happened, for instance, while I was pursuing a line of questioning about traumatic experiences in Iraq. Suddenly, Om-Yasameen and the participant began joking in Arabic and roaring with laughter. In these cases, she affected my ability to "control" the interview since I was forced to "share authority" with her in the interview space.[11] Initially, I found that these diversions into Arabic hindered the flow of the interview, especially when I was trying to stay on track and make my way toward more difficult questions about trauma and loss. Over time, I began to understand these outbursts of laughter as ways of releasing participants from remembering their traumatic pasts. As part of this communal remembering of past trauma and repression, Om-Yasameen's presence helped the women overcome their insecurities and hesitancy to divulge difficult pasts.

In most (but not all) cases, the women Om-Yasameen contacted and introduced to me led to a recorded interview. The initial exchange prior to the interview took place exclusively between her and the potential participant. As part of a community of displaced Iraqis in Amman, Om-Yasameen drew upon personal contacts to broker a tentative relationship on my behalf with each participant by first establishing my "good" reputation based on my father's status and good standing in the community.[12] Class position and reputation in Arab communities are traditionally based upon the social status of the father's blood relatives.[13] My position within the Al-Gailani family enabled me to later develop my own connections with Iraqi families living in North America. Most of the participants began the interview by referring to my father's family, partly out of respect and deference to Om-Yasameen,[14] and also as a means of legitimizing the interview and their part in it. When, with a knowing smile and a reverent nod, one woman told me: "I know who you are my dear. You come from an old family. You are a *good* girl,"[15] she was underscoring the common ideal of women's moral regulation, present in so many of the oral narratives of

Iraqi women. This was a reflection of her efforts to negotiate between dominant codes of femininity in the homeland and the diaspora.[16]

In order to draw me into this hybrid space, participants often invoked my background and identity at the beginning of the interview. I soon realized that this early exchange was part of the two-way negotiation of information in which I was expected to engage if participants were to divulge personal narratives. My precarious position on the margins of Iraqi culture and community as a half-Iraqi, half-Welsh immigrant to Canada provided me with a hybrid passport and the flexibility to shift between insider and outsider status. My already tenuous position of insider-outsider was further complicated by the imperial connotations of having a slight British accent, which continues to be a mark of status and prestige in Iraq. My own hybrid status reinforces the complications of belonging in the third space, at once a physical, psychological, and cultural grey area between traditional and Western cultures.[17] The interviewee saw an interviewer who "looked" Iraqi, but they heard a foreign language and an accent that immediately shaped my position as "other."[18] Om-Yasameen's presence not only legitimized my claims to belonging as an Iraqi, but also worked to elevate my status by emphasizing my British heritage, drawing on identifiable status markers in Iraqi society.

Language played an interesting part in solidifying my outsider status in the community and determining the information Iraqi women were willing to share in the interview. I had expected women to be uncomfortable with conducting interviews in English rather than in Arabic. This did not appear to be a source of discomfort, although it did have a significant impact on the kinds of relationships I formed with interviewees. Women treated me as a confidant and sometimes even as a counselor, often sharing personal secrets and, in return, asking my opinion on subjects such as love and intimacy in their lives. Given the anxieties women discussed about the role of gossip and bad rumors in shaping their reputation outside the homeland, I often wondered if they viewed me as a safe alternative to sharing this information with another woman from within their Iraqi community. It will be interesting to follow up on this idea in future research and explore the intricate networks of intimacy and gossip that shape the ways in which information is transmitted in female networks of diasporic Iraqis.

Languages of Interpretation: Concealing Trauma in the Interview

When I returned to Canada and began transcribing the interviews with Om-Yasameen's help, I noticed patterns in how participants manipulated narratives into the English formal account and the Arabic counternarrative; a response to the presence of an Arab-Muslim female translator. One particular example was in an interview where I asked the participant what daily life was like for women during the decade of international sanctions in the 1990s. The "golden years" of Iraq's economic boom coupled with the incorporation of women into the labor force during the 1970s and early 1980s were followed by an abrupt reversal of these opportunities during the decade of sanctions imposed upon the country following the invasion of Kuwait.[19] Travel was increasingly difficult, women were forced back into the home due to crippling cuts in child care programs, and many families found their fortunes significantly altered.[20] In English, the participant responded by saying that Sunnis hardly felt the difference since they were protected by the Sunni-dominated regime and were able to readily access education, health care, and travel. She then shifted the conversation toward a short and convivial exchange in Arabic with Om-Yasameen. Once transcribed, I found that the participant had joked with my stepmother in Arabic about the irony that, for the first time in decades, Sunnis were able to travel yet they were now reduced to being transported as *shroogi*[21] refugees.[22]

As we transcribed the interview, Om-Yasameen confessed her part in encouraging the formation of dueling narratives because she did not want the participant to reveal *their* (referring here to the Sunni elite) situation during the sanctions period. By manipulating the official narrative in this way, Om-Yasameen kept her own personal experiences as well as the collective memory of this dark decade in Iraq's past off the record, even though technically it was part of the recorded and formal interview transcript. I wondered later, given our personal relationship, if she also silenced these subjective experiences of life during sanctions to shelter me from the realities of my family's suffering during this period in Iraq. This example illustrates not only the problematic nature of sharing authority in the interview space with a family member, but also how Om-Yasameen's position as translator enabled her to influence the construction of the narrative, according to her own agenda and intimate knowledge of women's suffering during this period.

The transcription process uncovered patterns in Om-Yasameen's manipulation of participant narratives from English to Arabic in order to "protect" the women from unearthing personal memories of trauma. In a particularly emotional interview in Amman with a close family friend, I was very grateful for my stepmother's presence as she helped calm the participant who repeatedly beat her chest and cried profusely throughout the interview. The woman chose to conduct most of the interview in Arabic, and in her translation, Om-Yasameen explained that the participant was upset because it was painful for her to be away from her homeland. Only after the interview was over did my stepmother explain that the woman's brother had been missing for a few weeks and was feared dead. The woman proceeded to try to tell me about her brother, bringing out family photographs and explaining, in her broken English, how he was kidnapped.[23] As translator, Om-Yasameen once again had a hand in tailoring the narrative according to *her* interpretation of what should and should not be part of the formal narrative. The liberties she took with the translations, and her relationship to participants, informed how these narratives were recorded and the exchange of information that took place within the formal interview space. However, without her assistance in this particular case, and with her ability to genuinely empathize and connect with the participant, I likely would have ended the interview early having failed to record any of the participant's narrative. Thus, despite her manipulations of the narrative, Om-Yasameen's presence was an essential element to accessing narratives of war and trauma, even if these accounts were modified in the process of recording the interview.

There were, however, instances in which Om-Yasameen's social status and ethnoreligious affiliation significantly altered the course of my interviews and how participants shaped collective and counternarratives. In an interview with an Iraqi Shi'a woman from a lower socioeconomic class than her upper-middle-class Sunni heritage, these ethnoreligious differences became increasingly apparent and intrusive in the exchange between translator and participant. As with many Iraqi refugees in Jordan, the woman was struggling to sustain her family and was receiving support (including a housing allowance) from local agency branches of international organizations, such as Caritas. Having received a minimal education in Iraq, her English was poor and our primary means of communication was through the translator. The interview began relatively smoothly, as I communicated with her through Om-Yasameen to find out why she had left Iraq and how the family was coping with the transition to refugee status in Jordan. When I asked the participant if she had plans to apply through the United Nations High Commission for Refugees (UNHCR) for placement in Canada or the United States, she became increasingly agitated, raising her voice aggressively toward the translator. It was unclear at the time if Om-Yasameen had translated the questions directly into Arabic or if she had altered the information in translation. The interview soon devolved into an angry exchange between the two women, from which I was excluded. As the participant became more aggressive, we hurriedly made our exit with her shouts still audible in the distance.

Afterward, my stepmother explained that the participant had grown incensed with my question of whether or not she would seek refuge beyond Jordan because she considered her place to be in the homeland, defending the country from foreign invasion. She then asked the translator whether she agreed and Om-Yasameen was forthcoming about her plans to immigrate to Canada. Upon hearing this, the participant became increasingly agitated, which then led to a very angry exchange between the women over ethnoreligious difference and who constituted the "real" Iraqis. My own background was called into question, as she accused my father of neglecting his duties to raise a proper "Iraqi," an Arabic-speaking child raised in the Iraqi culture. Ultimately, the participant questioned the loyalty of Sunnis to Iraq, since most members of the professional class had either fled to neighboring countries or were in transit to Europe or North America by 2007. This embittered exchange is emblematic of ongoing hostilities in the homeland, heightened in diaspora as each group vies for control over the state in the aftermath of the Saddam Husayn regime. In the emotional space of the interview, these historic divides permeated the personal narrative of the participant, blurring the boundary between past and present.

By employing my stepmother as translator, and drawing on personal family contacts to interview Iraqi women, it became impossible to maintain a clear line between the academic and the personal within the interview space. In instances, such as the interview documented earlier with the Shi'i participant, this line ceased to exist, and my currency as a researcher was reduced to the social standing of my family within Iraqi society. The interviews conducted in Amman highlighted the benefits of making the personal political in my work, but also the pitfalls of being so personally engaged with my research topic. When I returned to conduct interviews in Canada and the United States, I made a point of accessing interviewees through professional contacts as much as possible, in an effort to reassert my own authority as a researcher, and also to maintain a certain distance between my own experiences and those of my family as part of the vast Iraqi diaspora. As Ruth Behar notes, writing and listening vulnerably flirts with the ultimate taboo in academia; it invites emotion into an academic setting.[24] Although my research is certainly devoid of "objectivity" in the traditional sense, striving to maintain an objective relationship to these women prevented this study from becoming a self-indulgent exercise.[25] Involving a translator who is also a close family member blurred the boundaries in ways that made me exceedingly uncomfortable, and yet opened up discussions of personal and intimate experiences that might otherwise have remained silenced. Displaying my vulnerability and involvement in the project is essential to understanding the organic development of the interview process, the multifaceted role of the translator, and how memories were recorded.[26]

The Ties That Divide: Negotiating Ethnoreligious Difference in the Interview

An interview conducted with a Sabean family in Amman highlighted the importance of ethnoreligious difference in shaping oral narratives as well as the realities of religious persecution and ongoing turmoil in the homeland.[27] Despite having ready access to networks of Muslim Arab and Kurdish Iraqi women in Amman, I faced an ongoing struggle to gain the trust and consent of Assyrian and Sabean families. Having worked with several community agencies (including Caritas and Mizan Law Group), I was eventually granted an introductory meeting with a Sabean family living in Amman's bustling first circle, a more traditional region of the city. There was no initial exchange by telephone between Om-Yasameen and the participant, and due to safety concerns I was urged to keep the identity and location of the family confidential. During the interview, the participant sat with her sons and spoke in a muted but monotone voice about the persecution her family had suffered and the family members she had lost over the past 30 years. Her official narrative differed significantly from that of the majority of my Arab interviewees in Amman, who, conforming to the official "myth of nation" narrative, detailed the unity between ethnoreligious groups and the freedoms and protections afforded to these groups by the state prior to the invasion of Iraq by US forces in 2003. Her narrative did not speak to the communal remembering of a united Iraq or a national bond between Iraqis. Instead she detailed the persecution of minority groups such as the Sabeans by the Ba'th government and thus constructed a formal counternarrative.[28]

Class and religious differences complicated how the translator and Shi'a/ Sabean minority participants negotiated their place within Iraq's collective past. The Sabean participant claimed that her personal reasons for leaving Iraq were to create better future opportunities for her sons. Having been informed in advance of the family's situation by the community worker who arranged the interview, I was aware that the family had suffered great personal trauma in Iraq, and concluded that her response to this question was a result of her desire to preserve the privacy of her family and prevent her trauma from becoming part of the public record. After the interview was over, Om-Yasameen began arguing with the Sabean woman in Arabic about the participant's version of the Iraqi past, culminating in a lengthy and heated debate. Their conflict over the place of non-Muslims in national collective memory quickly sparked the sharing of her subjective experience following the taped interview. The interviewee admitted to leaving Iraq due to death threats, and showed us evidence of ongoing threats sent from within Jordan by a fundamentalist Sunni militant group based in Iraq. She informed us that her sons had been unable to leave the apartment for months due to the nature of the threats. Informally, the participant detailed how her brother had been murdered in his home shortly before they decided to flee to a refugee camp on the border between Jordan and Iraq. Although the recorded interview contained a much different official account of ethnoreligious divides in Iraq's past, the counternarrative of trauma shielded the personal loss of the interviewee from the record.[29] In this particular case, proximity to the homeland informed the ways that life experiences were shared due to the physical threat of violence and the very recent loss of family members in the homeland. The immediate connection, both physical and emotional, to the homeland elicited a forthcoming account of state persecution and religious conflict, whereas the real physical threat of violence and the lived experience of trauma shaped a counternarrative shared only in the "third space," silencing personal trauma from the record.[30]

Om-Yasameen's participation within this interview space led the participant to construct a counternarrative about her lived experience. While her presence was certainly a contributing factor to the emotionally heightened tone of the postinterview exchange, without the negative reaction that she provoked, the contrasting account of persecution and loss would have remained off the record for fear of retribution. The interview with this Sabean family was especially indicative of the reality of retribution, resulting from an online video post made by one of the sons, which contained his filming of the assassination of Sabean Mandeans in Nasiriya by a radical Arab Sunni group. The family provided material proof of death threats left at the door of the apartment in Amman by members of this same radical militia group. As we left the interview, our cabdriver informed us that we were being followed, which served to highlight the imminent danger that this family faced on a daily basis. Although we were fortunate to escape unscathed, this interview greatly shaped how I dealt with discussions of fear, retribution, and loss in the interview space.[31]

The third space created a safe space within which marginalized minority experiences could be articulated beyond the recorded transcript. As a Muslim woman, Om-Yasameen herself is a product of nationalist colonial codes of power imprinted upon the Sunni middle classes in the homeland.[32] In her interactions with minority ethnoreligious Iraqi participants within the interview space, my stepmother embodied the colonizing force of the Iraqi national state, impeding the ability of certain participants to engage with their lived realities and personal experiences as persecuted minorities. These discursive transparencies are informed primarily by the Arab collective discourse of nationalism in Iraq, overlapping with imperial discourses of colonialism and the hegemonic male-dominated collective memories.[33] The layered hierarchy operating within this interview space, comprised of colonizer (British-born interviewer), subordinate colonial (Sunni upper-middle-class interpreter), and alien minority colonized (Sabean participant), might have resulted in the silencing of this woman's oral history. However, the third space invited the negotiation of female subjectivities because it was informed by these overlapping and competing codes of authority transposed from the homeland and enforced in diaspora.

The third space within the interview is perhaps best described as a feminine space where intimacies and personal subjectivities can be shared. Often, but not always "off the record," these exchanges highlight the many ways that women crafted narratives informed by masculine collective national memories as well as the trauma and loss they suffered under the Ba'th regime in Iraq. Om-Yasameen's presence in the interview allowed participants to use language to create this third space where personal accounts were modified in order to be kept off the official record of the interview. Traversing the space between the recorded and unrecorded material, interviewees manipulated the telling of life histories using language as a means of sharing secrets and intimacies. In interviews conducted without my stepmother's help, trauma, loss, and personal experiences were typically shared within the intimate and informal space following the taped interview, over coffee and sweets. In order to share these subjective pasts, women constructed these intimate spaces, enabling them to recount female experiences, their interpretations of the past, their place within the national and communal memory of the nation, and their subjective experiences as migrant women in diaspora.

Conclusion

As feminist oral historian Lynn Abrams notes, a focus on and respect for women's subjectivities helps correct the power imbalance in the interview space, and in official histories that marginalize women, gives equal weight to their experiences and interpretations.[34] In practice, however, Chandra Talpady Mohanty, Lila Abu-Lughod, and many other postcolonial feminists argue that the research methods employed by Western-trained feminist academics cater exclusively to secular constructions of womanhood, casting religious women as victims and diminishing the importance of their activism.[35] Incorporating a translator and facilitator from within the Iraqi community bridged these cultural and linguistic divides and served to correct the imbalance of authority and power within the interview space. Sharing authority with Om-Yasameen meant giving up control of the interview and embracing the unpredictable outcome of these exchanges as a vulnerable listener. In her role as cultural and linguistic translator, Om-Yasameen's presence and participation in the interview informed how female participants shaped narratives of migration and lived experience, uncovering personal trauma and unsilencing subjective pasts.

The complicated nature of my relationship with my stepmother, and her relationship with the participants, ultimately resulted in unsilencing the vulnerable realities of women on the margins of hegemonic collective memories. My family history and personal involvement in the project informed how the translator came to be a part of the interview space. The "personal" is essential to understanding how these interviews came to be, how they developed, and ultimately what was recorded.[36] Interviews with Sabean, Kurdish, and Arab Muslim women in Amman and Toronto suggest that it is essential to incorporate elements of both formal and informal narratives so that we may understand the whole, learning to "listen in stereo, receiving both dominant and muted channels clearly and tuning into them carefully to understand the relationship between them."[37] This process of "listening in stereo" to formal and informal and official and counternarratives enables us to reconstruct the composition of memory from women's experiences in the homeland as well as their gendered interpretations of nation and nationalisms and their lived realities of displacement. Ultimately, the third space is a site of resistance within which women can reproduce official narratives in conjunction with the subjective female experiences of trauma, war, and dislocation. Contesting the boundaries of ethical guidelines is an essential part of maintaining the authenticity of these voices by incorporating both recorded and unrecorded narratives in an effort to understand the intersecting realities that inform female migrants' lived experiences.

Notes

1. All names have been changed to protect the privacy of participants in this research project. Om-Yasameen translates loosely to "Yasameen's mother," which is a cultural term through which close friends or family members relate to parents according to their status as father, mother, or first-born child.
2. Interview by author, Jordan, Amman, September 22, 2008.
3. Franca Iacovetta, "Post-Modern Ethnography, Historical Materialism, and De-centring the (Male) Authorial Voice: A Feminist Conversation," *Histoire Sociale/Social History* 32, 64 (November 1999): 275–93.
4. Michael Frisch, *A Shared Authority: Essays on the Craft and Meaning of Oral and Public History* (Albany: State University of New York Press, 1990), 84–86; Stacey Zembrzycki, "Sharing Authority with Baba," *Journal of Canadian Studies* 43, 1 (Winter 2009): 219–38; Lisa Ndejuru, "Sharing Authority as Deep Listening and Sharing the Load," *Journal of Canadian Studies* 43, 1 (Winter 2009): 5–11.
5. Vijay Agnew, "A Diasporic Bounty: Cultural History and Heritage," in *Diaspora, Memory, and Identity: A Search for Home*, ed. Vijay Agnew (Toronto: University of Toronto Press, 2005), 171–87; Pamela Sugiman, "Memories of Internment: Narrating Japanese-Canadian Women's Life Stories," in *Diaspora, Memory, and Identity: A Search for Home*, ed. Vijay Agnew (Toronto: University of Toronto Press, 2005), 48–81; Isabel Kaprielian-Churchill, "*Odars* and 'Others': Intermarriage and the Retention of Armenian Ethnic Identity," in *Sisters or Strangers?: Immigrant, Ethnic, and Racialized Women in Canadian History*, eds. Marlene Epp, Franca Iacovetta, and Frances Swyripa (Toronto: University of Toronto Press, 2004), 341–65; Shahnaz Khan, *Zina, Transnational Feminism, and the Moral Regulation of Pakistani Women* (Vancouver: University of British Columbia Press, 2006).
6. Homi Bhabha, "DissemiNation: Time, Narrative, and the Margins of the Modern Nation," in *The Location of Culture*, ed. Homi Bhabha (London: Routledge, 1994); "The Third Space," in *Identity Community Culture Difference*, ed. Jonathon Rutherford (London: Lawrence and Wishart, 1990), 207–21.
7. See especially Eric Davis, *Memories of State: Politics, History, and Collective Identity in Modern Iraq* (Berkeley: University of California Press, 2005), 282–87.

8. This trend, regarding dual female perspectives, is elaborated in Kathryn Anderson and Dana Jack, "Learning to Listen: Interview Techniques and Analysis," in *Women's Words: The Feminist Practice of Oral History*, eds. Sherna Berger Gluck and Daphne Patai (New York: Routledge, 1991), 11.

9. Lynn Abrams, *Oral History Theory* (London: Routledge, 2010), 74.

10. Chandra Talpady Mohanty, "Under Western Eyes: Feminist Scholarship and Colonial Discourses," in *Third World Women and the Politics of Feminism*, eds. Chandra Mohanty, Ann Russo, and Lourdes Torres (Bloomington: Indiana University Press, 1991), 51–80; Lila Abu-Lughod, "Do Muslim Women Really Need Saving? Anthropological Reflections on Cultural Relativism and its Others," *American Anthropologist* 104, 3 (2002): 785.

11. Stacey Zembrzycki discusses how sharing authority with a third participant can create a more intimate setting, but at the same time this dynamic shapes the flow of discussions and can often change how narrators reconstruct shared memories: "Sharing Authority with Baba," 225.

12. The class structure in Iraq is defined according to the position of one family to the next, especially in disapora where class hierarchies are disrupted and realigned according to new fortunes and successes in the host country. An exhaustive description of the formation of the class structure in Iraq can be found in Hanna Batatu, *The Old Social Classes and the Revolutionary Movements of Iraq: A Study of Iraq's Old Landed and Commercial Classes and of its Communists, Ba'thists, and Free Officers* (Princeton, NJ: Princeton University Press, 1978).

13. See especially 'Ali Al-Wardi, *A Study of the Nature of Iraqi Society* (Baghdad: Matba'at al-'Ani, 1965); Sana Al-Khayyat, *Honor and Shame: Women in Modern Iraq* (London: Al-Saqi Books, 1990).

14. Om-Yasameen also brought an additional element of legitimacy through her own family background to the research, since her father was the renowned historian Dr. Salih 'Ahmad Al-'Ali, former president of the Iraqi Academy (Baghdad), and recognized throughout the Middle East for his work in establishing the foundations for British-style universities in the developing oil-rich Emirates. Political historian Eric Davis documents Dr. Al-'Ali in Davis, *Memories of State*, 250–51.

15. Interview by author, Jordan, Amman, September 12, 2008.

16. The regulation of femininity and sexuality by diasporic communities as well as Western onlookers has become the focus in women's histories of diasporic groups in North America. A discussion of female modesty as it relates to the example of Iraqi women can be found in: Shanaz Khan, *Aversion and Desire: Negotiating Muslim Female Identity in the Diaspora* (Toronto: Women's Press, 2002); Yvonne Haddad, "Islamic Values among American Muslims," in *Family and Gender among American Muslims: Issues Facing Middle Eastern Immigrants and Their Descendants*, eds. B. Bilge and Barbara Aswad (Philadelphia: Temple University Press, 1996), 1–13; Fatima Mernissi, *Beyond the Veil: Male-Female Dynamics in Modern Muslim Society* (Bloomington: Indiana University Press, 1987); Nadje Al-Ali, *Iraqi Women: Untold Stories from 1948 to the Present* (London: Zed Books, 2007).

17. Traversing between the cultural gulf of East and West is discussed in Salman Rushdie, *East, West* (New York: Vintage Books, Vintage International, 1996); R. Radhakrishnan, *Diasporic Mediations: Between Home and Location* (Minneapolis: University of Minnesota Press, 1996).

18. The colonial stereotype and the Orientalist construction of "other" derives from Edward Said's discourse and is further complicated by Homi Bhabha's commentary on the structured condition of ambivalence and simultaneous alienation of the colonial subject. See Said, *Orientalism* (London: Routledge and Kegan Paul, 1979); Bhabha, "The Other Question: Difference, Discrimination and the Discourse of Colonialism," in *Out There: Marginalization and Contemporary Cultures*, eds. Russell Ferguson, Martha Gever, et al. (Cambridge, MA: MIT Press, 1990), 71–88. Shanaz Khan discusses the specific ways that Muslim and Arab women are shaped by the simultaneous alienation that occurs at the nexus of desire and aversion, in *Aversion and Desire*.

19. Yasmin Husein Al-Jawaheri, *Women in Iraq: The Gender Impact of International Sanctions* (London: Boulder, 2008), 1–10.

20. Al-Ali, *Iraqi Women*, 744–45.

21. The definition of this word is somewhat contentious and certainly derogatory. The literal meaning of the term "*sharqi/sharqiyya*" means "Eastern" as in "East of the Euphrates," and in its modern usage it refers to poor Southern Iraqi farmers, the majority of whom were Shi'i Arabs who migrated to Baghdad in the 1930s and 1940s. As they formed slums on the outskirts of Baghdad, they were referred to as "*shargawi*" or "*shroogie.*" This derogatory term remains in the daily vocabulary (unofficially) of middle-class Sunni and Christian Iraqis when referencing the poor and peasant class of Iraq. The term retains its original ethnic connotations even when it is used in reference to other ethnic or racial groups. This is a slang term and thus is not cited in most academic texts. This information was compiled from a number of different oral sources.

22. Interview by author, Jordan, Amman, September 26, 2008.

23. Interview by author, Jordan, Amman, September 25, 2008.

24. Ruth Behar, *The Vulnerable Observer: Anthropology that Breaks your Heart* (Boston: Beacon Press, 1996), 19. Also see the chapters in part II of this collection.

25. Valerie Yow, "'Do I Like Them too Much?': Effects of the Oral History Interview on the Interviewer and Vice-Versa," in *The Oral History Reader*, second edition, eds. Robert Perks and Alistair Thomson (London: Routledge, 1998), 63.

26. Behar, *The Vulnerable Observer*, 14–15.

27. The ongoing struggle of the Sabeans in Iraq is detailed in Ma'oz Moshe, *Middle Eastern Minorities: Between Integration and Conflict* (Washington: Washington Institute for Near East Policy, 1999), 71–91.

28. Interview by author with Sabean family, Jordan, Amman, September 30, 2008.

29. Interview by author, Jordan, Amman, September 30, 2008.

30. J. D. Cohon, "Psychological Adaptation and Dysfunction Among Refugees," *International Migration Review* 15, 1 (1991): 255–75; J. Dyal and Y. Dyal, "Acculturation, Stress and Coping: Some Implications for Research and Education," *International Journal of Intercultural Relations* 5 (1981): 301–28.

31. Iraqis continue to live in fear of retribution generations after leaving the homeland, owing mainly to their ongoing ties to communities, family, and friends in Iraq. In the most recent displacement of refugees, these threats have become a reality, as many have suffered the loss of loved ones and acquaintances in the sectarian violence that continues to destabilize the country. In interviews with Iraqi women, approximately 80 percent of interviewees reported having lost family or

friends as a result of the Ba'th regime's repressive policies or in the most recent violence following its overthrow. My own family has suffered these threats, and my own life course was, in turn, shaped by the Ba'th regime's totalitarian presence in family life and the impossibility of maintaining relationships across national borders without the threat of suspicion and pending retribution upon close family members. In my dissertation, I also discuss the important presence of this fear of retribution in determining expatriate voting outcomes in North America, and how this ultimately shapes the diasporic citizen and the ways that Iraqis continue to connect with the homeland. Also see Joseph Sassoon, *The Iraqi Refugees: The New Crisis in the Middle East* (London: I.B. Taurus, 2009), 23–31.

32. Khan, *Aversion and Desire*, 3.

33. The distribution and arrangement of differential spaces and the overlapping codes of authority are discussed in Homi Bhabha, "Signs Taken for Wonders: Questions of Ambivalence and Authority under a Tree outside Delhi, May 1917," in *The Location of Culture*, ed. Homi Bhabha (London: Routledge, 1994), 109.

34. Abrams, *Oral History Theory*, 74.

35. Mohanty, "Under Western Eyes," 51–80; Abu-Lughod, "Do Muslim Women Really Need Saving?," 785.

36. Behar, *The Vulnerable Observer*, 14–15.

37. Anderson and Jack, "Learning to Listen," 11.

CHAPTER 10

"If you'd told me you wanted to talk about the '60s, I wouldn't have called you back": Reflections on Collective Memory and the Practice of Oral History

Nancy Janovicek

The cultural memory of the 1960s is a preoccupation in recent scholarship. Revisionist histories that challenge the progressive narrative of the decade argue that a romantic and uncomplicated collective memory of it makes interviews with political activists from this period unreliable. My current research project is about the back-to-the-land movement in the West Kootenays of British Columbia in the 1960s and 1970s. This region, located in the southeast part of Canada's most western province, became a hub of the countercultural back-to-the-land movement. Back-to-the-landers were attracted to this bucolic area because land was cheap. They also built relationships with the Doukhobors and the Quakers, communities that had moved to the region in the early and mid-twentieth century and shared the back-to-the-land movement's commitment to simplicity, self-reliance, and sustainability. I am interested in how the back-to-the-land community transformed the political, cultural, and economic landscapes of the region. In the 1970s, logging was the primary industry and the area suffered high unemployment due to the precariousness of mill closures. By the end of the 1980s, tourism became one of the most important industries, in part because of the influence of the rural counterculture. Promotion of the area as a tourist destination not only rests on the natural beauty of the area, but also invokes stereotypical images of "aging hippies" and the counterculture. The deeply political motivations of people who went back to the land are overshadowed by romantic 1960s narratives.

Interviews and "off-the-record" discussions with people who were involved in radical politics and countercultural communities have compelled me to question academic warnings about 1960s nostalgia. The need to interrogate scholarly skepticism about the usefulness of interviews with New Left activists became even clearer when I contacted Corky Evans to ask him about a community-based forest management project that he directed in the 1970s. When he responded to my message, he asked me how I had heard about the project, and how it fit into my research. After I described my interest in how the politics of the "new homesteaders" shaped economic and social changes in the West Kootenays, he said, "If you'd told me you wanted to talk about the '60s, I wouldn't have called you back." Although he did not want to revisit these difficult memories, he was excited to talk about his involvement in helping Slocan Valley residents become interested in sustainable forestry practices. According to him, this had been a moment of political possibility.[1] Other people who I have interviewed for this project talk about how the political ideas that came out of the 1960s influenced their decision to live an intentional lifestyle based on self-sufficiency and sustainability, but they share Evans's pragmatic analysis of the politics of "the long sixties."

Many of the interviews that I have conducted to date challenge the assumption that the cultural memory of the 1960s dominates all personal memories of the period.[2] As oral historians, we must question whether trendy academic skepticism impacts how we recruit narrators, how we listen to them, and how we analyze the data we collect from them. Colleagues joke about making sure that my "bullshit detector" is on when interviewing political activists from the 1960s generation. This advice flies in the face of my training, which emphasized respect, ethical obligations, and gratitude to the people who open their homes and share their stories.[3] Trust is the foundation of a good interview. Researchers have political and moral responsibilities to victims of political and social dislocation.[4] This is also true of projects involving people who are not "vulnerable narrators."[5]

In this chapter, I offer some reflections on how the cultural memory of the 1960s might influence the relationship between researcher and narrator. I begin with a discussion of skepticism about the reliability of people's memories about this decade. Recent reevaluations of the radical politics are a needed corrective to idealistic histories of the period, often written by people who were involved in those politics. But not all of those who were engaged in radical 1960s politics share a nostalgic analysis that is entrenched in popular history and culture. My narrators spoke about how broader politics informed their actions, but their investment in placing themselves in the local history of the area is just as important as the "sixties" narrative. I conclude with some old lessons from oral history theory to guide us through the skeptical scholarly stance that has developed in response to the simplified—and commercialized—cultural memory of the 1960s.

The Contested Legacies of the 1960s

My own research fits "uncomfortably" with the history of the 1960s, and therefore conversations with people have compelled me to question the prevailing periodization, which views the decade as a pivotal moment that defines our times. Although the migration of "new homesteaders" to the Kootenays began in the mid-1960s, the majority of my interviewees moved to the area in the 1970s.[6] Most of the political projects that I am interested in—those pertaining to the environment and sustainable economic development, alternative education, and feminism—also began in the 1970s. "The long sixties" attempts to recognize the precursors to the social movements of the decade and the continuing impact of "the Sixties generation." Yet this focus on youth does not capture connections to local history or the intergenerational cooperation that people in the Kootenays identify as important. While I do not consider myself to be a "sixties scholar," this is the historiography that informs my research. This section discusses how a reevaluation of the decade informs a skeptical stance toward the memory of those who lived through the decade and the ways that interviews compel me to question the dominant themes in the historiography on youth and generational conflict.

Historians interested in the late twentieth century are debating the legacy and meanings of the 1960s. Popular culture has generally ignored the complexities and contradictions of the period, focusing instead on youth culture, political protest, and, of course, an uncomplicated celebration of sex, drugs, and rock and roll. To some extent, this popular misrepresentation of the period has been reinforced by the first wave of historical scholarship about the 1960s, produced by former student activists who laid the narrative groundwork as the decade moved "from memory to history."[7] Emphasizing the impact of student activism and movements for social justice, this literature seeks to understand the legacies of social protest. While some have asked how the political activism of the decade laid the foundation for social and political gains in subsequent years, others examine how the hope of the early 1960s gave way to rage, violence, and political apathy.[8]

In recent years, some historians have rejected this focus on progressive politics, arguing that the idea of the 1960s, which has been carefully guarded by former student leaders, has precluded any meaningful discussion of the period. In referencing the celebration of mind-altering drugs during the 1960s, Gerard de Groot states that "time has proved an equally effective hallucinogen. As years go by, real events have given way to imagined constructs."[9] The social memory of the 1960s, this scholarship argues, can only be protected by preserving a social amnesia about the conservative political opinions and acceptance of Cold War politics that were just as prominent at the time.

These calls for a more nuanced history are reasonable. Evidence demonstrates that most people were not drawn to student groups or left politics, and historical research about conservatism is necessary to make sense of the continuities and changes in late-twentieth-century political and cultural history. Analysis of inter-generational cooperation complicates the dominant historiographical narratives that focus on generational conflict and youthful protest.[10] But what seems to me to be unreasonable is how these skeptical accounts of the impact of student and youth activism in the New Left tend to dismiss the memories of people involved in these politics. Critical analysis of the cultural memory, and concomitant social amnesia, about the 1960s is producing a necessary counternarrative to romantic recollections, which insists that this was a moment of political possibility and hope that it will never be repeated. Kristin Ross's important and provocative analysis of the "management of May's memory" is one example. She argues that the intellectual investment in keeping students at the center of the 1968 Paris general strike, by both left and conservative pundits, is a historical problem that must be unpacked to truly appreciate its legacy. She explained why she decided not to interview participants in the events:

> "Whom would I have interviewed? To convey something of the nature of a mass event, I was reluctant to turn to the people who have become major figures in the legends of May culture by virtue of the attention that has already been accorded them, many of whom can now be seen occupying those choice positions within the structure of power that are reserved especially for people who once publicly accused it?"[11]

I have no objections to her methodological decision to focus on the written record; historians do not have to interview people just because they are still alive. Yet her dismissal of the usefulness of interviewing 1960s radicals echoes early opposition to the reliability of oral history.[12]

I have also noticed this cynicism, about interviewing 1960s activists, at conferences and departmental colloquia. When doctoral students began to present conference papers about the 1960s that used oral histories, they faced questions about the reliability of the memories of their narrators. I recall one delegate who quipped that he was thinking about writing a methodological piece called "Why I never want to interview another 60s radical." The assump-tion behind these questions is that the narrators are always too nostalgic about the 1960s and are always aggrandizing their own participation in events. These are fair questions, and in some cases people do put themselves at the center of events when they played a less prominent role.[13] But for quite some time now, oral history theory has argued that the value of this approach is not only in the facts that can be gleaned from interviews, but also in the meanings produced by the relationship between personal and collective memories. Why is there a tendency to forget these theoretical insights when new scholars interview "the sixties generation?"

My interviews and encounters with Kootenay residents have led me to believe that these historiographical debates reflect a generational conflict within academia better than they do a shared nostalgia for the 1960s. Each generation rewrites history, but often the aim to advance historiographical debates is presented as an inherently "better history" that rejects the insights of foundational scholarship.[14] Moreover, cynicism about memories of the 1960s does not adequately consider how gender, class, and race shape them, an insight established by feminist oral historians many years ago.[15] The dominant narrative in the historiography also traps this generation in their youth. Focusing on student politics and youthful rebellion fails to recognize that these radicals took on adult responsibilities that often compelled them to modify their politics and change their lifestyles. For many of those who moved from the United States, protecting their children from increasing urban violence and drug use in communes was their key motivation for migrating. Canadians who moved from urban centers have talked about raising their children in a cleaner environment and growing food to ensure that their children ate well.[16]

During my travels in the Kootenays, I have met back-to-the-landers whose stories follow the popularized narratives of the 1960s and others who are modest and uncertain about the historical value of their experiences. When I interviewed Patricia Bambrick, for instance, she recalled her first meeting with me: "I think when I first saw you ... I felt almost cynical or defensive or something, what the heck. Also maybe feeling old, I mean, oh my god, I'm old enough to be having a history! (Laughter from both.) And to have done something of historical value, that was scary."[17] We first met at her friend's house, where I have stayed during two research trips. Bambrick asked me questions about my interest in the back-to-the-land movement and how I planned to approach the topic. I explained that my project explored the long-term impact of the back-to-the-landers on the social, cultural, and economic changes in the region and that I was more interested in relationships and coalitions that people built in the community than the countercultural experiments people created to exist outside of and in opposition to mainstream society. Reflecting on this meeting, I now realize that she was interviewing me before she agreed to be involved in the project. Her initial cynicism and defensiveness may have also been a reaction to the commercialization of 1960s nostalgia and the concomitant "gen x" disdain of the continued influence of the boomers in popular culture.[18] People also decide whether or not their life story belongs to the history I want to tell. Bambrick's initial concern, that her life was not of historical significance, suggests that she did not see her life portrayed in the dominant narratives of protest and self-indulgence. Perhaps asking me about my research was a way to determine whether I was listening to her when she shared her life with me, or if I was looking for stories to fit into a predetermined narrative.

When I talk to potential interviewees about the project, I tell them that I am less interested in "sex, drugs, and rock and roll" than I am in the political and economic goals of the back-to-the-land movement. I do think that farming, family, and feminism are inherently more interesting than the stereotypes about the period. But I also tell people about my interests to build trust. This surely influences how they prepare for the interview, but I also think that it has made people willing to talk to me. In some cases, like my first conversations with Bambrick and Evans, people have interviewed me before they agree to be a part of this project. They seem to be more receptive to sharing their memories when they are sure I take seriously the long-term impact of the political and economic alternatives they hoped to create. I also emphasize my interest in how they shaped local politics. Locating them in the place where many continue to live, rather than in the collective memory of the 1960s, means that I enter the interview attentive to what they will say.[19]

Back to the Kootenays

This is not the first time that I have been a researcher in the West Kootenays. Nelson was one of the case studies for my book about rural and small-town campaigns to open transition houses for abused women, a study that is based on my doctoral research.[20] Feminism thrived in the rural areas of the Kootenays, and most of the organizers of the Nelson and District Women's Centre, the first rural women's center in Canada, were from the back-to-the-land movement.[21] Almost all of the activists whom I interviewed during my doctoral studies lived rurally and moved to the Kootenays in the late 1960s and early 1970s. When I spoke to these women, I became intrigued by their decision to become farmers when they were in their twenties, in part because I grew up on a family farm and could not wait to move to the city at that time in my life. Based on my previous research in the area, I also knew that feminists formed coalitions with groups that did not always share their politics in order to develop services for abused women. This was necessary during the 1980s, because the Social Credit government would not fund new transition houses, and the 1983 Solidarity Coalition, a provincial protest to the drastic cuts under this government, was another opportunity for the newcomers to build political relationships with the community.

I came to this research with a critical analysis of the standard narrative that the early 1960s were days of hope and the 1970s were a time when radicals who became disillusioned, turned inward, and disengaged from politics.[22] The notion that the back-to-the-land movement is an example of the abandonment of the radical possibilities of the New Left is entrenched in the literature even though more recent research is challenging this uniform depiction of rural countercultural communities.[23] My frustration with the dismissal of the political possibilities of the back-to-the-land movement informs the ways that I have developed research relationships with Kootenays activists. The women I met during my doctoral studies are still political activists, and for this reason many of my interview questions pertain to politics. The relationships I established in my previous research no doubt influence how I recruit people. When I returned to the Kootenays, I visited the women's center, and reconnected with some of the women I had interviewed before. They have since referred me to people in their social and political networks.[24]

Analyzing the changing economy of the region is another key theme of this project. Urban refugees came to the Kootenays because land was cheap. When property in areas, which were hubs of the back-to-the-land movement in the United States, became more expensive, people migrated north. Similarly, when they could no longer afford land on the west coast, the interior of British Columbia and Nova Scotia became more attractive.[25] Communes that pushed the boundaries of social respectability were an important part of the region's transformation from a staid, resource-based community to a countercultural haven. Conflicts between the "hippies" and "the locals" attracted media attention. But these sensational stories about nudity, drug use, and youthful rebellion do not capture the complexity of the economic and political alternatives that the new homesteaders were trying to create. As Bob Ploss, who moved from California in the mid-1960s, explained in an email: "The economic side of alternate living was largely ignored by the outside world—the sex drugs and rock/roll stories were much more entertaining and vastly more likely to sell newspapers."[26] My interest in the movement's economic context is also based in my own background, as the daughter and sister of farmers. When we talk about organic farming, I tell people that I grew up on a cash crop farm, which was not organic. When they learn about my background, many become more relaxed, probably because they realize that I understand the precariousness of farm economies and the difficult work involved in farming.[27]

My questions focus on their experiences when they came to the Kootenays. Many people recall that the ideas of the 1960s and early 1970s influenced their decision to try to live an alternative lifestyle, and made it possible for them to do so. But what has struck me most is how people who have stayed in the area are more concerned with locating themselves in the history of the community rather than in a collective history of the 1960s. They are activists, and are also an inspiration for the most recent migration of young people who have moved to the area to live off of the land. The back-to-the-land movement has become part of the area's local history as well as tourism promotion. It is more important to be aware of how people want their contributions to local history to be remembered. Rather than the cultural memory of the radical 1960s, this is what shapes how they frame their stories.

Local Histories, Collective Memory, Sharing Authority

Sharing authority is a central theme in this collection. Developing collaborative projects that make the community a partner in all stages of research seeks to bridge the divisions between university-trained historians and the communities with which they work.[28] Early proponents of oral history explained that it gave voice to the powerless.[29] Sharing authority moves beyond giving voice to marginalized people, and compels oral historians to recognize that, as Alessandro Portelli states in the afterword to this volume, narrators give voice to us. Reflecting on his long collaborations with three of his narrators, Portelli explains that researchers should not always assume that their interest in the lives of ordinary people makes them realize the significance of their lives.[30] We are also empowered if we listen carefully to the stories people tell about their lives. If we do this and earn their trust, narrators give us not just their stories; their insights guide our analyses too. Unequal power relationships cannot be addressed if researchers assume that they are the experts who give voice to the marginalized.

Many of my interviewees are modest about the historical significance of their lives. There are, however, a number of local and public history projects that commemorate the back-to-the-land movement in the region. Some narrators have preserved newspapers, records, and ephemera from their political activism, and their history is scattered in the basements of the region. My university-based research project asks different questions than local histories, which commemorate their successes. Nevertheless, speaking to people in the community has influenced my project's design, particularly its focus on coalitions and the relationships that back-to-the-landers developed with their neighbors.

In her history of the Slocan Valley, which describes the Kootenays as a "hippie nirvana," Kathleen Gordon argues that by the end of the 1970s, the counterculture "had become absorbed into the valley's way of life."[31] Although Nelson's reputation as an interesting place to visit rests in part on the young and old hippies who congregate at the coffee houses and parks, and who continue to hitchhike on the country highways, the place of the counterculture in local history is contested. This is perhaps best illustrated by the 2004 debate about the proposal to erect a monument to Vietnam War draft-resisters in Nelson, British Columbia. A Fox-TV News report about the plan to build it drew vitriolic responses from veterans' associations in the United States.[32] Worried about the negative impact this would have on tourism, the municipal government withdrew its support for the project, and the monument has not been displayed publically. The cultural components of the back-to-the-land movement, which could be commercialized as part of the tourist industry, have become part of the local culture. There is reticence about the political challenges to social and economic inequalities that the newcomers introduced.

Within the countercultural community, there is division about the impact of the Vietnam draft resisters and other Americans who moved to the area. Some, but not all, people who moved from the United States argue that the American tradition of assertive politics they introduced to the area ended the community's passive political culture. Canadians have expressed frustration with the emphasis placed on the importance of Americans in recent local histories. They question the war resistors' impact on the area because many of them were the children of wealthy Americans and they were more interested in protecting themselves from military service than progressive politics. Rita Moir, who moved from Lethbridge, Alberta, to the Slocan Valley in the early 1970s, argues that focusing on the legacy of opposition to the war and American migration to the region ignores the fact that many people came from Canadian cities. According to her, the prairie cooperative tradition was more influential in her politics, as well as the Kootenays, than 1960s student radicalism.[33] In addition, people who were raised in the Kootenays were drawn to the lifestyles and politics of the local counterculture, and they found the roots for their politics in local labor organizations. They became an important bridge between the newcomers and longtime residents in environmental campaigns, negotiations to keep logging jobs in the area, and protests against government cuts to local services. In interviews, people have talked about the conflicts they had with people who were upset by the new ideas and lifestyles the counterculture introduced to the region. But they also insist that they were able to create coalitions with older political groups. Many people in the Slocan Valley bought old Doukhobor homesteads, recalling how this community taught them the rural skills they needed when they first arrived. The desire to find a place in a longer tradition of political dissidence in the region is not new. I was surprised and intrigued by the number of articles about local history in the alternative newspapers from the 1970s.

In recent years, the community has organized reunions and events to commemorate its past. In 2006, the "Our Way Home Peace Event and Reunion," held in Castlegar, brought together peace activists and Vietnam War draft resistors, and featured a performance by Buffy Sainte-Marie and a lecture by Tom Hayden. In August 2009, Argenta organized a reunion of students who had attended the Friends School. Filmmaker Peter Schramm, who was five when his parents moved to Argenta in 1970, attended the event to interview people for a film he is making about the optimism of the countercultural community.[34] Bob Ploss maintains a public Facebook page, "Slocan Valley

1968–1988," to reconnect with people who have left the area, encouraging them to post photographs, memories, and artifacts because "[those] who once made a community are older, and some have scattered. Their kids are now having kids. Let's share and laugh about how silly we were, back in the day."[35] Marcia Braundy, who was active in many Slocan Valley projects, has launched *Kootenay Feminism*, a digital history of feminist activism in the region.[36] To commemorate the fortieth anniversary of the construction of the Vallican Whole Community Centre, which was also home to the alternative school organized by back-to-the-land parents, she curated an exhibit, entitled *Building the Building—Building the Community*. When the back-to-the-land community built this center in 1972, it was quite controversial. Those who worried about the negative influence of the counterculture on the valley used it as an example of how government funds were being wasted and criticized the alternative lifestyles of the new homesteaders.[37] In the past 40 years, it has hosted political meetings, concerts, weddings, funerals, and educational programs that promote rural skills and self-sufficiency. Braundy helped to build the center and was a teacher at the school. As the title of the exhibit makes clear, she considers the building to be the foundation of her community.

I am one of many researchers who have been drawn to the West Kootenays and most of those I have interviewed have been involved in more than one project about the back-to-the-land movement.[38] I wonder whether some people have become weary of continued requests for interviews about the counterculture. Does the interview process shape how they think about their experiences after the interview? In one case, a woman who moved to Argenta in the early 1970s decided that she was not really a back-to-the-lander because she also worked in Nelson. She generously introduced me to people whom she believes are better suited for my project because they have maintained a self-sufficient lifestyle and continue to live off-grid, and even drove me to a farmer's field and invited him over for lunch so that I could interview him. She also informed me that Kathleen Rodgers, who is examining the influence of American back-to-the-landers on regional politics, had interviewed her. Perhaps she did not want to be a narrator for another project, or perhaps reflecting on her experiences made her less willing to identify as part of the back-to-the-land movement.[39]

Lessons from Oral History Theory

The relationship between individuals and collective memory is an essential question in oral history theory and practice. Lynn Abrams explains that we interview people for four reasons: to find out "what happened, how they felt about it, how they recall it, and what wider public memory they draw upon."[40]

Historians play a role in creating the public memory that shapes how people narrate their lives. As oral historians, we are trained to be aware that people will place emphasis on certain events, and likewise forget others, based on how historical events are collectively recalled or how they have been judged by history. There is an assumption that people who were young in the 1960s shape their narratives according to the popularized tropes of the period. But perhaps that is what we are listening for. The emerging critique of the historiographical emphasis on the progressive politics and antiauthoritarian ethos of the 1960s will certainly create new spaces for those who cannot fit their own personal experiences into the accepted and commercial memory of the period. But we need to pay attention to how the frustration with 1960s nostalgia, which seems to be gaining ground in academic circles, influences research relationships between younger oral historians and research participants.

My own experiences interviewing back-to-the-landers inform my frustration with the cynical attitudes that are becoming more common in the historiography of the baby boom generation. Reflecting on my first research trip to the Kootenays, I confess that I expected to encounter "aging hippies" who would explain why their generation's political, musical, and cultural contributions were superior to the apathetic conservatism that preceded and followed their youth. Instead, I met men and women who are quite reflective about the possibilities and limitations of their political and social experiments in the 1960s and 1970s. They laugh at their youthful naivety and mistakes. They insist on the importance of the legacy of the political dissidence of previous generations, and speak optimistically about the potential of young people, who have moved to the area as part of the more recent wave of the back-to-the land movement, to make meaningful change. These people have taught me to approach my interviews with humility so that I will hear the unexpected narratives that do not conform to the historiography.

Collective memory shapes individual recollections, but personal stories do not always depend on shared history.[41] In conversations and interviews about the impact of the counterculture in the Kootenays, people emphasize different aspects of political organizing, depending on their engagement in current politics. They have divergent memories of the relationships they had with the established community. The 1960s radicals grew up, and their politics changed. The debates and divisions about watersheds, logging, and the environment are part of the collective history that shapes their stories about the Kootenays, not a nostalgic recollection of the political possibilities of 1960s student protests. What has surprised me the most is the sadness that some people have expressed about the local political disputes that have deeply divided their community. The only way to make space for people to talk about these difficult issues is to pay attention to how local circumstances influence the ways they make sense of their place in the past.

The advice to never trust a 1960s radical seems to me to be unfair. Although a few historians continue to dismiss the validity of oral history, it is now established as a methodology that requires specific skills and training. Academics have not rejected the usefulness of oral history to understand war veterans, political leaders, and ordinary people from previous generations. There is a rich oral history theory that explains self-censorship, performance, and memory. And it has long been accepted that meaning is more important than factual accuracy. As Portelli argued in 1981, "Errors, inventions, and myths lead us through and beyond facts to their meanings."[42] Oral history's greatest strength is the unreliability of stories. The current emphasis on critiquing the management of the meaning of the 1960s is leading to an unwarranted skepticism over the experiences of politically engaged people. How people connect to and reject these narratives should play a role in the reevaluation of the 1960s, and will also influence the ways that we understand continuities and differences with previous and later politics.

Notes

1. Conversation with Corky Evans, July 16, 2010.
2. I have interviewed 31 people so far; 4 are with people who grew up in back-to-the-land families.
3. Nancy Janovicek, "Oral History and Ethical Practice: Towards Effective Policies and Procedures," *Journal of Academic Ethics* 4 (2006): 157–74.
4. Victoria Sanford and Asale Angel-Ajani, eds., *Engaged Observer: Anthropology, Advocacy, and Activism* (New Brunswick, NJ: Rutgers University Press, 2006). Also see the chapters by Alexander Freund, Sherna Berger Gluck, Julie Cruikshank and Tatiana Argounova-Low, Stacey Zembrzycki, and Nadia Jones-Gailani in this volume.
5. Joy Parr defines "vulnerable narrators" as "those who agree to speak with us not knowing what they will tell." See Parr, "'Don't Speak For Me': Practicing Oral History Amidst the Legacies of Conflict," *Journal of the Canadian Historical Association* 21, 1 (2010): 7.
6. About 420 people moved to the Slocan Valley between 1966 and 1971, a trend that reversed 13 years of population decline in the area. See Myrna Kostash, *Long Way from Home: The Story of the Sixties Generation in Canada* (Toronto: James Lorimer & Company Publishers, 1980), 118.
7. David Farber, "Introduction," in *The Sixties: From Memory to History*, ed. David Farber (Chapel Hill: University of North Carolina Press, 1994), 1–10.
8. Van Gosse and Richard Mose, eds., *The World the Sixties Made: Politics and Culture in Recent America* (Philadelphia: Temple University Press, 2003).
9. Gerard de Groot, *The Sixties Unplugged: A Kaleidoscopic History of a Disorderly Decade* (Cambridge MA: Harvard University Press, 2008), 1.
10. Catherine Gidney, "War and the Concept of Generation: The International Teach-Ins at the University of Toronto, 1965–1968," in *Cultures, Communities, and Conflict: Histories of Canadian Universities and War*, eds. Paul Stortz and Lisa

Panayotidis (Toronto: University of Toronto Press, 2012), 272–94; Van Gosse, *Rethinking the New Left: An Interpretive History* (New York: Palgrave Macmillan, 2005).

11. Kristin Ross, *May 68 and its Afterlives* (Chicago: University of Chicago Press, 2002), 17.

12. This is not the case for all 1960s scholarship. See, e.g., Luisa Passerini, *Autobiography of a Generation: Italy, 1968* (Hanover: University Press of New England, 1996); Stuart Henderson, *Making the Scene: Yorkville and Hip Toronto in the 1960s* (Toronto: University of Toronto Press, 2011); Jessica Squires, "A Refuge from Militarism? The Canadian Movement to Assist Vietnam Era Draft Resisters and Government Responses, 1965–1973" (PhD diss., Carleton University, 2009).

13. See Joan Sangster, "Telling Our Stories: Feminist Debates and the Use of Oral History," *Women's Review of History* 3, 1 (1994): 5–27.

14. My thanks to Joan Sangster for asking me this question at the "Off the Record" Workshop. She elucidates on the generational divisions in the introduction of her most recent book: *Through Feminist Eyes: Essays on Canadian Women's History* (Edmonton: Athabasca University Press, 2011).

15. Sherna Berner Gluck and Daphne Patai, eds., *Women's Words: The Feminist Practice of Oral History* (New York: Routledge, 1991).

16. Sharon Weaver's narrators shared similar concerns: "Coming from Away: The Back-to-the-Land Movement in Cape Breton in the 1970s" (MA thesis, University of New Brunswick, 2004).

17. Patricia Bambrick, interview with author, Nelson, British Columbia, November 1, 2010.

18. One recent example is "No Country for Old Men: Baby boomers: drop the watercolours, back away slowly," *This Magazine* (March–April 2009).

19. My thanks to Linda Shopes for helping me clarify my thinking on the relationship between local history and collective memories.

20. Nancy Janovicek, *No Place to Go: Local Histories of the Battered Women's Shelter Movement* (Vancouver: University of British Columbia Press, 2007).

21. For examples of the range of feminist activities in the region, see "Kootenay Feminism," http://kootenayfeminism.com/index.php (accessed August 8, 2011).

22. Todd Gitlan, *The Sixties: Years of Hope, Days of Rage* (New York: Bantam, 1987); David Farber, ed., *The Sixties: From Memory to History* (Chapel Hill: University of North Caroline Press, 1994); Gosse and Mose, *The World the Sixties Made*; Kostash, *Long Way from Home*; Bryan Palmer, *Canada's 1960s: The Ironies of Identity in a Rebellious Era* (Toronto: University of Toronto Press, 2009); Mark Kurlansky, *1968: The Year That Rocked the World* (New York: Random House Paperbacks, 2005).

23. Doug Owram, *Born at the Right Time: A History of the Baby-Boom Generation* (Toronto: University of Toronto Press, 1996); Kostash, *Long Way from Home*; Sean Mills, *The Empire Within: Postcolonial Thought and Political Activism in Sixties Montreal* (Montreal & Kingston: McGill-Queen's University Press, 2010); Stuart Henderson, "Off of the Streets and into the Fortress: Experiments in Hip Separatism at Toronto's Rochdale College," *Canadian Historical Review* 92, 1 (March 2011): 107–33; Michael William Doyle and Peter Braunstein, eds.,

Imagine Nation: the American Counterculture of the 1960s and 1970s (New York: Routledge, 2002); Sharon Weaver, "First Encounters: 1970s Back-to-the-Land, Cape Breton, NS and Denman, Hornby and Lasqueti Islands, BC," *Oral History Forum d'histoire orale* 30 (2010): 1–30; Andrew G. Kirk, *Counterculture Green: The Whole Earth Catalog and American Environmentalism* (Lawrence: University of Kansas Press, 2007); Jinny A. Turman-Deal, "'We were an oddity': A Look at the Back-to-the-Land Movement in Appalachia," *West Virginia History* 4, 1 (Spring 2010): 1–32.

24. I have also found people in unlikely places. My neighbors in Calgary, who grew up in back-to-the-land families in the Kootenays, have introduced me to their parents.

25. Sharon Weaver, "First Encounters," 1–30.

26. Email from Bob Ploss to author, August 12, 2010.

27. Amber Bakker, a graduate student who transcribed some of my interviews, has also noted a change of tone in some of the interviews when we start talking about farming.

28. Michael Frisch, *A Shared Authority: Essays on the Craft and Meaning of Oral and Public History* (Albany: State University of New York Press, 1990); Steven High, "Sharing Authority: An Introduction," *Journal of Canadian Studies* 43, 1 (Winter 2009): 12–34; "Sharing Authority in the Writing of Canadian History: The Case of Oral History," in *Contesting Clio's Craft: New Directions and Debates in Canadian History*, eds. Christopher Dummitt and Michael Dawson (London: Institute for the Study of the Americas, 2009), 21–46.

29. Paul Thompson, *The Voice of the Past: Oral History* (Oxford: Oxford University Press, 1978).

30. See Portelli's afterword in this collection.

31. Katherine Gordon, *The Slocan: Portrait of a Valley* (Winlaw, BC: Sononis Press, 2004), 248 and back cover.

32. Bodie Dykstra, "Monument to Peace or Monumental Insult? The Controversy over the Our Way Home Memorial in Nelson, B.C. and the Conflict between Opposing Memories and Interpretations of the Past" (Unpublished graduate paper, University of Calgary, December 2011).

33. Moir has emphasized this in personal conversations with me. Also see Gordon, *The Slocan*, 238.

34. Schramm has produced DVDs of these interviews: *Interviews of Argenta Quakers and Longtime Residents of Argenta B.C. Canada*, Volumes 1–6, Selkirk College Library, Castlegar, BC.

35. For more on this group, see: http://www.facebook.com/group.php?gid=114551021899186&v=info (accessed August 8, 2011).

36. I asked Braundy if she was interested in collaborating on a feminist history project. She reminded me that she was not paid a salary to write. In our efforts to share authority, we must think carefully about how much we ask of those who do not benefit financially from the projects that come out of these projects.

37. On the history of the center and school, see Nancy Janovicek, "'The community school literally takes place in the community': Alternative Education in the Back-to-the-land movement of the West Kootenays, 1959–1980," *Historical Studies in Education/Revue d'histoire de l'éducation* 24, 1 (Spring/printemps 2012): 150–69.

38. Other ongoing projects include Kathleen Rodgers, "For the Love of Our Water: How the West Kootenay Counterculture Politicized the Commons, 1968–1988," and Megan Davies, "Nature, Home, Spirit: Back-to-the-land Childbirth in the Kootenays," both presented at Countercultures and the Environment, Hornby Island, British Columbia, July 2011. Past projects include Harley David Rothstein, "Alternative Schools in British Columbia, 1960–1975" (PhD diss., University of British Columbia, 1999); Terry Simmons, "But We Must Cultivate our Garden: Twentieth Century Pioneering in Rural British Columbia" (PhD diss., University of Minnesota, 1979).

39. I thank Kathleen Rodgers for this insight.

40. Lynn Abrams, *Oral History Theory* (London and New York: Routledge, 2010), 77.

41. Alessandro Portelli, *The Battle of Valle Giulia: Oral History and the Art of Dialogue* (Madison: University of Wisconsin Press, 1997).

42. Alessandro Portelli, *The Death of Luigi Trastulli and Other Stories: Form and Meaning in Oral History* (Albany: State University of New York Press, 1991), 2.

The Ethical Murk of Using Testimony in Oral Historical Research in South Africa

Monica Eileen Patterson

> The story of apartheid is, amongst other things, the story of the system-
> atic elimination of thousands of voices that should have been part of the
> nation's memory. The elimination of memory took place through censorship,
> confiscation of materials, bannings, incarceration, assassination and a range of
> related actions. Any attempt to reconstruct the past must involve the recovery
> of this memory.
> —South Africa Truth and Reconciliation Commission Final Report[1]

From 1995 to 2002, South Africa's Truth and Reconciliation Commission
(TRC) gathered a range of evidence—mainly in the form of oral testimony—
about human rights violations committed during the last 34 years of apartheid rule. While the TRC is rarely viewed as an oral history project, I argue
that these testimonies, or public interviews, "count" as oral history; seeing
them through this lens enables a richer understanding of the TRC and oral
historical practice. As a practitioner of oral history and an observer of TRC
testimony, the last 15 years of my own anthropological and historical research
in South Africa has shown that this approach illuminates crucial but often
ignored ethical and epistemological questions about oral historical practice,
particularly concerning the risks and consequences of probing into people's
pasts and publicizing their stories.[2] These consequences can deleteriously
affect not only the subjects of oral historical research, but also the stories

themselves and the interpretations and meanings they inspire. To this end, the commission's prominence in contemporary attempts to examine the apartheid past has made it an important frame of reference in a wide range of historical inquiry, for both everyday keepers and scholars of South African history.

In oral history projects, historians typically conduct extensive interviews with community members, many of whom know each other, or know about one another. As potential interviewees agree to, decline, or (re)negotiate the terms of their participation, they become aware of the fact that their individual accounts will be placed within a context of others' narratives, alongside stories and documentary evidence that they may regard as incomplete, biased, or untrue. Thus, unlike many documents found in archives, an oral historical account simultaneously inhabits multiple temporal frames in very self-conscious ways: interviewees craft narratives of the past in a particular present and often with some attention to the possible future outcomes of the history they cocreate.

The TRC produced a body of testimony through different types of public hearings, but all were based on the dialogic format of the interview.[3] Clearly, the context of the TRC's public hearings differed greatly from the more intimate, private interview setting favored by oral historians. But too often, oral historians have a tendency to fetishize the transcripts that come out of their interviews, excising people's historical narratives from the multiple broader contexts in which they were produced. For every oral history interview or official recording of testimony, one must imagine a cluster of conversations and engagements around it.[4] One should also acknowledge the multiple social, political, and cultural domains in which these encounters take place. Following Astrid Erll and Ann Rigney, these structuring dynamics are forms of "intermediation," and reflect that "all representations of the past draw on available media technologies, on existent media products, on patterns of representation and medial aesthetics" in an ongoing process of mediation and remediation.[5] Intermediation includes dominant and shaping frameworks, tropes, various reproductions, appropriations, and (de)contextualizations, and the many ways in which historical narratives draw from, interact with, and shape one another.

Occurring at a period of transition marked by profound uncertainty and the wholesale creation of new social and political structures, the TRC, as an emergent entity, drew from a range of interview genres—including private, one-on-one encounters of participants' initial processing by TRC staff, public hearings, investigatory sessions, interviews with various media outlets, and informal conversations at boreholes and in beer halls—in its attempt to piece together a fractured and suppressed history of mass violence and oppression. The large-scale and public nature of the TRC's testimony collection project allows a clearer view of the intermedial processes at play in all oral historical work. Further, because of the intense scrutiny the TRC received in the relatively condensed period of concentrated story-gathering, from its establishment in

1995 through the last Amnesty hearings in 2000, many of oral history's most challenging issues were distilled, making dominant frameworks and intermediations more identifiable.

To this end, I make three key claims in this chapter. First, it is not enough to analyze testimonial texts or think only about the meanings embedded in the interview experience. We must consider the larger contexts—social, cultural, political, and economic—in which interviews take place. Within these broader contexts, a handful of what I call "good stories" were constituted through complex processes of (still ongoing) intermediation. These dominant narratives tend to blot out nuance of the original experience, while overshadowing or rendering invisible divergent experiences and accounts. Second, a prevailing economy of emotion at the TRC proceedings, and within the media coverage and analysis that followed, helped constitute "good stories" while constraining or even silencing others. Third, an examination of the TRC as oral history *in public* reveals the high stakes involved for the participants who shared their stories, and points to difficult ethical questions that surround oral history-based knowledge production more generally, particularly in the context of a postcolonial world still rife with deep inequalities. In considering these questions, I illuminate a challenging domain of *ethical murk* that surrounds the use of oral historical testimony—testimony of experiences of suffering—for the production of scholarly and public knowledge.

South Africa's TRC

After centuries of oppression and resistance, the first free and fair elections took place in South Africa in April 1994. With the toppling of the brutal and racist apartheid regime, the nascent democracy's leaders drew on a range of experience and expertise to design and implement the country's transition from authoritarian rule. From the beginning, the majority government recognized the importance of oral history for a number of crucial areas, including education, heritage, archives, museums, and the arts, and thereby established extensive legislation, infrastructure, and funding for oral history projects charged with democratizing these domains.[6]

As part of this impulse, in 1995, the Promotion of National Unity and Reconciliation Act established the Truth and Reconciliation Commission of South Africa. Along with the new constitution, the TRC was conceived as one of the cornerstones of nation building, designed to unite a divided people with the creation of a new moral economy based on the principles of reconciliation and human rights. An uncovering of truth and an extended public dialogue about the apartheid past would produce the conditions for this moral imperative.[7] Reflecting on the challenges of establishing a "shared past," the commission clarified its notion of truth in its Final Report, insisting on not one, but four definitions: (1) factual or forensic truth; (2) personal or narrative truth; (3) social or "dialogue" truth; and (4) healing and restorative truth.[8]

Structurally, the commission was comprised of three committees: the Human Rights Violations Committee (HRVC), the Amnesty Committee, and the Reparation and Rehabilitation Committee.[9] Much work went on behind the scenes of these committees, involving administration, investigations, research, public relations, translation, eventual efforts to track down remains of the dead, and defense of the commission's work in various lawsuits. For the purposes of this chapter, however, I will focus on the public nature of the TRC: namely, the hearings that South African and international observers heard, witnessed, recorded, interpreted, and circulated as testimony, memory, and fact. As a self-declared exercise in nation building, the TRC can be seen as a public and explicitly collective national oral history project of unprecedented scope and scale. But, as with all collective memory projects, the version of the "shared past" it produced inherently marginalized many citizens.

Perhaps the single most consequential characteristic of the TRC was its public nature. This differentiated it from the 16 truth commissions that preceded it, but was emulated by many of those that have followed.[10] Public proceedings were deemed crucial to uniting a divided country, guaranteeing transparency, and encouraging broad-based participation, particularly in the aftermath of extensive state oppression, censorship, and covert criminal activities, including torture, detention without trial, and extrajuridicial execution. Hearings typically occurred in large halls and were often broadcast live on television and radio. Intensive national and international media coverage amplified the impact of the TRC considerably.[11] An extensive range of informal audience circles also listened in and commented on the commission's proceedings in their quotidian lives and social networks.

Dominant Frameworks and Intermedial Processes

As an institution, the TRC formed an official structure for managing the history of trauma, complicity, and reconciliation based on a set of underlying frameworks, agendas, and priorities. Of the approximately 22,000 people who came forward to give statements to TRC staff members, about 10 percent gave their testimony in public HRVC hearings and more than 7,000 people applied for amnesty. Through the mobilization of key categories ("victim" and "perpetrator," "gross violation of human rights," and "political" crimes) and the daily workings of its proceedings, the commission engaged in particular kinds of memory making as part of its production of truth. Notions pertaining to reconciliation were at the heart of these efforts.[12] This concept was not clearly defined from the beginning, but emerged through various invocations, while being both subtly and overtly contested by participants. The African notion of *ubuntu* (often parsed in English as "a person is a person through other people"), the importance of forgiveness, the healing power of speaking about one's trauma, and Christian tropes were other key frames that commissioners drew on when shaping how—and what—stories were told.

Similarly, operative periodizations constrained and influenced the narratives that emerged. Critics have pointed in particular to the exclusion of events before and after the stipulated time frame of 1960–1994, and experiences of violence and suffering that did not qualify as "gross violations of human rights."[13] These delimiting parameters obscured the *everyday* suffering, exploitation, and oppression of the colonial period, the apartheid system, and the present day, where conditions of apartheid still thrive. In HRVC and Amnesty hearings, a temporal frame of "before," "during," and "after" the human rights violation(s) in question directed the flow and focus of participants' narratives. Although this orientation is at the center of many oral history projects that inquire into past events, typically forming the basis for interview guides, it tends to belie how past violence extends into the present, not only in terms of psychosocial effects on individuals and communities, but also in regard to socioeconomic circumstances.

The commission's reliance upon the binary division of participants into "victims" and "perpetrators" was another significant structuring framework.[14] Largely employed in mutually exclusive terms, this taxonomy often failed to accommodate the shades of coercion, force, desperation, and miscommunication that defined many people's lives during the apartheid era. Throughout my historical and ethnographic research in South Africa, I have encountered many people who felt alienated by the "victim" label and thus refused to participate in the TRC, arguing they either did not see or want to present themselves in this way.[15]

The failure of the TRC to adequately address, not to mention intervene in, the lasting economic consequences and largely unchanged distribution of resources resulting from apartheid is arguably its greatest shortcoming. With its emphasis on the redemptive framing of reconciliation as a largely emotional, spiritual, communicative, and symbolic phenomenon, structural inequality was only occasionally referenced, and not taken up as a challenge to be addressed in concrete, systemic, and economic ways. While a great deal of journalistic and anecdotal evidence points to epiphany-like acknowledgments among some white South Africans about the horrors of the apartheid system, the TRC process clearly fell short of forcing broad recognition of the deeply layered, and especially economic, ways that all whites benefitted from it, regardless of their political orientations. A deeper appreciation of the extent and continuation of these benefits may have generated more momentum to affect economic change. The absence of "beneficiary" as a meaningful category in TRC proceedings, along with an overly simplistic emphasis on the extremes of "victims" and "perpetrators," flattened out the complexity of witnesses' experiences, and enabled a perpetuation of the socioeconomic status quo.

Participants and observers did not, of course, just passively inhabit or reproduce the TRC's categories; many brought their own frameworks of understanding to the process. Within a complex, shifting web of power relations, they struggled to bring these understandings to bear, both in the hearings themselves and in related activity around the commission's public proceedings. Most prominently, members of the Azanian People's Organisation (AZAPO), and the families of Steve Biko, Fabian and Florence Ribiero, and Griffiths and Victoria Mxenge (antiapartheid activists assassinated by agents of the apartheid government) formally opposed the possibility of amnesty for torturers and killers, rejecting the option on principle and taking issue with the criteria used in its application. Deflecting sustained questioning and prompting from commissioners, not to mention much evidence to the contrary, former prime minister F. W. deKlerk insisted that he had no knowledge of gross human rights abuses perpetrated by his own security forces. During the public hearings, audience members often broke into song, erupted in laughter, held up placards with messages written on them, booed and hissed, and even heckled participants. But often the TRC's dominant frameworks were contested in more subtle and implicit ways, which I explore further later in the chapter.

The Emergence and Power of "Good Stories"

Individuals' understandings of the past are always informed by wide-ranging interpersonal and social dynamics. Cultural values, family dynamics, community rumors, generational conflict, religious mores and social stigmas, politics, and "selling out" are just some of the currents that speak to the complex backdrop within which these stories were told and evaluated. The intermedial networks and multilayered processes of meaning making that are always at play in oral history work are more visible in the South African case because of the density of engagement with public aspects of the TRC.

An examination of the TRC as oral history in public reveals insights about the relationality of participants' self presentations and positionings.[16] An unlimited audience intensely scrutinized those who testified in public, evaluating, commenting upon, and comparing their stories as well as their character to other TRC participants and testimonies. A range of critics, commentators, and interlocutors mediated participants' stories through summaries, selected excerpts, and various framings, further refracting their narrated experiences from the original accounts and experiences. While commissioners, journalists, scholars, and everyday citizens assessed participants, they also did their own assessing. With varying degrees of consciousness, people participated in the TRC not just as individuals, but as representatives of groups, providing an additional layer of intermediation that begs deeper analysis. As the commission hearings traveled across the country, the testimonies given in each town produced a kind of oral history of the area. The commission organized amnesty and thematic hearings in clusters, grouping related testimonies together for evaluation and public consumption. Through the process of telling stories about the past in public, "good stories" emerged.

My notion of "good stories" comprises many elements. On one level, they served as dominant narratives that helped scaffold the picture of the past that was publically unfolding. Through this collective process of memory making, certain truths and testimonies became foundational touchstones of the commission's work, celebrated for their symbolic resonance, emotional meaning, and historical truth. Of course, consensus about what counted as a "good story" or the sites of their production has been difficult to ascertain. Context is also crucial, as what counts as a "good story" in one place may have been scorned in another. But, for the purpose of my analysis, I point to the general tendency to privilege select witness testimonies from the time of the public hearings to the present. Many, including commissioners, TRC staff, journalists, filmmakers, artists, and academic and other writers, have played a role in the inevitable filtering out of certain stories—and parts of those stories—over others.

"Good stories" existed in a range of genres, only a few of which I can address here. What would become one of the narrative anchors of the TRC proceedings, celebrated especially in the international press and by TRC chairperson Archbishop Tutu, was the story of American Fulbright scholar Amy Biehl, an antiapartheid activist who participated in voter registration for black South Africans in preparation for the first open election. In August 1993, when she was on her way to drop off some friends in the black township of Gugulethu, a group of young men coming from a Pan African Student Organisation rally stoned and stabbed Amy to death. The youth were incited by the struggle slogan "One Settler, One Bullet," and PASO's decision to launch Operation Barcelona, aimed at stopping deliveries from towns into townships. When they saw Amy, a white woman driving a car, they viewed her as an enemy and attacked and killed her.

Responding to a barrage of requests to come to South Africa, Amy's parents, Linda and Peter Biehl, appeared before the TRC in support of its work. Part of the "good story" that emerged is how they openly forgave Amy's killers and publicly endorsed their application for amnesty. In a statement to the commission, Peter Biehl declared: "The most important vehicle of reconciliation is open and honest dialogue...we are here to reconcile a human life which was taken without an opportunity for dialogue. When we are finished with this process we must move forward with linked arms." These words have been quoted extensively, not least by Tutu in numerous interviews and public speaking events. However, direct quotes from both reveal a more complex picture. Reading a statement toward the end of the amnesty hearing, Peter Biehl stated:

> We unabashedly support the process which we recognize to be unprecedented in contemporary human history. At the same time we say to you it's your process, not ours. *We cannot*, therefore, *oppose* amnesty if it is granted on the merits. In the truest sense it is for the community of South Africa to forgive its own and this has its basis in traditions of ubuntu and other principles of human dignity. *Amnesty is not clearly for Linda and Peter Biehl to grant* [my italics].[17]

Following the hearing, members of the press asked the Biehls if they could forgive their daughter's killers. Linda Biehl responded: "I don't think I have anything to forgive, because I don't believe I ever felt hatred." Peter Biehl agreed that he did not feel angry, and had many things in his own life for which he would like to be forgiven. But he also seemed to draw a line in how far he was willing to embrace the TRC's public reconciliation project, stating, "I believe in forgiveness, but to be honest my forgiveness is for me not for the public."[18]

Within individual accounts, particular narrative portions were often decontextualized, gaining primacy to the exclusion of others. On a larger scale, further fragmentation and selection occurred as certain narratives became iconic in media coverage, popular culture, informal conversation, and academic texts. Amy's story, or the dominant version that emerged through the TRC process, presented her as a martyr, and her forgiving parents as paragons of reconciliation. Omitted from these accounts were her parents' private struggles to reach the decision to support their daughter's murderers' applications for amnesty and the ongoing challenges they faced after hiring two of the youths to work at the nonprofit foundation they established in her honor. Nevertheless, the Biehls came to embody the ideals of the TRC process and, in so doing, shaped how others viewed and evaluated the commission's work.

Often presented in Christian or spiritual frames, despite the fact that South Africa is officially a secular state, many "good stories" framed reconciliation as a liberating end point in a journey of healing. Such stories were widely celebrated not only in the words of commissioners (most often those of Tutu) during the hearings themselves, but also in press interviews and statements that drove home the TRC's agenda. One of the biggest problems with this process, which highlighted exemplary stories for disproportionate celebration and attention, was how it flattened lived experiences and rendered complex people into one-dimensional heroes or saints.

The inverse also occurred. The identification of perpetrators such as death camp commander Eugene "Prime Evil" de Kock and director of the Chemical and Biological Warfare project Wouter "Dr. Death" Basson reinforced ideas about the apartheid state—namely, that violent "excesses" were the result of "a few bad apples" rather than widely sanctioned and institutionalized practices. This emphasis on extreme cases deflected attention from the structural violence that was the foundation of the apartheid system. Although this approach helped to "restore dignity" for some, too often those celebrated were iconicized in ways that diminished their humanity, oversimplified their engagement with the TRC, and obscured important aspects of their realities—particularly socioeconomic ones—that should have been more closely addressed.

In addition to gathering histories from witnesses, TRC commissioners asked them to discuss what the commission could do for them. Many observers, including journalists and academics, have since referred to these responses as touchingly humble. The most common "victim" request was for the return and/or (re)burial of loved ones' remains. While a few people asked for financial assistance, these requests were usually not for the person testifying, but rather to meet the basic needs (such as medicine, rent money, or school fees) of young, sick, or poor family members.[19]

In his interdisciplinary analysis of TRC testimony, literary scholar Mark Sanders explains "why public requests for reparation after apartheid have widely assumed the form of appeals for funeral rites," requests that he believes are meant to "make good for the violations of apartheid."[20] Sanders seems to take these statements, uttered in the very particular context of public HRVC hearings, at face value, and further lauds them as agentive acts of commemoration—a way of taking back power. To the extent that participants' requests prompted the commission to create a new fund for exhumations, one can celebrate not only their ability to affect change, but also the commission's willingness to meet participants' needs. My own research and the ongoing demands of survivor groups, such as the Khulumani Support Group, suggests that Sanders's reading is overly sanguine, not least because it fails to account for the real demands for economic redress South Africans have articulated in multiple sites beyond the TRC. This particular celebratory interpretation reproduces and elides the very frame that the commission, reinforced by media coverage and the public nature of the hearings, produced: the TRC was strongly invested in producing and celebrating "good stories" of (overwhelmingly) black forgiveness and magnanimity in the face of incredible suffering and very limited expressions of white remorse. This is not to deny that proper burials and the attendant rites and rituals are not hugely important to many South Africans. But beyond requests made in these very particular, power-laden frameworks of public storytelling, many of the private conversations I had about reparation point to a much wider range of needs and desires. In the township of Khayelitsha where I volunteered at a crèche for two years, many residents pointed to the lack of basic services and facilities still plaguing their daily lives when we discussed reconciliation and the TRC. It is important to ask *why* and *how* TRC hearing participants may have felt constrained or compelled in the representation of their experiences, feelings, and wishes, in addition to acknowledging that, almost two decades after independence, these feelings and wishes may well have shifted.

The TRC's Economy of Emotion

One of the key conditions that constituted a "good story" was the TRC's prevailing economy of emotion. While always subject to contestation, negotiation, and refusal by participants, commissioners (and especially Chairperson Tutu) endorsed, modeled, and, at times, even explicitly enforced a normative code of acceptable emotional display. Words, expressed emotions, and embodied movements and gestures from witnesses, audience members, commissioners, and TRC staff members helped operationalize this economy, itself a powerful form of intermediation.

Within the unwritten rules of this code, grief and mourning were treated with the utmost reverence and respect. Commissioners established the tone for such reception early in the public proceedings. On the second day of the HRVC hearings in East London, wheelchair-bound activist Singqokwana Ernest Malgas testified about the three decades of arrest, detention, house arrest, assault, torture, and harassment that he experienced at the hands of the Security Police. He told listeners that officers set his house on fire in 1985 and poured acid over his son, who died as a result. While describing an experience of torture involving intense pain and suffocation, Mr. Malagas broke down and started sobbing. Chairperson Archbishop Tutu dropped his head into his hands and began crying as well. Commissioner Alex Boraine closed the proceedings as Commissioner Hlengiwe Mkhize rubbed his back and comforted Tutu. This was a pivotal moment that many journalists widely covered, viewing it as a moment of truth and even transcendence.[21] But not everyone agreed with this interpretation: some conservative presses later derided the TRC as the "Snot en trane Kommissie" (Afrikaans for "Snot and Tears Commission") or the "Kleenex Commission."

Throughout the public proceedings, Tutu presented a sometimes heavy-handed interpretive frame for understanding participants' expressed emotions. Witnesses who cried while testifying often slowed the pace of testimony as the chairperson offered them a bit of space to collect themselves. In these moments, Tutu frequently reflected upon the themes of suffering, reconciliation, and the African concept of *ubuntu*. He expressed gratitude to witnesses for sharing their experiences, proffered his belief in the restorative and therapeutic power of forgiveness, and stressed how telling one's story served as a means of restoring victims' dignity. Professional comforters—TRC employees—were also on hand, seated next to or behind the witness, ready to provide more intimate, and often, physical support. They offered tissues, glasses of water, hugs, a shoulder to lean on, and arms to fall into; sometimes comforters even helped carry witnesses who had collapsed out of the auditorium.

While victims' tears and grief were typically revered, and those who shed them sacralized, there were limits. Witnesses who could not regain control of their ability to speak within what the chairperson deemed to be a reasonable amount of time were escorted off the stage, possibly to return later, although not all did. The intensity of crying was also judged. The hearing chairperson ultimately determined if the threshold between self-expression, which could include grief and mourning, and loss of control was crossed. Of course there were ethical concerns at stake in these decisions as well. Commissioners prioritized protecting the welfare of the person providing testimony, and I do not doubt that they had witnesses' best interests at heart. But it is important to acknowledge that just as in oral history interviews, "the right thing to do" in such situations is not always clear. In my own viewing and reading of recorded TRC testimonies, I have often thought that a more prolonged encounter with gut-wrenching sobs or shrieks of despair would be more appropriate than the fleeting and constrained emotional ruptures that the TRC smoothed over, suppressed, and even effectively silenced during proceedings. While recognizing the risks of voyeurism and further violation, I cannot help but wonder how the economy of emotion that kept "excessive" displays of grief out of public view constrained South Africa's engagement with its apartheid past.

Furthermore, participants' and audience members' expressions of anger, desires for vengeance, and feelings of bitterness were often subdued when they surfaced. Reflecting the power of the structuring frameworks that defined the HRVC hearings, these more negative feelings arose more frequently in Amnesty hearings where former victims could ask their torturers questions, and in the more investigatory and court-like public enquiries. In the most widely publicized of these, the Special Hearing on Winnie Madikizela and the Mandela United Football Club, Archbishop Tutu reprimanded some of the witnesses for expressing their anger or bitterness, which he regarded as "threats to the dignity" of the commission's proceedings.

But again, the question bears asking: Who is to say that angry diatribes or incensed roars are not appropriate responses to the abuses that took place? If the TRC's central goal was for listeners and witnesses to confront the impact of apartheid on victim's lives, why was there not more space for expressing negative emotions? A tendency to fix, identify, and simplify complexity is often inherent in analytical projects based on testimony and oral history, particularly when such complexity threatens to undermine the various "good stories" that serve particular agendas, including the often unacknowledged biases of researchers.

The TRC managed emotions and oral testimony in ways that were too narrow for witnesses to be able to express a full range of emotions and recalled injustices. As Heidi Grunebaum argues: "Voices, lives, and stories were assimilated into testimony and testimonial sound bites that were split off from the real bodies and real lives of those in whose name the new nation, the reconciled community, was imagining itself into being."[22] Contrary to the linear, developmental model of healing that claims truth facilitates healing, my ongoing conversations with South Africans who were hurt in various ways by the apartheid system and its agents reveal that peoples' feelings of reconciliation, vengefulness, anger, indifference, or healing depend on the day, and even the moment. These encounters also underscore the *social* nature of feelings and the ways that they are generated and experienced in relation to their perceptions of how others have fared and how their own lives have unfolded in time. In other words, people's felt emotions are contingent upon intersubjective, complex circumstances. The lack of significant socioeconomic change in the democratic South Africa has contributed to rising feelings of bitterness, disillusionment, and resentment across many sectors of society and particularly among the poor. Although many TRC narratives were elicited and delivered in ways that fit into the dominant frame of reconciliation and forgiveness, many of the people that I have come to know continue to feel, if anything, *conflicting* emotions.

To return to my earlier consideration of how best to understand witnesses' requests for reburials or the repatriation of their loved ones' remains, it would seem that while the commission's attempt to survey witnesses' needs and hopes was well-intentioned, its approach was fundamentally flawed. Asking, at a single, heightened, and very public moment, what victims of human rights violations want from the commission prematurely fixed what for many continues to be a shifting and fraught experience of the *ongoing* impact of apartheid's past. Moreover, people's desires for the future are informed by not only their sense of injury about the past, but also how their present life circumstances compare to those of their peers. All of these factors are highly dynamic, subjective, and situational.

The limitations of the TRC were not part of a sinister plan to flatten out or exclude, but speak to the very nature of engaging with "difficult knowledge" through oral encounters, as "knowledge that does not fit...[and that] induces a breakdown in experience, forcing us to confront the possibility that the conditions of our lives and the boundaries of our collective selves may be quite different from how we normally, reassuringly think of them."[23] It is precisely these kinds of questions that oral history needs to explore through better, broader, and multiple contextualizations, and greater attention to the relevant intermediations—social, political, economic—as they continue to unfold.

The Ethical Murk of Testimony

Analyses of the TRC, including my own in this chapter, are often guilty of the very shortcomings they criticize. It is difficult to do justice to the dynamism of emergent processes, and to engage the intermedial dimensions of still-circulating testimonies, particularly in ways that recognize the power of explanatory frameworks without positing deterministic scripts. As in all historical inquiries, we are also challenged to resist the arc of teleology, in which our presentist knowledge of how historical events turned out informs our interpretation of them as they unfolded in the past. Historians must actively refuse to impose such linear inevitability onto what were complex, open-ended experiences. The TRC evolved over time and across space as it traveled throughout the country for its public hearings. According to many of the commissioners and researchers with whom I have spoken, it was a foray into what frequently felt like uncharted ethical territory.

The TRC's public components opened the process to a wide range of engagements and critiques. Watching testimonies, reading transcripts, and following news reports and the outpouring of secondary analyses still being generated, it is easy to criticize how commissioners foreclosed certain themes. We can point to the ways that they imposed hegemonic views, if often unwittingly. Indeed, this is also true of video and audio testimonies that have been recorded as part of many oral history projects. But beyond questions about structuring frameworks and privileged lines of historical inquiry, it is important to acknowledge the *ethical murk* that defines our engagements with past violence. Signed consent forms cannot guarantee that interviewees will not be hurt or negatively affected by how we choose to portray them, or the (often unpredictable) circulations and afterlives of these portrayals.[24] Should interviewers allow interviewees to continue speaking when they are upset? Should we push them when they are reticent? Should inconsistencies within and across testimonies be probed? Should we seek to elicit and engage interviewees' emotions? What costs come to those who share their stories of suffering? Despite the existence of ethics boards, graduate seminars, and oral history manuals and training sessions, we must admit that definitive answers, particularly in terms of "best practices," are often elusive, as much as we invest in protocols intended to pin them down.

Despite commissioners' best wishes, appearing before the TRC was not always a cathartic experience. Unanticipated negative consequences were at odds with the commission's claim (and hope) that talking would be restorative. As details surfaced—of victims' prolonged suffering before death, detainees' recollections about comrades under the duress of torture, or evidence of romantic infidelities—they often inflicted new pain and generated new questions for survivors and their family members. The architects of the TRC, like the authors of much recent scholarship on reconciliation, assumed that truth would facilitate recovery and thereby failed to account for the *renewed* pain and suffering that truth commissions can generate for participants. In engaging with the past and probing into people's memories, oral historians can also generate new pain or reopen old wounds. It is important to hold this possibility up alongside the more celebratory characterizations that have papered over the ethical murk at the heart of all oral historical inquiry.

In my conversations with some of the commission's witnesses and researchers, it was often remarked that participants could not have anticipated how their involvement in the TRC would impact their lives. While the TRC engaged with most of its participants primarily as individuals, they eventually returned to their communities and social worlds, to contexts very different from that of the TRC. While some witnesses were happy to have shared their stories, others experienced negative consequences. Regardless of whether they received reparations, several witnesses told me that most of their friends, family, and community members believed that their involvement in the TRC had resulted in significant monetary compensation. Such beliefs led to expectations, jealousies, and resentment that complicated their relationships in ever-unfolding ways. One man, who testified about his detention and asked for assistance in paying his children's school fees, described wanting to turn back the clock on that experience because his friends and family members have hounded him for money ever since his public testimony. People's participation reshaped communal and family dynamics in significant ways, and thus demands further consideration and research.

As individuals were thrust into public realms, they became subjects of ongoing scrutiny, analysis, critique, and questioning. With so many people watching and listening, the stakes of telling were high. As detained ANC activist Yazir Henri writes: "At the time of my testimony I had no idea what the consequences of 'public' could have meant in the context of public hearings. The fact that my testimony could be appropriated, interpreted, re-interpreted, re-told and sold was not what I expected."[25] Throughout the course of my research in South Africa, several TRC participants expressed a range of responses about how fragments of their larger testimonies were excised from the contexts in which they (at least in part) chose to frame them. One former activist, who attempted suicide while in detention, felt that this moment of shared despair and weakness overshadowed the strength and courage he demonstrated over years of involvement in the resistance movement. Many survivors of sexual violations still struggle with the consequences of being identified in the press and remembered by individuals solely as rape victims, to the exclusion of other aspects of their experience and identities.

For many, being reduced in a headline to "cheating spouse," "police informer," or "victim of torture" was a new kind of violation. As a form of shorthand, such decontextualized renderings have tremendous social force, often producing social tensions ranging from hurtful gossip and rumor-mongering to ostracism, attacks on friends and family members, or even murder. The selective fragmentation of testimony, the shock of learning about unknown political, sexual, and violent acts, and the public airing of intimate details about victims' torture also affected and continue to impact the loved ones of those who played various roles in the struggle against apartheid.

Conclusion

The proliferation of testimony in the past few decades has revamped global industries of expertise, posing legal challenges and blurring boundaries between scholarship and other domains of representation and expression. Testimony can produce powerful sites of resistance, and given its presumed therapeutic capacity—for speakers, listeners, and society more broadly—it has been touted as the foundation for community peace building in the wake of mass atrocity. But in privileging more interpretive aspects of narrative, scholarly and artistic engagements with testimony have often neglected to account for the political economy in which such work takes place.

What are the politics of testimony-based knowledge production? Who benefits from the industries that are created, and in what ways? With the transition to democracy, a host of researchers, journalists, and authors descended upon the former apartheid state, extracting stories of suffering that led to the production of dissertations, academic degrees, books, and articles. In South Africa today, foreign analysts of various stripes are often compared to vultures or vampires because of the extractive nature of their trades. As producers of scholarly knowledge, we, typically privileged foreigners like myself, have been rewarded socially and economically in direct and indirect ways that remain beyond the realm of possibility for the majority of South Africans.[26] In South Africa, the political economy of story extraction, which so closely mirrors the longer history of mineral extraction, disproportionately benefits the researchers, truth commissioners, journalists, filmmakers, artists, and transitional justice workers who have made careers of working with the raw material of others' stories over those who tell them. These are issues of pressing concern. While contemporary public practices and uses of oral history expand, the fight against apartheid has yet to be won, and the largely unexamined question of what should now be done with the knowledge that the TRC produced remains. How might we extend the processes of dialogue the TRC began in ways that not only uncover but also help break from the histories of violence with which they engage?

On the one hand, the TRC helped familiarize and legitimize core tenets and protocols of oral historical research, treating the stories of regular people with respect and reverence. But as oral history *in public*, it simultaneously magnified the challenges and limits of such research, in ways both specific to the TRC and shared with oral historical research more broadly. With its extensive publicity and the vast array of policy-shaping industries that it has generated and sustained, the TRC raised the stakes of telling stories of trauma in ways that impinge upon both the storytellers, and those who produce knowledge about them. As the subjects of such work increasingly articulate their concerns, anxieties, and frustrations with the manner in which they have been represented and the political economy of the representations themselves, they force to the surface many dilemmas that have in fact always been present in oral history practice.

In working with oral history testimony for the production of scholarly and public knowledge, we step into a fraught terrain of ethical murk. We need to better apprehend the *public* dimension(s) of these testimonies, regardless of where such interviews take place. As an example of the more recent formulations, and increasingly impactful ends to which oral history projects are being put, the TRC illuminates the importance of what happens off the record, on the sidelines, and in broader contexts in other sites of cultural and historical production and acts as a powerful reference point in many South Africans' minds, shaping their own understandings of not only the past itself, but what engaging with the past entails.

Notes

1. *Truth and Reconciliation Commission of South Africa Report (TRC Report)*, Volume 1 (Cape Town: Juta, 1998), 201.
2. See Monica Eileen Patterson, "Childhood, Memory, and Gap," in *Anthrohistory: Unsettling Knowledge and Questioning Discipline*, ed. E. Murphy et al. (Ann Arbor: University of Michigan Press, 2011), 81–96; *Constructions of Childhood in Apartheid's Last Decades* (PhD diss., University of Michigan, 2009).
3. Public hearings included six public enquiries, Amnesty hearings, and five types of Human Rights Violation Committee (HRVC) hearings, including regional "victim" hearings, political party hearings, and theme-based hearings that explored a range of institutions, special groups, and specific events. See *TRC Report*, 145–51.
4. I use the term "testimony" to denote the retelling of personal experience that occurs not only in the collection of oral histories, but also at other sites of cultural and historical production. In South Africa, these include the TRC, museum work, documentary projects, media coverage, community and commemorative events, and the publication of scholarly and literary works.
5. Astrid Erll and Ann Rigney, *Mediation, Remediation, and the Dynamics of Cultural Memory* (Berlin: Walter de Gruyter, 2009), 4.
6. "White Paper on Arts, Culture and Heritage." See http://www.dac.gov.za/white_paper.htm (accessed May 1, 2012).
7. No. 34 of 1995: Promotion of National Unity and Reconciliation Act, 1995, from the Office of the President, No. 1111, July 26, 1995.
8. *TRC Report*, 110.

9. The HRVC gathered close to 22,000 statements, covering almost 38,000 violations. From 1996 to 1998, about 2,200 people gave testimony in public HRVC hearings. Amnesty hearings took place from 1996 to 2000, with 5,392 people refused and 849 granted amnesty, out of 7,112 petitioners. Official Truth and Reconciliation Commission website, http://www.justice.gov.za/trc/ (accessed May 1, 2012).

10. For an overview of earlier commissions, see Priscilla Hayner's *Unspeakable Truths, Facing the Challenge of Truth Commissions* (New York: Routledge, 2002).

11. See Catherine M. Cole's *Performing South Africa's Truth Commission: Stages of Transition* (Bloomington: Indiana University Press, 2010) for an examination of the intermediating role played by the *Special Report*, in particular. A two-hour weekly news program produced by journalist Max du Preez for the duration of the commission's HRVC hearings, it broadcast 87 episodes from 1996 to 1998 and became the most-watched television show in South Africa.

12. See Madeleine Fullard and Nicky Rousseau, "Uncertain Borders: The TRC and the (Un)Making of Public Myths," *Kronos* (Bellville) 34, 1 (November 2008): 215–39, for their argument about how reconciliation was not central to HRVC hearings. Beyond the number of specific mentions it received within hearings, the fact that all public hearings were held quite literally under the banner of "truth and reconciliation" reinforced it as a central anchor of the TRC's proceedings and shaped people's understandings of the goals for the commission's accomplishments.

13. The Promotion of National Unity and Reconciliation Act, 1995, from the office of the president defined "gross violations of human rights" as "the killing, abduction, torture or severe ill-treatment of any person; or any attempt, conspiracy, incitement, instigation, command or procurement to commit [such] an act."

14. Later hearings problematized this categorization, particularly the political party hearings where it was revealed that liberation movement forces such as those of ANC also committed human rights violations.

15. Patterson, *Constructions of Childhood in Apartheid's Last Decades*.

16. In literary studies, the concept of "intertextuality" has drawn scholars' attention to similar processes.

17. From "Statement by the Truth and Reconciliation Commission on Amnesty Arising from Killing of Amy Biehl," South African Government Information website: http://www.info.gov.za/speeches/1998/98729_0w0699810056.htm (accessed May 1, 2012).

18. "Amy Biehl's Parents Believe Her Killers Are Genuinely Sorry," South African Press Association (Cape Town), July 9, 1997.

19. While women disproportionately gave testimony, they usually testified about violations committed against a loved one, not themselves. See Fiona Ross, *Bearing Witness, Women and the Truth and Reconciliation Commission in South Africa* (London: Pluto Press, 2003).

20. Mark Sanders, *Ambiguities of Witnessing: Laws and Literature in the Time of a Truth Commission* (Palo Alto: Stanford University Press, 2007), 76.

21. And yet, this iconic moment conveyed only part of Singqokwana Malagas's story, a man who "did not talk about his role as leader of the Amabutho youth

militants...who enforced the consumer boycotts and served as the shock troops in the fratricidal conflicts between the UDF and Azanian People's Organisation AZAPO." Fullard and Rousseau, "Uncertain Borders," 230.

22. Heidi Grunebaum, "Talking to Ourselves 'Among the Innocent Dead': On Reconciliation, Forgiveness, and Mourning," *PMLA* 117, 2 (March 2002): 306–10.

23. Parsing Deborah Britzman, *Lost Subjects, Contested Objects: Toward a Psychoanalytic Inquiry of Learning* (Albany: State University of New York Press, 1998), as cited in *Curating Difficult Knowledge: Violent Pasts in Public Places*, eds. Erica Lehrer, Cynthia Milton, and Monica Eileen Patterson (New York: Palgrave Macmillan, 2011), 8.

24. For a sensitive discussion about relevant approaches to oral history, see chapters 1 and 4 in this collection.

25. Yazir Henri, "Reconciling Reconciliation: A Personal and Public Journey of Testifying before the South African Truth and Reconciliation Commission," in *Political Transition: Politics and Cultures*, ed. Paul Gready (London and Sterling, Virginia: Pluto Press, 2003), 262–75.

26. For an earlier consideration of these issues, see Sherna Berner Gluck and Daphne Patai, eds., *Women's Words: The Feminist Practice of Oral History* (New York: Routledge, 1991).

PART IV

Considering Silence

Erin Jessee

Silence has long been a subject of interest among oral historians. Silences affect the stories we hear and how we interpret them, and it is widely accepted that in order to do justice to the oral historical narratives we collect, we cannot present them as complete, finished accounts.[1] However, the theoretical, ethical, and methodological negotiations central to oral historical engagements with silence are rarely presented in our documentaries, publications, and presentations. With few exceptions, the roles that silences play in shaping both our research projects and outcomes are too often relegated to the sidelines: something we acknowledge as important for understanding the bigger picture, but fail to address in depth. But of course, silences occur and are reproduced in every aspect of oral history, from the research design and ethics approval process to the analysis and dissemination of our research findings.

The chapters by Alexander Freund, Luis van Isschot, and Anna Sheftel thereby pave new ground for oral historians. They take us beyond the familiar terrain of examining how silences within the interview influence our understanding of the narratives participants share and the larger historical processes they illuminate.[2] Freund's piece initiates a timely discussion that advocates an "ethics of silence." Drawing upon encounters with two German immigrants to North America, he reflects on the discomfort he experienced when they purposely (and symbolically) omitted certain details about their lives from the interview but revealed them "off the record." Freund states that his anxieties about recording incomplete stories, combined with the fear and frustration he felt in trying to respond to his participants' needs, impeded his ability to act in an ethical manner. While he respected his participants' requests not to speak on the record, he failed to probe the underlying reasons for their silences—a behavior that led him to colonize these silences because he attached his own meanings to them, rather than those intended by his participants.

To this end, Freund's greatest contribution lies in the ethical guidelines he proposes for addressing the inevitable silences that emerge in the course of oral historical research. His call for an ethics of silence is long overdue in the discipline, particularly the need for oral historians to develop ethical ways of probing silences to ensure their meaning and purpose is fully understood, and not merely assumed, by researchers. Often we attribute silence to a reticence about discussing controversial subjects, painful memories, or other issues that we would normally sweep under the proverbial carpet.[3] Given the myriad factors that may influence an individual's decision to consent to an interview, for example, it only makes sense that similar complexities can lie behind their silences.

Van Isschot's chapter, "The Heart of Activism in Columbia," further demonstrates the value of considering silence beyond the interview space. In particular, he speaks to the challenges of conducting interviews with leftist guerillas and related activists in the aftermath of an occupation orchestrated by right-wing paramilitary forces in Barrancabermeja, Colombia. His research occurred in a dangerous context, under surveillance and interference from paramilitary forces and in a place where actors from all sides of the conflict perpetrated human rights violations. These factors left him wondering how frequently and in what ways his participants' narratives were simultaneously a product of the volatile political setting in which they were produced.

Like so many oral history projects that occur in settings of insecurity and political violence, not to mention those conducted under more peaceful circumstances, van Isschot found that his research questions regarding Barrancabermeja's more distant past were overwhelmed by the urgency of his participants' contemporary political agendas and the silences that surrounded certain subjects, such as the violent excesses of left-wing guerillas and right-wing paramilitary groups.[4] By considering the political, historical, and social factors shaping these silences, however, he manages to better contextualize his participants' lived experiences of the recent right-wing paramilitary occupation and its legacy of everyday violence.[5] What is particularly fascinating about van Isschot's efforts to probe these silences is how his insights into these social and political factors were revealed through his willingness to embed himself in the community, to experience the violence as an ethnographer of sorts. This unintentional merging of fieldwork strategies suggests that interdisciplinary approaches are one way to respond to Freund's call for an ethics of silence.

Last, Sheftel's piece, drawn from her fieldwork experiences in the small Bosnian city of Bihać, tackles silence from a different perspective: namely, the silences that emerge during the recruitment phases of our projects. By probing Bosnians' refusals to be interviewed, Sheftel came to understand that there were a variety of social, cultural, and political factors shaping, and hampering, her project. Analyzing these rejections enabled her to view the dynamics of wartime memory in new ways. In particular, refusing to be interviewed was a way for Bosnians to exercise agency and, in turn, resist the larger societal politics at play; politicians had a well-established tendency to revise history so as to incite ethnonationalist divisions within and outside of the country, and this typically reduced the region's history to the Bosnian War and genocide of Bosnian Muslims—a fact that disturbed some Bosnians.

Like van Isschot, Sheftel's insight was informed not only by a consideration of her would-be informants' refusals to participate, but also by her immersion in everyday life in Bihać. Living among her interviewees sensitized her to the highly politicized historical narratives that Bosnian politicians and various international actors have maintained for decades. Given this context, Sheftel is able to frame silence as an expression of the agency and resilience of citizens who reside in postconflict settings, rather than as the almost clichéd symptom of trauma.

Taken together, these three chapters articulate a more nuanced understanding of how and why silences occur, not just during interviews, but also within the practice of oral history as a whole. They also demonstrate how oral historians are uniquely situated to contribute to a conversation that ought to extend to other qualitative research practices in the humanities and social sciences. These questions might serve as a starting point for this type of discussion: What would an ethics of silence look like? In settings of peace? In settings of conflict or recent conflict? And where should the probing of silences begin? Ethnographers might begin by examining their research design as well as their biases, noting how they may initiate silences. But should oral historians, with their more concentrated interest in narratives and their deeper meanings, take a similar approach or is there another, more appropriate starting point for understanding silence? And to what end? Is caution warranted? Are there instances when we should remain silent about the silences that influence our research? Or, are the benefits of engaging with silences within and beyond the interview space worth blurring the already porous disciplinary boundaries of oral history? Certainly, the chapters by Freund, van Isschot, and Sheftel suggest that oral historical inquiry can benefit from interdisciplinary engagement and a broader understanding of how silence impacts oral history practice. But beyond settings of insecurity and discussions of difficult subject matter, is there potential for similar inquiries?

Notes

1. For example, see Laura Benadiba, "The Persistence of Silence after Dictatorships," *Oral History Review* 39, 2 (Summer–Fall 2012): 287–97; Martha Norkunas, "Teaching to Listen: Listening Exercises and Self-Reflective Journals," *Oral History Review* 38, 1 (Winter–Spring 2011): 63–108; Luisa Passerini, *Fascism in Popular Memory: The Cultural Experience of the Turin Working Class*, trans. Robert Lumley and Jude Bloomfield (Cambridge: Cambridge University Press, 1987); Joan Sangster, "Telling Our Stories: Feminist Debates and the Use of Oral History," *Women's History Review* 3, 1 (March 1994): 5–28.
2. See, e.g., Judith Zur's discussion of Guatemalan war widows' "forbidden memories" or Ulla-Maija Peltonen's discussion of the silences in one man's narrative about surviving Stalin's labor camps: Zur, "Remembering and Forgetting: Guatemalan War Widows' Forbidden Memories," in *Trauma: Life Stories of Survivors*, eds. Kim Lacy Rogers and Selma Leydesdorff (New Brunswick: Transaction Publishers, 2009), 45–59; Peltonen, "Memories and Silences: On the Narrative of an Ingrian Gulag Survivor," in *Memories of Mass Repression: Narrating Life Stories in the Aftermath of Atrocity*, eds. Nanci Adler, Selma Leydesdorff, Mary Chamberlain, and Leyla Neyzi (New Brunswick: Transaction Publishers, 2011), 61–79.
3. On reticence in the interview space, see Lenore Layman, "Reticence in Oral History Interviews," *Oral History Review* 36, 2 (Summer–Fall 2009): 207–30.
4. See Erin Jessee, "The Limits of Oral History: Ethics and Methodology Amid Highly Politicized Research Settings," *Oral History Review* 38, 2 (Summer–Fall 2011): 287–307; Susan Thomson, *Whispering Truth to Power: Everyday Resistance to Reconciliation in Post-Genocide Rwanda* (Madison: University of Wisconsin Press, forthcoming in 2013).
5. Ethnographers, such as Nancy Scheper-Hughes and Philippe Bourgois, first popularized the concept of everyday violence—those subtle forms of structural violence to which people gradually become habituated: Scheper-Hughes, *Death Without Weeping: The Violence of Everyday Life in Brazil* (Berkeley: University of California Press, 1993); Bourgois, "The Moral Economies of Homeless Heroin Addicts: Confronting Ethnography, HIV Risk, and Everyday Violence in San Francisco Shooting Encampments," *Substance Use & Misuse* 33, 11 (1998): 2323–51.

CHAPTER 12

Toward an Ethics of Silence? Negotiating Off-the-Record Events and Identity in Oral History

Alexander Freund

Silences are a constitutive part of oral history interviews. Silences may express individual or collective forgetting, collaborative remembering, discomfort, reluctance, (self-)censorship, noncompliance, confrontation, reticence, politeness, fear, anger, deceit, taboos, secrets, contemplation, concern for the other, reflection, conformity, or that which need not be told.[1] Some silences are explicit or obvious, others are not. Interviewees' silences may be an effect of oppression or agency. Interviewers may use silence to give narrators space to remember or to make them talk. Silences in an interview may be consensual or express a communicative struggle. This chapter attempts to address, in a preliminary, tentative way, oral historians' troubled and troubling relationship with silences.

The silences I speak of in this piece, more specifically, emerge from some specific dynamics of oral history practices and constitute events that are commonly described as "off-the-record" incidents. Literally everything that happens in an oral history relationship that is not recorded may be considered off the record. An interviewee may ask the interviewer to turn off the recorder to provide additional information; or he may put a written note on the table to communicate without speaking. Off-the-record silences, thus, are not simply absences of voice, acts of nonspeaking; rather, they are deferments of voice, relocations from "on" to "off," from speaking to writing and gesturing.

Several off-the-record incidents from my own practice immediately came to mind when I was invited to write about them.[2] Even though they had happened one or two decades earlier, they were still with me, ever-present in my mind, as intriguing anecdotes harboring secrets that might reveal otherwise unknowable truths about oral history. The two off-the-record incidents I discuss here come from interviews with German women and men who migrated to North America in the second half of the twentieth century; for one study, I explored German migrants' encounters with the history and memory of World War II and the Holocaust in North America, and, in particular, their relations with Jews (Dirk, the first case); for another study, I conducted interviews to find out about young, single women's identity constructions as postwar immigrants to Canada (Christel Meisinger, the second case).[3] After presenting the case studies and some preliminary analysis, I discuss the ways that oral historians' negotiations of off-the-record incidents are shaped by diffuse fears of silence and how our approaches to silence are entangled in negotiations of our professional and personal identities. Silences, oral historians fear, may signify a loss of information, a threat of incompleteness, a breakdown of rapport, a loss of trust, or an interviewer's ineptness—all constitute threats to our identities as skilled interviewers and people who want to be liked by others. We respond with methods and theories that attempt to contain silences and keep us in control of knowledge about our interviewees. Our conflicted attitudes toward silence pose a fundamental ethical problem: in our emotionally charged quest for a complete and perfect interview, we are insufficiently prepared to accept our interviewees' silence as a form of agency in the interview situation. Thus, next to methodological and theoretical responses, we need to develop an ethical response to interviewee silence, an ethics of silence, which I attempt to address in my conclusion.

"Why don't you turn off the tape recorder?" Difficulties in Hearing Silences

Silences texture life stories. In her guidebook *Recording Oral History*, Valerie Yow uses a short anecdote to alert novice oral historians to this reality: "Anthropologist John Gwaltney, in his book *Drylongo: A Self-Portrait of Black America*, quotes a narrator who told him, 'I know you must have sense enough to know that you can't make me tell you anything I mean to keep to myself.'"[4] We go into interviews knowing we will not get the complete story. Yet, throughout our interviews, we hope and attempt to get, if not the whole story, at least a fully self-contained story. In my own interviewing, based on practices developed by social psychologists and oral historians in Germany, I try to get at life histories in different ways, asking interviewees, in a first phase, to tell me their "life story," and following up with questions in a second phase, often spread over two or more sessions.[5]

I took this approach in my interview with Dirk (a pseudonym) in New York City on January 17, 2000. The description that follows is taken from my field notes at the time:

> I met Dirk through an advertisement for my research that was displayed at the German consulate in New York City. For the interview, we met at his place, a student dorm. Initially, it was easy to break the ice, because the doorman was very strict, which we both found amusing, especially Dirk. Speaking German, we continued to say the formal Sie instead of the informal Du. While he was only six years older than me, he was already a professor at a German university. We went to a nearby fish restaurant, which was actually too loud for a good taping of the conversation. But as this was the first interview, I agreed. Before and during dinner, we talked mainly about his work in Germany and the United States and a little about my own work.
>
> Dirk was very concerned about confidentiality. He said if I were to get the full scoop, it would have to be anonymous and the tape could not be deposited in an archive. I agreed to these conditions. The interview began well. After probably half an hour, however, he asked me to turn off the recorder, even though we had agreed to very strict rules of confidentiality. After some back and forth and me finally turning off the recorder, he proceeded to tell me an interesting story—as it turned out, it was the most illuminating story of the interview, [at least in terms of my research project, which focused on relations between German migrants and Jewish North Americans].

This in short was the story, according to my field notes taken right after the interview:

> When he lived in the United States, he had a Jewish lover. Dirk told me that he was gay, but this was not the reason why he did not want me to tape the story, because this was not a secret, he was out of the closet, so to speak. He told me in detail about having sex with this man. If I remember correctly, he said that while the two bodies were rubbing against each other, he thought how strange it was that those were the bodies of a German and a Jew. After sex, he told his friend about it. But his friend could only understand him theoretically, not emotionally. This was so, because for the Jewish friend, Germany had a very different connotation than one (at least as a German) would usually assume. He was from a small mid-western town, where his homosexuality was like a prison for him. He could not come out of the closet in his hometown. But he had been to Germany once, to Frankfurt on the Main. And it was in Frankfurt that he came out of the closet. Thus, for him Germany was

the great place of liberty, not the country of the Holocaust. Put crudely, he perceived Germany and Germans not from a Jewish perspective, but from a gay perspective. [...]

The evening after [the interview], I talked to [a colleague and friend] about it and he said there were ways of actually using this story in a metaphorical way. I need to talk to him about that and maybe raise this topic in one of our Friday meetings. Fellow oral historians have encouraged me to do this as this seems an important story.

A telephone conversation on January 27, 2000; the following is a translation of my German language field notes:

Dirk was friendly but unwilling to meet for another interview or to write down his story, which I could fully understand. I did not sell myself well. We came to the following decisions: 1. I will send him a transcript with all changes regarding anonymization and expect corrections from him and his written consent to deposit the interview at a public archive. 2. I am allowed to include his story about his lover if it is anonymous and I will then send him the excerpt and he will tell me if it is okay.

I have no record of sending Dirk the transcript or of me receiving a corrected transcript. Until now, I have not used his story. In preparation for this chapter, 11 years after the interview, I contacted Dirk, asking permission to use the field notes quoted earlier. He replied immediately and I emailed him both the text and the transcript of our interview. He replied within one week, asking me to take out details that could be used to identify him, which I did. After further correspondence, I further anonymized the field notes. Thus, although he agreed to my use of anonymized field notes, he continued to be concerned about confidentiality. Dirk's interview, then, is a good example of the multiple negotiations of off-the-record information that shape the dynamics of oral history relationships before, during, and (long) after the interview.

Before the interview began, there was little time to build rapport, a situation familiar to many oral historians, especially those working and traveling on shoestring budgets, always pressed for time, and under pressure to achieve a certain quorum of interviews for a dissertation committee or a funding agency. My life story approach and the professional desire to create an archival record had me concerned about getting the full story. When Dirk asked me to turn off the recorder, I was taken aback. After hearing the story, I became concerned about the integrity, coherence, and completeness of the interview. Dirk's story about his Jewish lover was, it seemed to me, the most important and telling story, and without it there was little of value in the interview itself, because it was both incomplete and incomprehensible. At the same time, I had little understanding or sympathy for my interviewee's silence. He had volunteered to be interviewed, he knew the topic, we had agreed to anonymity and confidentiality, and yet, he still wanted to go off the record. I was frustrated by the loss of control during and after the interview and by the loss of control over information that seemed to be of great value to me. These feelings were only exacerbated by having chosen a "poor" recording location (too noisy) and the wrong language (I had wanted to do the interview in English but then I started and we continued in German), and by Dirk's later decision not to be interviewed again.

I do remember the hesitation and feeling of impotence when Dirk said, "Why don't you turn it off." Our professional guides advise us to stall and try to convince narrators to continue.[6] Self-doubt about my skills as an interviewer crept in as I remembered the admonition to never stop recording. With trepidation I recalled, as I rested my thumb on the stop button, that Alessandro Portelli's only formal oral history lesson had been "never turn the tape recorder off."[7] As I closed my eyes and pushed stop, I also remembered Donald Ritchie's words: "An oral history is not a journalistic interview, so there is little to be gained by hearing a story 'off the record.'"[8] All of the compromises I had made bore no fruit. By all methodological standards of our profession, I had failed as an oral historian. As my comment "I did not sell myself well" indicates, I also felt that I had failed as a person who, like most, wants to be liked. Like every interviewing experience, this incident was not just about the narrator's identity, it was also about my own.

My response to Dirk's silences—both his request to go off the record and his refusal to be reinterviewed—was shaped by various emotions: an intellectually indefensible wish to get the full story; the fear of failure; frustration with the narrator. It was also influenced by a complex power relationship. I feared that rapport would diminish if I balked at turning off the recorder. Furthermore, I felt that, being just out of graduate school, I had little leeway in negotiating with Dirk, a professor, and particularly his request to go off the record. His off-the-record story left traces on the rest of the recording. I was flustered, disheartened, and no longer as focused as I wanted to be. Dirk had made very clear to me that this story was not to be repeated or published. I was therefore worried about not asking the wrong questions—questions that might somehow insinuate my knowledge of this story. I also wondered whether this interview was of any value at all if he kept the most interesting stories off the record. Inevitably, my mind was more preoccupied with what had not been recorded than with what had been put on the record.

One result of my emotionally charged response was that I did not "hear" what Dirk told me. Following conventional wisdom that I could not "use" what was not recorded, I had decided to "write off" this specific story. In rushing off to the next on-the-record story, I failed to ask why he wanted to tell me the story in the first place; after all, he could have chosen not to tell the story. I therefore did not realize that Dirk had led me in an interesting direction; I did not hear that he suggested a queering of my approach; and I did not hear Dirk's wish, perhaps even his need, to tell the story. After all, how many people had he been able to tell this story? Thus, because I focused so much on what I wanted "the record" to be and ignored Dirk's concept of "the record,"[9] I perceived a silence where there actually was none.

Yet, I also missed the silence in the room. Deviation from conformity, writes Robyn Fivush, "often leads to *being silenced*...Some deviations may be so threatening to the dominant narrative that they simply cannot be heard and so continue to be silenced."[10] Dirk's counternarrative was not fully silenced (he told me the story), but could also not be fully voiced (he did not go on record and thus tell a larger audience). Failing to pursue his story, I became implicated in his being silenced.

Pen and Paper: Written Communication in Oral History

Perceived silence, and implication in silencing, may be on or off the record in another form: as a written note, as was the case in an interview I did with Christel Meisinger (pseudonym) in Vancouver in 1993. Meisinger was born in 1931 and grew up in Kassel, Germany. She was 21 years old when she and her 18-year-old girlfriend Helga migrated to Vancouver in 1952 to work as domestic servants in private homes. Meisinger was happy at her place of employment, but her friend Helga was not:

> My girlfriend used to cry a lot. So, one day I told [my employer] Mrs. Manning that Helga wasn't too happy there. So she discussed it with her husband and then he said after supper: "Look: you phone Helga to tell her to pack her suitcase and Mr. Manning is going to pick her up, to be in front of the door at seven o'clock to pick her up." Well, the deal was to get her out of there as soon as possible and Mrs. Manning said: "She can stay with you downstairs" in my room and when Thursday came—I don't know what day the week this was—when Thursday came was my day off, then I would go with Helga to the Unemployment, on Robson it was and try to explain the situation there and then they would place her someplace else. And this is what we did.

As she recounted the story, I began to wonder what the cause of the problem might have been. The literature on domestic service in the early 1990s, although not nearly as comprehensive as now, had already told me that sexual harassment was a major threat to female domestic servants, especially those who lived in their employers' homes. I therefore assumed that Helga had experienced some form of sexual assault. Concurrently, I began to anticipate a silence on Meisinger's part. Considering that she felt the need to share the story, without going into details, and following my own ambivalent needs between getting the story and respecting my interviewee's privacy, I asked:

> *AF*: What was the situation that it was so urgent to get her out of there as fast as possible?
>
> *CM*: [At this moment, Mrs. Meisinger hesitated, remembering that the cassette-tape recorder was on, got up to get a piece of paper and pen, wrote down something and gave me the note. It had one word written on it: "Juden" ("Jews"). She made clear with her gestures that this topic was off the record and I was not to probe any further during the interview. As she was doing all of that, she continued to talk:] Uhh…Anyways, so that's what we did, Mr. Manning put me in the Cadillac and, and…Mr. Manning put me in the Cadillac and there was Helga with her suitcase and we put her in and she stayed with me for two weeks and they placed her almost across from me. Mr. Manning ate in the dining room, the kids and I ate in the kitchen. I don't know where Helga…and she had this great big room and one cheap little fold-away cot in the basement, not really privacy or anything, it was just so cold, the whole situation, the way they treated her and that was the way she couldn't handle it. So, Mr. Manning, I told him that and he pulled her out and they gave her that job. And I was always the one…she is younger than me, two years.

The written note continued to lie on the table between the two of us, and it served as a reference again later in the interview, when Meisinger recounted her own disappointment about domestic work in other employment situations: "Spring cleaning, washing walls, and, you know, and I did this for—few times, you know, for, uhm—[points to the word *Juden* on the note] you know, and hey, they wanted work done, you know, five, six hours washing the kitchen, washing the hallway, washing and, you know, it's hard work."[11] Here we have a silence that is both on and off the record. The tape was running, it recorded a person getting up and scribbling on a piece of paper. But it did not record the important information, which was captured only by my mind's eye. The silence this creates in the archival document is the same as the one in the interview with Dirk. Yet, it is a different kind of silence. Unlike Dirk's, it was not premeditated. It was a decision of the moment, in the flow of the narrative, within the dynamics of storytelling. It surprised Meisinger as much as me. During this interview sequence, Meisinger sounds flustered and her heartbeat must have quickened as she realized that she had talked herself into a situation that was difficult to escape.

My own emotions, in the span of just a few minutes, ran rampant. This was a great story, and every great story comes with an adrenaline rush. It was both secretive and taboo. There was, as in Dirk's case, the narrator's wish to tell me something she did not dare tell, a secret from her life. Dirk's and Meisinger's stories were confessions. How, I wondered, should I react to this? Should I read it out loud to get it on tape? Should I turn off the recorder to see whether she wants to talk about it? Neither seemed possible. Reading it out loud would have been a clear breach of confidence and probably the end of the interview or at least quickly diminishing rapport. Turning off the recorder might have broken the flow of the story.

This was no longer a story about female labor migrants; it was now about *Vergangenheitsbewältigung*—German society's emotionally charged attempt to "come to terms" with the Nazi past.[12] Out of the blue, it seemed to me at the time, Christel Meisinger, who had invited me into her home, fed me, and generously told her life story to a stranger, exposed a darker side of herself.[13] Yet, my attitude to her did not change. My main motivation for interviewing has always been curiosity. Every story I hear is new, strange (in its anthropological meaning: unfamiliar), and intriguing, and so this was yet another facet of an increasingly complex and fascinating person. The off-the-record note nevertheless affected the rest of the interview, because until we stopped the recording my mind continually wandered back to this note, as I was trying to figure out what it meant and how to mention it on the recording. Even though I was younger and much less experienced as an interviewer than when I interviewed Dirk seven years later, I was more willing to entertain the idea of getting this on the record. The more comfortable atmosphere—in someone's home rather than in a public place—and a much less pronounced hierarchical interviewer-interviewee relationship contributed to this attitude. Yet, I did not touch the topic, and this had to do with the broader context of the interview.

This particular context was convoluted. Much was negotiated before the interview with Meisinger. In the early 1990s, oral historians and Canadian universities were just beginning to work with national and university ethics guidelines and, as a new graduate student, I had no personal experience with research ethics formalities. If memory and my records serve me right, I sent a one-page description of my interview proposal to a person in charge of research ethics. Upon request, I provided a detailed list of questions. I agreed to anonymize all interviews. For reasons that I can no longer recall, it came to be assumed (by whomever, but eventually by me) that I could not ask my interviewees *why* they had left Germany because it would somehow insinuate that they had committed crimes during the war or that I would appear to hold them somehow responsible for the Holocaust.[14] I had in part been alerted to the idea that German immigrants may be sensitive when speaking about "the war," because I had received a few anonymous messages telling me to stop wallowing in "the past," and, specifically, to abstain from researching German immigrants' Nazi activities (which I was explicitly not doing). My own upbringing in Germany made me sensitive to the idea of talking with Germans who had lived through the Third Reich. Since the late 1960s there had been a general consensus among the postwar generations that the older generations had utterly failed in coming to terms with the past and had been complicit, to say the least, in forgetting and silencing the past after the war. At the time Meisinger put the note on the table, the months-long sensitization to potential ethical concerns about postwar Germans' presumed Nazi sympathies had made me particularly impressionable to such an incident.

Concerns about the completeness or coherence of the story and fears of failing as an interviewer or human being were not immediate, as the extensive description in the transcript documents: for me, the specific incident was not off the record. It was only many years later, when I began to write about this particular episode, that these concerns crept up. For a long time I wondered whether and how I could use this information, which I now understood to be off the record. I came to the conclusion that anonymity was sufficient protection for the interviewee. Yet, this did not address several questions. Why had Meisinger decided to start a story that she knew would likely end up the way it did? Narrative coherence is a powerful communicative force; once a story is begun, a narrator is no longer fully in control of it. It develops its own dynamic. It demands to be told and finished. What is our responsibility when we detect such dynamics? Experienced orators, like politicians and celebrities, know how to steer a story into safe havens. Many others, who, like Meisinger, tell a private story in public for the first time, do not.

At the same time, as I listened again to the interview and read the transcript, it is clear that I accepted Meisinger's "off-the-record" request, because I did not pursue the topic. The literature on sexual abuse in domestic service had prepared me to pursue one line of questioning, but the ethical concerns about German migrants' relationship to the Nazi past—concerns that lingered for eight years, until I began interviewing for a project that focused on just these encounters with the Nazi past—had closed off another line of questioning, implicating me in the postwar silence about the Nazi past that my generation and that of my parents had so vehemently rejected. There were no silences where I perceived them, and there were silences where I did not see them.

Oral Historians' Irrational but Understandable Fear of Silence

These off-the-record incidents tell us something about our troubled and troubling relationships with silence. We are faced with a dilemma. Intellectually, we know that there will always be silences in our interviews and that such silences are telling; we can write papers and books about them. Emotionally, however, we fear silence. Silences signal more than a loss of information. They signal a loss of control and a resistance to our wish to know, explain, and understand.[15] They constitute an attack on our professional and personal identity.

An oral history interview is a "conversational narrative"[16] that is the product of the moment and a specific situation. Our interviewers perform narratives in interaction with us; their lives are narrative constructions, their memories shaped by social and cultural conventions. Intellectually we know that there is not one true story out there, enclosed in a container called memory that can be excavated with the right tools. Yet, we do everything in our power to learn and use the right tools so that we may avoid silences. The better the interviewer (the better his handling/knowledge/development of the right tools), our guides tell us, the fewer silences there will be. I do not wish to discard this sentiment as positivist method, but I am perplexed by the disconnection between our documentary method and our constructivist understanding of life stories. Do we use positivist methods in our interviews to arrive at postmodern truths in our books?

Oral historians have developed a methodological apparatus that, through sophisticated interrogation techniques and capturing technologies, aims to record and archive people's memories in a finite form: an analog or digital medium stored in a warehouse. Our guidebooks tell us to buy the best equipment we can afford and on the listserve H-OralHist we discuss whether we should use audio or video recording, because we wonder which of these technologies captures more information. According to those standards, recordings ideally are uncompressed, not just in digital format but also in content—we want people's memories in WAV, not in mp3. All of these aspects of the apparatus insinuate that the final product is complete; it has a beginning and an end—it is secured in a container.

Oral historians have also developed a theoretical apparatus, one that tells us that the data we captured are far from fixed, finite, or complete. Memories are fleeting, products of encounters between interviewers and interviewees, effects of social discourses and narrative conventions, and only residually and indirectly connected to lived experiences. We draw on this apparatus as we write our own stories about the captured memory fragments, we use bits and pieces—fragments of fragments—and we draw on our memories and notes of everything that happened off the record, to explain the incompleteness of the ostensibly complete, archived record.

Emotionally, however, silence is difficult for us on several levels. As people interacting with others, we find that "silences are particularly disturbing if they disrupt the conversational flow." What is at stake here are "feelings of belonging, self-esteem, and social validation." Even a brief silence can result in "negative emotions and feelings of rejection."[17] We are comfortable with silences in interviews only as long as we control them.

Silence troubles us also as professionals. There is little that oral historians—just like other researchers in the humanities, social sciences, and even natural sciences—fear more. What happens if our sources, our informants, our lab experiments do not speak (to us), or at least not in a way that we can share with other researchers? Silences call into question our identity as good and successful researchers.

Silence is a double-edged sword.[18] It is a symbol and tool of oppression. Those who are silent are so because they have been silenced (oppressed, subjugated, and discriminated against), not because they chose to remain silent. By giving the silenced an opportunity to interrupt this silence, to fill this silence with words, to give voice, to speak up and out, they can be liberated. Our conviction that oral history is a tool to overcome oppressive silence, to liberate through speaking, to democratize history by giving people a forum for their testimonies provides motivation and drives much of our work. When our interviewees fall silent, we are troubled: did we silence them? Why do they reject our generous offer of a public forum for their voices?

For the subaltern, however, silence may also be a powerful weapon, and often it is their only one: "Lies, secrets, silences and deflections of all sorts are routes taken by voices or messages not granted full legitimacy in order not to be altogether lost."[19] Both Dirk and Meisinger revealed secrets and taboos. By speaking off the record, they ensured their experiences did not become "altogether lost."

We fight silence with silence. Ritchie suggests combating interviewees' silences with silence itself. If an interviewee's answers are short and perfunctory, he advises, the interviewer may need to keep quiet: "Silence indicates that an interviewer expects more. Ten seconds can seem excruciatingly long if neither party is speaking, but can encourage the interviewee to give a more detailed response."[20] Valerie Yow counsels that the length of interviewer silences depends on the "narrator's pacing." She also mentions the ten-second pause, but warns that long pauses may disaffect the interviewee.[21] For Ritchie and Yow, interviewer silence is legitimate as long as it does not diminish rapport.

Even if our interviewees choose to remain silent, we often do not let them. We make our interviewees speak through theory.[22] Now trained to "listen to silences," oral historians, Luise White charges, have turned silence into "another site of interpretation." This, she argues, "got out of hand...Anyone whose voice was not included had been silenced, and any number of interviews were interpreted for what was unsaid, rather than what was said. This gave interviewers much more power than they would admit wielding...Not speaking was not seen as resistance but as oppression."[23] We have then developed methodological and theoretical responses to our interviewees' silences. But we have not developed ethical responses. An ethical response will have to balance two concepts that are at times in conflict with each other, as Yow explains: "Protection of the well-being of the persons studied and truth in publication."[24]

Toward an Ethics of Silence

What may an ethics of silence entail? The following are tentative and hesitant suggestions that use my own, limited off-the-record experiences as a springboard. First, simply accepting interviewee silence seems to be neither constructive nor responsible, at least not if we accept Portelli's claim that a good interview is hard work for both interviewer and interviewee and should leave both parties changed.[25] Silences may be the most uncomfortable spaces in our interviews, for both, interviewee and interviewer. Luisa Passerini, Kathryn Anderson, and Dana C. Jack focused in their interviews on the difficult choices their female narrators had to make in their lives.[26] Tracy E. K'Meyer and A. Glenn Crothers "pushed [their interviewee] to talk about topics we considered more important than she did."[27] Accepting silence may implicate the interviewer in the narrator's silence (Meisinger) or silencing (Dirk). Persistence in asking questions about silences can be positive if we keep in mind not only our own interests but also those of the interviewee.

Indeed, we should talk about silences during our interviews, not just afterward. Writing about reticence in oral history interviews, Lenore Layman states: "I do push against reticence within an individual interview if only to be certain that the narrator is definite about it."[28] But is leaving it at that and moving on to the next topic the best interviewing strategy? In my interviews with Meisinger and Dirk, I should have taken the time to address these silences. In my interview with Dirk, leaving the tape recorder off, I could have asked questions after he told me the story. In my interview with Christel Meisinger, I could have continued the interview and, at the very end, asked questions about it, on or off the record. There are many questions to ask about silence: Why did they feel this was an important story? Why did they believe they could not say this on record? What would have to change to have them talk about it on record? And finally, what part or version of the story, if any, would they consider saying on the record? Such questions may encourage narrators to reflect further on their decision to go off the record. This probing leads to "thick dialogue"[29] that transcends "a rehearsal of comfortable and conventional formulas"[30] and gets at "the story behind the story."[31] Responding to silence during interviews means learning more about different kinds of silences and attempting to find out what exactly our interviewees are expressing through their silences.

Second, we need not worry about silence as being destructive of "the record" if, instead, we broaden our own concept of a "complete archival record" to include our interviewee's concept of "the record." From an archival perspective, silence connotes a loss of information. But silence includes both verbal and nonverbal communication.[32] Narrators, as Julie Cruikshank and Tatiana Argounova-Low, point out, have their own concept of "the record" in mind and it may include more than one version.[33] Dirk and Meisinger had different ideas about the record they wished to leave for me and a broader audience. Narrators are aware "that they speak through their interviewers to a larger audience,"[34] but they nevertheless draw a distinction between the stories they tell us and those they tell an anonymous audience.

Third, we need to acknowledge the power of silence as a rhetorical tool, and we have to study how we and our narrators use it in oral history projects. For Donald Ritchie, who interviews savvy politicians, it makes sense not to go off the record. But going off the record may also be the only means an interviewee has of asserting agency. Ritchie must be read against Dwight Conquergood, who writes that "subordinate people do not have the privilege of explicitness, the luxury of transparency, the presumptive norm of clear and direct communication, free and open debate on a level playing field that the privileged classes take for granted."[35] Different relations of power in interviews create different regimes of silence.

Fourth, in our theoretical approach to silence, we need to negotiate a dilemma posed by Luise White: how should we write about silences? Is our writing a colonization of our interviewees' silences? Does our listening to and writing about silences construct a Benthamian panopticon around our narrators? White argues for a return to Michel Foucault's notion of silence as a discursive strategy.[36] In his exploration of the excessive discourse about sex in the Victorian period, Foucault found that it was important not only to locate what was and was not said, but also how the speakers and the silent were "distributed" in society and which discourses were "authorized."[37]

Finally, and this is connected to the first point, silence shapes our interviewees' identities as well as our own. Giving narrators time to reflect instead of rushing in with the next question makes us skilled interviewers; as the narrator tells a story, questions come to us, but we must remain silent and enjoy its fruit when most of our unasked questions are eventually answered. Conversely, however, if we lose control over our interviewees' silences, they threaten our identity. When an interviewee asks us to stop recording or begins to communicate via paper scraps, there is a break—often unexpected—in the conversation. Such "severe breaches of conversational and interview etiquette...also implicate the interviewer by suggesting implicitly that the question was inappropriate."[38] It is quite understandable that we fear, in such situations, that there may also be a rupture of rapport or even a break of trust. We cannot help but react emotionally, we cannot help but take this personally, we cannot help but doubt ourselves at such moments. As we attempt to control these situations, we often wonder, "What did I do wrong?" Going off the record and other silences are assaults on our identities as both oral historians and human beings who wish to be liked.

But going off the record is not always an outright refusal to answer. Both Dirk and Meisinger wanted to tell me a story, as a lecture and as a confession. This was *their* use of the interview, *their* agenda. In sharing authority with the interviewee, the interviewer accepts that oral history is not just "history-telling"[39] but an interactive communication guided in part by the interviewee's objectives. If we fail to listen to and probe these silences, we may become complicit in perpetuating them.

Perhaps, understanding silences, both our own and our interviewees', as constructive rather than destructive may be a first step toward an ethics of silence. "Patient listening"[40] must be combined with a more active engagement and questioning of silences that may resist understanding by both interviewer and interviewee. Accepting silences may be the most beneficial way forward after we have collaboratively, with our interviewees, probed the deeper meanings of such silences. Only then will we find a balance between protecting the well-being of our interviewees and "truth in publication."[41]

Notes

1. Mary Jo Maynes et al., *Telling Stories: The Use of Personal Narratives in the Social Sciences and History* (Ithaca: Cornell University Press, 2008), 9–10, 109–10, 119; Patricia A. Adler and Peter Adler, "The Reluctant Respondent," in *Inside Interviewing: New Lenses, New Concerns*, eds. James A. Holstein and Jaber F. Gubrium (Thousand Oaks: Sage Publications, 2003), 153–73; Lenore Layman, "Reticence in Oral History Interviews," *Oral History Review* 2 (Summer/Fall 2009): 207–30; Tracy E. K'Meyer and A. Glenn Crothers, "'If I See Some of This in Writing, I'm Going to Shoot You': Reluctant Narrators, Taboo Topics, and the Ethical Dilemmas of the Oral Historian," *Oral History Review* 34, 1 (Winter/Spring 2007): 71–93; Werner Enninger, "Focus on Silences across Cultures," *Intercultural Communication Studies* 1, 1 (1991): 1–38; Namkje Koudenburg, Tom Postmes, and Ernestine H. Gordijn, "Disrupting the Flow: How Brief Silences in Group Conversations Affect Social Needs," *Journal of Experimental Social Psychology* 47, 2 (2011): 512–15; on a family's collaborative remembering through "empty speaking," see Alexander Freund, "A Canadian Family Talks About Oma's Life in Nazi Germany: Three-Generational Interviews and Communicative Memory," *Oral History Forum d'histoire orale* 29 Special Issue "Remembering Family, Analyzing Home: Oral History and the Family" (2009): 1–26; on conformity, see Robyn Fivush, "Speaking Silence: The Social Construction of Silence in Autobiographical and Cultural Narratives," *Memory* 18, 2 (2010): 88–98.
2. I thank Anna Sheftel and Stacey Zembrzycki for inviting me to speak at the "Off the Record" workshop.
3. Alexander Freund and Laura Quilici, "Exploring Myths in Women's Narratives: Italian and German Immigrant Women in Vancouver, 1947–1961," *BC Studies* 105–106 (Spring/Summer 1995): 159–82; Alexander Freund, "Troubling Memories in Nation-Building: World War II—Memories and Germans'

Interethnic Encounters in Canada After 1945," *Histoire sociale/Social History* 39, 77 (May 2006): 129–55.

4. Valerie Raleigh Yow, *Recording Oral History. A Practical Guide for Social Sciences* (Thousand Oaks et al.: Sage, 1994), 136; Adler and Adler, "Reluctant Respondent," 153.

5. Alexander von Plato, "Contemporary Witnesses and the Historical Profession: Remembrance, Communicative Transmission, and Collective Memory in Qualitative History," trans. Edith Burley, *Oral History Forum d'histoire orale* 29 (2009): 1–27; Alexander v. Plato, trans., Christoph Tonfeld, ed. Alexander Freund, "Interview Guidelines," *Oral History Forum d'histoire orale* 29 (2009): 1–5; Almut Leh, "Ethical Problems in Research Involving: Contemporary Witnesses," trans. Edith Burley, *Oral History Forum d'histoire orale* 29 (2009): 1–14.

6. Donald A. Ritchie, *Doing Oral History: A Practical Guide*, second edition (Oxford University Press, 2003); Yow, *Recording Oral History.*

7. Betsy Brinson, "Crossing Cultures: An Interview with Alessandro Portelli," *Oral History Review* 28, 1 (Winter/Spring 2001): 87–113; for an expanded and more widely circulating version of this story, see Alessandro Portelli, *The Battle of Valle Giulia: Oral History and the Art of Dialogue* (Madison, WI: University of Wisconsin Press, 1997), 183–98, 186.

8. Ritchie, *Doing Oral History*, 98.

9. See chapter 2 in this volume.

10. Fivush, "Speaking Silence," 96; emphasis in original.

11. Christel Meisinger (pseudonym), interview by author, Burnaby, British Columbia, Canada, December 1, 1993.

12. Freund, "Canadian Family"; "A German Post-1945 Diaspora? German Migrants' Encounters with the Nazi Past," in *German Diasporic Experiences: Identity, Migration, and Loss*, ed. Mathias Schulze, et al. (Waterloo, ON: Wilfrid Laurier University Press, 2008), 467–78; "Troubling Memories."

13. Alexander Freund, "'How Come They're Nice to Me?' Deutsche und Juden nach dem Holocaust in Nordamerika," in *Migration und Erinnerung. Reflexionen über Wanderungserfahrungen in Europa und Nordamerika*, ed. Christiane Harzig (Göttingen: v & r unipress 2006), 143–56.

14. On some of the negative effects of formalized ethics requirements, see Adler and Adler, "Reluctant Respondent," 154–56; Portelli, *The Battle of Valle Giulia*, 55–71, 56.

15. Maggie MacLure, Rachel Holmes, Liz Jones, and Christina MacRae, "Silence as Resistance to Analysis: Or, on Not Opening One's Mouth Properly," *Qualitative Inquiry* 16, 6 (2010): 492–500.

16. Ronald J. Grele, *Envelopes of Sound: The Art of Oral History*, second revised and expanded edition (Chicago, IL: Precedent Publishing, 1985), 136.

17. Koudenburg et al., "Disrupting the Flow," 512.

18. Fivush, "Speaking Silence," 88.

19. B. Johnson, *A World of Difference* (Baltimore: Johns Hopkins, 1987), 31, quoted in MacLure et al., "Silence as Resistance," 497.

20. Ritchie, *Doing Oral History*, 94.

21. Yow, *Recording Oral History*, 98–99.

22. Smith, "Analytic Strategies," 348.

23. White, *Speaking With Vampires*, 75.

24. Yow, *Recording Oral History*, 130.

25. Portelli, *The Battle of Valle Giulia*, 55–71. Also see his afterword to this collection.

26. Cited in Richard Candida Smith, "Analytic Strategies for Oral History Interviews," in Holstein and Gubrium, *Inside Interviewing*, 347–37, 353.

27. K'Meyer and Crothers, "'If I See Some of This in Writing,'" 90.

28. Layman, "Reticence," 226.

29. Portelli, *The Battle of Valle Giulia*, 11.

30. Smith, "Analytic Strategies," 364.

31. K'Meyer and Crothers, "'If I See Some of This in Writing,'" 91.

32. Michal Ephratt, "Linguistic, Paralinguistic and Extralinguistic Speech and Silence," *Journal of Pragmatics* 43, 9 (2011): 2286–307.

33. See chapter 2 in this volume.

34. Smith, "Analytic Strategies," 363.

35. Dwight Conquergood, "Performance Studies: Interventions and Radical Research," in *The Performance Studies Reader*, ed. H. Bial (London: Routledge, 2004), 311–22, 312, quoted in MacLure et al., "Silence as Resistance," 498.

36. White, *Speaking With Vampires*, 77.

37. Michel Foucault, *The History of Sexuality, Volume 1: An Introduction*, trans. Robert Hurley (New York: Vintage Books, 1990 [1978]), 27.

38. Eva M. McMahon, "A Conversation Analytic Approach to Oral History Interviewing," in *Handbook of Oral History*, eds. Thomas L. Charlton, Lois E. Myers, and Rebecca Sharpless (Lanham et al.: Altamira Press, 2006), 353.

39. Portelli, *The Battle of Valle Giulia*, 24–39.

40. As recommended by MacLure et al., "Silence as Resistance," 498.

41. Yow, *Recording Oral History*, 130.

CHAPTER 13

The Heart of Activism in Colombia: Reflections on Activism and Oral History Research in a Conflict Area

Luis van Isschot

A catastrophic rupture with the past caused by the surge of right-wing paramilitary groups in Colombia's oil capital of Barrancabermeja since 2000 has led social activists to reflect candidly on the role that once-dominant leftist guerrilla groups played in local history. In an attempt to understand how right-wing forces came to dominate the city, known as the "heart of activism" in Colombia, many of the people I interviewed spoke about how their perceptions of the guerrillas changed over time. I lived and worked as a human rights observer in Barrancabermeja in 1998, the first year in a devastating siege during which more than one thousand people were killed.[1] Between 1999 and 2002 I traveled regularly between Washington, DC, Ottawa, Canada, Bogotá, and Barrancabermeja on behalf of an international human rights organization, enabling me to discuss current events with local activists as they unfolded. When I returned to Barrancabermeja to conduct oral history interviews in 2005, I found the city completely transformed. Progovernment paramilitary forces were now in charge,[2] and the insurgent guerrillas that held sway in the city's poor neighborhoods for more than two decades were in full retreat. The violence that has gripped Barrancabermeja since the mid-1980s has been directed mainly against progressive social movements by the Colombian military and their paramilitary allies.[3] Many of the people I interviewed were under constant threat, and just starting to come to terms with the new reality of right-wing dominance. This, significantly, included a critical reappraisal of the role played by insurgent groups in the Colombian conflict.

This chapter is about the mutually constitutive nature of social memory and current events. As Luisa Passerini observed in her study of postauthoritarian Italy, oral history narratives are shaped by contemporary social and cultural concerns.[4] In my conversations with embattled social movement leaders in Barrancabermeja, conducted between 2005 and 2007, many people relived the circumstances that gave rise to the most recent crisis and asked tough questions about how events unfolded. The guerrillas were never as brutal as the right-wing nexus of paramilitaries, armed forces, and drug-traffickers that emerged during the late Cold War period. But social movements were by no means immune from how armed insurgent groups exerted themselves. Had the actions of the guerrillas also contributed to the foreclosure of the political space claimed by Colombia's oldest and most vibrant popular organizations? The original purpose of my oral history interviews was to speak with the protagonists of Barranca's social movements about the origins of human rights activism in the strategically important oil producing and refining center. I wanted to know how the city's culture of popular radicalism was transformed by the dirty war of violent repression during the 1980s. However, our conversations were pulled, time and again, into the present, as we sought to make sense of the *toma de Barranca*, or the occupation of the city by paramilitary forces.[5] These first-person accounts provide valuable insight into the possibilities and limitations of human rights organizing in conflict zones. It is a way of accessing the hidden transcript, not just of resistance, but of frustration, disillusionment, and adaptation.[6] These narratives raise the kinds of complex philosophical and political questions posed by social activists seeking to maintain their autonomy in the midst of armed conflict. It is not that Barranca activists have all of a sudden come to question the role of armed guerrilla groups, but that the abrupt and brutal paramilitarization of the city brought long-held anxieties to the fore. While tracing my own journey from activist to academic, this chapter explores how activists living in conflict areas respond to traumatic change and the ways that these experiences inform the construction of social memory. This is not an attempt to tell the fullest or most revealing version of the "truth" about life and work in a conflict area. It is, rather, about the contingency of oral history, and how conversations about the past can open new fields of enquiry. My education as an oral historian is also central to the construction of the narratives that I listened to while conducting interviews. Despite my background as a human rights activist, I embarked on this project somewhat naively. I set out to learn from activists who daily interact with state bureaucracies, security forces, and illegal armed groups. Yet my focus was narrowly historical in the sense that I was intent on resurrecting an idealized past. What was Barrancabermeja like prior to the onset of counterinsurgent violence?

This was partly a survival strategy. Having been a human rights activist I was well aware of the need to exercise caution while in the field, not to give anyone an excuse to either accuse me of meddling in current affairs, or deny me access to valuable archives, or worse. Being a historian, I believed, would inoculate me from accusations that my research was overly political. It was not until I reread my transcripts that I realized the history I was attempting to write would be incomplete without some reflection on the interplay between past and present.

The "Heart of Activism" in Colombia

The longevity and combativeness of Barrancabermeja's social movements is due to the city's unique history as an oil refining center as well as widespread identification among *barranqueños* with radical nationalist, working-class, anti-establishment politics. Its strategic importance has made the city of 300,000 a focal point in Colombia's armed conflict. Barrancabermeja is the unofficial capital of the large resource-rich Magdalena Medio region that includes parts of five Colombian states, or *departamentos*. It serves as a key regional base of operations for the Colombian army, navy, and national police. Since the late 1960s, multiple leftist guerrilla and right-wing paramilitary formations have been active in Barranca and its environs.

Colombia is well into the fifth decade of an armed conflagration that most people refer to simply as *el conflicto*, the conflict. The Colombian guerrillas were born in the mid-1960s at the height of the Cold War, inspired both by local traditions of popular resistance and the Cuban Revolution. Through the latter half of the twentieth century, Colombia's two major political parties shut out opposition voices through a combination of violent repression, emergency legal measures, and a bipartisan power-sharing agreement.[7] The guerrillas' influence grew in the 1980s as frustration with conventional politics persisted. While several smaller insurgent groups disbanded or sued for peace, the Revolutionary Armed Forces of Colombia (FARC) and the Army of National Liberation (ELN) remained at arms. In response to the challenge posed by the guerrillas, the Colombian military aided and abetted the deployment of right-wing paramilitary forces. Beginning in the early 1980s, army officials worked with drug traffickers to set up death squads in the countryside, just south of Barrancabermeja. At the same time, official security forces began carrying out their own covert terrorist operations in the city. The guerrillas pursued a parallel strategy of military expansion, fueled in part by the extortion of profits from the drug trade.[8] By the end of the 1990s, the country's guerrilla groups were nearly 30,000 fighters strong.[9] Paramilitary groups also continued to grow during this period.[10] A massive influx of American military aid following the approval of the $1.3 billion Plan Colombia in 1999, contributed significantly to the overall militarization of the country.[11] Although their stated mission was counterinsurgency, the paramilitaries targeted any persons they considered to be their ideological enemies, especially trade unionists, social movement activists, and organized indigenous and African Colombians.

Marxist-inspired and nationalist ideologies were significant forces in Barranca politics in the twentieth century. In the 1920s, radical socialists helped organize the city's first oil strikes.[12] Popular radical tendencies in the region culminated in 1948 with an armed uprising known as *la Comuna de Barrancabermeja*, the Barrancabermeja Commune. The *Comuna* rebels then formed small rural guerrilla bands that continued fighting for the next decade. The Army of National Liberation (ELN) launched its war on the Colombian state in 1964 in the foothills of the eastern *cordillera* of the Andes Mountains, just a few kilometers from Barranca. Legal activists from movements that shared the guerrillas' revolutionary politics, such as the Communist Party (PCC), the Patriotic Union (UP), and ¡*A Luchar!*, were among the first to be attacked by paramilitaries in the city. But the hardest blows were dealt to ordinary citizens with no political affiliations, who participated in popular forms of protest. A massive military and police presence in Barranca limited the guerrillas to outlying suburbs. When I worked in Barranca, the city was divided between the center and the *barrios*, where the guerrillas operated. When crossing the boundary into guerrilla-dominated areas at night, taxi drivers would turn on the inside light so that whoever was watching could see who you were. The presence of guerrillas, and the military response this engendered, posed serious challenges to the city's social movements and, particularly, their right to maintain space for civilian activism.

Oral History and the Study of Human Rights

This chapter recognizes ambiguity in a highly polarized context. The social narratives of war often reproduce overly simplistic interpretations of extremely complex issues. The competing versions of historical events advanced by warring parties, backed as they are by lethal force, tend to marginalize independent voices. During the year I spent in Colombia, my colleagues and I were extremely judicious in how we used and shared sensitive information. Human rights activists know that it is not always wise to broadcast accusations against human rights violators. The effects of an ill-considered missive denouncing local military leaders can be very serious. An "urgent action" or declaration to the media can increase the reach of terrorist actions. Amnesty International (AI) recognized early on that publicly denouncing repression, though a strong impulse, was not always the best strategy. In its 1968–1969 annual report, AI observed: "The publication of criticism always produces retaliation. Criticism does not always need to be public and great care is taken to avoid publicity if reasonable progress seems possible without it."[13] Human rights activists have learned to engage carefully with political and moral complexities. While the objectivist discourse of human rights may help to shield them from some criticism, Colombians' experiences suggest that there is no way of avoiding hostile responses on the part of abusive states and armed groups.

Many foreign academics who work on the history of Latin America's most chronically violent country have sought to give voice to popular resistance and political repression. The impulse to do so is strong in the Colombian case, a country that scholars often describe as having a weak history of social movement organization. I am part of a new cohort of international scholars working on Colombia, with direct activist experience and leanings, who have become engaged in human rights debates since the escalation of the Colombian conflict in the 1990s.[14] In her ethnographic study of human rights claims and counterclaims in Colombia, entitled *Counting the Dead*, anthropologist Winifred Tate correctly observes that the term "human rights violation" is used by human rights workers to make violence socially legible, establish accountability, and locate specific acts within broader histories. She adds that the framework of human rights has been used by different groups to advance profoundly different ideological projects. I chose to utilize an oral history methodology precisely because I wanted to explore the contentious politics that give rise to human rights movements.[15] While the history of human rights activism cannot ignore the prevailing narratives of atrocity that human rights movements themselves reproduce, we can use oral sources to look critically at why, how, and with what impact people organize collectively around human rights.

Human rights struggles are not merely humanitarian struggles. No social activist can separate human rights from political principles. In Colombia, the movement to protect human rights has been led by the veterans of social, labor, and left political movements.[16] However, human rights defenders are often held up to putative standards of objectivity that cannot be met. Anthropologist Flor Alba Romero observes: "The movement for the defence of human rights [emerged] during the 1970s in open conflict with the state."[17] Colombian progressives deserve to be credited for their leadership and creativity in the development of socially and politically engaged notions of human rights. In Barrancabermeja, the human rights movement was rooted in a deep current of activism that predated the rise of the guerrillas by several decades. One way of acknowledging this legacy is by sharing activists' stories.

Even before I moved to Barranca, I had heard about the workers' strikes and civic protests of the 1970s and 1980s. An exiled *barranqueña* living in Canada in the late 1990s, who encouraged me to join the human rights group Peace Brigades International in Colombia, was the first person to tell me about this extraordinary place. I would later interview her in her home in Bogotá while conducting my doctoral research. Like most of my interviewees, she expressed a nostalgic view of Barranca's activist past, as well as a deep sadness. Recalling the times that she participated in searches for people who had disappeared, she said: "Don't ask me about those experiences, they are too painful."[18] Despite the sting of loss and the danger of reprisal, activists continue to draw inspiration from the social memories of popular protest.[19] Felipe, who works for the oil workers' union, was raised in the Communist Party. During our interview, he remembered a time when "throwing rocks" at the police was part of growing up.[20] These were the years prior to the rash of killings of social activists in the 1980s, after which human rights became the language of popular protest. I wanted to tell the stories of the community organizations and trade unions that made Barranca such a hotbed of activism.

Barranca residents who came of age in the late 1960s and 1970s, prior to the onset of dirty warfare, were inspired by the romance of the revolutionary struggle. Former student leader Francisco, the son of an oil worker, recalled feeling that radical change was possible in Colombia. Francisco was expelled from university in 1971 following a series of bitterly fought student strikes. He returned to Barranca emboldened.[21] In our interview, conducted in the office where he works with the Catholic Diocese of Barrancabermeja, he described his journey to activism:

> My father was an oil worker and I was able to study at the seminary in Barrancabermeja and was in contact with a kind of elite, so I had many contacts and relationships with those people. When I finished high school I had big expectations, as a young person, to become a professional and fill my pockets with money and get a pretty girl, but after I caught the revolutionary fever, let's just say, I became obsessed. I took it on with all of my strength. I had a new perspective. I have thought a lot about the past, and I feel that my own personal history is starting to open up, and at times I think to myself... what would have become of me if I had not gone to live in the northeast of the city? If I had been a good student, studied hard, been responsible, and all of that?[22]

Francisco was part of a generation of community organizers in Barranca who, over the next decade, claimed a prominent place alongside the oil workers' union. The longing he expressed about his education as an activist and the role he played in building the city's civic movements were typical of the stories I heard in most of my interviews. The "what would have become of me" was an assertion of pride in what he achieved, and the fate he avoided by embracing service to the community over career goals.

A respected former leader within the *Pastoral Social*, the social service branch of the Catholic Church in Barranca, Francisco did not seem at all shy about discussing his process of coming to consciousness. The combined political and moral force of Marxism and liberation theology shaped his worldview. Camilo Torres Restrepo, a Jesuit priest and sociology professor at the National University in Bogotá, inspired a generation of Catholic progressives.[23] Torres had literally given up his life as a teacher and intellectual to join the armed movement. Killed in 1966 during his first combat mission in the hills east of Barranca, Torres remains a nationally recognized martyr and symbol of self-sacrifice. As Francisco explained, young radicals aspired to the same ideals and ethic of personal sacrifice:

> When I graduated from secondary school in 1967, I went to study at the Industrial University of Santander (UIS). When I was at university, it was a hotbed of revolutionary theories . . . It was during this time that I was first exposed to Marxism and to the practices of activist Christians, activist Catholics. I was a member of Catholic Student Youth and became active with the student movement at the UIS. Then I was expelled in 1971. I returned to Barrancabermeja defeated, but having made a heroic gesture on behalf of the popular and social cause. It was the time of great influence of Camilo Torres, of the theology of liberation, of the influence of the Golconda Group. It was a time of great political and social reflection within the Catholic Church.[24]

Not long after his expulsion from university and return to Barranca, Francisco moved from his parents' home to the squatters' neighborhood of Las Granjas. He spent the next 12 years living and working there as a community organizer on behalf of the *Pastoral Social*. Backed by Catholic Church leaders in Barranca, Francisco and others helped to provide legal representation to local communities as they fought for decent public services, including potable water, education, and health care. Living among the hard-working migrants who settled in Las Granjas, and marrying into a local family, Francisco's political convictions were strengthened.[25]

Barranca's reputation as a leftist bastion is widely known, though often exaggerated and oversimplified. The notion that the city was "controlled" by the guerrillas was something I heard many times from outside observers during the late 1990s, ranging from foreign diplomats to international aid workers. There is no evidence that Barranca's social movements worked on behalf of insurgent groups. Depicting Barranca as a rebel city has been the pretext for the systematic repression of civil society by Colombian state security forces. It also denies the historical evidence demonstrating how church, trade unions, and community-based organizations built up an expansive and pluralist popular social movement in the city over many decades. Scores of Barranca-based activists have been murdered for allegedly supporting the guerrillas. The list of victims includes dozens of trade unionists as well as members of the city's main human rights group, the Regional Committee for the Defense of Human Rights (CREDHOS). In 1991, CREDHOS secretary Blanca Valero was shot and killed on the street in front of the organization's downtown office. Valero's murder coincided with the publication of an opinion piece by CREDHOS president Jorge Gómez Lizarazo in the *New York Times*, in which he accused the Colombian military of working with paramilitaries, "forcing human rights activists to abandon their regions and try to do their work from Bogotá or abroad."[26] Claims by officials that human rights defenders secretly support the guerrillas continue to justify attacks on all critics of the state.[27]

Reflecting on the Guerrillas' Legacy

The activists I interviewed were keen to reflect on the guerrillas with hindsight. At the center of many of these retrospective criticisms are memories of how the presence of armed guerrilla members in the city, beginning in the late 1980s, changed popular protest. Of special interest to Barranca-based activists is the way that the *paro cívico*, or civic strike, a form of citizen-led general strike pioneered by neighborhood groups and trade unions, was transformed into the *paro armado*, or armed strike, by the guerrillas.[28] As paramilitary repression increased, the guerrillas grew more brazen. Whereas they had previously distributed leaflets or raised banners at protests, they were now convening and leading the protests themselves. A *paro armado* would often be announced with the burning of a bus on the bridge separating Barranca's poor eastern *barrios* from the main part of the city, sending residents hurrying to the safety of their homes.

As Colombia's political violence deepened in the 1980s, in response to the collapse of peace talks between the guerrillas and the government and the concurrent rise of paramilitary groups, the imperative to protect social movements increased. If civil society groups were to survive the onslaught of official repression and retain their autonomy, there would have to be a clear separation from the guerrillas. María, a Bogotá-based activist who worked in support of the ELN guerrillas in the 1980s, and traveled regularly to Barranca as a "fixer" for journalists wanting interviews with guerrilla militants, recalled her own process of disillusionment. In our preinterview conversations she expressed strong feelings that the role of the guerrillas had become a blind spot for academics, many of whom seem unable to address the contradictions that previous generations of Colombian activists faced. I was keen to hear more:

> This was the 70s and 80s, the period of revolutionary fervor in Latin America. There were all sorts of reasons for this fervor, in the sense that change was absolutely necessary in terms of improving peoples' lives, and that revolutionary struggle involving arms was a legitimate thing to do. In terms of my own experience, it was very much about the discourse that it was a peoples' revolution, it was not about 10,000 guys in arms taking power. It was about building

a base of support for change, and without that base of support, it would never happen, that was the discourse. There really did seem to be the possibility of a historical political project making a difference… and revolution was one of the viable ways to produce a radical change. What that looked like on the ground was, in retrospect, quite different. First of all, you are dealing with an army. An army has a certain kind of structure, a certain way of dealing with the world. Clandestinity was another element of revolutionary organizing. So, how do you build a base of support amongst popular organizations, social movements, with a clandestine military leadership, which is what the guerrillas were proposing? It was very complicated. There was interference, there was control, there were disputes about what needed to be done… when it came down to the crunch, Daddy was always there saying you can do this, you can't do that.[29]

Throughout our interview, María continued in the same vein, expressing disappointment and resentment about what she perceived to be guerrilla interference in social movement organizing. In hindsight, she concluded, it was too difficult to try and combine legal and clandestine forms of popular organization.[30] María's personal decision to cut ties with the revolutionary struggle illustrates perennial tensions between social movements and the guerrillas.

The guerrillas learned that they would never achieve their revolutionary aims without popular support. Fabio Vásquez, who served as top commander of the ELN from 1964 through 1974, had once maintained that the guerrillas represented a revolutionary elite. It is estimated that Vásquez ordered or approved the execution of 200 ELN members and collaborators in internal purges carried out during his tenure with the guerrillas.[31] Vásquez stepped down in 1974 after a crushing military defeat that saw the ELN's fighting force reduced by 90 percent. He fled to Cuba, where he continues to live in self-imposed isolation. Through the next decades, the ELN reached out to organized civil society. But, as María remarked, the effort to build a mass movement was complicated:

You cannot build a popular organization from a clandestine military leadership. I mean, it is just a contradiction in terms. But this is with a lot of hindsight. It was not simply manipulative. They really wanted that popular support. But it was really a contradiction that was impossible to overcome, because clandestinity is a very difficult thing to manage when you are talking about a mass movement. I mean, they just don't go together. A mass social movement may want to take off in directions that collide with what the military structure would like to happen. And there were many of those kinds of confrontations.[32]

The men who emerged as leaders of the ELN following this period—Manuel "el Cura" Pérez and Nicolás "Gabino" Rodríguez—defined the organization's new political-military direction for the next 25 years. But the goal of moving beyond the vanguardism of the past proved difficult.

The contradictions between different forms of struggle were acutely felt in Barrancabermeja, where social movements have strong roots. While their leadership style was less authoritarian than that of Vásquez, the second generation of ELN leaders remained protective of their power. There have been many politically motivated homicides in Barranca's short history, but few have been as significant or as confounding as the murder, in 1985, of ELN cofounder and Barranca native Ricardo Lara Parada. Lara Parada's complex personal journey from student militant to guerrilla leader and back to civilian life parallels the recent history of the Magdalena Medio region. The former guerrilla had left the ELN a decade earlier and was branded a traitor. His assassination on November 14, 1985, in Barranca by members of the organization he helped to build was one of the events that marked the start of a dirty war between the state, paramilitary forces, and guerrillas. According to Betty, a longtime teacher and activist, the murder of Lara Parada foreshadowed an increase in guerrilla actions that ran counter to Barranca's tradition of pluralist civil protest:

> When the guerrillas began to take control of the *paros cívicos*, many leaders were afraid. If [the guerrillas] had behaved differently, in a more civilized way, the history of Barrancabermeja would have been very different from what it is now. I am totally convinced that the death of Ricardo Lara Parada changed everything. The ELN killed Lara Parada, and that intolerance, that thinking that the armed struggle was going to lead to liberation... the guerrillas just were not capable of seeing the very important role that Ricardo Lara was playing. This changed the struggle in Barranca. Because until that time, everyone, ELN [*elenos*], FARC [*faruchos*], right wing, left wing, whatever... we could listen to one another and tolerate one another. But the death of Lara Parada brought out the differences between us. In spite of all of this, we were able to join together, organize ourselves and defend our lives. But we lost leadership.[33]

The killing of Lara Parada drove a wedge between factions of the left in Barranca, and opened the door to the encroachment by armed groups on civilian organizing spaces. This shift toward the militarization of protest is remembered by Betty and others as something that upset the spirit of nonviolence that had guided social organization in the city. Another longtime activist told me: "Barranca has a libertarian spirit, it is a city of convergence... death is foreign to the popular imaginary of native *barranqueños*."[34] The battle for armed dominance in Barranca thus had disastrous consequences for social movements.

From her office in an elementary school in the city's low-income southeast district, Betty has had a direct view of the transformations that have taken place in Barranca. The final offensive undertaken by the paramilitaries and security forces in the late 1990s seemed to push the guerrillas into a corner. Before leaving the city, the guerrillas became engaged in a war against *sapos* (literally "toads," a pejorative term for informants). The final disarticulation of the guerrillas' urban militias was devastating, as some individual fighters joined the paramilitaries.[35] As Betty lamented, multiple abuses were committed on all sides, and confusion reigned:

> The guerrillas lost their way. They lost sight of the interests of the people…and their own interests. In the end, the guerrillas were very cruel. The only thing that they have done in this neighborhood is change their uniforms. The paramilitary occupation, it is a degenerated version of the guerrillas. Here it was not like in other parts of the country where outsiders came. No, here those who were guerrillas one day were paramilitaries the next. It is very sad.[36]

By 2002 the guerrillas had no armed presence in the city. For the first time since the urban guerrilla militia was established in the 1980s, Colombian military personnel now patrol the streets of the *barrios orientales* on foot. According to many of my interviewees, the paramilitary takeover of the city was occasioned by the decline of grassroots social processes relative to the power of guerrilla groups. The ability to inspire social change had previously rested with social movements, not with the guerrillas.

Conclusion

One of the main challenges in writing the history of Barranca is to make sense of what may seem to an outside observer, and perhaps a good number of local residents, as a litany of tragic events. A while ago I wrote to a friend in Barranca to tell her that I had completed my doctorate. Her response was full of warmth and congratulations but it ended with the following: "Here we are living the worst sort of monotony in the universe. Deaths, accidents, accusation, misery. This is our daily bread."[37] How can we use activists' perspectives to make sense of the tragic and oftentimes baroque reality that is the Colombian conflict? The stories that can help us illuminate Colombian history are often too terrible or too dangerous to recount. How do you tell the history of a war that is, for the most part, fought by clandestine forces? Do you trust your own eyes?

Barrancabermeja was the most violent city in Colombia from 1998 to 2002. The city experienced a profound political transformation during that period. The new reality of paramilitary dominance has caused many activists to reflect on the losses suffered during one of Latin America's longest, bloodiest, and least-known dirty wars. The paramilitary takeover of the city has prompted some people to reflect on the contributions and contradictions of leftist insurgent groups. In our interview, human rights activist Yedira attempted to make sense of the contradictions at play: "In terms of the guerrillas, we had certain things in common ideologically, but not in terms of defending human rights. Questioning the guerrillas was an attempt to elevate them to ethical standards they claimed."[38]

If it is true, as has been argued by historian Charles Bergquist, that Colombia resists social scientific explanation, then we need to employ alternative methodologies.[39] Anthropologists Michael Taussig and Winifred Tate have observed something similar. The "frantic fear" and the sense of a "permanent state of emergency" experienced by people living in the midst of armed conflict and repression is often lost in the retelling. How do we resolve the problem of the inscrutability of violence?[40]

Human rights activists and oral historians both work hard to maintain their powers of trust and discretion, albeit for different reasons. Returning to Colombia to undertake academic research after having spent five years as an advocate for human rights there, I was granted rare access to community activists and archives. Networks that exist for the protection of human rights in conflict areas differ from other civil society networks because their members are frequently required to respond to emergencies. When the telephone rings, you may answer to find a colleague in distress on the other end of the line. It is not unusual for such crises to occur on the weekend, in the early morning, or late evening. You have to be able to retain key pieces of information, while being sensitive to the emotional state of the person in danger. During the course of my research, I cautiously explored new pathways of dialogue with interviewees and confidants, friends and colleagues. At no point during my interviews did I knowingly ask anyone to step outside of their comfort zone. More often than not, I was the one being tested. I wanted to avoid the conceit of "insider information." I did not want to claim authority, based on a false idea that as a former activist I had access to deeper, uncomfortable truths. Oral history methodology teaches us how historical narratives are acted upon by the present. Contemporary circumstances influence not just how historians interpret past events, but which events they choose to focus on. The dialogue between oral history and human rights can help us problematize and deepen debates around the impact of armed conflict on popular organization.

Notes

1. Banco de Datos de Violencia Política, Centro de Investigación y Educación Popular (CINEP) and Corporación Regional para la Defensa de los Derechos Humanos (CREDHOS), "Barrancabermeja, la otra versión: paramilitarismo, control social y desaparición forzada, 2000–2003," *Noche y Niebla Caso Tipo No. 3* (Bogotá: CINEP/CREDHOS, 2004).

2. There is a small but growing literature in English on the paramilitarization of Colombia: Winifred Tate, "From Greed to Grievance: The Shifting Political Profile of the Colombian Paramilitaries," in *Colombia: Building Peace in a Time of War*, ed. Virginia Bouvier (Washington, DC: United States Institute of Peace Press, 2009); Jasmin Hristov, *Blood and Capital: The Paramilitarization of Colombia* (Athens, Ohio: Ohio University Press, 2009); "Self-Defense Forces, Warlords or Criminal Gangs? Towards a New Conceptualization of Paramilitarism in Colombia," *Labour, Capital, and Society* 43, 2 (2010): 13–35. On recent developments in Barrancabermeja, see Lesley Gill, "Durable Disorder: Parapolitics in Barrancabermeja," *North American Congress on Latin America Report* 42, 4 (July/August 2009): 20–24.

3. There were between three thousand and five thousand murders committed in Barranca between 1982 and 2002. See Vicepresidencia de la República de Colombia, "Panorama actual de Barrancabermeja" (Bogotá: Observatorio del Programa Presidencial de Derechos Humanos y Derecho Internacional Humanitario, 2001), 8. The Coroner's Office concluded that more than 80 percent of the 754 homicides committed in 2000 and 2001 were politically motivated: Centro de Referencia Nacional Sobre la Violencia, "Lesiones infligidas por otros," published between 1999 and 2008.

4. Luisa Passerini, *Fascism in Popular Memory: The Cultural Experience of the Turin Working Class*, trans. Robert Lumley and Jude Bloomfield (Cambridge: Cambridge University Press, 1987), 19.

5. Michael Taussig's *Law in a Lawless Land: Diary of a Limpieza* allows us to see the process by which paramilitaries lay siege to a town in the Valle de Cauca through the eyes of a concerned outside observer: *Law in a Lawless Land: Diary of a Limpieza* (Chicago: University of Chicago Press, 2005).

6. James C. Scott, *Domination and the Arts of Resistance: Hidden Transcripts* (New Haven: Yale University Press, 1990).

7. Paul Oquist, *Violence, Conflict, and Politics in Colombia* (New York: Academic Press, 1980).

8. Nazih Richani, *Systems of Violence: The Political Economy of War and Peace in Colombia*, second edition (New York: State University of New York Press, 2013).

9. For an overview of the Colombian conflict at the time, see Charles Bergquist, Ricardo Peñaranda, and Gonzalo Sánchez, eds., *Violence in Colombia 1990–2000: Waging War and Negotiating Peace* (Wilmington, DE: Scholarly Resources Books, 2001).

10. Forest Hylton, *Evil Hour in Colombia* (New York: Verso, 2006), 116.

11. Ibid.

12. Medófilo Medina, *Historia del Partido Comunista de Colombia*, vol. 1 (Bogotá: Editorial Colombia Nueva, 1980).

13. James N. Green, *We Cannot Remain Silent: Opposition to the Brazilian Military Dictatorship in the United States* (Durham, NC: Duke University Press, 2010).

14. Notable individuals, who were or remain close to activist causes in Colombia, include former Washington Office on Latin America (WOLA) associate and anthropologist Winifred Tate, as well as Lesley Gil, Jasmin Hristov, Leah Carroll, and journalists Gearóid Ó Loingsigh and Gary Leech.

15. Luis van Isschot, *The Social Origins of Human Rights: Protesting Political Violence in Columbia's Oil Capital, 1919–2010* (Madison: University of Wisconsin Press, forthcoming).

16. Winifred Tate, *Counting the Dead: The Culture and Politics of Human Rights Activism in Colombia* (Berkeley: University of California Press, 2007).

17. Flor Alba Romero, "El movimiento de derechos humanos en Colombia," in *Movimientos sociales, estado y democracia en Colombia*, eds. Mauricio Archila and Mauricio Pardo (Bogotá: Centro de Estudios Sociales, Facultad de Ciencias Humanas, Universidad Nacional de Colombia, 2001), 445.

18. All interviewee names within this chapter have been changed to pseudonyms. Anonymous interviewee, interview by author, Bogotá, Colombia, March 14, 2006.

19. The concept of social memory is attributed to sociologist Maurice Halbwachs, who argued that social groups or communities may develop "agreed upon" versions of the past by means of public communication and the sharing of stories. See Jacob C. Climo and Maria G. Catelli, eds., *Social History and Memory: Anthropological Perspectives* (London: Alta Mira Press, 2002), 4.

20. Felipe, interview by author, Barrancabermeja, Colombia, October 26, 2006.

21. Francisco, interview by author, Barrancabermeja, Colombia, October 26, 2006.

22. Ibid.

23. Spanish priests Jose Antonio Jiménez, Domingo Laín, and Manuel Pérez were also members of the ELN. See Joseph Novistski, "Radical Priests in Colombia, Heirs to Slain Guerrilla, Have Forged an Open Marxist-Catholic Alliance," *New York Times*, February 16, 1970.

24. Francisco, interview.

25. Ibid.

26. Ibid.

27. Colombian President Álvaro Uribe Vélez (2002–2010) delivered his first public attack on Colombian human rights activists on September 8, 2003. Throughout the speech, he referred repeatedly to human rights "traffickers" who profit from making the Colombian state look bad. Presidencia de la República, "Palabras del Presidente Uribe en posesión de Nuevo Comandante de la Fuerza Aérea de Colombia, Bogotá," Álvaro Uribe Vélez, http://www.presidencia.gov.co/prensa_new/discursos/fac.htm.

28. "Civil strikes essentially involve the total or near-total paralysis of all activity in a city, to demand that the government resolve problems related to public services, issues that effect the whole population." See Jaime Carrillo Bedoya, *Los paros cívicos en Colombia* (Bogotá: La Oveja Negra, 1981), 13.

29. María, interview by author, Bogotá, Colombia, October 28, 2006.

30. Ibid.

31. Alfredo Molano, "La justicia guerrillera," in *El caleidoscopio de las justicias en Colombia*, volume 2, eds., Boaventura de Sousa Santos and Mauricio García Villegas (Bogotá: Siglo del Hombre Editores, 2001), 332.

32. María, interview.

33. Betty, interview by author, Barrancabermeja, Colombia, March 8, 2006.

34. Anonymous interviewee, interview by author, Bogotá, Colombia, March 14, 2006.

35. Examples of such desertions have been documented since the 1980s. See Francisco Cubides, "From Private to Public Violence: The Paramilitaries," in Berquist, Ricardo Peñaranda, and Gonzalo, *Violence in Colombia 1990–2000*, 136.
36. Ibid.
37. Anonymous author, personal correspondence with author, December 2009.
38. Yedira, interview by author, Bogotá, Colombia, September 27, 2005.
39. Charles Bergquist, *Labor in Latin America: Comparative Essays on Chile, Argentina, Venezuela, and Colombia* (Stanford: Stanford University Press, 1986), 270.
40. Tate, *Counting the Dead*, 22.

CHAPTER 14

"I don't fancy history very much": Reflections on Interviewee Recruitment and Refusal in Bosnia-Herzegovina

Anna Sheftel

All of them have their own stories, I mean they watch from their own point of view, and there are three different histories, and that is one of the reasons why I don't fancy history very much, because the winners always write the history.

—Elvir[1]

When I undertook an oral history project for the first time, during my doctoral studies in history, it was for many of the usual idealistic reasons. My research examined the construction and evolution of individual and local memories of twentieth-century violence in Bosnia-Herzegovina and how the state's frequent manipulation of its official histories impacted them. I wanted to not only learn how history is experienced on the ground, but also understand how peoples' experiences and memories affect the dynamics of postconflict societies. I therefore loved the disciplinary literature's focus on speaking truth to power and giving voice to the voiceless.[2] Once I found myself in the field trying to put these lofty ideas into practice, however, I discovered that giving voice to the voiceless was more difficult and ambiguous than I had realized. I struggled to find willing interviewees. At the time, as a doctoral student desperate to get her research done, this was a source of stress and shame. Now that I am able to reflect on the process, I view my refusals as part of an important reality: people have far more complex relationships to remembering and speaking about the past than we often acknowledge. My recruitment challenges therefore got to the heart of the mnemonic phenomena that I was interested in studying.

Most oral histories are still written with little mention of the context in which interviews took place. Such discussion tends to be relegated to introductions and conclusions. This absence has significant consequences for budding oral historians: when your experiences in the field do not match the ideal scenarios found in methodological essays, you panic. I arrived in Bosnia-Herzegovina with the naïve expectation that a group of people who had survived mass violence, and who had been largely ignored or marginalized in public and academic discussions of that violence, would be banging down my door to speak with me. This did not happen. It took me three months to get my first interview. Many people turned down my requests to be interviewed. While many also agreed, I have only recently begun to admit and discuss my recruitment difficulties. I began doing so when, during "off the record" conversations with other oral historians, I learned that my experience was relatively common. Friends and colleagues confessed that it had taken them a great deal of effort to find willing interviewees as well.[3] I therefore wondered if my experience had any significance both for my specific study, and for oral history as a craft. The Achilles' heel of oral history is that we only hear the stories of the people who are willing to speak to us; we can never learn about the full range of experiences and memories within a given community because there will always be some who will not speak. To deepen our understandings of what it means to remember a complex past, we should, at the very least, attempt to understand why those who refuse us make this choice.

In this chapter, I reflect on my experiences recruiting interviewees in Bosnia-Herzegovina, and how these refusals contributed to my overall understanding of the dynamics of wartime memory in the region. I then ask how oral historians can develop ways to interpret and write about these previously ignored parts of the process. I argue that within the context of my own research, a refusal to talk to me, on the record, was part of a larger regional phenomenon that speaks to a distrust of history and historical narratives. I ask how one can conduct oral histories in a place where, as Elvir succinctly told me, people "don't fancy history very much."

Contextualizing Refusal

I chose to situate my case study around the city of Bihać, which is located in the northwestern corner of Bosnia-Herzegovina, for various reasons. While it is difficult to find a truly ethnically diverse area of Bosnia because the country is currently divided into two separate entities, this region does boast considerable populations of the three major ethnicities: Bosniaks (the majority),[4] Croats, and Serbs.[5] The Bihać area has also been understudied due most probably to its distance from Sarajevo—it has less of an international presence than anywhere else in Bosnia.[6] The only other foreigners I met while I lived there in 2005–2006 were a handful of peacekeepers and Christian missionaries, an English teacher, and a couple of nongovernmental organization (NGO) workers. Most foreigners simply pass through the area, and so my presence was obvious and noteworthy in this city of approximately 40,000 people. I hoped that this would help me with interviewing. At the time, I owned a bright red trench coat that I wore throughout the fall and spring, so I quickly became known as "the Canadian in the red coat." Notoriety, however, did not immediately translate into formal interviews.

Bihać also made for an interesting case study location because it was an important location during World War II and the Bosnian War. People there are most proud of the fact that the city hosted the first meeting of the Anti-Fascist Council for the People's Liberation of Yugoslavia (AVNOJ) in the fall of 1942.[7] This was the first organized congress of Josip Broz Tito's communist partisans, which took place during a brief ten-month period when the region around Bihać was unoccupied, making it one of the few unoccupied zones in Europe during the war. Many see it as a foundational event of the second Yugoslav state.[8] Today, this historical moment is a defining feature of Bihać's identity as a city. This is in stark contrast to the more general experience of World War II in the former Yugoslavia, which included fascist occupation, a fascist Croatian state and genocidal movement named the Ustaša, and violent clashes between competing resistance groups, such as the Communist Partisans and the largely Serb-led loyalist Četniks.[9]

When Tito inherited a profoundly fragmented Yugoslavia in 1945, he paid special attention to how the war would be historicized. He constructed a sterilized account of World War II, which overlooked the complex dynamics briefly described earlier, and united all Yugoslavs in a joint struggle against fascist occupying powers and their few internal collaborating traitors. This narrative was the Yugoslav state's founding myth, glorifying the partisan resistance[10] while deliberately silencing anything that challenged this narrow interpretation.[11] This vision of World War II worked well within Bihać because it boasted such an important part of that story of resistance.

This politic of remembering resistance and forgetting ethnic violence unraveled quickly following Tito's death in 1980 with the near immediate publication of many dissenting histories.[12] History became an increasingly political tool in the 1980s, employed by nationalist leaders so as to convince citizens of their nationalist agendas. Franjo Tudjman revived the memory of the Ustaša, while Slobodan Milošević exhumed the mass graves of Serbs massacred during World War II.[13] It is in this historically charged environment that war broke out in the

1990s, marking the physical end of the Yugoslav state and shocking Yugoslavs and the world with the brutality of the violence, ethnic cleansing, and genocide that took place in Croatia, Bosnia, and Kosovo. I provide this summary to show that history has, throughout the twentieth century, been politically instrumentalized in the region, leading both to stability and violence.

Bihać's experience of the Bosnian War, which took place between 1992 and 1995, was considerably less glamorous than its World War II story. The area around Bihać was ethnically cleansed early in the war, while the United Nations (UN) declared the city a safe area in April 1993 along with Sarajevo, Tuzla, Srebrenica, Žepa, and Goražde. By this time, many Bosniak civilians had already fled to these cities, and so their designation meant that they became demilitarized zones, protected by UN peacekeepers as a means of ensuring the safety of civilians while avoiding a massive exodus of refugees to neighboring European states.[14] Safe areas actually became targets for Serb aggression, precisely because they regrouped civilians so effectively. The July 1995 Srebrenica massacre was the most well-known attack on a safe area; an estimated 8,000 Bosniak boys and men were killed. Žepa fell a week later.[15] While Bihać itself was liberated during a notoriously controversial offensive by the Bosnian Fifth Corps in the summer of 1995,[16] the end of the war came with the signing of the Dayton Accords.

The historical revisionism that began in the 1980s has only continued since the end of the war. There is not a single Titoist truth. There is not even a single Bosnia. Dayton divided the country into two entities as it remains today: 49 percent of the country belongs to the Serb entity of the Republika Srpska and 51 percent belongs to the Federation of Bosnia and Herzegovina. Local communities are thereby more ethnically homogenous than they were before the war. The two entities also makes it difficult for the Bosnian state to function: the presidency is shared by the three ethnicities; and these divisions add an excess of administration that leads to corruption and endless bureaucracy.[17] Croats, Bosniaks, and Serbs in Bosnia have different banks, telephone service providers, beers, schools, media, and alphabets.[18] Narratives of the Bosnian War, and even World War II, are divided as well. Each group of ethnic nationalists has its own story, and each of these serves to advance its own cause.

This is the local and national context that greeted me when I arrived in Bihać in 2005. I provide both contexts because they are crucial for understanding why people responded as they did when I approached them for interviews. They also highlight the regional specificities that are particular to my study. The very purpose of oral history, as I understand it, is to capture the diversity of historical experiences in a way that can only be done by sitting down with the people who have lived them. I therefore do not mean to represent the Bihać experience as universal to Bosnians as a whole. The country is too fragmented to make this possible. The question of how Bihać's particularities interact with the larger politics of postconflict Bosnia is precisely what is interesting. This piece is intended as an instructive example.

I lived in Bihać for eight months and I was affiliated with the local university during that period. I avoided affiliations with NGOs so that I would not be perceived as having particular allegiances. I chose to interview broadly, across generations, genders, ethnicities, and religious and political leanings.[19] I used two complementary interview guides: one for the older generation that had lived through World War II and the Bosnian War, and a second for the younger generation that only had direct memory of the Bosnian War. I asked my interviewees to not only recount their experiences, but also reflect on memory and commemoration in their communities.[20] With the exception of three cases in which my interviewees were fluent in English and insisted on conversing in it, I conducted all of my interviews in Serbian-Bosnian-Croatian. I made a conscious decision to learn the language and interview in it because I believed that working with a translator would complicate the interview space. Specifically, I did not want the ethnicity and personal history of the interpreter to affect my interviews.[21] I recorded all of my interviews on a digital audio recorder, which was small and unobtrusive.

This chapter is not about the interviews in and of themselves. It is about the process of getting to them, and especially about the many times that I did not, in fact, get to them. In the following pages, I will draw on excerpts from those interviews that elucidate the dynamics of memory and silence in the Bihać area, as well as on my own reflections on the process, to contemplate why so many people declined interviews. Researchers do not arrive in the communities where they intend to work without their own baggage. However, just as I brought my position as a Canadian, a historian, a human rights advocate, and a former community worker to Bihać, the people whom I wished to interview brought their own experiences of memory and history, and their uses and abuses, to the table.

Encountering Refusal

Before I arrived in Bihać, I expected—given the history I described earlier—that people in the region would be angry about the hegemonization of memory that took place under Tito, and starved for open ways of discussing their violent past without falling into ethnic nationalist traps. Instead, I arrived to a place where people did not "fancy history very much." When I asked interviewees how one ought to remember violence or speak about Bosnia's history, I received many responses like Elvir's. Perhaps the most direct statement of Bosnians' distrust of history came from Irma, who told me: "We have too much history here. That is why we have so many wars."[22] This spoke to the trajectory that I describe in the previous section, which, combined with the local context, has created a paradigm in which the Titoist project of forgetting is associated with an era of relative prosperity and interethnic harmony. The post-Titoist project of remembering, on the other hand, has almost uniquely manifested itself in divisive ethnic nationalist narratives and mass violence. After several people repeated variations on the theme of having "too much history," I began to ask myself how, exactly, I as an oral historian could work with those who explicitly rejected the idea of history.

While distrust of history came up frequently during my interviews, it manifested itself most prominently during interviewee recruitment. Since Bihać is a relatively tight-knit community, it was not hard to make myself known in the area. Bosnia-Herzegovina has an infamous hospitality culture, and within a few weeks of arriving in town, I found myself on a perpetual caffeine high due to all the coffee dates I was summoned to attend. I was also an invited guest in many homes, and in the interest of building trust and accepting people's hospitality, I abandoned 15 years of vegetarianism so that I could partake in the three-course meals that inevitably appeared during these visits. These often featured meticulously cooked steaks that had been purchased on my behalf, despite people's precarious finances. All of this thick Turkish coffee and grilled meat did not, however, translate into interviews. I was interesting to people in the local community because I was one of a handful of foreigners who had ever elected to live in their region, without being sent by some larger organization. That I had learned to speak the local language made me even more novel. People were curious about me and they warmly welcomed me. However, whenever conversations turned to my research, their faces fell. They would ask polite questions about my project, but it was clear that their hearts were no longer in the conversation. This made the prospect of requesting interviews daunting and socially awkward.

Why was this? One reason that came up especially when speaking with younger people was frustration at how Bosnia has come to be seen, internationally, as a backward place prone to violent conflict. Here they were, looking westward and identifying with Europe, while Europe itself only viewed them as downtrodden victims.[23] Bihać's citizens are also very proud of their beautiful mountains and rivers, and their extensive history. I have heard variations on this pride echoed in informal conversations in other parts of Bosnia; it is indeed a beautiful country with a rich culture and history. That yet another person had arrived and was only interested in the ugliest details of their lives was disappointing. I often felt ashamed when I brought up my research topic.

This frustration spoke to many of the broader themes that I explored in my interviews. Contrary to much of the Western literature about the region, many Bosnians see their history as being rooted in interethnic cooperation. This was true long before, and during, the Titoist period. For example, when I would reveal during small talk that I was Jewish, people often commented that the former Yugoslavia, under Ottoman rule, was one of the safest places for Jews in Europe, and amassed its Jewish population from refugees who had fled from other European locations.[24] Bosnia was once a model of cosmopolitanism and multiculturalism, but in the present day it was understood as the opposite. These sentiments are often cited as a reason for Bosniaks' naïveté during the beginning of the war; they thought it was not possible. When I spoke to Elvir about what he knew of the Croatian War, which took place between 1991 and 1992 right across the border from Bihać, as it was happening, he told me how his neighbor had fought for the Jugoslav National Army (JNA) and had come back to tell them stories of the slaughters he had witnessed there. This was the very same JNA that went on to fight the Bosnian Army later that year. When I asked him if his neighbor's stories made him worry about the future of his own city and country, he responded: "No... It was very interesting... How people are naïve, if you can say that, how they always thought, 'Oh that's too far away, it will not happen to us.' We love Serbs, Serbs love us. I mean they're our neighbors, they're our godfathers, whatever."[25] Such statements and mentions of naïveté came up repeatedly during interviews, and are present throughout other oral histories with Bosnians.[26] Some have suggested that by positioning themselves as naïve, and by idealizing prewar Yugoslavia as a multicultural utopia, Bosniaks attempt to evade any responsibility for the resulting violence. Whether or not recollections like Elvir's are ethnically motivated or consciously constructed, most Bosniaks stayed in their towns and cities as violence erupted in the region and crawled rapidly toward them. My interviewees characterized their own city and country as having been so peaceful and idyllic that it was inconceivable to believe it could be hit with such violence; this was at odds with research that seeks to focus almost entirely on violence.

This relates to the second reason why people did not want to speak with me about the war. Elvir's and other's invocations of naïveté suggested that this was not meant to be Bosnia's history; they also communicated a sense of shame about what occurred. The Bosnian War is still physically present in the Bihać area: buildings are pock-marked with bullet holes; windows are covered with plastic sheeting that was provided by the United Nations High Commissioner for Refugees (UNHCR) during the war; and many people, due to a lack of funding, live in half-constructed homes consisting almost entirely of bricks and mortar.[27] These physical reminders were not, however, discussed in the personal or public memories that my interviewees shared with me. For them, the Bosnian War was an embarrassment; it was not something to be commemorated as thoroughly as the World War II Titoist narrative. The latter had led to a state of global stature and the former had destroyed it.

Furthermore, as a researcher, the context in which I was proposing to interview was, no matter how much I tried to avoid it, necessarily institutional. Considering the historiographic context, Irma's concern about having "too much history" seemed to refer to too much institutionalized and subsequently instrumentalized history. Disinterest in remembering and commemorating the Bosnian War was an expression of distrust and alienation from the top-down actors who institute avenues for public remembering. As Ivo told me:

> The last person I want to talk about the war is a politician in this country. We do not like Bosnian politicians generally. Many Bosnian politicians became politicians actually because the war happened. And many citizens of Bihać who were anonymous before the war promoted themselves through war and became really important people in Bihać. And they became rich, they were like warlords. And those people are ruling the country now...Opinions are different. We have an expression in Bosnia. It says *nekom rat, nekom brat,* do you know what it means?...It means, like...war is someone's brother, and the war is for someone else, just the war. Because it helps someone to get what he never had, and the other guy loses everything and is left stranded. Most of the people in the population in Bosnia were screwed by the war, not looking at religion or nationality or...The ordinary citizens were destroyed...I witnessed a lot of injustice, and I am still witnessing a lot of injustice from Bosnian politicians. The Bosnian politicians are the ones that I...belong to, actually, but a lot of injustice is being done all around Bosnia, at this point, and I think the situation will still be the same for a while.[28]

Many interviewees declared that it was good that I was the one doing this research, as it required an outsider to be able to say anything true about the region; Bosnians themselves were too influenced by their ethnic narratives or corruption. I thought that my outsider status, especially as a Jew, since I was not Catholic, Orthodox, or Muslim, allowed me to be seen as a neutral party who could be trusted. Despite this sentiment, reflection of my many refusals made me realize that I was hardly a neutral party. The international community, which has been at the forefront of the institutionalization of Bosnian War memory through such bodies as the International Criminal Tribunal for the Former Yugoslavia (ICTY) as well as various NGO initiatives within Bosnia, is not uncontroversial in the region. Accused of contributing to the protracted violence through the failure of the UN safe areas; of brokering the Dayton Accords, which rewarded aggression and left contemporary Bosnia politically paralyzed; and of running bodies such as the ICTY, which have failed to bring the principal instigators of the genocidal violence to justice; the international community itself is perceived as an actor in the region's violence and therefore my own position as a researcher there could never be neutral.[29]

Finally, the war was not just a topic that presented Bosnia badly to the outside world, that was a source of shame, and that indicted internationals like me. It was also a distraction. As Alen told me: "I don't need to remember the past. I need a job."[30] Frustrated with how ethnic narratives of war kept the country divided and impeded economic progress, the last thing many of my interviewees thought they needed was more discussion of the war. Alen himself was a recent graduate of a local engineering program, but the only job he could get was delivering bottles of mineral water to convenience stores for a salary of under 300 euro a month. This job had to support his entire family, as he was the only one with steady work. Interviewees said that it was difficult for them to mind Titoist limits on freedom of speech when they had work, food, and relatively comfortable lifestyles, with frequent trips to the seaside and opportunities to study and advance themselves. As Alen relayed at another point in our interview:

> But comparing those two situations, before and now, now people are saying that they have more religious freedom than before...I did not experience those kinds of problems before, maybe because I was not involved in a religious community before the war...But that system before had flaws, but no system is perfect. But this present system is really bad for us.[31]

When I offered to interview people, was I, like many other international actors, perpetuating the idea that speaking about the war was more important than day-to-day survival?

With all of this baggage in mind, why did people say yes or no when I finally worked up the nerve to awkwardly ask for an interview? I did not count how many turned me down, but I am certain that they far outnumbered those who agreed to speak with me. This is one of the reasons why writing about my interviews necessitates writing about my rejections; it would be dishonest not to. But why did people also say yes? Those who agreed to be interviewed fell into three categories: they were either interested in discussions about World War II, which was a topic that many older people genuinely loved; or they identified with Bosniak politics that promoted narratives of the Bosnian War as evidence of Serb (and to a lesser extent, Croat) wrongdoing, and this story had become central to their identities as Bosnians; or they thought I was a nice young woman and wanted to do me a favor. As far as I can tell, this middle group, composed of those who actually wanted to speak about the war, consisted of two interviewees, total. The rest fell into either the first or the third groups, or both. My very first interviewees, who later connected me to many others, were friends. While we agreed that we both learned a lot from each other, as they had rarely gone "on the record" with their experiences, it was clear to me that the only reason they had agreed in the first place was as a favor.

Other people, despite being among my closest friends in the region, still turned me down. They told me that it was just not the kind of thing they had anything to say about; that this was not a topic that interested them; or that their stories were not valuable. The first two reasons speak to the themes I have discussed earlier, regarding why people may reject public or institutionalized remembering. Turning me down was yet another way of turning down the whole project of wartime memory. The last idea, that people did not value their own stories, is one that has come up often when I have swapped interview stories with fellow oral historians. Our interviewees often do not immediately understand why we want to listen to them. I considered this devaluing of personal experience within the Bosnian context, where memory was so suspect; was this devaluing a way of rejecting postcommunist mnemonic divisiveness and a throwback to the collectivism of Titoist memory? If people say that their stories are not important, it is perhaps presumptive for oral historians to assume that they need to be "enlightened" as to why they should want to have their most intimate memories recorded. People might have very good reasons for choosing not to value the personal, as Alen told me, when I asked him when and with whom he talked about the war:

> We talk a lot about funny things that happened to us... I talk with friends that were here. When I was in the States, I tried to talk with... people were asking me, "How was it like?" like it was a cowboy movie or something. They were asking me "How was it like?" and then I caught myself, explaining things, trying to explain things in a way, in a way I try to explain it to my friends who actually understand me. And then I realize I can't explain it in a way... it's just really, really hard. They don't understand it in a way that somebody else like [my girlfriend] or my friends, as the people who were here understand you. And then, in the end, it turns out to be, the best thing is to talk with people who stayed here in Bihać during the war, because they understand you, they know what you've been through, they've been through the same thing... So it's the easiest way, to talk to them.[32]

Alen viewed speaking about the past with anyone other than those who had shared similar experiences to be needlessly frustrating. Sometimes oral historians assume that giving personal stories a spotlight, and asking people to share the most intimate details of their suffering, will always make for positive experiences. When I consider my own assumptions, I see how they come from a very Western, Judeo-Christian understanding of what it means to live with difficult memories. As I have demonstrated earlier, there are both political and personal reasons why speaking "on the record" about the war might not be appealing, and they relate to the very subject that I was in Bosnia-Herzegovina to study: the complex dynamics of postconflict memory.

Studying Refusal

I have now had six years not only to think about why recruitment was so difficult, but also to reflect on what I learned from that process. The question I am currently faced with is how to analyze and write about those silences. Luisa Passerini, in considering silence when studying memories of totalitarianism, writes that "the twentieth century has been for the most part a time of cancellation of memory, and . . . it has prolonged the tendency to remove the past—a process . . . deriving from the crisis of memory and experience typical of modernity."[33] She suggests that oral historians' work allows us to counter the repression described earlier and she advocated for paying attention to what goes unsaid within interviews.[34] As I have argued, however, what I encountered in Bihać was not repressed memory yearning to be excavated. Rather, people negotiated the many ways that memory has been used and abused when deciding when and how they would or would not speak. It is important to remember that just because people did not want to speak to me, or to other researchers, does not mean that they did not remember the war, or that they never remembered it out loud. What they were refusing, specifically, was having their memories recorded, interpreted, and historicized. Of course they talked about the war, as Alen's comments noted. They just did not want to talk about it with somebody like me.

While oral historians are increasingly apt to pay attention to silences within interviews,[35] we still lack ways to talk about structural silences, such as refusals to be interviewed. Instead of seeing these refusals as challenges that impede the research process, we should view them as important information that is integral to our research. After all, in studying how war is remembered in this community, and in asking people to recount those memories on a recording that would or would not be public, but that would at the very least be cited in publicly available scholarship, I was becoming part of how war was remembered there. I went to great pains when I was establishing myself in Bihać to communicate that I was not there to be an authority on what happened in the war, but that I was there to try to understand my interviewees' subjectivities. Nevertheless I now realize that the moment I pressed "record" on my audio recorder I of course became another conduit for public remembering. Many scholars of the former Yugoslavia have written very critically about the region's historiography, and because that is a site of so much controversy, historians themselves have been treated as actors, and not impartial observers, in Yugoslavia's unraveling.[36] There has been a tendency, however, to draw a line between insider and outsider historians, with the former being the primary objects of suspicion. When Elvir told me that he does not "fancy history very much," did he mean history written by local, national, or international historians? Do people outside academia care about making such distinctions? While some interviewees urged me to write an objective history, others, in their resistance, clearly did not see me as an impartial observer at all. This was, again, instructive and relevant for understanding how Bosnians navigate the region's complex historiography. Therefore, if I can contribute one piece of insight into how we may study and write about topics like the refusal to be interviewed, it is simply that we *should*.

We must be open to understanding silence and refusal as legitimate ways of interacting with the oral history process and, consequently, with the idea of remembering difficult pasts more generally. My biggest mistake, when conceptualizing my project, was in assuming that the utopian language of truth and reconciliation, and of healing through open dialogue about the past, would automatically resonate with people.[37] In many places in Bosnia, it does.[38] However, my own biases as a Western scholar, which are steeped in this kind of language, blinded me to the reality that this was but one way of grappling with memories of violence, and not the default. Anthropologist Robert Hayden has similarly argued that Western scholars writing about the region have been unable to see beyond their own perspectives of how one manages postconflict challenges, to how Bosnians themselves perceive their challenges.[39] We must be open to listening to all modes of communicating about the difficult past, even those that contradict our own perspectives. It is especially important to unpack the assumptions that oral historians make about what we are doing when we historicize and interpret people's lives.

Opening ourselves up, however, requires us to develop more thorough ways of listening, researching, and writing. I could not adequately write about the dynamics of silence in Bihać if I were to rely entirely on my recordings. Silence was in the chats I had when I ran into friends and acquaintances on the street; when I brought up my project during those infamous coffee dates; when I introduced my consent form before an interview; and when I attended community events that often had nothing to do with any war.

How do I write about these portentous moments? Academic writing is steeped in footnotes and fact-checking. I can offer neither when writing about my recruitment process. Yet, I am convinced that it was full of meanings, which allowed me to more profoundly understand what I was hearing in my interviews. As oral historians, we acknowledge that our work entails the cocreation of primary sources,[40] and so our writing must take that reality seriously. In the same way that an archival historian contextualizes when, where, how, and why their source was created, placing that source within the debates and challenges that led to its existence, we must put our own processes under the same degree of scrutiny. The difference is that our contexts are more subtle, mired in issues of consent and ethics, and often not recordable. I have been understanding my refusals through two different angles: first, by listening for cues about refusal and silence in my interviews; and second, by reflecting on my informal experiences in the community, which I had never actually imagined as being "part" of my research. How do I footnote that moment where my acquaintance's face fell upon my uttering the words: "I want to interview you about your memories of the war"?

Conclusion

My research in Bosnia-Herzegovina grappled with questions about how people remember war and atrocity; why they choose or refuse to speak; and how all of this interacts with other, more formal levels of memory, such as top-down ethnic narratives of violence. The challenges I faced when trying to recruit interviewees for my project helped me answer those questions. I argue that oral historians must be open to the possibility of refusal as an important, meaning-laden act in the research process, and not just an impediment. If we want to understand how people remember violence beyond what they tell us, we necessarily need to adopt a holistic, interdisciplinary approach.[41] Specifically, we must learn from both ethnographers and communications scholars so that we may expand our notions about where "research" happens [42] and learn to better interpret how and why people communicate with us in all the complex ways that they do.[43] Taking the research process seriously will enable us to see memory as the shifting, situational phenomenon that it is.

My interviewees told me, explicitly, that the issue of when, how, and what to remember was more difficult than simply choosing a side. They were well aware of their own, as well as historians', subjectivities, and this influenced the ways that they interacted with the process. This awareness speaks to how Bosnia has served as a classroom for the ways that history is a living, political, and fallible creature, and not something objective that is dictated from on high. Refusals to be interviewed may thus demonstrate sophisticated understandings of what historical research is, and what its effects can be. People were communicating with me about Bosnia's difficult history when their faces fell and they said no. A refusal is not nothing. It is, itself, a story.

Notes

1. Elvir, interview by author, Bihać, Bosnia-Herzegovina, March 21, 2006. All interviewee names within this chapter have been changed to pseudonyms.
2. See, e.g., Paul Thompson, *The Voice of the Past* (Oxford: Oxford University Press, 2000); Michael Frisch, *A Shared Authority: Essays on the Craft and Meaning of Oral and Public History* (Albany: State University of New York, 1990); Luisa Passerini, ed., *Memory and Totalitarianism* (Oxford: Oxford University Press, 1992).
3. In her forthcoming manuscript, Stacey Zembrzycki explains that she could not get any interviews in her own Ukrainian community in Sudbury, Canada, until she involved her grandmother in the project. Speaking with Stacey about her own difficulties with recruitment was tremendously helpful for my own reflections

on process. See Stacey Zembrzycki, *Sharing Authority with Baba: Wrestling with Memories of Community* (Vancouver: University of British Columbia Press, forthcoming).

4. "Bosniak" is the term most commonly used in the current literature to describe Bosnian Muslims as an ethnicity.

5. Federation of Bosnia and Herzegovina Federal Statistics Office, *Population of the Federation of Bosnia and Herzegovina, 1996–2006* (Sarajevo: Federal Office of Statistics, May 2008).

6. I have only found two English-language academic studies that looked at war in the region: Azra Hromadzic, "Challenging the Discourse of the Bosnian War Rapes," in *Living Gender after Communism*, eds. J. E. Johnson and J. C. Robinson (Bloomington: University of Indiana Press, 2007), 169–84; Max Bergholz, "The Strange Silence: Explaining the Absence of Monuments for Muslim Civilians Killed in Bosnia during the Second World War," *Eastern European Politics & Societies* 24, 3 (2010): 408–34.

7. M. Vukmanović et al., *Bihać u Novijoj Istoriji (1918–1945): Zbornik radova sa Naučnog skupa održanog u Bihaću 9. i 10. oktobra 1986. godine, Tom I* (Banja Luka: Institut za istoriju, 1987); G. Jokić, *Bihać: grad prvog zasjedanja AVNOJ-a* (Bihać and Belgrade: Turističko društvo, 1977).

8. This period is most extensively immortalized in a two-volume collection published by the local AVNOJ museum, which contains thousands of documents related to those ten months: M. Krivokapić et al., eds., *Bihaćka Republika, Prva Knjiga: Zbornik Članaka* (Bihać: Izdanje Muzeja Avnoja i Pounja, 1965); M. Krivokapić et al., eds., *Bihaćka Republika, Druga Knjiga: Zbornik Članaka* (Bihać: Izdanje Muzeja Avnoja i Pounja, 1965).

9. For an overview of World War II in the region, see Noel Malcolm, *Bosnia: A Short History* (London: Macmillan, 1994); Walter R. Roberts, *Tito, Mihailovic and the Allies, 1941–1945* (New Brunswick: Rutgers University Press, 1973); Richard West, *Tito and the Rise and Fall of Yugoslavia* (London: Sinclair Stevenson, 1994).

10. Wayne S. Vucinich, "Postwar Yugoslav Historiography," *The Journal of Modern History* 23 (1951): 41–57.

11. This strategy was first espoused at the Fifth Yugoslavian Communist Party Congress in 1948. See Josip Broz Tito, "Politički Izvještaj," in *Fifth Yugoslavian Communist Party Congress: Information and Reports* (Belgrade: Savez komunista Jugoslavije, 1948). It was later encoded into a law that forbade any type of speech or publication that threatened the health of the communist state. See Amnesty International, *Yugoslavia: Amnesty International Briefing* (London: Amnesty International Publications, 1985).

12. These included, e.g., soon-to-be Croatian president Franjo Tudjman's doctoral thesis, which questioned Croatian guilt in World War II, to a revised biography of Tito by Vladimir Dedijer, who had once been Tito's official biographer. See Franjo Tudjman, *Horrors of War: Historical Reality and Philosophy*, revised edition, trans. Katarina Mijatovic (New York: M. Evans, 1996); Vladimir Dedijer, *Novi Prilozi za biografiju Josipa Broza Tita* (Zagreb: Mladnost, 1980).

13. On the Croat issue, see Dunja Rihtman-Auguštin, "The Monument in the Main City Square: Constructing and Erasing Memory in Contemporary Croatia," in

Balkan Identities: Nation and Memory, ed. Maria Todorova (London: Hurst and Company, 2004), 180–96. On the Serb issue, see Bette Denich, "Dismembering Yugoslavia: Nationalist Ideologies and the Symbolic Revival of Genocide," *American Ethnologist* 21 (1994): 367–90.

14. United Nations Security Council, Resolution 836, June 4, 1993, http://daccess-dds-ny.un.org/doc/UNDOC/GEN/N93/330/21/IMG/N9333021.pdf (accessed March 2, 2010).

15. D. Rohde, *Endgame: The Betrayal and Fall of Srebrenica: Europe's Worst Massacre since World War II* (New York: Farrar, Straus & Giroux, 1997).

16. Bihać's liberation came as part of Operation Storm, the Croat offensive that ethnically cleansed the Croatian *Krajina* region of its Serb minority. See Brendan O'Shea, *Crisis at Bihać: Bosnia's Bloody Battlefield* (Gloucestershire: Sutton Publishing, 1998).

17. P. Andreas, "The Clandestine Political Economy of War and Peace in Bosnia," *International Studies Quarterly* 48 (2004): 29–51; M. Pugh, "Post-War Political Economy in Bosnia and Herzegovina: The Spoils of Peace," *Global Governance* 8 (2002): 467–82; T. Donais, "The Political Economy of Stalemate: Organised Crime, Corruption and Economic Deformation in Post-Dayton Bosnia," *Conflict, Security and Development* 3, 3 (December 2003): 359–82.

18. M. Hanson, "Warnings from Bosnia: The Dayton Agreement and the Implementation of Human Rights," *The International Journal of Human Right* 4, 3–4 (Autumn 2000): 86–104; M. Weller and S. Wolff, "Bosnia and Herzegovina Ten Years after Dayton: Lessons for Internationalized State Building," *Ethnopolitics* 5, 1 (March 2006): 1–13; F. N. Aolain, "The Fractured Soul of the Dayton Peace Agreement: A Legal Analysis," in *Reconstructing Multiethnic Societies: The Case of Bosnia-Herzegovina*, eds. D. Sokolovic and F. Bieber (Aldershot: Ashgate, 2001), 63–94.

19. One serious exception to my multiethnic interviewing approach is that I did not interview any Roma people. This was not intentional, but rather a question of access to that community and also interest in the topic of this thesis. Roma people in the region have a unique story of ethnic persecution that is certainly ripe for academic exploration. Unfortunately it was beyond the scope of my study.

20. My approach to interviewing was influenced by the work of people like Alessandro Portelli, who argues that oral history is about searching for meaning; Ronald Grele, who sees interviews as negotiating the dialectical tension of history and myth in people's minds; and Henry Greenspan, whose methodology brings academic interpretation into the interview space, as an important part of it, rather than as a result of it. See Portelli, *The Death of Luigi Trastulli* (Albany: State University of New York Press, 1991); Grele, "Movement Without Aim: Methodological and Theoretical Problems in Oral History," in *The Oral History Reader*, first edition, eds. Robert Perks and Alistair Thomson (London: Routledge, 1998), 38–52; Greenspan, *On Listening to Holocaust Survivors: Beyond Testimony*, second edition (St. Paul, MN: Paragon House, 2010).

21. For a more profound reflection on using interpreters in politically contested interview spaces, see chapter 9 in this collection.

22. Irma, interview by author, Bihać, Bosnia-Herzegovina, January 26, 2006.

23. My youngest interviewee was 22 years old, and I very much believe that this dynamic is why I failed to recruit any interviewees younger than that.

24. See, e.g., Malcolm, *Bosnia*; John B. Allcock, *Explaining Yugoslavia* (New York: Columbia University Press, 2000).

25. Elvir, interview.

26. See, e.g., Stevan M. Weine, *When History Is a Nightmare: Lives and Memories of Ethnic Cleansing in Bosnia-Herzegovina* (New Brunswick: Rutgers University Press, 1999).

27. On rebuilding, see G. Hovey, "The Rehabilitation of Homes and Return of Minorities to Republika Srpska, Bosnia and Herzegovina," *Forced Migration Review* 7 (2000): 8–11.

28. Ivo, interview by author, Bihać, Bosnia-Herzegovina, March 14, 2006.

29. For critiques of the international community's involvement in various aspects of the conflict, see, e.g., David Rieff, *Slaughterhouse: Bosnia and the Failure of the West* (New York: Simon & Schuster, 1995); Pierre Hazan, *Justice in a Time of War: The True Story behind the International Criminal Tribunal for the Former Yugoslavia* (College Station, TX: Texas A&M University Press, 2004); Isabelle Delpla, "In the Midst of Injustice: The ICTY from the Perspective of Some Victim Associations," in *The New Bosnian Mosaic: Identities, Memories and Moral Claims in a Post-war Society*, eds. X. Bougarel, E. Helms, and G. Duijzings (Aldershot: Ashgate, 2007), 211–34.

30. Alen, interview by author, Bihać, Bosnia-Herzegovina, March 6, 2006.

31. Ibid.

32. Ibid.

33. Luisa Passerini, "Memories between Silence and Oblivion," in *Memory and Totalitarianism*, ed. Luisa Passerini (Oxford: Oxford University Press, 1992), 196.

34. On a similar note, Stacey Zembrzycki and I wrote a piece reflecting on our work with Holocaust survivors, which argued that the places survivors would not go in their recounting were instructive to understanding their identities as survivors. See Anna Sheftel and Stacey Zembrzycki, "Only Human: A Reflection on the Ethical and Methodological Challenges of Working with 'Difficult' Stories," *Oral History Review* 37, 2 (2010): 191–214.

35. See Lenore Layman, "Reticence in Oral History Interviews," *Oral History Review* 36, 2 (Summer/Fall 2009): 207–30.

36. David Campbell, "MetaBosnia: Narratives of the Bosnian War," *Review of International Studies* 24 (1998): 261–328; Ivo Banac, "The Dissolution of Yugoslav Historiography" in *Beyond Yugoslavia: Politics, Economics, and Culture in a Shattered Community*, eds. S. P. Ramet and L. S. Adamovich (Boulder, San Francisco and Oxford: Westview, 1995), 39–65;Sabrina Ramet, *Thinking about Yugoslavia: Scholarly Debates about the Yugoslav Breakup and the Wars in Bosnia and Kosovo* (Cambridge: Cambridge University Press, 2005).

37. On a similar note, Susan Sontag argued that the mere representation of violence and atrocity, such as through war photography, was not in and of itself necessarily a condemnation of violence, and that it is a mistake to assume otherwise. See Sontag, *Regarding the Pain of Others* (London: Picador, 2004).

38. For example, the association that represents the widows and mothers of the men who were murdered at Srebrenica has been very vocal in the fight for a just public record of what happened there. See Association the "Mothers of Srebrenica," http://www.srebrenica.ba (accessed April 5, 2011).

39. Robert M. Hayden, "Moral Vision and Impaired Insight: The Imagining of Other Peoples' Communities in Bosnia," *Current Anthropology* 48, 1 (2007): 105–31.

40. See, e.g., Luisa Passerini, *Autobiography of a Generation: Italy, 1968* (Hanover: University Press of New England, 1996).

41. To this end, I explore how dark humor about the Bosnian War presents an alternative, nonliteral way of remembering the past in my article: "'Monument to the International Community, From the Grateful Citizens of Sarajevo': Dark Humour as Counter-Memory in Post-Conflict Bosnia-Herzegovina," *Memory Studies* 5, 2 (April 2012): 145–64.

42. See Barbara Myerhoff, *Number Our Days* (New York: Dutton, 1979); Ruth Behar, *The Vulnerable Observer: Anthropology That Breaks Your Heart* (Boston: Beacon Press, 1996); Lisa M. Tillmann-Healy, "Friendship as Method," *Qualitative Inquiry* 9, 5 (2003): 729–49.

43. Wulf Kansteiner makes a similar argument in his critique of Memory Studies: "Finding Meaning in Memory: A Methodological Critique of Collective Memory Studies," *History and Theory* 41, 2 (2002): 179–97. For examples of communications and rhetoric-based analyses of difficult memory, see Stephanie Houston Grey, "Wounds Not Easily Healed: Exploring Traumas in Communication Studies," in *Communication Yearbook 31*, ed. C. S. Beck (New York and Abingdon: Lawrence Erlbaum, 2007), 174–223; Marouf Hasian, "Authenticity, Public Memories, and the Problematics of Post-Holocaust Remembrances: A Rhetorical Analysis of the *Wilkomirski* Affair," *Quarterly Journal of Speech* 91, 3 (2005): 231–63.

Afterword

Alessandro Portelli

In November 2012, I was attending a conference in Sanremo, about five hundred kilometers from Rome. On the last night, a young man I vaguely recognized approached me and asked if we could talk. We moved aside and he reminded me that I had interviewed him a few years before in Monterotondo, near Rome, about the town's antifascist history. With tears in his eyes, he told me that he had driven all night because his uncle—a former partisan, who I had also interviewed—read that I was at the conference and wanted me to know that he was nearing death. Also, he had something to say about the Resistance, which he had never told anyone, and he would tell me the story if I went to see him. For me, that initial interview with this man was interesting but it was one of many. I did not realize that to him it was a significant moment of self-expression and its meaning lasted well beyond the duration of our encounter.

In an essay I wrote 30 years ago, I described the oral history interview as an "experiment in equality" in which two individuals, separated by class, age, gender, ethnicity, education, or power endeavor to speak to each other as if all of these inequalities were suspended, and human beings could talk to one another as in a utopian world of equality and difference.[1] For this reason, I have always felt uneasy about the fact that I interview many people and I often never see them again, leaving the relationship, as it were, suspended—at least, on my part. This leaves me with a sense of being inadequate and selfish. Therefore, I took the opportunity offered by the 2011 "Off the Record" workshop, which gave rise to this collection, to dedicate my remarks to three of the people with whom the interview led to a lasting, lifelong relationship that inspired and sustained the writing of most of my work. This afterword evolved out of those remarks. This volume explores the tensions, challenges, and meaningful encounters that emerge out of different oral history experiences. By discussing how I came to know and work with the three people that I describe in the following pages, I hope to highlight just how central relationships are to the varying negotiations found throughout this book, and how they can be transformative, personally and professionally. An ethnography of my own practice would necessarily revolve around these people, whom I have been lucky enough to know and learn from.

I have done three major projects in my life: one focused on the steel workers of Terni; another on the history of Resistance and the Fosse Ardeatine massacre in Rome; and my latest work was about the people of Harlan County in Kentucky. While the Terni and Harlan County projects originated in my interest in the relationship between traditional cultures and modernity in contexts of intense industrialization brought in from the outside, the one on the Ardeatine Caves was meant to correct the historical revisionism, which by "debunking" the narrative of the Italian antifascist Resistance that is at the root of Italian democracy attempts to undermine the foundations of our democratic constitution.[2] Each of these projects has a person that not only made it possible because they told the story, but also made it necessary because I owed it to that person to keep the story going: Dante Bartolini, in Terni, who revealed to me the history and culture of the working-class town where I grew up; Annie Napier, in Harlan, who took me in as a brother and shared her passion for the culture, history, and people of her county; and Mario Fiorentini, a partisan and world-class mathematician, whose stories drew me to the complicated history of the Fosse Ardeatine massacre and the living heritage of the Resistance.

I will start with Dante Bartolini. He was a fighter, a worker, and a poet; I will introduce him with one of his "philosophical" musings:

> See what old folks tell you, my son? We talk about things we lived through, we don't say things like, what they call philosophy. This is a model of the trials we went through and a memory that goes on forever. Sometimes there are comrades who say, when you ask about these things, they'll say, "Forget it, this is philosophy!" What do you mean, philosophy? Is the truth philosophy? Philosophy is the priest that tells you "this is God, this is heaven..." That is philosophy, that moves you, and you think you're going to heaven and instead you go under the earth. And when you're down there, forget it, because we have seen all of the ancestors—none of them has sent us back, what do I know, through the air, through the spirit, a hint to tell us "We're doing fine," or "We're not doing fine." They've suffered, they've died, their trials are over, they're in there, and have turned into air, into ashes, into earth. We are worms of the earth. She made us, and to her we return.[3]

This passage eloquently states Dante's worldview and it has a reflexive style that is very different from some of his epic narrative moments. I also like it because he addresses me as "my son." Much of an interview's meaning is implicit in the way an interviewee addresses you: and he really did become a father figure to me, even beyond our obvious age difference. In fact, Dante Bartolini is the reason I became an oral historian.

I was looking for folk songs, and I was introduced to him as a folk singer, a former partisan, a factory worker, an herb doctor, and many other things. He had composed songs about the Resistance and the labor movement, but he would not sing them without telling their story. He is the first person who told me about the death of Luigi Trastulli, which has since become a sort of standard piece in oral history literature.[4] He made me realize that stories, which are not factually accurate, may be sites of imagination, desires, and dreams. They are as important as mere facts. I worked with Dante from 1972 to 1976 and then moved on to other things and we did not see each other for a while. When he died suddenly in 1978, at the age of 62, I felt that I owed it to him to write the history that he had taught me. My first oral history book was a response to missing Dante Bartolini.

When I first met Dante, he had not sung or told stories in public for years. I told him what I was looking for, and he took me to his cellar, where his notebooks and papers, in which he had written all of his songs and poems, were literally buried underneath a heap of coal. Digging out these papers from the coal was, for me, a metaphor for unearthing memories and reviving gifts and talents that had been buried by a working-class life. He basked in my admiration and the praise he received from many young people to whom I introduced him. Like many artists, he was very narcissistic. He was an actor and a performer, and in many of the stories he told us over the years he played to the expectations of the young revolutionaries in his new audience. He talked about the violence in the Resistance and how he viewed it as a revolutionary war, very much in terms he thought his audiences might like. We found other people in the area—the Nera River Valley, the rural backyard to Terni's steel mills—who could also sing and tell stories, and so we put together a group of traditional singers and storytellers and arranged for them to travel and perform. Not all of their repertoire was politically correct, especially in gender terms, so we had discussions about what was proper to sing. To many of us Dante became a mentor, guru, and father figure. Many of his songs and stories became standards in the oral and folk music revival. In turn, he was very much concerned about me and my life, which he viewed as disorganized and wasteful. This is something I found again and again: once you strike up a relationship with the people you are learning from, they become concerned about you, your life, and your relationships. He was happy when I told him my girlfriend, whom he very much approved of, and I were getting married.

I met Dante as a consequence of one of my most egregious mistakes. I had met an excellent folk singer before him and I failed to explain to him fully who I was and what I was doing. I played the neutral, objective researcher who does not talk about himself, and, of course, if you do not talk about yourself, people will draw conclusions about you on the basis of their own stereotypes. So this man saw me as some kind of bourgeois academic, and he gave me an image of himself that corresponded with this stereotype: he only sang religious or ritual songs, and even a couple of para-Fascist pieces. Only by sheer accident did I later learn that he was a committed communist. When he discovered that I was on the same side, he introduced me to Dante, his daughter's fiancé's uncle. This time I clearly stated that I was a fellow comrade in search of working-class history and culture.

But after he introduced me to a number of partisans and labor activists, I began to notice that he did not introduce me as a "comrade" but as "professor" Sandro. It was the early 1970s, and the Communist Party—of which I was not and have never been a member—was getting over 60 percent of the vote in Terni, so who needed another comrade? Which side I was on was proved by the fact that I was with him; but what they needed was an intellectual, someone with the skills and the means to write their history. This taught me that our contribution to the people and communities we work with depends on how they perceive us, which is not necessarily what we expect.

The relationship between intellectuals and members of the working class, in places like Terni, can be very complicated. In the Communist Party archives I found a 1927 report, at a time when the party was being forced underground, which said that the working-class comrades were frustrated because they were being silenced by the educated people who were joining the party and could speak the jargon of politics better than them. Indeed, the workers were being silenced by "us."

Dante reversed the relationship: he and his comrades were in charge and they actually used me. I learned through Dante that the idea of us "giving voice" to the voiceless is nonsense. Dante was not voiceless, I was. I could not sing, I had no stories to tell, and I was only able to write because people like Dante gave *me* a voice. I returned the favor by listening and amplifying their voices. When my Terni book finally came out, they were not overly impressed: "OK, Sandro's been pestering us for years with this project, now it's out, and it's no big deal." It was just another book—not something to which most of them related immediately. Not all of these storytellers were readers, and their age and eyesight made reading even more difficult. Also, the book contained nothing new to them— they had told me those stories to begin with.

They only recognized the impact of our work when other historians started to quote them from my book. Then they realized that by talking to me they had become part of the canon of sources through which history was being written. They would be heard well beyond their small valley. This is our contribution as oral historians: we give them and their stories exposure and access to a broader public discourse. Taking Dante to sing and tell stories in Rome, Parma, Florence, and even Germany was a way of making these singers and storytellers relevant not just to their comrades, neighbors, and families, but to a national and international audience.[5]

Another person who had a similar impact on me was Annie Napier, from Harlan County in Kentucky. I met her in 1986 and stayed at her house every year after that, for 20 years. I will introduce her with an excerpt from a 1996 interview that was done as part of an audio documentary project that we put together with Charles Hardy III.[6] Again, this was about bringing Annie's voice out of its immediate environment, to a broader audience. As the quote that follows indicates, in our long-standing relationship we had shared the stories many times; but repeating them made sense because this time she would not be talking to just me but to people beyond the boundaries of her everyday community. The concern about whether the tape recorder is on indicates this awareness. Like most of Annie's stories, this story is about life, hardship, and survival, the basic themes of our shared research.

AN: You got it working, huh?

AP: I got it working.

AN: Okay. That'll work.

AP: One thing we should remember is, we've talked to each other so many times that we can—it's hard to say anything new. But we're probably going to use this tape for people who haven't heard about you, so let's just keep it natural, but remember that there's another possible audience for this.

AN: Another possible audience for this.

AP: Okay. Just to get started.

AN: What do you want to know about me?

AP: Oh, everything. Why don't you just tell me about what you did today, what time you got up, you know, these things, your workday.

AN: Well, I got up at six o'clock this morning, and then I went out and drove a school bus until one, and come back in home to referee the kids until bedtime. And it's not too bad. Well, we're going to play music after a while. At least that's fun. That's not working. Yeah.

[...]

If you think about the way we growed up, it was a miracle that we survived. When a baby's born, the first thing is, when a baby's born, all odds in the world is against it, back when I was growing up. The first thing, the houses are so cold, they're lucky to survive. Most of them is born underweight because of nutrition. But then after you get the little critters here, they start doctoring them with these homemade remedies. First thing you do is make you a sugar tit. You know what a sugar tit is?

AP: Like a piece of cloth with water and sugar?

AN: Right. Then they give you catnip tea, which gives you a chronic bellyache. I know that for a fact. Liked to kill Becky Ruth. And then you got all the childhood diseases to go through—measles, mumps, chicken pox, whooping cough. Typhoid fever went around here back in the fifties. I guess it was back in the fifties, late forties, early fifties, from a flood, which one of my uncle's little babies died. And you just think about survival, you know. Before you're ever two years old, you've already beat the odds of survival.[7]

Asking Annie to "keep it natural" was superfluous. She was always natural. She came to the Columbia Oral History Institute in New York City and to the University of Rome, and she was just herself all the time. Yet, it reminds us that this conversation is also about our relationship: we had known each other for years, yet she still needed to make sure I understood what she said: "[Do] you know what a sugar tit is?"

I had always wanted to go to Harlan County because I had heard the struggle songs that came from its working-class history. I mentioned this to Guy Carawan from the Highlander Center[8]—he taught us all the song "We Shall Overcome"—and he suggested that I look up the Cranks Creek Survival Center, which was run by Annie's half-sister. So I called her, and asked if I could come and do an interview, and she said: "Come on over." Only ten years later did Annie mention that, after my call, her sister called her, and said, "This guy called me and he wants to do an interview, what are we going to do?" They talked it over, and concluded: "If he ain't too stuck up, we'll talk to him."[9] It took me another two years before I got around to asking Annie "What made you think I *wasn't* too stuck up?"

In order to understand her reply, you must imagine her. She was very poor. Her husband was a disabled and unemployed coal truck driver. She had two daughters with three children from different fathers while still in their teens and was raising them all. She had worked in a factory to make sure her younger daughter could get an education. She played music. She worked with the Cranks Creek Survival Center, driving a truck halfway across the United States to pick up donated clothes and food and then she would help give these supplies out to people even poorer than she. She would drop everything when I visited, to come with me and do interviews. There was just one thing she did not have time for: housekeeping. Her house had not been cleaned in years. A proud person, she was sensitive about this. When I managed to invite her to Rome and she stayed at my house—not a shining example of organization either—she kept making remarks about how nice and well-kept it was. So, when I asked her what made her think I was not stuck up, she said: "You came in, and you didn't look for a clean place to set you butt on."

To this day, I cannot remember whether I really did not look, because I was so excited to be there, or I quickly decided it was useless. But then, it was a test. I learned early that the distinction between the observer and the observed is a myth. An inter-view is about two people looking at each other. The observed observe us, and they are often shrewder than we are, because they judge us from our body language and from behavior of which we are not even aware. This is not just personal. For over a century, the people of the Southern Mountains have been "observed," judged, and humiliated by well-meaning onlookers—missionaries, sociologists, folklorists, and politicians.[10] They have been exposed to this stigmatizing gaze, which explains their poverty as a consequence of their culture, or even their biology. So they are used to "stuck-up" visitors looking down at them. Not surprisingly, they resent them.

So I passed a test I did not even know I was taking. Annie became my sister. I loved her dearly and her family became my Harlan County kinfolk. The time I shared with them, as with Dante and Mario Fiorentini, was not just about interviewing and recording, but included sharing meals, taking train and car trips, and being present during family visits. We grew to know each other as people and friends well beyond the interviewer/interviewee, historian/informant relationship. This is the reason why I grieved so much when Annie and Dante passed away.

The typical scene in Annie's home was centered around two old couches, set at an angle, one facing the television and the other facing the stove. She would sit by the stove, facing the television but never really looking at it, with a cup of coffee and a cigarette. You can hear her cough on the tape. Smoking eventually killed her. I sat on the other couch, and I would just turn the tape recorder on, and the stories would pour out of her. Often she accompanied me on drives around the county, introducing me to people that I would never have reached without her—the most marginal who were not included in the grapevine of recognized authorized speakers and storytellers. As we drove along, I would just hang the microphone on the rear-view mirror in front of her, and we would talk. In the book, I have a harrowing description, although without some of the goriest details, of the birth of her first child. Annie told me this story when we were stalled in a traffic jam in Rome. It was always like being at the fountainhead of storytelling:

AN: Well back then we didn't have no TV, or no radio or anything and at night time when it got dark you had to go in on account of snakes.

AP: They come out a lot?

AN: We got rattlesnakes and copperheads around here, but at night time we'd go in and build a fire in the fireplace and mommie and my daddy would sit around and tell us stories about when they were growing up. And stories that their parents had told *them* about growing up. That's where the storytelling started from. And when you trace it back it's all fact. It's real you know, it's been real all the time.[11]

The first time I saw Annie, we were at her sister's house, and she came out on the stoop at dusk and called out: "Children, come on in, it's getting dark, and they're craw-w-w-lin'..." So my introduction to her had to do with snakes. Stories in Harlan County are mainly about two things: snakes and "ghosties." One literally dark and stormy night we were sitting on the couch as usual, in this isolated house on top of Stone Mountain, and she asked: "Do you believe in ghosties?" I said: "No." And she replied: "I don't either. However,"—and she paused—"there's one that walks every night from the porch to the kitchen."[12] There is a classic Italian play by Eduardo De Filippo and the title is "It's not true but I believe it."[13] She was just the opposite: "I don't believe it, but it's true." Later on she told me that each time they moved the ghost moved with them because it was attached to two of their possessions: an antique rocking chair and a gun that was actually used, she said, to kill people in the union wars in the 1920s. I come from an urban environment where you rarely see a snake or a ghost, or think about them; so I was both scared and fascinated. On my first visit, Annie's husband Chester explained: "We have copperheads and rattlesnakes right in the backyard." He gave me a detailed description of the different types of snakes in the backyard, and then reassured me: "Don't worry: snakes are more afraid of you than you are of them. They can hear you coming and just crawl away." I gave a sigh of relief, but he went on: "However, this time of the year they can't hear you because they're shedding their skins and they're deaf."[14] So when Annie told me about the ghost, I was not sure whether I wanted to sleep in the house with the ghost, or in the car outside with the snakes. Finally, I decided that I believe in snakes more than I believe in ghosts, and, in fact, the ghost never bothered me. To me this was an introduction to a deep sense of otherness. The poverty, the religion, the language, the ghosts, the snakes, and the ways that people's patterns of thought were so different from what I had experienced. It was only when I came back into the "normal" world that I realized I had spent a week in an alien cultural environment and yet the relationship with the people in it made me feel very much at home. Being exposed to these differences also enabled me to understand Annie and her stories.

The third person to leave a lasting impression on me is Mario Fiorentini, a partisan leader in 1943–44 and a world-class mathematician. This is a much more complicated, ambivalent, and unresolved relationship than the other two, partly because Mario belongs to the same class and environment as me, and has his own ideas about the purpose of the oral history work we have been doing together, and partly because, at the age of 94, his rich and varied life makes it impossible for me to hold him to one subject and agenda. This man is probably the most difficult person I have ever interviewed—which is why I have more than

30 hours with him: he has never answered any of my questions because he always feels the urge to talk about something else. As he told me in a rare self-critical moment: "The form that senility has taken with me is that I can't stop talking, I just ramble on and on." But all of his rambles are full of meaning.

Mario and I met in 1997. Earlier on, I had attended an international conference on the memory of Nazi war crimes in Europe[15] and the organizer, Leonardo Paggi, asked me to expand on some occasional comments I had made about the Fosse Ardeatine massacre into a paper for another conference. It was not my field, so I said that I could not do it; however, I went to the conference, and someone pointed out that Mario Fiorentini, a hero of the Resistance and one of the partisans involved in the partisan action that prompted the German retaliation and the Fosse Ardeatine massacre, was in the audience. I was introduced, we exchanged a few words, and I was so impressed that, though I still did not think I would write anything on the subject, I asked him to do an interview.

A couple of days later we sat in an outdoor café in piazza San Silvestro, across from Rome's main post office. On its front, a plaque I had never noticed before listed the names of the post office workers killed in the Resistance and at the Fosse Ardeatine. I was awed. It was like being in the presence of a legend. And then Mario began to talk:

> On the 10th of September of 1943 I witnessed a terrible and shocking event: the entry of the German armored column and the beginning of the occupation of Rome. [My future wife] Lucia Ottobrini and I were on via del Tritone, the corner of via Zucchelli, a hundred meters from via Rasella.[16] Some said that the German tank column was "overbearing." No—to me, there was a solemnity. They entered Rome as its masters. And, frankly, it made me shiver, because I remembered the newsreels that showed Hitler and his generals occupying Paris. To me it was a chilling sight.[17]

The streets that he mentioned were only a couple of blocks away. After our conversation ended, as I walked home, I began noticing the plaques on the walls and the street names, commemorating historical figures as well as members of the Resistance. And I caught myself thinking, "I didn't know this town had a history." I mean, Rome, one of the world's most historical places! But precisely because Rome has so much of a past, we tend to forget it is a modern city with a living history too. Mario embodied this insight for me. From then on, the memory of the Fosse Ardeatine became the vantage point for the reconstruction of the city's history over the previous 150 years. Two years later, *The Order Has Been Carried Out* came out, and Mario was the one who started it all.

This encounter led to an important relationship with Mario's wife, Lucia Ottobrini, too. Indeed, she is mentioned in the very first sentence on the tape of our first interview. In fact, one aspect of interviewing that often remains "off the record" is that even when an interview occurs on a one-on-one basis, other people, like family members, are also involved or touched. This was the case with Annie's husband Chester and her daughter Marjorie and with Dante Bartolini's circle of political and musical friends.

The reason why my relationship with Mario became a personal friendship was Lucia's understated and often silent or even reluctant but always encouraging presence. She endeavored to check her husband's gushing narcissistic narration, but encouraged him to talk to me because she liked the way I looked at him: "This person's eyes light up when he looks at you." Once again, as in my first encounter with Annie, I did not realize that I was being evaluated by my body language and that, as I "observed" her husband, Lucia observed me.

Mario and Lucia have been married for over 65 years. Their deeply loving relationship led me to notice an often disregarded aspect of the Resistance: the fact that many of its members married one another (there were many women in the guerrilla underground) as soon as the war was over. The Resistance was a war, a confrontation with death, but to many it was also an experience of love.

Lucia fought in the Resistance, but she refused to be interviewed. However, she was interested. Often, when I was interviewing Mario in their living room, she would come in, ostensibly with a cup of coffee or a glass of water, but also as a way of being there, of participating in silence—perhaps, of checking in on Mario. Once, when she came in, Mario asked her if she remembered a name that he could not think of right then. "Of course I do," she said. She spoke about that person, and went on for another two hours, standing up with the coffee tray in her hand. This was not an interview, because we were not sitting down: it was more of an everyday conversation, like those chats with Annie on the couch by the stove and the television. It was then that she told me the most moving thing I ever heard about the Resistance. She is a very spiritual person and she said: "In those two years when I was fighting in the Resistance..."—she was in armed conflict, she planted bombs, and she caused the death of enemy soldiers ("even the enemy is human," she says)—"During those two years, I never talked to Him." And I asked her, "Was it because you thought that Jesus would not understand what you were doing?" And she said: "Yes, I didn't think he would. I started talking to Him only after it was over."[18] When people today talk about the violence and killings during the partisan war, they rarely realize that these were very reluctant warriors: what they were doing was so alien to their own deep selves that they could only countenance it in absolutely alien circumstances like the war and the Nazi invasion.

Although Mario is proud of his role in the Resistance, he also insists on talking about other aspects of his life: he does not want to be identified only as a man of war, but also as a scientist and a man of culture. Thus, after all of these years and all of these interviews, there are still gaps in his story. For instance, I can never get him to talk about the time when he was parachuted to Northern Italy beyond the Germans lines, fought on the Swiss border, was arrested, and escaped. This gap is not due to reticence on his part, but to the fact that he resents being identified only with his war past. He seeks a fuller recognition of his personality. He always has his own agenda: "OK, Mario, tell me about when you went up North to fight." "No, no, today we will talk about the teaching of mathematics and the role of the teacher." I once outwitted Mario by asking him to talk about mathematics. As expected, he responded: "Yes, we will, but first I must tell you about the situation in Rome in February 1944."

Mario has lived such a rich life that it cannot be controlled by narrative form. Though he only received a technical-vocational education, he was a friend and cohort of painters, actors, and filmmakers. After the Resistance, he experienced what he describes as a conversion experience ("I fell off my horse, like Paul on the road to Damascus") and discovered mathematics. Since his educational background did not allow him to enter university, he taught himself Latin and Greek, passed the exam, got a degree, and started teaching high school math in a disadvantaged Roman neighborhood: "Revolution meant making mathematics available to all." During this time, he kept up with advanced research going on in the university and with visiting foreign professors, and by his late fifties he made the unusual jump from high school teacher to full professor and cutting-edge researcher: "I am very lonesome," he once mused, "because only about twelve people in the world understand what I do, and most of them are in Japan." Though this was beyond the range of my immediate interests, as a professor myself, I could not help but be attracted to his passion for teaching and his democratic approach: "A good teacher always speaks to the last rows."

Mario has so many stories and thoughts to pass on, so many opinionated views to voice—and so little time: regardless, he continues to associate and digress as the moment's urgency moves him. When Rome's House of Memory and History organized a celebration of his partisan background on his ninety-fourth birthday, he turned it into a conference on the relationship between Italian and Romanian mathematicians, much to the dismay of most of the audience.

Mario Fiorentini has taken to the extreme the lesson I learned from Dante Bartolini: I was his mouth-piece, he was using me to make his public mark. Dante and his comrades expected me to write their history; Mario expects me to write his biography. I often feel like a traitor because I know I never will; I have fallen short of his expectations about what he wants us to accomplish together.

Mario still plies me with documents and calls me up to talk for hours about the books, articles, lectures, and films we must plan together. When the telephone rings and it is Mario calling I know that I can forget my plans for the rest of the day. That said, I am still awed by him, and I do not mind listening even to his wildest plans, most of which will be forgotten and replaced by other equally implausible but often fascinating ideas the next time he calls. I owe it to him. Like Dante and Annie, he has done so much for me and for all of us—for our democracy and our freedom.

I am not sure whether these stories have a moral. Oral history deals with stories, and stories cannot be reduced to any single meaning. To me, part of the lesson is summed up in a line by the American singer-songwriter Charlie King: "Our work is more than our jobs / And our lives are more than our work."[19] Oral history is not something one does just for a living; in my case, it was literally not my job. Good oral history has a purpose, even a mission. It aims to make a mark in the world. It does not end with the turning off of the recorder, with the archiving of the document, or with the writing of the book—to quote Emily Dickinson, "it just / Begins to live / That day."[20] All of the experiences contained in this volume attest to this reality.

But because it is something we do with other people, it also goes beyond our "work," or, at least, our "work" cannot be accomplished unless we place it in a broader context of human relationships. Work is something useful, but personal relationships, friendships that last a lifetime, and dialogue and confrontation with others are an end in themselves. In an oft-quoted passage, the Italian ethnologist Ernest de Martino writes: "I entered those peasants' homes as a 'comrade,' a seeker of men and of forgotten human stories. I went as one who is intent on observing and verifying his own humanity."[21] I was always aware that I was entering other people's homes, which may be why I often made such "classical mistakes" as "a television blaring in the background, family members walking through the room."[22] On the one hand, I was afraid of being intrusive; on the other, I felt like all of these "little disturbances" are an essential part of the experience and provide information about context, relationships, and, literally, background; a radical political interview takes on strange overtones if there is a variety show playing in the background, for instance.

The way I went into those homes defined how I walked out of them. I feel that unless one comes out of an interview changed from the way he entered it, one has been wasting time. The changes may be imperceptible, but they add up over the years, and make us who we are as individuals, not just as scholars or activists. This is what Dante, Annie, Mario, and countless others have done for me. I hope—and the story of the old partisan in Monterotondo suggests that it may be true sometimes—that by listening I have done something for them, too. I offer these reflections in the spirit of this book, which has similarly tried to capture the complexities and nuances of oral history practice and the relationships we forge as a result.

Notes

1. Alessandro Portelli, "Research as an Experiment in Equality," in *The Death of Luigi Trastulli and Other Stories: Form and Meaning in Oral History* (Albany: State University of New York Press, 1991), 29–44.

2. See Portelli, *The Death of Luigi Trastulli and Other Stories*; *Biografia di una città: Storia e memoria, Terni 1831–1985* (Turin: Einaudi, 1985); *The Order Has Been Carried Out: History, Memory, and Meaning of a Nazi Massacre in Rome* (New York: Palgrave, 2003) (originally published in Italian as *L'ordine è stato eseguito. Roma, le Fosse Ardeatine, la memoria* (Rome: Donzelli, 2003); *They Say in Harlan County: An Oral History* (New York: Oxford University Press, 2010).

3. Dante Bartolini, interview by author, Terni, Italy, April 4, 1972. Also see Portelli, *The Death of Luigi Trastulli and Other Stories*; *The Battle of Valle Giulia: Oral History and the Art of Dialogue* (Madison: The University of Wisconsin Press, 1997).

4. Portelli, *The Death of Luigi Trastulli and Other Stories*.

5. For a full documentary of this experience, see Valentino Paparelli and Alessandro Portelli, *La Valnerina ternana. Un'esperienza di ricerca-intervento* (Rome: Squilibri, 2011).

6. Charles Hardy III and Alessandro Portelli, "I Can Almost See the Lights of Home: A Field Trip to Harlan County, Kentucky. An Essay-In-Sound," *Journal for MultiMedia History* 2 (1999), available at http://www.albany.edu/jmmh/vol2no1/lights.html.

7. Ibid. Also see Portelli, *They Say in Harlan County*.

8. For more information about this center, go to: http://highlandercenter.org.

9. Portelli, *They Say in Harlan County*, 6.

10. See David Whisnant, *All That Is Native and Fine: The Politics of Culture in an American Region* (Chapel Hill: University of North Carolina Press, 1983); Steve Shapiro, *Appalachia on Our Mind: The Southern Mountains and Mountaineers in the American Consciousness, 1870–1920* (Chapel Hill: University of North Carolina Press, 1977).

11. Portelli, *They Say in Harlan County*, 13.

12. Ibid., 25.

13. Eduardo De Filippo, *Non è vero … ma ci credo* (1942), in *I capolavori di Eduardo*, Turin, Einaudi, 1971.

14. Portelli, *They Say in Harlan County*, 22–24.

15. Alessandro Portelli, "Lutto, senso comune, mito e politica nella memoria della strage di Civitella," in *Storia e memoria di un massacro ordinario*, ed. Leonardo Paggi (Rome: manifestolibri, 1996); Leonardo Paggi, ed., *Le memoria della Repubblica* (Florence: la Nuova Italia, 1999).

16. Via del Tritone is a major thoroughfare in the fashionable and historic center of Rome; via Rasella is where, later on, the partisan unit of which Fiorentini was a member attacked a Nazi battalion, which resulted in the Nazi retaliation—the massacre of 335 victims at the Fosse Ardeatine.

17. See Portelli, *The Order Has Been Carried Out*.

18. Ibid., 108.

19. Charlie King, "Our Life is More than our Work," in the l.p. record *Vaguely Reminiscent/Somebody's Story*, RSM Records, 002.

20. Emily Dickinson, "A word is dead," in Thomas H. Johnson, *The Poems of Emily Dickinson* (Cambridge: Harvard University Press, 1955), no. 1212.

21. Ernesto de Martino, "Etnologia e cultura nazionale negli ultimi dieci anni," *Società* IX (1953): 3.

22. See Alexander Freund's reflections in the introduction to this book.

Contributors

Tatiana Argounova-Low is lecturer in the Department of Anthropology, University of Aberdeen. She received her PhD from the University of Cambridge, Scott Polar Research Institute. Argounova-Low has wide-ranging research interests in the history and ethnography of Siberian Indigenous peoples and has conducted fieldwork in Evenkiia and Sakha (Yakutiia). Her recent research, focused on the social and economic aspects of native communities in Northern Russia, has been published in *Ethnohistory, Arctic Anthropology, and Landscape Research*. She is also the author of *The Politics of Nationalism in the Republic of Sakha (Northeastern Siberia) 1900–2000* (Edwin Mellen, 2011).

Hourig Attarian is a Social Sciences and Humanities Research Council of Canada (SSHRC) postdoctoral fellow at the Centre for Oral History and Digital Storytelling at Concordia University. Her work focuses on storying memory and identity through visual and narrative explorations. Her research interests include autobiographical and visual art-based inquiries, oral history, genocide, and Diaspora studies.

Julie Cruikshank is professor emeritus in the Department of Anthropology at the University of British Columbia. Her research focuses on practical and theoretical developments in oral tradition studies, and specifically how competing forms of knowledge become enmeshed in struggles for legitimacy. Her ethnographic experience is rooted in the Yukon Territory, where she lived and worked for many years recording life stories with Athapaskan and Tlingit elders. Her books include *Life Lived Like a Story* (in collaboration with Angela Sidney, Kitty Smith, and Annie Ned); *The Social Life of Stories*; and *Do Glaciers Listen?*

Alexander Freund holds the chair in German-Canadian Studies at the University of Winnipeg, where he is also an associate professor in the Department of History and codirector of the Oral History Centre. Recent publications include two edited essay collections: *Oral History and Photography* (with Alistair Thomson; Palgrave, 2011) and *Beyond the Nation? Immigrants' Local Lives in Transnational Cultures* (University of Toronto Press, 2012); and a special coedited journal issue: Edición Especial/Special Issue "Historia Oral en América Latina/Oral History in Latin America," *Oral History Forum d'histoire orale* 32 (2012) (with Pablo

Pozzi et al.). Freund's current research focuses on an oral history of refugees in Manitoba, Canada, since 1945; a digital storytelling and oral history project with children of survivors of Indian residential schools in Canada; and an essay collection on space, transnationalism, and borderland studies in North America (with Benjamin Bryce).

Sherna Berger Gluck, professor emeritus in women's studies and history and the former director of the Oral History Program at California State University Long Beach, both started and is ending her career as a US women's historian. In between, as an activist-scholar, she spent time in Palestine interviewing women's movement leaders and grassroots activists. Her wide-ranging publications include *Women's Words: The Feminist Practice of Oral History; Rosie the Riveter Revisited: Women, the War, and Social Change;* and *An American Feminist in Palestine: The Intifada Years.* While an early advocate of orality and the potential of the digital revolution (www.csulb.edu/voaha), she has also been warning of the new ethical challenges and political implications posed by it.

Henry Greenspan is a psychologist and playwright at the University of Michigan where he is chair of the Program in Social Theory and Practice. He has been interviewing and teaching about Holocaust survivors since the 1970s and is the author of *On Listening to Holocaust Survivors,* now in a second and expanded edition. In 2012, he was the Fulbright Visiting Research Chair at Concordia University in Montreal, Canada, affiliated with the Centre for Oral History and Digital Storytelling.

Steven High is a professor in the Department of History at Concordia University where he also holds the Canada Research Chair in Public History. He is also codirector of the Centre for Oral History and Digital Storytelling (http://story-telling.concordia.ca/) and was lead researcher for the *Montreal Life Stories* project (http://www.lifestoriesmontreal.ca/). He has published extensively on oral history, working-class history, and deindustrialization.

Nancy Janovicek is an associate professor in the Department of History at the University of Calgary. She is the author of *No Place to Go: Local Histories of the Battered Women's Shelter Movement* (University of British Columbia Press, 2008) and is coeditor, with Catherine Carstairs, of *Writing Feminist History: Productive Pasts and Future Directions* (University of British Columbia Press, 2013). She has published on ethics policy and oral history.

Erin Jessee is a Banting Postdoctoral Fellow with the Liu Institute for Global Issues at the University of British Columbia in Vancouver, Canada. Jessee works primarily in Rwanda where she uses ethnographic and oral historical methods to elicit a view from below of history, memory, politics, and rural life in the aftermath of the 1994 genocide and related mass atrocities. In addition to several recently published peer-reviewed articles, she is writing a manuscript on the political uses of history surrounding the Rwandan genocide in 1994 and the Bosnian War from 1992 to 1995. She has also just launched a new research program that assesses domestic and international efforts to locate, identify, and repatriate the victims of the 1994 Rwandan genocide from the perspective of Rwandan survivors.

Nadia Jones-Gailani is currently a Provost Postdoctoral Fellow at the University of South Florida, Tampa. Her dissertation research explored networks of displaced Iraqi women in Toronto, Detroit, and Amman who arrived between 1980 and the present day. In her work, she examines the ways that identity, religious practice, and historical memory are negotiated across generations of women living in Diaspora, and how these factors inform the organization and activism of ethnoreligious Iraqi communities. Her first article, "Iraqi Women, Identity and Islam in Toronto: Reflections on a New Diaspora," was published in 2008 in the *Journal of Canadian Ethnic Studies*.

Elizabeth Miller is a documentary filmmaker, community media artist, and professor in the communication studies program at Concordia University in Montreal, Canada. Miller is on the board of the International Association of Women in Television and Radio, and, for the last 15 years, she has developed documentary and transmedia advocacy projects with women, youth, senior citizens, and a wide range of human rights organizations including Witness, based in New York City. Her last documentary, *The Water Front*, which powerfully connects water privatization to environmental justice, has won seven awards, and has been integrated into classrooms around the world. Her latest project, *Mapping Memories: Participatory Media, Place-Based Stories & Refugee Youth* (www.mappingmemories.ca), is a free online resource developed for teachers and includes 20 digital stories.

Leyla Neyzi is an anthropologist and oral historian. She is a professor in the Faculty of Arts and Social Sciences at Sabancı University in Istanbul, Turkey. Neyzi's work concerns the experiences of minorities vis-à-vis the construction of national identity; studies of youth, generation, and age; and debates that focus on history and memory in Turkey's public sphere. Most recently, she created a website and a multimedia exhibition, with an accompanying book, as a means of introducing oral history to a wide audience and contributing to contemporary debates on the Kurdish issue in Turkey (www.gencleranlatiyor.org).

Martha Norkunas holds a DEA in history from the Université de Provence, France, and a PhD in Folklore from Indiana University. She is the author of *The Politics of Public Memory* (State University of New York Press, 1993) and *Monuments and Memory* (Smithsonian Press, 2002). From 1999 to 2009, Norkunas directed the Project in Interpreting the Texas Past (ITP) at the University of Texas at Austin where she taught interdisciplinary teams of graduate students to think critically about memory and history and to apply their knowledge to social and cultural issues, including creating more inclusive interpretations at Texas historic sites. In 2009 Norkunas became professor of oral and public history in the Public History Program at Middle Tennessee State University in Mufreesboro, Tennessee, where she developed a graduate concentration in oral history.

Monica Eileen Patterson received her PhD in anthropology and history from the University of Michigan. She is currently a Banting Postdoctoral Fellow at the Centre for Ethnographic Research and Exhibition in the Aftermath of Violence (CEREV) at Concordia University in Montreal, Canada. Patterson is coeditor of *Curating Difficult Knowledge: Violent Pasts in Public Places* (Palgrave, 2011) and *Anthrohistory: Unsettling Knowledge, Questioning Discipline* (University of Michigan Press, 2011). Her scholarly and teaching interests address the intersections of memory, childhood, and violence in postcolonial Africa, and the ways in which they are represented and engaged in contemporary public spheres.

Alessandro Portelli is an Italian scholar of American literature and culture at the University of Rome, *La Sapienza*. He is also a renowned oral historian whose work has compared workers' accounts of industrial conflicts in Harlan County, Kentucky, and Terni, Italy. His newest book, *They Say in Harlan County*, was published in 2010.

Joan Sangster, a fellow of the Royal Society of Canada, has pioneered labor, working-class, and women's studies in Canada while contributing to international debates about these fields. Her award-winning work has shed light on the experiences of both girls and women in relation to labor, politics, the law, and social policy. Her 1994 article, "Telling Our Stories," and her highly acclaimed book *Earning Respect* (University of Toronto Press, 1995) continue to be important for their insights into the deeper meanings implicit in oral narratives. She is affiliated with gender and women's studies, as well as the Frost Centre for Canadian and Indigenous Studies, at Trent University, in Peterborough, Canada.

Anna Sheftel is an assistant professor of Conflict Studies at Saint Paul University in Ottawa, Canada. She received her doctorate from the University of Oxford, and her dissertation asked how contemporary Bosnians negotiate their wartime memories within the context of politicized local, ethnic, and national narratives. She has significant experience working on issues related to oral history methodology and ethics, and she founded and administers H-Memory, the H-Net.org discussion network for memory studies. She is interested in the ways in which memories of violence are utilized, politicized, resisted, and subverted, and in how ordinary people experience, remember, and organize themselves around experiences of conflict.

Pamela Sugiman is a professor and chair of the Department of Sociology at Ryerson University. Her research is in the areas of Canadian working-class women's history, work and labor, racism and racialization, the history of Japanese Canadians, oral history, and memory. The author of *Labour's Dilemma. The Gender Politics of Auto Workers in Canada, 1937–1979* (University of Toronto Press, 1994), Sugiman is currently completing a manuscript on personal memory and World War II internment of Japanese Canadians. She is also undertaking a new project, "Gendered Livelihoods," which is an examination of how different groups of racialized working-class women across Canada remember and narrate their ways of making a living, from girlhood to old age.

Luis van Isschot is an assistant professor of history and human rights at the University of Connecticut. He holds a PhD in Latin American history from McGill University. He worked for the human rights organization Peace Brigades International from 1995 to 2005.

Alan Wong recently completed his PhD in Concordia University's Special Individualized Program and he teaches in Vanier College's English Department. His current research involves collecting the oral histories of lesbian, gay, bisexual, transsexual, transgendered, queer, or allosexual (LGBTTQA) racialized, ethnicized, or colonized (REC) activists and community organizers in Montreal, Canada. In doing this work, Wong's goal is to explore strategies and approaches to activism, ascertain the place of such activists in the broader historical LGBTQ activism context in Montreal, and analyze the role that their personal histories have played in their development as activists. In addition, he is examining the applications of Playback Theatre in an oral history context.

Stacey Zembrzycki is an adjunct assistant professor in the Department of History at Concordia University. A modern Canadian oral and public historian of ethnic and immigrant experience, she is the author of *Sharing Authority with Baba: Wrestling with Memories of Community* (University of British Columbia Press, 2014) and its accompanying website: www.sudburyukrainians.ca. Zembrzycki's current research uses multiple, life story, oral history interviews to understand the postwar narratives and educational activism of child Holocaust survivors in Montreal.

Index

Printed in the United States of America